Autonomy and Pregnancy

Technology has come to dominate the modern experience of pregnancy and childbirth, but instead of empowering pregnant women, technology has been used to identify a second patient, the foetus, characterised as a distinct entity separate from the pregnant woman, with its own needs and interests. Often, the interests of the foetus and the woman will be aligned and their care intertwined; nevertheless, in legal and medical discourses the two 'patients' are frequently framed as antagonists with conflicting interests.

This book focuses upon the permissibility of encroachment on the pregnant woman's autonomy in the interests of the foetus. Drawing on the law in England and Wales, the United States of America and Germany, Samantha Halliday considers the tension between a pregnant woman's autonomy and medical actions taken to protect the foetus, addressing circumstances in which courts have declared medical treatment lawful in the face of the pregnant woman's refusal of consent.

As a work that calls into question the understanding of autonomy in prenatal medical care, this book will be of great use and interest to students, researchers and practitioners in medical law, comparative law, bioethics and human rights.

Dr Samantha Halliday is an Associate Professor in Law at the University of Leeds.

Biomedical Law and Ethics Library

Series Editor: Sheila A. M. McLean

Scientific and clinical advances, social and political developments and the impact of healthcare on our lives raise profound ethical and legal questions. Medical law and ethics have become central to our understanding of these problems, and are important tools for the analysis and resolution of problems – real or imagined.

In this series, scholars at the forefront of biomedical law and ethics contribute to the debates in this area, with accessible, thought-provoking, and sometimes controversial, ideas. Each book in the series develops an independent hypothesis and argues cogently for a particular position. One of the major contributions of this series is the extent to which both law and ethics are utilised in the content of the books, and the shape of the series itself.

The books in this series are analytical, with a key target audience of lawyers, doctors, nurses, and the intelligent lay public.

Available titles:

Human Fertilisation and Embryology
Reproducing regulation
Kirsty Horsey & Hazel Biggs

Intention and Causation in Medical Non-killing
The impact of criminal law concepts on euthanasia and assisted suicide
Glenys Williams

Impairment and Disability
Law and ethics at the beginning and end of life
Sheila A.M. McLean & Laura Williamson

Bioethics and the Humanities
Attitudes and perceptions
Robin Downie & Jane Macnaughton

Defending the Genetic Supermarket
The law and ethics of selection the next generation
Colin Gavaghan

The Harm Paradox
Tort law and the unwanted child in an era of choice
Nicolette Priaulx

Assisted Dying
Reflections on the need for law reform
Sheila A.M. McLean

Medicine, Malpractice and Misapprehensions
V.H. Harpwood

Euthanasia, Ethics and the Law
From the conflict to compromise
Richard Huxtable

The Best Interests of the Child in Healthcare
Sarah Elliston

Values in Medicine
What are we really doing to patients?
Donald Evans

Autonomy, Consent and the Law
Sheila A.M. McLean

Healthcare Research Ethics and Law
Regulation, review and responsibility
Hazel Biggs

The Body in Bioethics
Alastair V. Campbell

Genomic Negligence
An interest in autonomy as the basis for novel negligence claims generated by genetic technology
Victoria Chico

Health Professionals and Trust
The cure for healthcare law and policy
Mark Henaghan

Medical Ethics in China
A transcultural interpretation
Jing-Bao Nie

Law, Ethics and Compromise at the Limits of Life
To treat or not to treat?
Richard Huxtable

Regulating Pre-Implantation Genetic Diagnosis
A comparative and theoretical analysis
Sheila A.M. McLean & Sarah Elliston

Bioethics
Methods, theories, domains
Marcus Düwell

Human Population Genetic Research in Developing Countries
The issue of group protection
Yue Wang

Coercive Care
Rights, law and policy
Bernadette McSherry & Ian Freckelton

Saviour Siblings
A relational approach to the welfare of the child in selective reproduction
Michelle Taylor-Sands

Human Population Genetic Research in Developing Countries
The issue of group protection
Yue Wang

Stem Cell Research and the Collaborative Regulation of Innovation
Sarah Devaney

The Legitimacy of Medical Treatment
What role for the medical exception?
Sara Fovargue and Alexandra Mullock

The Jurisprudence of Pregnancy
Concepts of conflict, persons and property
Mary Neal

Revisiting the Regulation of Human Fertilisation and Embryology
Kirsty Horsey

Pioneering Healthcare Law
Essays in honour of Margaret Brazier
Catherine Stanton, Sarah Devaney, Anne-Marree Farrell and Alexandra Mullock

End of Life Decision Making for Critically Impaired Infants
Resource allocation and difficult decisions
Neera Bhatia

Forthcoming titles include:

Values and Institutions in Health Research Regulation
The case of regenerative medicine
Shawn Harmon

The Umbilical Cord Blood Controversies in Medical Law
Karen Devine

Revisiting Landmark Cases in Medical Law
Shaun D. Pattinson

The Ethical and Legal Consequences of Posthumous Reproduction
Lewis Browne

About the Series Editor
Professor Sheila A.M. McLean is Professor Emerita of Law and Ethics in Medicine, School of Law, University of Glasgow, UK.

Autonomy and Pregnancy

A Comparative Analysis of Compelled Obstetric Intervention

Samantha Halliday

Routledge
Taylor & Francis Group
LONDON AND NEW YORK

First published 2016
by Routledge
2 Park Square, Milton Park, Abingdon, Oxon OX14 4RN

and by Routledge
711 Third Avenue, New York, NY 10017

Routledge is an imprint of the Taylor & Francis Group, an informa business

British Library Cataloguing in Publication Data
A catalogue record for this book is available from the British Library

Library of Congress Cataloging in Publication Data
Names: Halliday, Samantha, author.
Title: Autonomy and pregnancy : a comparative analysis of compelled obstetric intervention / Samantha Halliday.
Description: Abingdon, Oxon ; N.Y., NY : Routledge, 2015. | Series: Biomedical law and ethics library | Includes bibliographical references and index.
Identifiers: LCCN 2015003884| ISBN 9781859419182 (hbk : alk. paper) | ISBN 9780415423038 (pbk : alk. paper) | ISBN 9781843147206 (ebk : alk. paper)
Subjects: LCSH: Perinatology--Law and legislation--United States. | Perinatology--Law and legislation--Germany. | Perinatology--Law and legislation--England. | Involuntary treatment--Law and legislation--United States. | Involuntary treatment--Law and legislation--Germany. | Involuntary treatment--Law and legislation--England. | Fetus--Diseases--Law and legislation--United States. | Fetus--Diseases--Law and legislation--Germany. | Fetus--Diseases--Law and legislation--England.
Classification: LCC K4367.G96 H35 2016 | DDC 344.03/219832--dc23
LC record available at http://lccn.loc.gov/2015003884

Zugl.: Gießen, Univ., Fachbereich Rechtswissenschaft, Diss., 2016.

ISBN: 978-1-85941-918-2 (hbk)
ISBN: 978-0-415-42303-8 (pbk)
ISBN: 978-1-843-14720-6 (ebk)

Typeset in Galliard
by Taylor & Francis Books

For Saskia

Denn nur durch Vergleichung unterscheidet man sich und erfährt, was man ist, um ganz zu werden, was man sein soll.

For only through comparison can one distinguish oneself and discover who one is, in order to become all that one should be.

(Thomas Mann, *Joseph in Ägypten*, 1933)

Contents

Acknowledgements

This book is based on my doctoral thesis, 'Constructing the Foetus as a Patient: A Comparative Analysis of Compelled Obstetric Intervention,' supervised by Walter Gropp. I owe him a great debt of gratitude for the stimulating conversations we shared, his insightful comments and his enthusiasm for my research. I am also grateful to his colleagues at the Justus-Liebig Universitât Giessen, particularly Bernhard Kretschmer for his enthusiastic support and perceptive comments.

Over the course of writing this monograph I have been inspired, supported and encouraged by many people, especially Elizabeth Macdonald, Paula Case, Jean McHale, Roger Brownsword and Gillian Hundt – your support is hugely appreciated. Thanks are also due to colleagues and students who have encouraged and joined me in my broader study of comparative medical ethics and the law over the years at the Universities of Warwick, Liverpool and Leeds.

I would like to thank my parents John and Sheila for their loving support; my sisters Vicki and Sarah, both huge sources of strength (and chocolate); and most of all, very special thanks are due to my partner Jörg Richter and our wonderful daughter Saskia. Jörg has been an unwavering source of support, believing in me and this project even when I doubted my ability to complete it, and commenting upon and proof-reading drafts along the way. Saskia has consistently brightened my day, has distracted me when I most needed it and has regularly reminded me that a cuddle will make everything seem possible! Thank you both for allowing me the time to complete this work, for giving me the space and strength to carry on, for believing in me and loving me – I love you both to the moon and back!

Foreword

This monograph by Samantha Halliday is based upon her doctoral dissertation "Constructing the Foetus as a Patient: A Comparative Analysis of Compelled Obstetric Intervention" submitted to the Faculty of Law at the Justus-Liebig University of Gießen, Germany. The thesis was graded as *summa cum laude* (outstanding) in January 2016. Samantha first visited the University of Giessen at the invitation of Professor Günter Weick, as part of the collaboration he nurtured between the Universities of Giessen and Warwick. The idea to undertake a comparative criminal law study of the variable conceptions of protection afforded to the foetus and the pregnant woman (above all where the performance of a blood transfusion, or a caesarean is indicated to save the foetus) arose in 2012. In 2014 she spent some time in my department, analysing the jurisprudence of the *Bundesverfassungsgericht* and the concept of a derivative crime of omission.

The results are surprising. Although the constitutional position of the foetus in German law appears to be strong, that counts for little in the case of a conflict of interests because the criminally relevant omission of the pregnant woman will only rarely give rise to criminal liability due to the criterion of reasonableness. The foetus has better prospects in the USA and England and Wales. In recognising a state interest in unborn life, the author argues that some American state courts have demonstrated a surprising willingness to disregard the refusal of a blood transfusion or a caesarean, even in the case of a *competent* pregnant woman. In England and Wales the woman's capacity is portrayed as the central issue. It is well recognised that medical treatment without consent will constitute a trespass to the person and that an individual with capacity has the right to refuse treatment. However, as Halliday argues, the courts appear to have been extremely willing to find women to lack the capacity to refuse a caesarean necessary to save the life of the foetus, thereafter designating the safe delivery of the foetus as the defining element of the woman's best interests. As a result of her comparative analysis Halliday argues that it is imperative to set the woman back in the centre of the discussion about the boundaries of prenatal diagnosis and therapy. She therefore advocates the use of an anticipatory pregnancy or birth directive by pregnant women, drafted at a time when their capacity is not in question, and the implementation of procedural safeguards to ensure that the woman remains part of, and the central focus of, decision-making.

This monograph is extremely topical; questions from doctors' circles are repeatedly addressed to lawyers as to whether, and if so which, interventions can be imposed upon a pregnant women in the interests of the unborn child, or her own health. More often than not, questions of liability are at the fore: could a doctor face liability for failing to act to protect the unborn child? The clarification provided by this work about when and to what extent the consent of a pregnant woman can be expected is of vital importance. Halliday's preferred approach, to relocate the decision-making from during birth to an earlier stage where the woman's capacity is undiminished, through the use of an advance pregnancy directive intended to take effect in the case of intervening incapacity, is admittedly not unproblematic. Such a directive is conceptually distinct from the more usual advance directive intended to set out the manner in which the patient would like to die. Whilst the refusal of treatment in a typical advance directive will inevitably lead to the patient's death, that is not necessarily the case in the context of a pregnancy directive. In this context it will be essential to undertake a detailed assessment of the woman's capacity and resort to the presumed will of the woman cannot be excluded.

The contribution to the literature made by this work is not only significant in the field of medical law; its contribution to comparative criminal law cannot be underestimated. The comparing and contrasting of common law and civil law is exceptionally successful. Whilst the analysis of the case law dominates the common law analysis, the author approaches the civil law by centring her analysis upon the abortion jurisprudence of the Federal Constitutional Court, before providing a sophisticated analysis of the German law in relation to derivative crimes of omission. Worthy of particular note is her analysis concerning the fundamental difference between the prohibition of the active termination of pregnancy and enforced acquiescence to an obstetric intervention in the context of a blood transfusion, a caesarean and other similarly invasive treatments. Halliday is capable of such high level analysis due to her outstanding knowledge of both the common law and the specific area of criminal liability for omissions in the German civil law system. This ability also enables the author to accurately develop her analysis, reasoning from the disproportionality of a forcible donation of blood in the so-called blood donor case, to the unlawfulness of obstetric treatment provided against the will of the pregnant woman.

In conclusion, Samantha Halliday has produced an innovative and groundbreaking contribution to the literature that will influence both German and European medical (criminal) law in the area of obstetrics.

Prof. Dr. Dr. h. c. Dr. h. c. Walter Gropp,
Professor of Criminal Law, Criminal Procedure Law and
Comparative Criminal Law,
Justus-Liebig-Universität Giessen

A. Introduction

I. The context: the evolving status of the foetus, from non-person to patient, to adversary

This book is concerned with the permissibility of encroachment on the pregnant woman's autonomy in the interests of the foetus.[1] Although the foetus has not been accorded the status of person in any of the jurisdictions under consideration, it has increasingly been accorded the status of patient, an acquisition of status largely attributable to technology. Technology has effected a seismic shift in the relationship between the pregnant woman and the healthcare professionals treating her, reducing the reliance of professionals upon knowledge imparted by the woman, and indeed largely reversing the flow of information between the two. For example, doctors are no longer reliant upon women informing them that the foetus has quickened, or even when her last period was; rather, ultrasound scans are used to date the pregnancy and monitor foetal well-being. Technology has come to dominate the modern experience of pregnancy and childbirth, with professionals informing the woman of what is happening, both during the pregnancy, for example through the use of ultrasound, or during the birth through the use of electronic foetal monitoring, increasingly rendering birth a medical event, rather than a natural occurrence. The medicalisation of pregnancy has thus led to the situation where both pregnancy (the process) and birth (the outcome) are subject to oversight by a healthcare professional. This professional is, however, not a neutral observer; she[2] will have her own attitudes about what constitutes appropriate antenatal behaviour, attitudes often based to at least a degree upon clinical evidence, but those attitudes may not correspond with the pregnant woman's own views as to how she wishes to live, or indeed how she wishes to be treated during her pregnancy and labour.

1 Throughout this work I have followed the conventional usage in the literature, making reference to 'foetus' whenever referring to the developing human organism from conception to birth, unless a distinction needs to be drawn between an embryo (the developing organism up to the end of the 8th gestational week) and a foetus.

2 The use of feminine pronouns throughout this work is intended to encompass both genders.

Instead of empowering pregnant women, technology has been used to identify a second patient. As Mark Kilby recognised, 'One of the most significant advances in antenatal care has been the introduction of ultrasound. This has allowed the visualisation of our second patient, the fetus'.[3] Similarly, in 1971 one of the leading American obstetrics texts stated:

> Since World War II and especially in the last decade, knowledge of the fetus and his environment has increased remarkably. As an important consequence the fetus has acquired status as a patient to be cared for by the physician as he long has been accustomed to caring for the mother.[4]

As acknowledged by these excerpts, the use of techniques such as ultrasound and foetal surgery has led to the characterisation of the foetus as a second patient, a distinct entity separate from the pregnant woman, with its own needs and interests. Often, foetal and the woman's interests will be aligned and their care intertwined; nevertheless, in legal and medical discourses the two 'patients' are frequently framed as antagonists with conflicting interests, a trend graphically illustrated by the title of Jeffrey Phelan's article, 'The maternal abdominal wall: a fortress against fetal health care?'[5] Thus technology has transformed the relationship both between the pregnant woman and the foetus she carries and between the pregnant woman and her healthcare professionals. Within this triadic relationship, the role of foetal protector is therefore often ascribed not to the pregnant woman but to the healthcare professional who may intercede on its behalf to secure its well-being and/or treatment, if necessary by protecting it from the pregnant woman. Indeed, as Ingrid Zechmeister suggested, technology may shift the focus of antenatal care from caring to surveillance:

> The growing foetus which had always been hidden in the uterus has become visible, a development which, without doubt, has made pregnancy much less mysterious for the medical profession. This, on the other hand, poses the danger that antenatal care no longer emphasises, as the name might suggest, caring but that the focus shifts from caring to technical surveillance. Hence, women become the object of medical surveillance. What inevitably follows as another consequence is that because technique of visualisation opens up the new possibility of seeing the foetus, the focus of surveillance will be less on the mother but increasingly on the foetus. For the profession it becomes 'their' patient rather than the mother's baby. There might be two patients in pregnancy, however, as Overall … suggests, 'the fetus is medically and technically

3 M. D. Kilby, 'Prenatal Diagnosis: The Way Ahead? (1998) 59(10) *Hospital Medicine* 752.

4 J. W. Williams; L. M. Hellman and J. A. Pritchard (eds) (1971) *Williams Obstetrics*, 14th edn, New York: Appleton-Century Crofts, at 199.

5 J. Phelan, 'The Maternal Abdominal Wall: A Fortress against Fetal Health Care?' (1986) 65 *Southern California Law Review* 461.

> by far the more interesting one'. Women solely function as environment and space to be explored in the interests of science.[6]

The recognition of the foetus as a separate patient has severed the unitary construction of the pregnant woman and her foetus, emphasising that it may be necessary to protect the foetus from its host, the pregnant woman. Foetal protection policies may be pursued at a state level – for example, through the statutory recognition of the foetus as a separate entity capable of being the victim of child abuse – or by healthcare institutions seeking court orders to override a woman's refusal of consent to treatment believed to further the best interests of the foetus or to be necessary to safeguard its life. Notably, these policies construct the foetus not only as separate but as an innocent third party or victim in need of protection; the uterus ceases to be a place of safety and is portrayed instead as a place of danger. In this manner an adversarial relationship may be created between the woman and the foetus, pitting each against the other, despite the fact that there is only one person involved because at most the foetus can only be characterised as a potential person. As McLachlin J recognised in *Winnipeg Child and Family Services (Northwest Area) v G (DF)*,[7] the concept of

> the unborn child and its mother as separate juristic persons in a mutually separable and antagonistic relation ... is belied by the reality of the physical situation; for practical purposes, the unborn child and its mother-to-be are bonded in a union separable only by birth... . Judicial intervention ... ignores the basic components of women's fundamental human rights – the right to bodily integrity, and the right to equality, privacy, and dignity... . The foetus's complete physical existence is dependent on the body of the woman. As a result, any intervention to further the foetus's interests would necessarily implicate, and possibly conflict with, the mother's interests.

As McLachlin J noted, the concept of the foetus as a separate patient is belied by its location – whilst the foetus may be regarded as a patient in its own right, it is not an independent being; it is located within the woman's uterus and thus a unique situation arises whereby access to patient A (the foetus) must be gained through the body of patient B (the woman). While most women will willingly accept medical advice about what is best for the foetus, a dilemma arises when the wishes, or indeed interests, of a pregnant woman conflict with the perceived interests of the foetus. As will be seen from the cases discussed in the following chapters, women have rejected treatment that could benefit the foetus, or even save its life, for a number of reasons, including fear, religious beliefs, cultural practices or simply because they disagree with the doctor's prognosis. In all other

6 I. Zechmeister, 'Foetal Images: The Power of Visual Technology in Antenatal Care and the Implications for Women's Reproductive Freedom' (2001) 9 *Health Care Analysis* 387, at 391.

7 (1997) 3 B.H.R.C. 611, at 620–2 (Canadian Supreme Court).

areas of medical law, patient autonomy has become the gold standard, the principal determination of medical care of an adult with capacity, but the addition of a foetus into the equation, particularly a viable foetus, has posed a potent challenge to the autonomy of pregnant women. In many of the cases discussed below, the courts in England and Wales and in the United States of America have been prepared to authorise, or indeed order, medical treatment to be given for the benefit of the foetus, notwithstanding the woman's refusal of consent. Moreover, in some states of America child abuse statutes have been extended to cover the foetus so that the pregnant woman's lifestyle may be restricted.[8]

II. The general principle that consent is a prerequisite to medical treatment

There is a general principle that everyone's body is inviolate, as Cardozo J stated in *Schloendorff v Society of New York Hospital*:[9]

> Every human being of adult years and sound mind has a right to determine what shall be done with his own body.

Therefore, consent will generally be a prerequisite to any medical treatment; without it the doctor may be liable in negligence or battery. Moreover, it is well recognised that generally in each of the jurisdictions under consideration every patient with the requisite capacity has the right to refuse medical treatment, even that which may save his or her life.[10] Nevertheless, an exception to this general

8 See, for example, *Whitner v State* 528 U.S. 1145 (1998) and *In re Baby Boy Blackshear* No. 99CA00018, 1999 Ohio App. LEXIS 4274 (Sept. 7, 1999). As at 1 July 2015, 'One state allows assault charges to be filed against a pregnant woman who uses certain substances [Tennessee]. 18 states consider substance abuse during pregnancy to be child abuse under civil child-welfare statutes, and 3 consider it grounds for civil commitment'. Guttmacher Institute *State policies in brief: substance abuse during pregnancy*, available at www.guttmacher.org/statecenter/spibs/spib_SADP.pdf (accessed 13 August 2015). For discussion of this, see, for example, J. Ehrlich, 'Breaking the Law by Giving Birth: The War on Drugs, the War on Reproductive Rights, and the War on Women' (2008) 32 *N.Y.U. Review of Law & Social Change* 381; R. Roth, *Making Women Pay: The Hidden Costs of Fetal Rights*, Ithaca, NY: Cornell University Press, 2000; L. Paltrow, 'Pregnant Drug Users, Fetal Persons, and the Threat to *Roe v Wade*' (1999) 62 *Albany Law Review* 999; M. Mills, 'Fetal Abuse Prosecutions: The Triumph of Reaction over Reason' (1998) 47 *DePaul Law Review* 989; K. Moss, 'Substance Abuse during Pregnancy' (1990) 13 *Harvard Women's Law Journal* 278; S. Balisy, 'Maternal Substance Abuse: The Need to Provide Legal Protection for the Fetus' (1987) 60 *Southern California Law Review* 1209; C. R. Daniels, *At Women's Expense: State Power and the Politics of Foetal Rights*, 1993, Cambridge, MA: Harvard University Press.

9 105 NE 92 (1914), at 93.

10 *Re T (An Adult) (Consent to Medical Treatment)* [1993] Fam 95; *Airedale NHS Trust v Bland* [1993] 1 All ER 821; *Re MB (Medical Treatment)* [1997] 2 FLR 426; *Ms B v An NHS Hospital Trust* [2002] EWHC 429 (Fam); *BGHSt* 11, 111 at 113;

principle appears to have been developed in the US and to some extent in England and Wales and Germany, in relation to pregnant women, particularly where the foetus is viable.

Given that the courts in the US and England and Wales have refused to accord the foetus a right to life, it is rather surprising that they have been prepared to override a woman's refusal of consent to medical intervention deemed necessary for the foetus. By contrast there are no reported decisions of cases concerning court-authorised obstetric intervention in Germany. This may be due to the low level of reporting in such cases, or simply due to the fact that no case has been brought to court, but it is significant given the fact that the *Bundesverfassungsgericht* has held that the foetus has a constitutionally protected right to life from implantation and that the foetal right to life operates even against the pregnant woman.[11] Moreover, under German law both the woman and her attending doctor are classified as guarantors, owing a duty to protect the life of the foetus. As discussed below, this means that German law imposes a *prima facie* duty upon doctors to operate to save the life of the foetus, notwithstanding the woman's objection, and that women have a duty to accept treatment needed to save the life of the foetus.

III. The focus of this book

This book will focus upon that tension between the pregnant woman's autonomy and actions taken to protect the foetus. It will address the circumstances in which courts have declared medical treatment lawful in the face of the pregnant woman's refusal of consent, considering first the English and American case law relating to court-authorised caesareans and blood transfusions. Thereafter, the duties imposed by German law upon the pregnant woman and her doctor with regard to safeguarding foetal life will be considered, assessing to what extent the pregnant woman's duty to protect the foetal life gives rise to an obligation to accept medical treatment for its benefit. Finally, it will comparatively analyse the way in which courts and healthcare professionals, relying upon technology, have enabled the foetus to displace the woman as the primary patient, restricting or even overriding her autonomy, in the name of protecting the entity that will only gain the status of person after live birth.

BGHSt 11, 111 at 113; *BGHZ* 154, 205; *BGHZ* 163, 195; *Cruzan v Director, Missouri Dept of Health* 111 L ed 2d 224 (1990).

11 Art. 2 II GG; *BVerfGE* 39, 1 (1975); *BVerfGE* 88, 203 (1993).

B. Legal responses to a pregnant woman's refusal of medical treatment required for the benefit of the foetus

I. Court-ordered obstetric intervention: the American case law

1. Introduction: the application of *Roe v Wade* outside the abortion context

Although a patient with capacity may generally accept or refuse even life-sustaining treatment, where the patient is pregnant some courts in the United States of America have shown themselves to be willing to override the women's autonomy in order to protect the foetus. In *Roe v Wade*,[1] the Supreme Court held that the state has an important and legitimate interest in protecting the potentiality of human life throughout pregnancy and that this interest becomes compelling from the third trimester onwards.[2] Therefore it has been argued that if a caesarean is medically indicated and vaginal delivery would have the same effect as an abortion, in that it would result in the death of the foetus, the court may order that a caesarean be performed, notwithstanding the woman's refusal of consent. As will be seen in the following discussion, this interpretation of *Roe* has been relied upon a number of times by the courts in the United States as a justification for ordering that medical treatment be performed against a woman's wishes. However, it should be remembered that although the state's interest in potential life becomes compelling at viability, it never becomes absolute. In *Roe* and its progeny, the Supreme Court stressed that, whilst the state's compelling interest in potential life meant that it could restrict or even prohibit abortion after viability, the state's interest could never outweigh the woman's right to elect an abortion where the continuance of her pregnancy posed a threat to her life or health.[3] Moreover, the

1 *Roe v Wade* 410 U.S. 113 (1973).

2 *Roe v Wade* (note 1), at 162–4. In *Webster v Reproductive Health Services* 492 U.S. 490 (1989) and *Planned Parenthood v Casey* 505 US 833 (1992) the Supreme Court held that the state's interest in potential life become compelling at 24 weeks' gestation – that is, when the foetus achieves viability. This is not really inconsistent with the decision in *Roe v Wade*; it simply acknowledges that advances in medical science have led to a foetus being considered viable at an earlier stage of pregnancy than in 1973. Moreover, in *Casey* the court stressed that the state has 'a substantial interest in potential life *throughout* pregnancy', at 876.

3 *Roe v Wade* (note 1), at 165, *per* Blackmum J; *Planned Parenthood v Casey* (note 2), at 846.

fact that the state may restrict or even prohibit abortion, in cases where there is no threat to the life or health of the woman, is a very different proposition to that suggested above, whereby courts have suggested that the state's interest may suffice to mandate treatment for the benefit of the foetus.[4]

Notwithstanding the poor fit of the third-trimester rule, or indeed child abuse statutes when applied to the foetus (an alternative justification sometimes adopted by the courts), the courts in some US states have shown themselves willing to mandate the performance of a blood transfusion or a caesarean, despite the woman's refusal to consent to the procedure. It may be argued that the degree of invasion entailed in a blood transfusion is of a much lesser degree than that involved in a caesarean, a major operation; for that reason the case law relating to the two forms of intervention is considered separately. Nevertheless, the common feature is that in both cases US courts have been willing to overrule a woman's refusal to consent to obstetric intervention because she was pregnant at the time of the ruling and her refusal jeopardised the life or health of the foetus.

2. Court-ordered blood transfusions

As will be apparent from the following cases, the issue of court-ordered blood transfusions (for the benefit of the foetus) has arisen mainly in relation to Jehovah's Witnesses who believe that blood transfusions are contrary to the tenets of the Bible[5] and that the receipt of blood endangers eternal life. Although the courts have given varying reasons for overriding the woman's refusal of consent to a blood transfusion, in a number of cases they have done so in order to protect the foetus, showing scant regard for the woman's autonomy or her genuinely held religious beliefs.

*a. Pre-*Roe v Wade*: the recognition of the unborn child's right to the law's protection*

Raleigh Fitkin-Paul Morgan Memorial Hospital v Anderson[6] was one of the first cases in which a court accepted that a woman's refusal of consent to medical treatment could be overruled. The hospital sought a declaration that it would not be unlawful to administer a blood transfusion to Willimina Anderson if it were considered necessary to save either her life or that of the foetus. Mrs Anderson was 32 weeks pregnant and so the foetus had achieved viability. According to medical opinion, there was a real risk that she would haemorrhage and that a transfusion would be necessary to save both lives. However, Mrs Anderson had stated that even if a transfusion were to become necessary, she would not consent due to the fact that she was a Jehovah's Witness. The trial court refused to grant the order sought, holding that it could not intervene to protect the life of either

4 In *In re Brown*, 689 N.E.2d 397 (1997) the Illinois Court of Appeals accepted that abortion is not the same as a refusal of treatment, at 405.

5 Acts 15:28–9.

6 42 N.J. 421 (1964), NJ Sup Ct.

Mrs Anderson or the foetus. The hospital appealed, but Mrs Anderson left the hospital, so the judgment was given *per curiam* as the situation was likely to occur again. The New Jersey Supreme Court held that the 'unborn child' was entitled to the law's protection and that

> The welfare of the child and the mother are so intertwined and inseparable that it would be impracticable to attempt to distinguish between them with respect to the sundry factual patterns which may develop. The blood transfusions (including transfusions made necessary by the delivery) may be administered if necessary to save her life or the life of her child, as the physician in charge at the time may determine.[7]

It is notable that this case predates the Supreme Court's decision in *Roe* and thus proceeds on the basis that the foetus, rather than the state's interest in potential life, is capable of protection. The court's decision clearly demonstrates the potential for a woman's right to self-determination to be nullified by the fact of pregnancy. Indeed, as the court held, in the case of a pregnant woman, the power to determine whether or not medical treatment should be provided may rest not with the woman, but may be transferred to the doctor if there is a threat to her life, or that of the foetus, in the view of that same doctor. The doctor is thus designated as the sole decision-maker, empowered to determine how she should treat her patient, without reference to that patient's views. Of course, if Mrs Anderson had not been pregnant, she would have remained entitled to refuse all treatment, including life-sustaining treatment.

*b. Post-*Roe v Wade*: balancing the state's interest in potential life against the pregnant woman's right to autonomy/privacy*

The relevance of the refusal's impact upon the foetus is underlined by the Maryland case of *Mercy Hospital, Inc. v Ernestine Jackson.*[8] Mrs Jackson was 25 weeks pregnant and in premature labour. The doctors advised that a caesarean was necessary and she consented to the performance thereof, but refused to consent to a blood transfusion even if her life were at risk. Her doctors accepted that she had the capacity to refuse a transfusion; she had previously undergone surgery without consenting to a blood transfusion and throughout her pregnancy she had made her doctors aware that she would not consent to a blood transfusion in any circumstance. Unlike the case of Mrs Anderson, the doctors believed that the failure to perform a transfusion would pose no risk to the life or health of the foetus; rather, any risk involved only the life of Mrs Jackson. Nevertheless, the hospital petitioned the court for the appointment of a temporary guardian of Mrs Jackson, with the authority to consent to a blood transfusion on her behalf.

7 Ibid., at 423.

8 62 Md. App. 409 (1985) (Court of Special Appeals of Maryland), 510 A. 2d. 562 (Md. 1986) (Court of Appeals of Maryland).

Unlike many of the other cases involving women refusing obstetric intervention, counsel was appointed for Mrs Jackson and an *inter partes* hearing took place, albeit it in an emergency setting at the side of her bed. Concluding the emergency hearing, Judge Greenfeld said:

> This Court is of the opinion that a competent, pregnant adult does have the paramount right to refuse a blood transfusion in accordance with her religious beliefs, where such decision is made knowingly and voluntarily and will not endanger the delivery, survival or support of the fetus. This conclusion is consistent with a patient's right of informed consent to medical treatment, ... and the corollary right to refuse that medical treatment.[9]

Thus Greenfeld J stressed that a woman's right to refuse medical treatment was not diminished by pregnancy ***provided that*** that refusal did not endanger a foetus, and there being no risk to the foetus in this case he refused the hospital's application. The surgery was performed immediately, no transfusion was performed and both Mrs Jackson and her baby survived unharmed. Despite the fact that the issue was rendered moot by the safe delivery of the baby, the hospital appealed against the court's refusal to appoint a guardian, but Greenfeld J's decision was affirmed by the Court of Special Appeals of Maryland.[10]

The appellate decision in *Anderson* predated the US Supreme Court's decision in *Roe v Wade* by nine years. Thus it could be argued that the reasoning adopted by the New Jersey Supreme Court – namely that the foetus, rather than the state's interest therein, was entitled to the law's protection – could not be adopted to compel a blood transfusion after the US Supreme Court had held that the foetus was not a person within the meaning of the constitution.[11] Certainly in *Jackson*, Greenfeld J did not address the issue of foetal rights or the state's interest in potential life, merely holding that as the foetus was not at risk, Mrs Jackson had the right to refuse the transfusion recommended by her doctors. However, in two New York cases decided during 1985 the pregnant woman's refusal of consent to a blood transfusion was overruled in order to safeguard the foetus's life or health. In the first of these cases, *Crouse Irving Memorial Hospital, Inc. v Paddock*,[12] the pregnant woman had, like Mrs Jackson, agreed to the performance of a caesarean, accepting medical advice that it was necessary, but refused to consent to a blood transfusion due to her religious beliefs. The medical evidence was that a transfusion would be necessary to save Stacey Paddock's life, particularly due to the fact that in performing the caesarean the doctors would have to cut the placenta due to its anterior position. The hospital sought an order authorising the transfusion of

9 Cited by Gilbert CJ, 62 Md. App. 409 (1985), at 417–18.

10 Subsequently the Maryland Court of Appeals held that the Special Court of Appeals should not have considered the hospital's appeal because it was moot and vacated that court's decision, *Mercy Hospital, Inc. v Ernestine Jackson* 306 Md. 556 (1986).

11 *Roe v Wade* (note 1), at 158.

12 485 N.Y.S.2d 443 (1985).

'mother and child' during the performance of the surgical procedure,[13] by which, of course, the transfusion of Mrs Paddock was meant as the foetus was still within her body and could thus not be separately transfused.

It is not clear from the judgment that the failure to transfuse Mrs Paddock would endanger the foetus; the medical evidence cited merely referred to the necessity of a transfusion to safeguard Mrs Paddock's life and makes no reference to its impact upon the foetus's welfare. Nevertheless, the New York Supreme Court, Onondaga County, considered the proposed transfusion of Mrs Paddock and the foetus separately. Hayes J considered the law regarding 'blood transfusions to save the baby's life and health', reviewing the case law where the refusal of parents to consent to a blood transfusion for their child had been overridden. However, he failed to distinguish between the foetus and a child, referring to the foetus as 'the baby', and indeed he failed to differentiate between cases where a woman refuses a blood transfusion for herself and those where she refuses to consent to a blood transfusion on behalf of her child. This case did not involve a woman refusing to consent to her child receiving a blood transfusion; it concerned a woman refusing to consent to a blood transfusion for herself. However, Hayes J held that Mrs Paddock could be required to undergo a blood transfusion, despite the fact that he recognised her to be 'an adult obviously of sound mind and deep religious conviction'.[14] Holding that 'the State has a vital interest in the welfare of children, an interest that will override even the parents' most fervently held religious beliefs', he authorised the hospital and attending doctors to administer blood transfusions as medically indicated.[15]

Moreover, the subjection of Mrs Paddock to a compelled blood transfusion was not only justified by concern for the foetus; rather, the judge admonished Mrs Paddock, stating that given she wanted the caesarean to be performed, she was putting the medical professionals in an untenable position by refusing a blood transfusion that was likely to be necessary as a result of the procedure. Hayes J found that

> when a patient puts her doctor in charge of a surgical procedure, she necessarily makes him responsible for the conduct of the operation. Every such grant of responsibility should be accompanied by authority sufficient to properly carry out the delegated responsibilities.[16]

Therefore he granted the order, authorising the doctors to transfuse Mrs Paddock not only prior to the birth of her child, but also thereafter until such a time as her condition had stabilised. Thus in this case Mrs Paddock's autonomy and religious beliefs were subordinated not only to the welfare of her foetus but also to the ethical integrity of the medical profession, a factor that was found to continue to

13 Ibid., at 443.
14 Ibid., at 445.
15 Ibid., at 444–5.
16 Ibid., at 445–6.

justify transfusion even after the foetus had been delivered, at a time when the failure to perform a transfusion could not impact upon its health or life.

Three months later, in *In re Jamaica Hospital*[17] the New York Supreme Court, Queens County, also had to consider the issue of a woman refusing a blood transfusion on religious grounds, but, unlike the cases of *Jackson*, *Paddock* and *Anderson*, in this case the foetus was not viable. Lonschein J held that despite the fact that the foetus was not yet viable, the state still had a significant interest in protecting its life and dismissed the fact that 'the state interest in protecting its life would be less than "compelling" in the context of the abortion cases'.[18] Holding that the state's interest in a 'mid-term fetus' outweighed the woman's right to refuse a blood transfusion,[19] Lonschein J recognised that were the woman not pregnant her refusal of treatment would be respected, stating: 'If her life were the only one involved here, the court would not interfere … Her life, however is not the only one at stake. The court must consider the life of the unborn fetus'.[20] Designating the foetus as 'a human being, to whom the court stands in *parens patriae*, and whom the court has the obligation to protect', he appointed her doctor as special guardian of the 'unborn child', ordering him to 'do all that in his medical judgment was necessary to save its life, including the transfusion of blood into the mother'.[21] Thus the judge effectively gave the doctor *carte blanche* to treat the woman as he felt necessary to safeguard the foetus, but noticeably without any requirement that the doctor consider the woman's health and welfare or indeed her wishes. Thus, whilst Lonschein J recognised the foetus as a human being, he appears to have considered the woman as rather less human; indeed, he appears to reduce her status to that of a foetal container.

The decisions in both *Crouse* and *In re Jamaica Hospital* completely disregarded the woman's autonomy and religious beliefs, but both decisions were cited with approval by the New York Supreme Court, Appellate Division, in another case involving a Jehovah's Witness who refused a blood transfusion, *Fosmire v Nicoleau*.[22] Unlike the two above-mentioned cases, Mrs Nicoleau was no longer pregnant at the time that doctors believed a blood transfusion to be necessary, having safely delivered her son. However, a few hours after giving birth she began haemorrhaging and the hospital applied for a court order authorising a transfusion. The order was granted and Mrs Nicoleau was transfused twice against her will. The Supreme Court, Appellate Division vacated the order, holding that the first instance court had erred in granting the order and had violated her right to due process. In doing so it distinguished both *Crouse* and *In re Jamaica Hospital*, stating:

> On this point, we note that this case does not present a situation in which a pregnant adult woman refuses medical treatment and, as a result of that

17 491 N.Y.S.2d 898 (1985).
18 Ibid., at 900.
19 Ibid., at 900.
20 Ibid., at 899, internal citations omitted.
21 Ibid., at 900.
22 *Fosmire v Nicoleau* 144 A.D.2d 8, 536 N.Y.S.2d 492 (1989).

> refusal, places the life of her unborn baby in jeopardy. Clearly, in such a case, the state's interest, as *parens patriae*, in protecting the health and welfare of the child is deemed to be paramount.[23]

Thus the court emphasised that it was the state's interest that must be weighed against the woman's right to self-determination, although it did appear to suggest that in all cases where the foetus's life was at risk the court would override the woman's refusal of treatment. On a further appeal the New York Court of Appeals failed to consider the question of whether a pregnant woman could refuse a blood transfusion, holding that in this case Mrs Nicoleau's right to self-determination could be restricted if it were outweighed by state interests, but that in the current circumstances no evidence would support a finding of such compelling state interest,[24] there being no threat to her son or the ethical integrity of the medical profession.

Both *Paddock* and *In re Jamaica* were first instance decisions that were not subject to an appeal; following the Supreme Court decision in *Roe v Wade* the first appellate consideration of whether a pregnant woman has the right to refuse a blood transfusion on the basis of her religious beliefs, even if that transfusion is necessary to save both her own life and that of the foetus, was provided in *In re Brown*.[25] During surgery to remove a urethral mass Darlene Brown lost a lot of blood. She had not previously mentioned that she was a Jehovah's Witness, but she refused a transfusion on the basis of her faith during the surgery and the doctors completed the operation without recourse to blood products. Her doctors believed that she had the capacity to refuse the transfusion, but, in the days that followed the procedure, doctors were unable to increase her haemoglobin level, raising fears for the health of both Mrs Brown and her viable foetus. Her doctor estimated that if she continued to refuse blood, her chances of survival, as well as those of the foetus, were only 5 per cent. The state applied for the appointment of a temporary custodian of the foetus, a custodian who would be able to consent to a blood transfusion for the benefit the foetus, even though that transfusion would have to be administered to Mrs Brown against her wishes. At the hearing the Browns, the state and the foetus were separately represented, illustrating the adversarial nature of the dispute.

The trial court held that the transfusion was necessary to preserve the life of both Mrs Brown and the foetus, that the state had a strong interest in protecting Mrs Brown's existing children from becoming orphans, that the transfusion would be minimally invasive and therefore that the state's interests outweighed Mrs Brown's interest in refusing treatment. It appointed the hospital administrator as the temporary custodian of the foetus and held that he could consent to such blood transfusions as were deemed necessary by the doctors. Mrs Brown was subsequently forcibly restrained and sedated so that a blood transfusion could be administered against her will.

23 Ibid., at 496.
24 *In the matter of Francis J. Fosmire v Denis J. Nicoleau* 75 N.Y.2d 218 (1990), at 234.
25 *In re Brown* (note 4).

After giving birth Mrs Brown appealed against the appointment of a temporary custodian with the ability to consent to a blood transfusion for sake of the foetus. The Illinois Court of Appeals held that the state may not override a competent patient's refusal of treatment to save the life of a viable foetus and confirmed that Mrs Brown's right to refuse medical treatment should be weighed against the state's interest in the viable foetus, rather than any rights the foetus might be considered to have.[26] In balancing these interests, the court considered the limits of the right to refuse treatment. As the US Supreme Court accepted in *Cruzan*, a competent person has a constitutionally protected liberty interest in refusing unwanted treatment, but that interest must be balanced against the countervailing state interests,[27] namely the preservation of life, the prevention of suicide, the protection of third parties and the ethical integrity of the medical profession.[28] The Illinois Court of Appeals took notice of the American Medical Association's view that 'judicial intervention is inappropriate when a woman has made an informed refusal of a medical treatment designed to benefit her fetus'.[29] On that basis the court held that the state's interest in the ethical integrity of the medical profession could not be dispositive. There was no suggestion that Mrs Brown wished to commit suicide or that her existing daughters (the relevant third parties) would be abandoned by her husband if she died. Whilst the trial court had considered the state interest in the preservation of life in relation to the preservation of Mrs Brown's life *and* that of the foetus, the Court of Appeals stressed that the only life to be considered was that of the decision-maker, Mrs Brown. Moreover, it held that the state's interest in the preservation of life has to be considered alongside the state's interest in protecting the autonomy of the individual,[30] recognising that the right to refuse treatment would be meaningless if it could always be overridden by the state's interest in preserving life. Thus the court found that the countervailing state interests would not outweigh Mrs Brown's right to refuse a blood transfusion.

In assessing the state's substantial interest in protecting the viable foetus, the court distinguished the case of refusing medical treatment from cases involving abortion or where the pregnant woman could be considered to be abusing the foetus through, for example, the use of drugs. It also noted that absent legislative action the foetus could not be considered a minor and therefore the refusal of medical treatment that would benefit a foetus could not be equated with child neglect.[31] The state had argued that a blood transfusion was a minor procedure and the Illinois Court of Appeals had previously left open the question of whether

26 *In re Brown* (note 4), at 405.
27 *Cruzan v Director, Missouri Dept of Health* 111 L ed 2d 224 (1990), at 279.
28 See, for example, *Application of the President & Directors of Georgetown College, Inc.*, 331 F.2d 1000, 1006–07 (D.C.Cir. 1964).
29 Report of American Medical Association Board of Trustees 'Legal Interventions during Pregnancy' (1990) 264 *Journal of the American Medical Association* 2663, at 2670.
30 Ibid., at 403–4.
31 Ibid., at 405.

it would be appropriate to compel a woman to undergo a blood transfusion for the benefit of a foetus.[32] Nevertheless, in *Brown* the court rejected the suggestion that a blood transfusion is a relatively non-invasive procedure and that it was distinguishable from cases concerning compelled caesareans on that basis.[33] Whilst it accepted that the state had an important and legitimate interest in potential life, the Court of Appeals stressed that the state's interest in potential life could not override Mrs Brown's valid refusal of consent.

Therefore, it is clear that the courts in some of the states have been willing to override a pregnant woman's competent refusal of a blood transfusion for the sake of the foetus, prioritising the state's interest in potential life and, in the case of *Paddock*, even subordinating the woman's autonomy to the ethical integrity of the medical profession. Given the AMA's statement in 1990, suggesting that judicial intervention will almost always be inappropriate, it is unlikely that the state's interest in the ethical integrity of the medical profession could be held to outweigh the woman's right to refuse medical treatment; however, it is clear that some states will continue to prioritise the state's interest in potential life over the woman's right to autonomy. Although there is a real dearth of reported case law concerning compelled blood transfusions, subsequent to the appellate decision in *Brown*, the Broome County Surrogates Court cited *In re Jamaica Hospital* in support of the view that New York has accepted that the state has the ability to protect foetal life and health,[34] suggesting that in New York the courts may still be prepared to override a woman's refusal of treatment to protect the state's interest in potential life.

Moreover, whilst the Illinois Court of Appeals did hold that a pregnant woman's valid refusal of consent could not be overridden by the state's interest in potential life, it did so when there was no longer any risk to a viable foetus – Mrs Brown had already been forcibly transfused and her baby had been safely delivered. It may be easier for an appellate court to reach a principled decision with the benefit of hindsight and outwith an emergency situation than for a court of first instance to apply those principles when a foetus is at risk. The Court of Appeals stressed the fact that the woman had to be competent to refuse the proposed treatment, giving rise to the question as to how competent a pregnant woman has to be in order to refuse treatment required for the benefit of her foetus. This approach emphasising capacity has also been taken in relation to court-ordered caesareans in Illinois and by the Court of Appeal in England and Wales, and is discussed in detail below, but it should be noted that the assessment of capacity is an extremely flexible tool, capable of eliminating a pregnant woman's autonomy. It is suggested that courts in Illinois and some other states will follow the lead of the Illinois Court of Appeals in prioritising the pregnant woman's

32 *In re Baby Boy Doe, a Fetus v Mother Doe* 632 N.E. 2d 326 (1994), at 333, discussed below, at text accompanying note 61.

33 *In re Brown* (note 4), at 405.

34 *In the Matter of the Guardianship of Baby K, an Infant* 188 Misc.2d 228 (2001), at 231. This case related to the appointment of the pregnant woman's parents as the guardian of her foetus in order to extend the potential grandfather's health insurance cover to the foetus.

autonomy and thus her right to refuse a blood transfusion. However, this will only be the case as long as no doubts are raised about her capacity, doubts that may be difficult to quell in an emergency situation where a foetus is imperilled by the refusal of what some may still consider a relatively minor medical procedure.

3. Court-ordered caesareans

Whilst some may argue that a blood transfusion is a relatively minor procedure, that description is certainly not applicable to the case of a caesarean section, a major operation which exposes the woman to the risk of haemorrhage, infection and damage to her bladder and other abdominal organs. In addition, it poses a significantly increased risk to the woman's life as compared with the risks involved in vaginal delivery, with maternal death being three times more likely to occur in the case of an elective caesarean, or nine times more likely to occur in the case of an emergency caesarean delivery when compared with vaginal delivery.[35] At the same time, a caesarean exposes the foetus to a heightened level of risk of suffering respiratory distress and being cut during the procedure. Nevertheless, courts in the US and England and Wales have ordered women to undergo a caesarean against their will, for the benefit of the foetus, despite the increased risk this posed to the pregnant woman. Indeed, in one case the caesarean ordered by the court to safeguard a foetus was listed as a contributing cause on the woman's death certificate.[36]

a. The application of Roe v Wade*'s third-trimester rule in the caesarean context*

One of the first cases in which an American court held that a woman could be forced to undergo a caesarean for the benefit of the foetus was *Jefferson v Griffin Spalding County Hospital Authority*.[37] Jessie Mae Jefferson was 39 weeks pregnant and suffering from placenta previa, a condition where the placenta lies over the cervix. This condition meant that she was likely to need both a caesarean and a blood transfusion. According to medical advice presented to the court, there was a 99 per cent chance that the foetus would not survive vaginal delivery and a 50 per cent chance that Mrs Jefferson would also not survive vaginal delivery. By contrast, doctors suggested that if the baby were delivered by caesarean, it was almost certain that both lives could be saved. Nevertheless, Mrs Jefferson refused both a caesarean and a transfusion because of her religious beliefs and left the hospital. The hospital sought an order authorising both procedures notwithstanding her lack of consent if she returned to the hospital. The Georgia Supreme Court granted the order, stating:

35 F. G. Cunningham, K. J. Leveno, S. L. Bloom et al., *Williams Obstetrics*, 23rd edn, New York: McGraw-Hill Medical, 2010, at 547, citing M. H. Hall and S. Bewley 'Maternal Mortality and Mode of Delivery' (1999) 354 *Lancet* 776.
36 *In re AC* 573 A.2d 1235 (1990), discussed below.
37 274 SE 2d 457 (1981).

> Because the life of [Mrs Jefferson] and of the unborn child are, at the moment inseparable, the court deems it appropriate to infringe upon the wishes of the mother to the extent it is necessary to give the child an opportunity to live.[38]

The court authorised the doctor to do anything he considered necessary to save the life of the 'unborn child' if Mrs Jefferson were to return to the hospital, but refused to grant an order forcing her to submit to surgery before the onset of labour.

The next day the Georgia Department of Human Resources brought an action for temporary custody of the foetus, alleging that it was a deprived child without proper prenatal care, and asking for an order forcing the mother to submit to a caesarean. The Georgia Supreme Court granted the department a temporary custody order in respect of the foetus and full authorisation to make all decisions relevant to its birth, including giving consent to a caesarean. The court also ordered Mrs Jefferson to submit to an ultrasound and, if the placenta was found to be still blocking the cervix, to submit to a caesarean. In reaching its decision, the court relied[39] on the third-trimester rule set out in *Roe v Wade*, namely that post-viability 'the State in promoting its interest in the potentiality of human life may, if it chooses, regulate, and even proscribe, abortion except where it is necessary, in appropriate medical judgment, for the preservation of the life or health of the mother'.[40] However, as Nancy Rhoden points out, 'There is a quantum leap in logic between prohibiting destruction and requiring surgical preservation' of the foetus.[41] Moreover, in addition to reading into *Roe* the ability for states to proactively intervene in pregnancy to compel women to undergo medical procedures, the terms of the court order appear to suggest that the foetus has constitutional rights that must be protected. In fact, the court appears to have weighed the interests of the woman against those of the foetus, rather than the state's interest in potential life:

> To abort this child would be a criminal offense in Georgia ... A viable unborn child has the right under the U.S. Constitution to the protection of the State through such statutes prohibiting the arbitrary termination of the life of an unborn fetus [citing *Roe v Wade*].[42]

That conclusion is not supported by the majority's judgment in *Roe* which stressed that the foetus is not a person and thus not capable of holding rights. Instead, the Supreme Court found the counterbalance to the woman's right to privacy/ autonomy in the state's interest in potential life.

38 *Jefferson v Griffin Spalding County Hospital Authority* (note 37), at 458.
39 Ibid., at 460.
40 *Roe v Wade* (note 1), at 165 *per* Blackmum J.
41 N. K. Rhoden 'Cesareans and Samaritans' (1987) 15(3) *Law Medicine and Health Care* 118, at 119.
42 *Jefferson v Griffin Spalding County Hospital Authority* (note 37), at 458.

Mrs Jefferson was rescanned and her placenta was found to have moved so that a caesarean delivery was no longer indicated. Worryingly, doctors had (correctly) testified that such movement is impossible, suggesting that this application was made on the basis of a mistaken reading of the ultrasound and highlighting the danger of courts merely accepting medical opinion without seeking independent confirmation of that evidence.

A common feature in cases where the woman's refusal of medical treatment is overridden is that the woman (the defendant) is portrayed as abusive, as selfish and uncaring; in sum she is undeserving of sympathy or respect. The typical case was inverted, however, at least at the appellate level, in what was to become the high-water mark of the American decisions concerning court-ordered caesareans, *Re AC*.[43] Angela Carder was in the terminal stages of cancer and pregnant. She was aware that she might die before her pregnancy reached full term and so she agreed to the performance of a caesarean if it should prove necessary, but only after the 28th week when she felt the foetus would have a better chance of survival. During the 25th gestational week a tumour was found on her lung and she was admitted to hospital where she drifted in and out of consciousness. Her doctors advised her against the performance of a caesarean, and both she and her family accepted their advice that a caesarean might hasten her own death and that the foetus would be unlikely to survive as it had already been deprived of oxygen due to Mrs Carder's condition.

However, the hospital sought a declaration that it would not be unlawful to perform a caesarean without Mrs Carder's consent. Separate counsel were appointed for the foetus, Mrs Carder and her family, and the hospital, emphasising the severability of Mrs Carder and the foetus; the foetus and Mrs Carder were seen as separate individuals with separate interests in need of representation, reducing Mrs Carder's status to little more than a foetal environment, albeit an environment that was becoming increasingly toxic for the foetus as her condition worsened. Although the doctors treating Mrs Carder advised against the performance of a caesarean section, a neonatalist estimated that the foetus had up to a 60 per cent chance of surviving if a caesarean were performed immediately. The court ordered that a caesarean be performed, following the Georgia Supreme Court's decision in *Jefferson* by relying upon the third-trimester rule set out in *Roe v Wade* and the Superior Court's decision in *Re Madyun*, discussed below.[44]

Mrs Carder's obstetrician refused to perform the operation without her consent and she was conscious long enough to hear of the court order and to refuse. An emergency appeal upheld the court order and questioned Mrs Carder's ability to make an informed decision. It was successfully argued that as she had already agreed to a caesarean being performed at 28 weeks, it was reasonable to perform one at this stage of the pregnancy, only two weeks earlier. Thus the fact that Mrs Carder was prepared to sacrifice her own life at 28 weeks was used to justify

43 537 A 2d 1235 (1990).

44 573 A 2d 1259 (DC, 1990). 114 Daily Wash Law Rptr. 2233 (D.C. Super.Ct. July 26, 1986). Published as appendix to *Re A.C.*, 573 A.2d 1235, 1262 (D.C.App. 1990).

martyring her at 26 weeks. The District of Columbia Court of Appeals held that as the foetus had achieved viability, its interests must be balanced against those of the woman. In weighing these interests, the court found that the performance of a

> Caesarean section would not significantly affect Mrs Carder's condition because she had, at best, two days left of sedated life; the complications arising from the surgery would not significantly alter that prognosis. The child, on the other hand, had a chance of surviving delivery, despite the possibility that it would be born handicapped.[45]

Thus the trial court and appellate court entirely disregarded Angela's autonomy and indeed her other interests. They did not merely treat her as a foetal container; rather, as George Annas pointed out, they indulged themselves in a rescue fantasy and dehumanised the dying. They

> treated a live woman as though she were already dead … and then justified their brutal and unprincipled opinion on the basis that she was almost dead and her fetus's interests in life outweighed an interest she might have in her own life or health.[46]

The caesarean was performed. The 26-week-old foetus died within two and a half hours, and Mrs Carder died two days later. Reviewing the case *en banc*, the District of Columbia Court of Appeals held that the trial court had been wrong, and that a patient, even when pregnant, still had a right to autonomy, albeit with a potential caveat:

> We do not quite foreclose the possibility that a conflicting State interest may be so compelling that the patient's wishes must yield, but we anticipate that such cases will be extremely rare and truly exceptional. This is not such a case … Indeed some may doubt that there could ever be a situation extraordinary or compelling enough to justify a massive intrusion into a person's body, such as a caesarean section, against that person's will.[47]

Therefore it was held that it would be 'extremely rare and truly exceptional' for the court to overrule a competent woman's refusal of consent. The court offered no advice as to when such a circumstance might arise that would justify intervention, but tellingly, despite this affirmation of the woman's autonomy, the Columbian District Court of Appeals did not overrule the Superior Court's decision in *Re Madyun*.[48] That case concerned a Muslim woman who was still in labour more

45 533 A 2d 611 (1987), at 617.

46 G. J. Annas, 'She's Going to Die: The Case of Angela C' (1988) 18(1) *Hastings Center Report* 23, at 25.

47 Ibid., at 1252, *per* Terry J.

48 573 A 2d 1259 (DC, 1990). 114 Daily Wash Law Rptr. 2233 (D.C. Super.Ct. July 26, 1986). Published as appendix to *Re A.C.*, 573 A.2d 1235, 1262 (D.C.App. 1990).

than 60 hours after her waters had broken. Her doctors recommended that she undergo a caesarean as the continuance of labour increased the risk of infection to the foetus. However, Ayesha Madyun and her husband both refused to consent to the performance of a caesarean on two grounds: first, their religious belief that, as a Muslim, Mrs Madyun was entitled to decide whether to endanger her health in order to eliminate a possible risk to the life of the foetus; and, second, the main source of their objection to the proposed intervention, their conviction that a caesarean was unnecessary. The hospital sought the court's authorisation to perform a caesarean, arguing that the risk of foetal sepsis was 50–75 per cent, whilst the risk to Mrs Madyun's life and health, from the performance of a caesarean, was only 0.25 per cent. This comparative risk assessment proved extremely persuasive, leading the court to hold that 'Given the significant risks to the fetus versus the minimal risks to the mother, ... there is a compelling interest to intervene and protect the life and safety of the fetus'.[49] The court not only evoked *Roe* in justifying intervention on the basis of a compelling state interest in potential life, but also conflated the foetus with a child extant. Thus the court relied upon the oft-cited passage from the Supreme Court decision in *Prince v Massachusetts*, 'Parents may be free to become martyrs themselves. But it does not follow they are free, in identical circumstances, to make martyrs of their children before they have reached the age of full and legal discretion when they can make that choice for themselves';[50] concluding that 'On these facts, the parents may not make a martyr of their unborn infant' and granting the order.[51]

The order sought was granted by the Superior Court of the District of Columbia at 1.05am and affirmed by the Court of Appeals at 2.08am, despite the fact that there was no evidence of infection at the time. There was no question that Mrs Madyun was competent, but the case differed from that of *Re AC* in that there was only a very small risk to the woman if the caesarean were to be performed, whereas the performance of a caesarean undoubtedly shortened Angela Carder's life. Moreover, in the case of *Madyun* it was argued that the caesarean would benefit not only the foetus but also Mrs Madyun herself, and, unlike *AC*, Mrs Madyun's pregnancy was at full term.[52] Whether this is sufficient to make the *Madyun* case 'extremely rare and truly exceptional' can be doubted, but the Court of Appeals did refuse to overrule the *Madyun* decision in *re AC*. However, it is suggested that *Re Madyun*, rather than *Re AC*, represents the typical case. As the Court of Appeals recognised in *re AC*, 'There was no clear maternal-fetal conflict in this case arising from a competent decision by the mother to forego a procedure for the benefit of the fetus'.[53] Moreover, a further point of contrast that the court did not highlight was that Mrs Carder did not fit the standard profile of women subjected to treatment against their will. The majority of court orders granted

49 573 A 2d 1235, at 1264.
50 321 U.S. 158 (1944), at 170.
51 *Re Madyun* (note 44), at 1260.
52 *In re AC* (note 36), fn 23 at 1252.
53 *In re AC* (note 36), at 1243.

overriding treatment refusals for the benefit of a foetus have been granted in cases where the woman was not white, were being treated in teaching hospitals or receiving public assistance and often did not speak English as their first language.[54] This difference, together with all of the other factors, confirms that it is the case of *Re AC* that should be considered atypical and suggests that the strong affirmation of the woman's autonomy set out in that case may be similarly atypical.

The case of *Re AC* also diverged from the norm in the way that the narrative of the case was constructed. The Court of Appeals made it clear that the villains of this piece were the doctors, the professionals who were prepared to sacrifice Mrs Carder in the hope of saving the foetus. The trial court had suggested that she might lack the capacity to make a decision and that it was illogical to consent to a caesarean being performed in the future, but not at the present time when medical opinion clearly viewed it as imperative that the foetus be delivered now. By contrast, the Appeals Court portrayed Mrs Carder as a thoroughly decent, moral woman, a woman who wanted the best for her child, rather than a capricious, selfish woman who was refusing to comply with medical advice. Of course, by the time of the review there was no longer a foetal life hanging in the balance, a factor that makes it significantly easier for a court to expound the importance of recognising and protecting a woman's right to autonomy.

b. The legacy of Re AC*: differing interpretations of 'extremely rare' and 'truly exceptional'*

The shocking way in which Angela Carder was mistreated by the medical and legal apparatus led the medical professional bodies to give significant consideration to how such scenarios should be managed in the future. Thus in 1990 the American Medical Association's House of Delegates adopted the recommendation that 'Judicial intervention is inappropriate when a woman has made an informed refusal of a medical treatment designed to benefit her fetus'.[55] However, echoing the court in *re AC*, the AMA did not foreclose the possibility that intervention might not be justified in exceptional circumstances, noting that if 'a medical treatment poses an insignificant or no health risk to the woman, entails a minimal invasion of her bodily integrity, and would clearly prevent substantial and irreversible harm to her fetus, it might be appropriate for a physician to seek judicial intervention'.[56] Thus, although appearing to support the pregnant woman's autonomy, the AMA's qualification regarding what might constitute an exceptional circumstance would appear to reflect the arguments used to justify intervention in *Re Madyun*, arguably a very typical case, rather than the exceptional circumstance suggested. Moreover, it is argued that the person who determines the significance of the risk or degree of invasion involved should be the person who will bear that risk and

54 V. E. B. Kolder, J. Gallagher and M. T. Parsons, 'Court-Ordered Obstetrical Interventions' (1987) 316 *New England Journal of Medicine* 1192, at 1193.

55 Report of American Medical Association Board of Trustees (note 29), at 2670.

56 Ibid.

whose bodily integrity will be invaded, particularly in view of the fact that minor risks are only ever those undergone by other people!

Despite the AMA's recommendation that judicial intervention would be inappropriate in all but exceptional circumstances, a further instance of a doctor seeking just such intervention arose in *In re Baby Boy Doe, a Fetus v Mother Doe.*[57] Somewhat surprisingly, the same doctor testified that he was not advocating that the caesarean be performed over the woman's objection,[58] perhaps believing that the court would succeed in persuading her to have a caesarean where he had failed! At 35 weeks' gestation, doctors advised Tabita Bricci (referred to as Mother Doe) that the foetus was not receiving enough oxygen and that a caesarean should be performed, or at the very least labour should be induced. Due to her religious beliefs, Mrs Bricci refused both courses of action, saying that she wanted to await natural childbirth. The obstetrician referred the matter to the State's Attorney who requested the appointment of the hospital as the foetus's custodian and an order requiring Mrs Bricci to submit to a caesarean. The Appellate Court of Illinois followed the Illinois Supreme Court's decision in *Stallman v Youngquist*,[59] holding that no balancing exercise should be undertaken between the rights of the foetus and those of the pregnant woman. Moreover, relying upon the Supreme Court's decision in *Thornburgh v American College of Obstetricians and Gynecologists*,[60] the court stressed that the woman's health is always the paramount consideration and that any degree of increased risk to the woman's health is unacceptable. Having accepted that a caesarean does increase the risk to a woman's life and health, as compared with the risks associated with vaginal delivery, the court held that a woman's competent choice to refuse invasive medical treatment should be honoured, even if that might harm the foetus.[61] However, the court did draw a distinction between invasive treatment (such as a caesarean) and relatively non-invasive, relatively risk-free procedures (such as a blood transfusion), saying that the question of whether a woman could be required to submit to the latter for the benefit of the foetus should be considered at a later date.[62] Of course, this question was resolved by the Illinois Supreme Court in *In re Brown*[63] where it was held that a pregnant woman may refuse any medical treatment regardless of whether that refusal might lead to the foetus suffering harm or indeed death.

Thus the Appellate Court of Illinois reached a decision strongly supporting the woman's autonomy and stressing that a caesarean was a major operation entailing serious risks for the pregnant woman. Following the detailed consideration given

57 *In re Baby Boy Doe, a Fetus v Mother Doe* (note 32).

58 Ibid., at 328.

59 125 Ill.2d 267 (1988).

60 476 U.S. 747 (1986) at 769.

61 *In re Baby Boy Doe, a Fetus v Mother Doe* (note 32), at 393. The court accepted that the maternal morbidity risk associated with a caesarean is about 1:10,000, whilst in relation to vaginal delivery the morbidity risk is much lower, being set at between 1:20,000 and 1:50,000, at 328.

62 *In re Baby Boy Doe, a Fetus v Mother Doe* (note 32), at 333.

63 *In re Brown* (note 4).

to this issue by the superior courts in *Baby Boy Doe* and *Re AC*, coupled with the guidance issued by the medical professional bodies,[64] it might have been expected that hospitals would no longer intervene in treatment refusal cases. However, five years later, in *Pemberton v Tallahassee Memorial Regional Medical Center*,[65] a federal district court dismissed the notion of a woman's autonomy entitling her to refuse a caesarean and minimised the risks involved in a caesarean by remarking that no medical procedures are without risk! Laura Pemberton had undergone a caesarean the previous year, and upon becoming pregnant again she sought advice from a number of doctors, insisting that she wanted to give birth naturally and did not want another caesarean. Unfortunately, her previous caesarean had been unusual in the sense that a vertical rather than horizontal incision had been made and this meant that there was a much greater risk of uterine rupture during any subsequent vaginal delivery than would be the case with a more typical caesarean section. All the doctors she consulted told her that a vaginal delivery was not a viable option and that she would have to undergo a further caesarean. Therefore, Mrs Pemberton decided to give birth at home, attended only by a midwife. After a day in labour she was becoming dehydrated and so she went to the emergency room of the Tallahassee Memorial Regional Medical Center and requested an intravenous infusion of fluids. The doctors advised her that she needed a caesarean, and when she refused to consent to one, they refused to supply her with the IV she had requested. Mrs Pemberton left the hospital with her husband, and the State Attorney sought a court order requiring Mrs Pemberton to submit to a caesarean. A hearing was convened at the hospital and following medical testimony that vaginal birth would pose a substantial risk of uterine rupture and result in the death of the foetus, the judge ordered Mrs Pemberton to return to the hospital. The State Attorney went to Mrs Pemberton's home, together with a police officer, and forced her to return to the hospital. The hearing reconvened in Mrs Pemberton's room and the judge ordered that a caesarean be performed.

After the caesarean was performed, Mrs Pemberton filed for damages, claiming that the caesarean had been unnecessary and that her constitutional rights (including her rights to bodily integrity, to refuse unwanted medical treatment, to make important personal and family decisions regarding the bearing of children without undue governmental interference and her right to religious freedom) had been violated. The federal district court dismissed all her claims. Hinkle J held that Mrs Pemberton's rights had to be weighed against the interests of the State of Florida in preserving the life of the unborn child. Relying upon the third-trimester rule set out in *Roe v Wade*, he dismissed the distinction between affirmative intervention and mere prohibition of abortion as superficial,[66] reasoning that

64 American College of Obstetricians and Gynecologists, Committee on Ethics, Committee Opinion 321 'Maternal Decision Making, Ethics and the Law' (2005) 106 *Obstetrics & Gynecology* 1127; American Medical Association Board of Trustees Report: 'Legal Interventions during Pregnancy' (1990) 264 *Journal of the American Medical Association* 2663.

65 66 F.Supp.2d 1247 (N.D. Fla. 1999).

66 Ibid., at 1251, n.9

> a third-trimester mother can be forced against her will to bear a child she does not want; this is in fact a substantially greater imposition on the mother's constitutional interests than requiring a mother to give birth by one method rather than another.[67]

Therefore it was held that because the birth was imminent and Mrs Pemberton only wanted to avoid giving birth in a particular manner, the state's interest in preserving the life of the unborn child outweighed her own constitutional rights.[68] Indeed, the fact that Mrs Pemberton was merely trying to avoid delivery by caesarean section appears to have been a predominant factor in the judge's reasoning, as he stressed:

> The balance tips far more strongly in favor of the state [in preserving the life of the foetus] in the case at bar, because here the full-term baby's birth was imminent, and more importantly, here the mother sought only to avoid a particular procedure for giving birth, not to avoid giving birth altogether... . The state's interest here was greater, and the mother's interest less, than during the third trimester situation addressed in *Roe*.[69]

Moreover, the court dismissed the Appellate Court of Illinois' decision in *In re Baby Boy Doe* by saying that a court may decide to hold that the interests of a foetus cannot be considered under state law, but that this did not mean that, as a matter of federal constitutional law, another state must follow that approach.

A typical feature of these cases is the substantial weight given to medical evidence and the immense impact it has in displacing the woman's own wishes and beliefs. The way in which judges appear to simply accept medical evidence almost without question might simply reflect professional courtesy, but given the high level of medical negligence litigation that is now conducted on both sides of the Atlantic, it seems rather quaint, not to say unwarranted, that judges are prepared to accept medical evidence so readily. In this case Hinkle J emphasised that on the 'clear and uncontradicted' medical evidence, the interests of the foetus required a caesarean section in order to avert the serious threat to its life. In fact, the medical evidence was not unanimous. Expert testimony on behalf of the hospital was offered by five doctors; one suggested that the risk of uterine rupture was 4–6 per cent; another, specifically described by the judge as a national expert, assessed the risk to be from 6 to 10 per cent at the low end, or even as high as 60 per cent. By contrast, Mrs Pemberton's expert (Dr Wagner) placed the risk of uterine rupture at 2–2.2 per cent and said that in the eventuality of rupture the risk to the life of the foetus was around 50 per cent.[70] Hinkle J was noticeably dismissive of Dr Wagner's testimony: whilst accepting his credentials as impressive, he noted that he had

67 Ibid.
68 Ibid., at 1251.
69 Ibid., at 1251–2.
70 Ibid., at 1253.

been living and working outside the US for a long time when the operation was performed and that he did not appear to have practised during that time. Dismissing Mrs Pemberton's belief that she could have safely delivered the foetus vaginally as 'bravado', and Dr Wagner's evidence, the judge flippantly remarked, 'Presumably there would still be no passengers on a plane if the risk of a crash was only two percent and if, in any crash, only half the passengers would die'.[71]

Therefore, Hinkle J concluded that the risk to the foetus was substantial, regardless of whether the risk was set at 1 or 60 per cent. Clearly, if a 1 per cent risk to the foetal life would justify intervention overriding the woman's autonomy, the threshold for intervention is being set very low. Indeed, the risks posed by a caesarean to both the woman and the foetus appear to have been given minimal weight in the judge's balancing of interests. Hinkle J accepted that caesarean sections are not without risk, saying:

> Medical procedures rarely are. The risk from a caesarean was far less, by orders of magnitude, than the risk from vaginal delivery … This case is thus markedly different from *In re A.C.*, 573 A.2d 1235 (D.C.App.1990), in which the court held that a caesarean could not properly be ordered for a terminally ill woman in her 26th week of pregnancy whose death would be hastened by the performance of the proposed caesarean.[72]

Moreover, Hinkle J concluded that the current case was one of the 'extremely rare and truly exceptional' cases referred to in *re AC*, where it was held that a non-consenting patient's interest could yield to a more compelling countervailing interest in such a case, thus allowing a woman to be forced to submit to a caesarean for the purpose of protecting the state's interest in potential life. He stated:

> In anything other than an extraordinary and overwhelming case, the right to decide would surely rest with the mother, not with the state. But based on the evidence disclosed by this record, this was an extraordinary and overwhelming case; no reasonable or even unreasonable argument could be made in favor of vaginal delivery at home with the attendant risk of death to the baby (and concomitant grave risk to the mother).[73]

In fact, in four subsequent pregnancies Mrs Pemberton went on to have successful vaginal deliveries, despite Hinkle J and the medical experts he relied upon being unable to conceive of this possibility.

A further 'extremely rare and truly exceptional' case, at least in the view of the Pennsylvanian court, appears to have arisen in *Wyoming Valley Health Care*

71 Ibid. In fact, Marsden Wagner M.D. is a former Director of Women's and Children's Health at the World Health Organisation. He campaigns for less intervention in labour; see, for example, M. Wagner, *Born in the USA: How a Broken Maternity System Must Be Fixed to Put Women and Children First*, Berkeley: University of California Press, 2008.

72 *Pemberton v Tallahassee Memorial Regional Medical Center* (note 65), at 1254.

73 Ibid.

Systems, Inc. & Baby Doe v Jane Doe and John Doe (2004).[74] Amber Marlowe had been in labour for two days; she first attended Mercy Hospital, but following an ultrasound was advised that the foetus was likely to weigh in excess of 13 pounds and that due to the size of the foetus a caesarean delivery would be necessary. Mrs Marlowe had already given birth to six children, each of whom had been large, and believed that she could give birth to the seventh vaginally as well. She was also extremely reluctant to have a caesarean due to the fact that her friend had died whilst undergoing the procedure. Therefore Mr and Mrs Marlowe refused to consent to the performance of a caesarean and left the hospital. Later that same day they went to WVHCS seeking assistance, but were again advised that a vaginal delivery posed a risk to both Mrs Marlowe and the foetus, and that a caesarean should be performed. Doctors tried to convince the Marlowes to consent to a caesarean, but the following day, when Mrs Marlowe discharged herself whilst still in labour, the hospital applied to the court for the appointment of itself as guardian of the foetus and for an injunction restraining the Marlowes from refusing to consent to a caesarean if such were considered necessary by the attending doctors.

The court granted the injunction and appointed the hospital as guardian of the foetus 'to preserve and protect the rights of Baby Doe regarding its health and survival before, during and after delivery'. Throughout this time there was no indication that the foetus was in distress and there was no suggestion that there was an immediate need to deliver the foetus, but the doctors believed that a vaginal delivery would endanger the foetus's health and both lives, and were prepared to go to court to seek an order to compel Mrs Marlowe to comply with their advice. Indeed, the Marlowes were not informed of the application and the court granted the order sought without even speaking to the couple who were neither present nor represented at the hearing due to the *ex parte* application. The court simply accepted the hospital's testimony and medical opinion that a caesarean was necessary to safeguard the foetus. As in *Madyun*, it was suggested that the Marlowes' decision was not entirely rational and that it was based on their religious beliefs – the hospital's application stated that the Marlowes made 'vague references to their religious beliefs, among other things as reasons for their refusal'.[75] The Marlowes disputed that their refusal was religiously motivated in interviews they gave to the press after the birth of their daughter. As the case was not appealed, there is no clear record of why the court felt there was sufficient cause to justify overriding Mrs Marlowe's refusal of consent. However, the caesarean was not performed as, ignorant of the fact that the hospital had applied for guardianship of their foetus, the Marlowes left WVHCS Hospital and went to a third hospital where Mrs Marlowe gave birth to a baby girl weighing 11 pounds and 9 ounces. The baby was delivered vaginally without incident, illustrating once again that doctors are

74 *WVHCS-Hosp., Inc.* v. *Doe*, No. 3-E-2004, 1–2 (Pa. Ct. Com. Pl. Jan. 14, 2004), unreported. A copy of the court order and the hospital's application for the appointment of a guardian of the foetus together with an injunction to enable the hospital to perform a caesarean to deliver the foetus is available at http://advocatesforpregnantwomen.org/WVHCSBabyDoevJaneandJohnDoe.pdf (accessed 13 August 2015).

75 Ibid., point 11 of the hospital's verified complaint.

not always correct when they say that a caesarean is necessary to protect the life and/or health of the foetus.

The most recent reported US case in which a court ordered a woman to undergo a caesarean section again involved the Tallahassee Memorial Hospital in Florida.[76] Samantha Burton was 25 weeks pregnant and was admitted to the hospital because her doctor believed that she was at risk of miscarriage. He advised that she stop work, should stay in the hospital with complete bed rest for the remainder of her pregnancy and give up smoking immediately. Given that the normal duration of pregnancy is 40 weeks, this could have entailed her remaining in hospital for 15 weeks, an unrealistic prospect for the mother of two young children. Ms Burton refused to accept this medical advice and the hospital informed the State Attorney that she had refused medical treatment. Upon the application by the State Attorney, Cooper J granted an order compelling Ms Burton to submit to any medical treatment, including a caesarean and detention in hospital for enforced bed rest, deemed necessary by her obstetrician to 'preserve the life and health of [her] unborn child'.[77]

Somewhat surprisingly, given the Supreme Court's ruling in *Roe* and the recognition that the counterbalance to the woman's right to refuse treatment was the state's interest in potential life, Cooper J made the order not on the basis that the state had a compelling interest that would override Ms Burton's right to refuse treatment but on the basis of the foetus's best interests. He held that 'as between parent and child, the ultimate welfare of the child is the controlling factor' and that the state's interests in the matter 'override Ms Burton's privacy interests at this time'.[78] Moreover, finding that if Ms Burton did not comply with the recommended course of treatment there was 'a "substantial and unacceptable" risk of severe injury or death to the unborn child', the judge purported to exercise the state's *parens patriae* authority (used to override a parent's refusal of treatment for a child extant) to require Ms Burton to undergo treatment. He also refused Ms Burton's request to transfer to a different hospital, stating that 'such a change is not in the child's best interest at this time'.[79]

Ms Burton did submit to the order, was confined to hospital and underwent a caesarean section two days after the order was made, but the foetus had already died in utero. On appeal to the District Court of Appeal of Florida, it was held that the trial court had erred in considering whether the treatment was in the foetus's best interests. Clark J held that the proper test to be applied was whether

76 *Samantha Burton v Florida* 39 So. 3d 263 (Fla. Dist. Ct. App. 2010).

77 There is no transcript of the circuit court's decision. Details have been taken from the Brief of Amici Curiae American Civil Liberties Union, American Civil Liberties Union of Florida and American Medical Women's Association in Support of Appellant, at 2, citing Appellant's Ex. D, at 1–2. Brief available at www.aclu.org/files/pdfs/reproductiverights/burton_v_florida_acluamicus.pdf (accessed 13 August 2015).

78 Quoted by Clark J in the appellate opinion (note 76), at 265.

79 Taken from Brief of Amici Curiae American Civil Liberties Union, American Civil Liberties Union of Florida and American Medical Women's Association in Support of Appellant, citing Appellant's Ex. D, at 3.

the state's interest was sufficiently compelling to override the woman's right to refuse medical treatment and that action taken on this basis must be narrowly tailored so as to limit the intrusion upon the rights of the individual as far as possible.[80] However, the appeal court did not indicate whether the state's interest would have been sufficiently compelling in this case to require Ms Burton to spend the remaining four months of the pregnancy in a hospital bed, to refrain from work and from smoking and to consent to a caesarean to further that interest, or whether the state's interest could have been protected in a less intrusive manner.

Although no further court orders compelling women to undergo caesareans have been reported, two further cases of the coercion of pregnant women in the United States have been widely reported in the press during 2014 and have been the subject of legal proceedings. The Florida case concerned Jennifer Goodall, a woman who had previously had three caesarean deliveries.[81] She had discussed the delivery of her fourth baby with her healthcare providers and wanted to have a trial of labour, although she was willing to consent to a caesarean should it become necessary. At a prenatal check-up, when she was 38 weeks pregnant, she received a letter from the hospital where she was being cared for, stating that the hospital ethics committee had reviewed her case and intended to contact the Department of Children and Family Services about her refusal to consent to a caesarean, to start legal proceedings for a court order regarding the delivery and that should she attend the hospital and doctors deem it clinically necessary they would perform a caesarean with or without her consent. Ms Goodall sought a temporary restraining order preventing the hospital from carrying out its threats, but the application was refused. Steele J held that there was no legitimate basis to forbid the defendant notifying the Department of Children and Family Services, initiating judicial proceedings if warranted, and that

> The Court also finds that Plaintiff has not established she is substantially likely to succeed on the merits of her claim that she has a right to compel a physician or medical facility to perform a medical procedure in the manner she wishes against their best medical judgment.[82]

However, Ms Goodall was not trying to compel doctors to perform a medical procedure in a manner contrary to their best medical judgment – labour is not a medical procedure performed by doctors upon a pregnant woman. Instead, Ms Goodall wanted to have a trial labour; it was the doctors who wanted to

80 *Samantha Burton v Florida* (note 76), per Clark J, at 266.

81 *Jennifer Goodall v Comprehensive Women's Health Center, Bayfront Medical Health Group, Bayfront Health Port Charlotte*, Case No: 2:14-cv-399-FtM-38CM, unreported. United States District Court, M.D. Florida, Fort Myers Division, 18 July 2014, unreported. A copy of the court order is available at http://advocatesforpregnantwomen.org/documents/Goodall%20-%20Order%20Denying%20TRO.pdf (accessed 13 August 2015).

82 Ibid., at 6.

compel Ms Goodall to consent to them performing a medical procedure in the manner they wished contrary to her desire for a vaginal birth. Ultimately, Ms Goodall did have a caesarean, but she did so having consented once it became clear that a caesarean was clinically necessary.

The other case occurred in New York and allegedly involved doctors overriding Rinat Dray's refusal of consent to caesarean without a court order. Ms Dray had had two previous caesareans, but hoped to deliver her third child vaginally. After a number of hours in labour, she alleges that doctors delivered her son by caesarean despite her refusal of consent and protests; during the course of the operation her bladder was perforated. The *New York Times* has reported that the hospital's director of maternal and foetal medicine wrote on her notes, 'I have decided to override her refusal to have a C-section'.[83] There is no suggestion that Ms Dray lacked the capacity to make an effective refusal of consent, and it appears that, as in the case of Ms Goodall, she was told that her refusal amounted to child abuse and that her child would be taken away from her. Ms Dray is currently suing the hospital for malpractice.

In both of these cases it would appear that the hospitals were willing to override refusal of consent to major surgery made by a woman with capacity. In both cases threats appear to have been used to try to 'persuade' the women to acquiesce, but neither case would appear to be such that it could be termed 'extremely rare and truly exceptional'. Moreover, it is extremely concerning that in both cases doctors appear to have been willing to override a woman's refusal of consent without seeking a court order, indicating a significant degree of confidence that such actions would be regarded as legitimate in any subsequent litigation.

4. The use of pregnancy exceptions in advance directive legislation

a. Precedent autonomy: advance directives as a means of extending decisional autonomy past the onset of incapacity

It is well accepted that 'every person's body is inviolate'[84] and that an adult patient with the requisite capacity may refuse medical treatment, including life-sustaining treatment. The logical extension of this principle is that individuals with capacity should also be enabled to exercise precedent autonomy, making choices during times of capacity that will take effect in the future where the individual lacks the capacity to make a contemporaneous decision, rather than treatment decisions being taken by a third party based on the patient's best interests or substituted judgment.[85] However, as the cases discussed above demonstrate, the general principle that an individual with capacity may give a contemporaneous binding

83 A. Hartocollis, 'Mother Accuses Doctors of Forcing a C-Section' *New York Times*, 16.05.2014, A18.

84 *In re F (Mental Patient: Sterilisation)* [1990] 2 A.C. 1, per Lord Goff, at 72.

85 S. Halliday, 'Legislating to Give Effect to Precedent Autonomy: Comparative Reflections on Legislative Incompetence' (2011) 11 *Medical Law International* 127.

refusal of treatment does not appear to apply in equal measure to pregnant women. Despite the strong affirmation of a woman's autonomy irrespective of pregnancy set out by the superior courts in *Baby Boy Doe* and *Re AC*, a number of state courts have recognised that the state's interest in potential life may justify the overriding of a woman's autonomy through compelled obstetric intervention. The inequality between treatment refusals made by pregnant and non-pregnant individuals is, however, even more marked in relation to precedent autonomy; most states, including Illinois, restrict or disqualify a woman's advance refusal of treatment if she is pregnant.

The principle of patient autonomy stresses respect for the patient as an individual, rather than as an object of concern, and attempts to promote precedent autonomy aim to extend that respect to those no longer capable of exercising autonomy and thereby to prioritise the patient's wishes over her welfare. An important mechanism for conveying that precedent autonomy is an advance directive, an instrument that originated in the United States of America during the 1960s,[86] which is designed to act as a communication bridge in the event of incapacity and provide a clear statement of how the patient wants to be treated, or more usually what treatment the patient does not wish to be afforded. However, whilst an important tool, an advance directive is a mono-directional form of communication that takes effect only once the patient lacks capacity and is therefore no longer able to discuss alternative treatment and care options, to clarify her wishes or, indeed, potentially to rescind her previously expressed wishes. The temporal and psychological distance that separates the anticipatory decision from the time at which it should be implemented differentiates anticipatory choices from contemporaneous ones, and the asymmetries between such decisions will be particularly important where there has been a significant change in circumstances since the drafting of the advance directive.[87] One such change might be the fact that the woman is pregnant at the time the directive falls to be implemented.

Arguably, the fact of pregnancy may have a significant impact upon the woman's decision to refuse treatment. It may be argued that she would not have intended her anticipatory decision to apply where the refusal of treatment would deprive the foetus of the opportunity to develop to a point at which it could be safely delivered. Alternatively, her critical interests and values may be unchanged by pregnancy so that she would still wish her decision to be implemented, notwithstanding the impact this would have upon the foetus. Therefore, both in Germany and in England and Wales questions about the validity and applicability of an advance decision may arise in the case of a pregnant woman; however, advance directives remain valid unless it is shown that the woman would not have intended her refusal to apply whilst pregnant. By contrast, the legislation relating to advance directives in the individual US states underscores the inequality

86 L. Kutner, 'Due Process of Euthanasia: The Living Will, a Proposal' (1969) 44 *Indiana Law Journal* 539.

87 S. Halliday, 'Legislating to Give Effect to Precedent Autonomy: Comparative Reflections on Legislative Incompetence' (note 85), at 128f.

between pregnant women and their non-pregnant counterparts, with advance directives generally being invalidated, or at least restricted, during pregnancy.

b. The basis for a pregnancy-based exclusion or limitation clauses in advance directive legislation

Following the Supreme Court's decision in *Cruzan*,[88] recognising the right to refuse life-sustaining treatment, Congress passed the Patient Self-Determination Act requiring health care providers that accept Medicare funding to inform all patients of their rights under state law to refuse medical treatment and to formulate an advance directive.[89] Whilst advance directives are regulated within the broader legislative context relating to those lacking capacity in Germany and in England and Wales,[90] in the United States legislation regulating precedent autonomy has been enacted at the individual state level through legislation dealing specifically with advance directives. Thus in every state and the District of Columbia legislation has been introduced giving effect to anticipatory decision-making in the form of an advance directive and/or the ability to appoint a healthcare proxy.[91] Whilst each state has adopted its own legislation, there are two distinctive features worthy of note from the outset: first, the US Acts restrict advance directives to situations where the patient is terminally ill or will not recover;[92] second in the majority of the Acts an advance directive is either automatically invalidated in the case of pregnancy or rendered inapplicable in certain circumstances when the declarant is pregnant. As the cases discussed above demonstrate, on one interpretation of the third-trimester rule set out in *Roe*, the state has an interest in potential life throughout pregnancy that becomes compelling from viability, and the state may act to protect that interest by requiring that the woman accept medical treatment for the benefit of the foetus. Thus, it may be suggested that just as the state's interest can justify the prohibition of abortion after viability (subject to the necessary health and life exceptions for the pregnant woman),[93] the state should be able similarly to require women to accept life-sustaining treatment, at least from the point of viability, in order to preserve foetal life.

In the context of anticipatory refusals, this interest was recognised by the Superior Court of Richmond Count, Georgia in *University Health Services Inc. v Piazzi*.[94] Donna Piazzi was discovered unconscious and not breathing in a public

88 *Cruzan v Director, Missouri Dept of Health* (note 27), at 278.

89 42 U.S.C. § 1395cc(f) (2011).

90 See s.24ff., Mental Capacity Act 2005; § 1901a Iff., Bürgerliches Gesetzbuch (BGB).

91 For an excellent overview of advance directive legislation, see B. J. Horttor, 'A Survey of Living Will and Advanced Health Care Directives' (1998) 74 *North Dakota Law Review* 233. In this chapter I will focus upon advance directives as a means of anticipatory decision-making.

92 See also D. Sperling, 'Do Pregnant Women Have (Living) Will?' (2005) 8(2) *Journal of Health Care Law & Policy* 331, at 333.

93 *Roe v Wade* (note 1). At 164.

94 4 August 1986, reprinted in (1987) 2 *Issues in Law & Medicine* 415.

toilet; she was 16 weeks pregnant. Her condition deteriorated and doctors pronounced her brain dead. The foetus was not viable, but doctors advised that if life support were maintained, the foetus would continue to develop until such a point as it could be delivered by caesarean and survive outside the uterus. Mrs Piazzi's husband wanted the hospital to terminate life support for his wife; however, David Hadden claimed to be the father of the foetus (a claim not disputed by Robert Piazzi) and wanted the hospital to maintain life support so that the foetus could continue to develop. Mrs Piazzi's own wishes were unknown, but in any event the court held that the woman's privacy rights terminated upon brain death. Moreover, it held that:

> The law is settled that ... after viability the state can both prohibit abortions and require that the mother undergo necessary treatment to protect the life of the fetus... . Although *Jefferson v Griffin Spalding County Hospital Authority* is factually distinguishable because the fetus in that case was viable, the court's ruling clearly showed the state's interest in, and preference for, the preservation of life or potential life.[95]

Moreover, the court recognised that the Georgia advance directive statute contained a pregnancy exclusion,[96] so that 'even though the law permits a patient to choose whether or not life support systems will be maintained for that patient, the legislature has specifically provided that the patient cannot make the decision if it will affect an unborn child'.[97] Thus the court concluded that life support must be maintained. In doing so, it treated Mrs Piazzi and the foetus as separate entities, holding that whilst Mrs Piazzi could refuse treatment for herself, she could not do so on behalf of the foetus. Thus, as the only way to maintain the foetus was to provide life support to the pregnant woman, the court declared that life support should be maintained as long as there was a reasonable possibility that the foetus could develop and survive. Once the foetus could be delivered, life support to Mrs Piazzi could be terminated; her role as incubator would be complete.

As Mrs Piazzi had not written an advance directive, her wishes regarding whether or not she would have wanted to have been maintained on life support after brain death were not known; however, as the court made clear, her wishes were irrelevant. In this case the court held that brain death extinguishes the right to autonomy, but it relied upon the Georgia advance directive legislation in emphasising that Georgia public policy required the maintenance of life support for the benefit of the foetus. Thus it would appear that even in other cases, cases where the patient is not brain dead and therefore her privacy/autonomy interests remain intact, the state's interest in potential life can override an anticipatory refusal of treatment.

95 Ibid., at 417.
96 Georgia Code § 31–32–2 stated that an advance directive 'shall have no force and effect during the course of pregnancy'.
97 Ibid., at 418.

c. Forms of pregnancy-based limitation and exclusion clauses

The pregnancy exclusions found in advance directive legislation fall broadly into six categories. The most extreme form can be found in legislation from states including Texas, Alabama and Connecticut, where the Acts automatically invalidate an advance directive for the duration of pregnancy, regardless of whether the woman has specifically addressed the circumstance of pregnancy or not.[98] For example, § 22–8A-4(e) Alabama Code states: 'The advance directive for health care of a declarant who is known by the attending physician to be pregnant shall have no effect during the course of the declarant's pregnancy'. Significantly, the provision refers to the doctor's knowledge of the pregnancy; it does not impose a duty upon the doctor to determine whether or not the woman is pregnant. Moreover, the provisions invalidate the advance directives regardless of whether the continued treatment of the woman might subject her to pain, or otherwise extend her suffering, and without regard to the stage of foetal development. It is suggested that such clauses are best regarded as incubator clauses as they elevate concern for the preservation of foetal life above any recognition of the woman's right to self-determination, or indeed her welfare.

By suspending the validity of an advance directive in all cases, without consideration of whether the foetus may be capable of surviving even if treatment is given to the woman, these states show complete disregard for the woman's autonomy. A more nuanced approach is taken by other states which exclude the applicability of advance directives where treatment might possibly lead to a live birth. For example, the Illinois legislation states:

> The declaration of a qualified patient diagnosed as pregnant by the attending physician shall be given no force and effect as long as in the opinion of the attending physician it is possible that the fetus could develop to the point of live birth with the continued application of death delaying procedures.[99]

Clearly, 'possible' is an extremely broad term in this context and thus it is suggested that this clause will justify the treatment of a pregnant woman in most circumstances, regardless of whether the foetus has achieved viability or not; indeed, it is possible that a foetus in the very early stages of pregnancy could develop to the point of live birth.

A slightly narrower type of clause excludes the applicability of an advance directive where treatment will probably lead to live birth, the clause favoured by the model Uniform Rights of the Terminally Ill Act (URTIA).[100] The URTIA is intended only to apply to the terminally ill and thus would not apply to, for example, someone in a persistent vegetative state. S.6(c) states:

98 Texas Health and Safety Code § 166.049; Alabama Code § 22–8A-4(e); Connecticut General Statutes § 19a-574 (2011) Sec. 19a-574.

99 755 Ill. Comp. Stat 35/3 § 3(c).

100 Pregnancy is not mentioned in the Uniform Health-Care Decisions Act 1993 that superseded URTIA.

> Life-sustaining treatment must not be withheld or withdrawn pursuant to a declaration from an individual known to the attending physician to be pregnant so long as it is probable that the fetus will develop to the point of live birth with the continued application of life-sustaining treatment.

No indication is given of how probable it must be that further treatment will enable the foetus to develop to the point it can be delivered, or even of whether the foetus should have achieved viability. Moreover, whilst the original version (1985) of the URTIA contained an exception for the case where the woman had specifically stated that the directive should apply in the case of pregnancy, the revised version contains no such limitation and thus renders the pregnant woman's wishes irrelevant.

In contrast to the previous two pregnancy exceptions, a further variant avoids the need to assess the likely probability, or indeed possibility, of the foetus developing to live birth by adopting viability as the threshold for invalidating an advance directive. Thus the Colorado and Georgia legislation both limit the validity of advance directives to cases where the foetus within the declarant's uterus has not achieved viability.[101] Such an exception is more consistent with the Supreme Court's abortion jurisprudence, but it still fails to try to balance the state's interest in potential life against the pregnant woman's autonomy interest.

The fifth category of pregnancy exception to be found in advance directive legislation is premised on the continuance of treatment in order to secure the further development of the foetus, but takes account of the woman's health interests by providing that her anticipatory refusal of treatment will be effective if the treatment would be physically harmful to her, or would prolong severe pain which cannot be alleviated by medication. Such an exception is found in the Kentucky legislation and that of New Hampshire.[102] Whilst this form of exception takes account of the woman's physical well-being, and therefore reflects the state's interest in protecting the woman's health and life, it does so by treating her as an object of concern, rather than as an individual with critical interests that outstrip her claim to be free of pain. Her autonomy, her right to bodily integrity and her dignity are totally disregarded in the quest to save the foetal life.

The final class of pregnancy exception takes the form of a rebuttable presumption that the woman would have wanted treatment to be continued where there is a real possibility that the foetus could develop to the stage where it could be born alive. A good example of such a presumption is set out in the Minnesota legislation which recognises that such a presumption can be displaced either by an advance decision to the contrary or by clear and convincing evidence of her wishes to the contrary.[103] Although the presumption is set out in favour of treatment to preserve the potential for continued foetal development, such a provision does recognise the woman as an autonomous being with a right to refuse medical

101 Colorado Revised Statutes § 15–18–104; Georgia Code § 31–32–9.

102 Kentucky Revised Statutes § 311.629(4); New Hampshire Revised Statutes 137-J:10.

103 Minnesota Statutes § 145C.10(g). A similar presumption is set out in the Oklahoma legislation: Oklahoma Statutes title 63, § 3101.4.

treatment, despite the fact that she is pregnant. However, it expresses the expectation that a woman will accept treatment for the benefit of her foetus, treatment that would not be imposed upon her in other circumstances.[104]

Not all living will statutes restrict the validity of advance directives during pregnancy. Thus, for example, the Vermont statute states:

> (a) An adult may do any or all of the following in an advance directive: ... (8) direct which life sustaining treatment the principal would desire or not desire if the principal is pregnant at the time an advance directive becomes effective.[105]

However, the recognition of a woman's right to refuse life-sustaining treatment in the event of pregnancy is often accompanied by an invitation to opt in to treatment in the case of pregnancy. Thus, for example, the Arizona legislation contains a sample living will, where one of the provisions that female declarants are invited to tick states:

> Notwithstanding my other directions, if I am known to be pregnant, I do not want life-sustaining treatment withheld or withdrawn if it is possible that the embryo/fetus will develop to the point of live birth with the continued application of life-sustaining treatment.[106]

Similarly, the Maryland advance directives legislation invites women to set out their wishes in the case of pregnancy.[107] Whilst recognising the woman's autonomy, such provisions reinforce the expectation that women will seek to protect and provide for their foetus, even when they are terminally ill.

Moreover, other state statutes simply do not address the question of the validity of an advance directive during pregnancy, leaving them open to challenge. In such cases it is likely that a declaration will be sought from the court before treatment is withdrawn from a pregnant woman, particularly if the potential father wishes treatment to be maintained. Furthermore, it is also possible that healthcare professionals may choose to exercise their right to conscientious objection (usually enshrined within advance directive legislation), refusing to withdraw treatment from a pregnant woman.

d. Challenging the constitutionality of pregnancy exceptions in advance directive legislation

In *Casey*, writing for the majority, Justice O'Connor stated:

> At the heart of liberty is the right to define one's own concept of existence, of meaning, of the universe, and of the mystery of human life. Beliefs about

104 See also L. C. Fentiman, 'The New Fetal Protection: The Wrong Answer to the Crisis of Inadequate Health Care for Women and Children' (2006) *Denver University Law Review* 537, at 565.

105 Vermont Statutes § 9702.

106 Arizona Revised Statutes § 36–3262.

107 Maryland Health-General Code § 5–603.

> these matters could not define the attributes of personhood were they formed under compulsion of the State.[108]

It is submitted that by restricting a woman's ability to make a legally binding anticipatory refusal of treatment the state reduces the woman to a foetal environment, disregarding her human dignity. In seeking to protect its interest in potential life, the state fails to seek a balance between that interest and its interest in recognising and respecting the woman's (precedent) autonomy. Thus it is argued that the pregnancy exclusion and limitation clauses built into advance directive legislation are unconstitutional, both in terms of violating the equal protection clause and the woman's right to autonomy.

The constitutionality of such exceptions has been challenged before the American courts on two occasions. In the first case, JoAnn Lynn DiNino challenged the constitutionality of the Washington Natural Death Act which recognised that a terminally ill individual could refuse life-sustaining treatment, and that such refusals could be set out in an advance directive.[109] It included a model directive which stated: 'If I have been diagnosed as pregnant and that diagnosis is known to my physician, this directive shall have no force or effect during the course of my pregnancy'. Ms DiNino drafted an advance directive, but modified the model directive to state that it was to continue to apply in the event that she was pregnant and that prior to the withdrawal or withholding of treatment the pregnancy should be terminated. Thus she purported to exercise her right to refuse treatment, but also required treatment through the termination of any existing pregnancy.

Ms DiNino, together with her doctor, sought a declaration that the directive was valid and enforceable and that a doctor would incur no civil or criminal liability for implementing it. In the alternative they sought a declaration that the Act was unconstitutional and void.[110] At first instance the court held that the NDA pregnancy provision was unconstitutional because it violated Ms DiNino's right to privacy. On appeal the Supreme Court of Washington reversed the trial court's decision, holding that it was non-justiciable. It held that as Ms DiNino was neither pregnant nor terminally ill, this was a purely hypothetical and speculative controversy so that any opinion issued as to its effect would be purely advisory. Moreover, it declined to exercise its discretion to grant a declaration about the constitutionality of the Act.[111]

Similarly, in *Gabrynowicz v. Heitkamp*[112] Joanne Gabrynowicz challenged the constitutionality of North Dakota's Uniform Rights of the Terminally Ill Act, which excluded the applicability of an advance directive throughout pregnancy and imposed a positive duty to provide a terminally ill pregnant woman with medical treatment unless it 'will not maintain the patient in such a way as to

108 *Planned Parenthood of Southeastern Pennsylvania et al v Casey* (note 2), at 851.
109 *DiNino v Gorton* 684 P. 2d 1297 (Wash., 1984).
110 Ibid., at 330.
111 Ibid., at 331f.
112 904 F. Supp. 1061 (N.D. 1995).

permit the continuing development and live birth of the unborn child or will be physically harmful or unreasonably painful to the patient or will prolong severe pain that cannot be alleviated by medication'.[113] The United States District Court for North Dakota found that this case was non-justiciable as well, pointing out that Mrs Gabrynowicz was not, and did not wish to become, pregnant and that she was not terminally ill. However, it did acknowledge that the Act raised constitutional questions.

Thus on both occasions the courts chose not to address the constitutionality of pregnancy exceptions in advance directive legislation. However, as Dimmick J pointed out in a strongly worded dissent in *DiNino*:

> If there is no justiciability at the time a woman drafts a directive under the Natural Death Act (NDA), there never will be. By the majority's reasoning, a woman must be pregnant and terminally ill before the issue is ripe for determination. Whatever the impact of the NDA in that circumstance, the woman whose directive will then be 'justiciable' will never benefit from a ruling on the matter. In fact, the case would run a very real danger of being declared moot before a judicial decision could be made.[114]

It is suggested that Dimmick J is quite correct in his analysis: if the courts are not willing to address the constitutionality of such clauses when the plaintiff is healthy and not pregnant, it is difficult to conceive of an effective means to challenge the validity of the clauses.[115]

I return to the question of how advance directives should be treated in relation to pregnant women in Part C, below, considering the extent to which pregnancy should displace an otherwise valid and applicable advance decision. It is argued that pregnancy exclusion and limitation clauses have the effect of compelling women to be not merely minimally decent Samaritans but extremely good Samaritans,[116] and that normative expectations of what a 'good' mother would do should not be supplanted for the views and wishes of the individual woman.

5. Interim conclusion

The American case law relating to obstetric intervention demonstrates a lack of unity, with state courts adopting different lines of reasoning. The question of whether the courts will prioritise the protection of autonomy or the state's interest in the life of the foetus essentially depends upon the state in which the case is heard. Unfortunately, the US Supreme Court did not take the opportunity afforded to it to give a federal ruling upon this matter in *Baby Boy Doe*, refusing to grant

113 § 23–06.4–07(3).

114 Ibid., at 333.

115 See also L. C. Fentiman (note 104), at 566.

116 Cf. Judith Jarvis Thomson, 'A Defense of Abortion' (1971) 1(1) *Philosophy and Public Affairs* 47, at 62f.

certiorari.[117] Thus two lines of jurisprudence are apparent from the case law considered above. On the one hand, the Appellate Court of Illinois and, in a more qualified manner, the Appeals Court for the District of Columbia have emphasised that a woman's autonomy is not diminished by pregnancy and that her refusal of treatment may not be overruled to protect the foetus.[118] By contrast, other state courts have been willing to authorise, or even order, treatment to protect the foetus on the basis of the state's interest in potential life, an interest that becomes compelling at viability. These decisions have largely echoed *Re AC* in stressing that cases where a woman's refusal may be overridden will be 'extremely rare and truly exceptional', yet the case law demonstrates the opposite – namely that a woman's refusal will only rarely be upheld. Indeed, of all the cases cited above, in only one case did the courts refuse to grant an order compelling a woman to undergo a caesarean where doctors advised that it was necessary to protect the foetus – *In re Baby Boy Doe*.[119] In that case both the circuit court and the Illinois Appellate Court refused to grant the injunction sought, compelling Mrs Bricci to submit to a caesarean. She gave birth vaginally at a later date to a baby boy who was apparently healthy, despite the view expressed by the doctors seeking the order, namely that 'the chances of the unborn child surviving natural childbirth ... are close to zero... . [and that] if the child were to somehow survive natural childbirth he would be retarded'.[120]

Thus in the US the question of whether a competent woman will be compelled to undergo treatment for the benefit of her foetus, be it a blood transfusion or a caesarean, will often depend upon in which state she is being treated. However, as noted above, the determination of capacity leaves substantial discretion to the courts. If the woman is found to lack capacity, the state's interest in protecting potential life will prevail; in fact, most of the states that have living will legislation, including Illinois, restrict or disqualify a woman's advance refusal of treatment if she is pregnant. Moreover, even in those states where the woman's refusal is likely to be respected, the very fact that she has refused medical treatment intended to benefit the foetus may have far-reaching impact. Thus in 2004 Melissa Rowland was arrested and charged with homicide following the stillbirth of one of her twins after she refused to have a caesarean section. Ms Rowland later pleaded guilty to the charge of child endangerment due to her drug use whilst pregnant (the surviving twin tested positive for cocaine), but the fact that she refused to accept medical advice to have a caesarean was a contributing factor in the decision to charge her with homicide.

Similarly, a refusal to undergo a caesarean has been used as evidence of child neglect in *New Jersey Div. of Youth & Fam. Servs. v. V.M. and B.G., in the matter of J.M.G., a minor*,[121] where the trial court held that VM's refusal to consent to a

117 114 S.Ct. 1198, 127 L.Ed.2d 547 (1994).
118 *In re Baby Boy Doe, a Fetus v Mother Doe* (note 32) and *In re AC* (note 36).
119 *In re Baby Boy Doe, a Fetus v Mother Doe* (note 32).
120 Ibid., at 328.
121 974 A.2d 448 (2009).

caesarean was a 'major consideration' when deciding to terminate her parental rights. The trial judge concluded that 'in the end with the mother's life and baby's life in balance, ... it was negligent ... not to accede to what the doctors requested'.[122] Although the facts described in the appellate judgment note that an examination revealed a non-reassuring foetal status, the record is silent upon whether a caesarean was considered medically necessary at this time. VM's capacity was assessed twice whilst she was in labour by psychiatrists; the first found her to have the capacity to refuse a caesarean and the second had not yet completed his assessment when VM successfully delivered her baby vaginally.[123] On appeal, the Superior Court of New Jersey held in a majority opinion that it did not need to consider the question of whether failure to consent to a caesarean could constitute an element of abuse or neglect.[124] However, in a concurring opinion Carchman J held that consideration of her refusal was 'improper and beyond the legislative scope of the child-protective statutes'.[125] It may well be the case that there was ample evidence of abuse and neglect to support the termination of VM's parental rights, but the fact that the trial judge considered her failure to consent to a caesarean as part of the proceedings is extremely worrying.

What is clear from the discussion above is that the protection of foetal life in the United States of America is multifaceted but by no means consistent, and that all too often the woman's autonomy is sacrificed upon the altar of foetal life. As will be discussed in the following chapter, the courts in England and Wales have also demonstrated considerable willingness to override a woman's refusal of consent to obstetric intervention, but have done so on the basis of holding her to lack capacity to determine how to give birth, rather than recognising foetal interests directly or a state interest in the foetus capable of protection.

122 Ibid., at 464.
123 Ibid., at 451.
124 Ibid., at 449.
125 Ibid., at 450.

II. Court-authorised obstetric intervention: the English case law

1. Introduction: the categorisation of the issue as a question of capacity, rather than as engaging foetal interests

As discussed in the previous chapter, the courts in the United States of America have used a variety of mechanisms to override a woman's refusal of consent to medical treatment in order to safeguard the foetus, ranging from declaratory relief (*Re AC*[1]), to granting custody of the foetus to a third party (*Jefferson*[2]), to invoking the *parens patriae* jurisdiction (*Burton*[3]). In England and Wales the only route open to the courts is to grant a declaration that it would not be unlawful to perform the medical procedure against the woman's wishes. There are no reported cases involving the overruling of a pregnant woman's refusal of consent to a blood transfusion in England and Wales. However, in a spate of cases during the 1990s the courts in England and Wales declared that it would be lawful for caesareans to be performed, notwithstanding the pregnant woman's refusal of consent. After a significant period without any similar cases being reported, in 2013 and 2014 a flurry of orders were granted, authorising the performance of a caesarean upon women suffering from a mental disorder or, in one case, a woman with learning difficulties. It is suggested that the lull in cases during the last ten years reflects the low level of reporting of such cases, rather than that such cases no longer occur.

Whilst the majority of the US courts have engaged with this issue by considering foetal interests, often in the guise of the state's interest in potential life, the English courts have refused to consider foetal interests, at least explicitly, except in the very first case where a caesarean was authorised to save the life of both the pregnant woman and the foetus. Instead, this matter is dealt with by the English courts as a question of capacity – if the woman has capacity, she may refuse all treatment, including that required to safeguard a foetus. The problem is that thus far no court has considered the question of capacity in such a case, where the issue was still live, rather than on appeal, and found the woman to have the necessary capacity to refuse treatment, leading to questions about the suitability of relying on capacity determinations to resolve this issue. It should be noted that as the first

1 537 A 2d 1235 (1990).

2 *Jefferson v Griffin Spalding County Hospital Authority* 274 SE 2d 457 (1981).

3 *Samantha Burton v Florida* 39 So. 3d 263 (Fla. Dist. Ct. App. 2010).

spate of cases were determined prior to the enactment of the Mental Capacity Act 2005, reference is made to competence and incompetence rather than capacity when referring to that case law. The Act has not changed the law pertaining to court-authorised obstetric intervention and the language used throughout this section reflects that used by the judges.

2. Pregnancy: an exception to the general principle that consent to medical treatment is required?

Consent will generally be a prerequisite to medical treatment; without it the doctor may be liable in negligence or battery. Moreover, it is well recognised that every patient with the requisite capacity has the right to refuse medical treatment, even that which may save his or her life. Nevertheless, the first mention in the UK of a potential exception in the case of pregnant women was made by Lord Donaldson MR in *Re T (An Adult) (Consent to Medical Treatment)*[4] where he stated:

> An adult patient who ... suffers from no mental incapacity has an absolute right to choose whether to consent to medical treatment, to refuse it or to choose one rather than another of the treatments being offered. The only possible qualification is a case in which the choice may lead to the death of a viable foetus.[5]

T was 20 years old and 34 weeks pregnant. She had been involved in a car accident and although she had not been seriously injured in the accident she had developed pneumonia and was admitted to hospital. Following a visit from her mother (a Jehovah's Witness) T informed hospital staff that she would not consent to a blood transfusion should it become necessary. Soon afterwards T went into labour and she was advised that a caesarean might be required. She repeated her refusal of consent to a blood transfusion, but was advised by the healthcare professionals that a transfusion was not always needed as other, less effective, procedures could be used. T signed a form recording her refusal of consent to a blood transfusion, despite the fact that the contents of the form were not explained to her. The caesarean was performed, but the baby was stillborn. T's health deteriorated to the extent that she had to be admitted to the intensive care unit and a transfusion was medically indicated. Two days later her father, supported by her partner, applied for a declaration that a transfusion would not be unlawful. At an emergency hearing the declaration was granted on the basis that at the time T signed the form she was not fully rational due to her condition and the drugs she had received. Later, at the full hearing, Ward J decided that T had in fact made a rational decision to refuse a blood transfusion, but that she had not appreciated how serious the situation might become and that her refusal of consent did not

4 *Re T (Adult: Refusal of Treatment)* [1993] Fam 95.
5 Ibid., at 102.

apply to the critical situation in which she now found herself. He further held that a transfusion was in her best interests and granted the declaration. On appeal the decision was upheld, but the Court of Appeal held that T's refusal of consent was invalid because she had been subject to undue influence from her mother and thus the refusal was not a free expression of her wishes.

Despite the fact that this case did not involve intervention to protect a viable foetus, Lord Donaldson indicated that the right to refuse consent to medical treatment might be qualified where such a refusal might lead to the death of a viable foetus. This suggests that pregnancy may transfer a woman from that category of patient who has the right to consent or refuse consent to any treatment, namely an adult with capacity, to the category of patient with a much more limited ability to determine their own treatment – for example, the mature minor. As the courts in England and Wales have demonstrated, the fact that a mature minor may consent to treatment does not mean that she may refuse treatment which accords with her best interests, such a refusal being subject to recidivism by either the court or a parental responsibility holder.[6] In *Re T* Lord Donaldson appeared to suggest that a similar limitation might hold true for a pregnant woman where the foetus has achieved viability. However, if a competent woman's refusal is capable of being overridden, some other recognised right or interest must be considered sufficiently important to justify the disregard of her autonomy. Lord Donaldson clearly suggested that a risk to the life of a viable foetus might be sufficiently important, but, unlike German law, Anglo-American law has refused to recognise that even a viable foetus has any rights until birth.[7]

Re F (in utero)[8] dealt with the question of whether or not the foetus of a woman suffering from mental illness could be made a ward of court. At first instance Hollings J held:

> As the law and practice at present stands, wardship can only apply to a living child. For it to apply to a child still within the body of the child's mother, very serious considerations must arise with regard to the welfare of the mother. I do not intend to spell out by examples in this judgment the difficulties that one would anticipate, but one can well imagine that there would be a repugnance on the part of a right thinking person in certain instances to think of applying the principle of paramountcy in favour of the child's welfare at the expense of the welfare and interests of the mother.[9]

6 See, for example, *Re W (a minor) (medical treatment: court's jurisdiction)* [1992] 4 All ER 627; *South Glamorgan County Council v W and B* [1993] 1 FLR 574; *Re E (a minor) (wardship: medical treatment)* [1993] 1 FLR 386;*Re M (a child) (refusal of medical treatment)* [1999] 2 FLR 1097.

7 *Paton v British Pregnancy Advisory Service Trustees* [1979] QB 276, at 279, QBD, *per* Sir George Baker P; *Paton v UK* (1980) 3 EHRR 408, at 413 (European Commission on Human Rights); *C v S* [1988] QB 135, at 140, *per* Heilbron J; *Re F (in utero)* [1988] 2 All ER 193; *Roe v Wade* 410 U.S. 113 (1973), at 158, *per* Blackmum J. Cf. *BVerfGE* 39, 1 (1975), *BVerfGE* 88, 203 (1993).

8 *Re F (in utero)* (note 7).

9 [1988] 2 FLR 307, at 315.

Whilst Hollings J is undoubtedly right that applying the paramountcy of the foetus's welfare is very controversial, in almost all of the cases discussed below the courts in England and Wales have applied just that principle, even if not explicitly, in order to justify overriding a woman's refusal of treatment that would benefit the foetus. Rejecting the appeal in *Re F*, May LJ stated:

> I think that there would be insuperable difficulties if one sought to enforce any order in respect of an unborn child against its mother, if that mother failed to comply with the order. I cannot contemplate the court ordering that this should be done by force, nor indeed is it possible to consider with any equanimity that the court should seek to enforce an order by committal.[10]

In fact, what May LJ could not contemplate – that is, the use of force or committal to enforce any such order against the woman – is exactly what has happened in England and Wales, as can be seen from the analysis of the cases discussed below.

3. The English case law

a. Overriding the woman's refusal of consent in order to save her own or the foetus's life

Lord Donaldson's possible exception arose for consideration just two months later in *Re S*,[11] the first case in which an English court granted a declaration that a caesarean could be performed despite the refusal of consent of the pregnant woman. S had been in labour for two days, but there was a risk that her uterus would rupture and so a caesarean was medically indicated. However, both S and her husband were born-again Christians and S refused to consent to such an operation due to their religious beliefs. Sir Stephen Brown P accepted the surgeon's evidence that the only way of saving the life of the woman *and* the foetus would be to perform a caesarean, and he ordered that it should be performed, in order to save *both* lives. Throughout his judgment he emphasised the separation of the foetus and S, referring to the patient S on the one hand and 'the baby', 'the child' and 'the unborn child' on the other.[12] This case is the first example of the courts' recognition of Lord Donaldson's possible exception to the rule that consent is generally a prerequisite to lawful medical treatment, although it is inconsistent with the legal position outlined by Lord Donaldson to the extent that the decision is based on saving the *woman*'s life rather than merely that of the foetus.[13]

There was absolutely no suggestion that S was incompetent; in fact, her competence does not even appear to have been considered. Instead, the primary consideration was that a caesarean could save not only her own life but, as Sir Stephen

10 [1988] 2 All ER 193, at 196.
11 [1993] Fam 123.
12 Ibid., at 124.
13 *Re T (Adult: Refusal of Treatment)* (note 4), at 653.

Brown P emphasised, also that of the foetus. Of course, had S not been pregnant, her refusal of consent to even life-sustaining treatment would have been upheld. In reaching his conclusion in *Re S*,[14] Sir Stephen Brown P relied upon the American case *Re AC*,[15] stating that 'if this case were being heard in the American courts the answer would be likely to be in favour of granting a declaration in these circumstances' and citing the District of Columbia Court of Appeals' decision. In that case the majority held that a patient, even when pregnant, had a right to autonomy, albeit with a potential caveat:

> We do not quite foreclose the possibility that a conflicting State interest may be so compelling that the patient's wishes must yield, but we anticipate that such cases will be extremely rare and truly exceptional. This is not such a case … Indeed some may doubt that there could ever be a situation extraordinary or compelling enough to justify a massive intrusion into a person's body, such as a caesarean section, against that person's will.[16]

If this statement is taken at face value, it would appear that Sir Stephen Brown P misunderstood the majority view adopted in that case, as it is submitted that the case of *Re S* would not fall into the category of extremely rare and truly exceptional cases. However, as discussed above, it is the case of *Re AC* and the strong affirmation of the woman's autonomy set out in that case that are atypical.[17] When the body of the American case law is considered, the majority of decisions would appear to support the finding made by Sir Stephen Brown P in overriding S's refusal of consent to the performance of a caesarean.

Re S is very similar to *Jefferson v Griffin Spalding County Hospital Authority*,[18] considered above, where the Georgia Supreme Court authorised a hospital to perform a caesarean section and any necessary blood transfusions upon a pregnant woman in spite of her religious beliefs. In that case the Georgia Supreme Court summed up by stating that it had 'weighed the right of the mother to practice her religion and to refuse surgery on herself, against her unborn child's right to live. We found in favour of her child's right to live'.[19]

In neither of these cases was there any suggestion that the women were incompetent. However, in both cases the court held that their refusals could be overridden, in the case of *Jefferson* to save the life of the foetus and in *Re S* to save both lives, with Sir Stephen Brown P emphasising that S's refusal would lead not only to her own death but also to that of the 'unborn child'.[20] In both cases the paramountcy principle was applied so that the woman's autonomy could be overridden in order to achieve a perceived higher purpose, namely to save the life

14 *Re S* (note 11), at 672.
15 *Re AC* (note 1).
16 Ibid., at 1252, *per* Terry J.
17 See above, B I 3.
18 274 SE 2d 457 (1981).
19 Ibid., at 460.
20 *Re S* (note 11), at 672.

of the foetus. However, Jefferson's baby was delivered vaginally without complications, despite medical evidence suggesting that there was only a 1 per cent chance it would survive vaginal delivery, and in the case of *Re S*, when the foetus was delivered it was found to be dead. Thus in this case the court, whilst eschewing the notion of a foetus having legal rights, appears to have endowed it with sufficient interests to warrant a woman's autonomy being disregarded, not only on the paternalistic basis of protecting her from her own 'irrational' decision to refuse medical treatment, which might save her own life, but also on the basis that it would preserve the life of the foetus. Although this decision has been severely criticised, Thorpe LJ, writing extra-judicially, suggested that most judges would have made the same decision:

> The President chose to override patient autonomy in order to maximise the chance of survival for mother and unborn baby. I was then a Family Division judge and I would have reached the same decision. More speculatively I say that the majority, if not all, the judges of the Family Division would have so decided.[21]

b. Indirectly safeguarding the foetus via the categorisation of a caesarean as a treatment for a mental disorder

In *Tameside and Glossop Acute Services Trust v CH*[22] a declaration was granted stating that a caesarean could lawfully be performed upon a woman detained under s.3 of the Mental Health Act 1983. CH suffered from paranoid schizophrenia and during her pregnancy CH's mental health had deteriorated due to the fact that she could no longer take her medication. Throughout her pregnancy CH had been reluctant to cooperate with her doctors and, by the 37th week of pregnancy, fears were expressed about the safety of the foetus. The foetus was suffering from interuterine growth retardation (i.e. it was smaller than might be expected for the stage of the pregnancy) and it was argued that unless the foetus were delivered in the near future, it would die in CH's uterus. CH had agreed to be induced, but the doctors were worried that she might change her mind and so the Trust sought a declaration that it would not be unlawful to perform a caesarean and to restrain her in order to do so, if it became necessary. Unlike *Re S*, CH was not in labour, was not at full term and was not refusing to follow the advice of her doctors. Thus the application was pre-emptive, the order being sought for the eventuality that a caesarean became necessary and CH refused to consent to the operation at that time, rather than on the basis of an existing medical situation.

The consultant psychiatrist considered that CH was incapable of making a balanced, rational decision about treatment. She already viewed the healthcare professionals as a threat to the foetus, and he said that if the foetus were to die she

21 M. A. Thorpe, 'Consent for Caesarean Section: Part 1 – Development of the Law' (1999) 5 *Clinical Risk* 173, at 175.

22 [1996] 1 FLR 762.

would blame them, which in turn would make it unlikely that she would cooperate with the further treatment of her mental illness. It is important to note that an individual detained under the Mental Health Act 1983 does not automatically forfeit his or her autonomy,[23] as the patient retains the right to consent, or refuse consent, to medical treatment not provided to treat the mental disorder from which he or she is suffering, provided that the patient is judged to be competent to make that decision. Nevertheless, relying on *B* v *Croydon Health Authority*,[24] Wall J held that the caesarean could be performed without CH's consent under s.63 of the Mental Health Act 1983, whereby 'The consent of a patient shall not be required for any medical treatment given to him *for the mental disorder from which he is suffering*' (emphasis added). Thus, because the caesarean was categorised as medical treatment for her mental disorder, the woman's consent was not required. It is, however, highly questionable whether the performance of a caesarean can truly be said to be medical treatment for schizophrenia.

There is clearly room for interpretation in determining what will constitute medical treatment for the mental disorder from which the patient is suffering. *B* v *Croydon Health Authority*, one of the cases relied upon by Wall J in reaching his decision in *Tameside and Glossop Acute Services Trust v CH*, concerned a patient detained under s.3 Mental Health Act 1983. B was suffering from a psychopathic disorder, one of her symptoms being that she tried to harm herself. She was refusing to eat and so the question for the court was whether tube feeding could be considered treatment for her mental disorder within s.63 of the Act, so that her consent could be dispensed with. Hoffman LJ considered the fact that the only treatment for her mental disorder was psychoanalytical psychotherapy; however, he concluded that not 'every act which forms part of that treatment ... must in itself be likely to alleviate or prevent a deterioration of that disorder'; rather, such treatment includes ancillary acts.[25] Artificial feeding was held to be an ancillary act and thus treatment could be afforded to B under s.63 of the Act. Similarly, in *Re KB (Adult) (Mental Patient: Medical Treatment)*[26] KB was anorexic and it was held that artificial feeding could be given without her consent as the feeding was held to constitute treatment for a symptom of her mental disorder. Nevertheless, in *B* v *Croydon Health Authority* Hoffman LJ did stress that the treatment afforded must be directly linked to the mental disorder, distinguishing the case of *Re C (refusal of medical treatment)*[27] where the court accepted a schizophrenic's refusal of consent to the amputation of his gangrenous leg. Referring to that case, Hoffman LJ said that an amputation would have been too remote from the mental disorder from which C was suffering, schizophrenia.[28] These decisions would suggest that, in the case of a pregnant woman detained under the Mental Health Act, the Act would only permit a caesarean to be performed without her consent if

23 *Re C (refusal of medical treatment)* [1994] 1 FLR 31.
24 [1995] 1 All ER 683 (CA).
25 Ibid., at 687.
26 (1994) 9 BMLR 144.
27 *Re C (refusal of medical treatment)* (note 23).
28 *B* v *Croydon Health Authority* (note 24), at 688.

it were treatment for the mental disorder, in CH's case schizophrenia, or ancillary to that treatment.

Nevertheless, in *Tameside and Glossop Acute Services Trust v CH* Wall J adopted a very wide interpretation of the requirement that the treatment be for the mental disorder, arguing that the caesarean would prevent a deterioration in CH's mental state, that it was necessary for her to give birth to a live baby in order for the treatment of her schizophrenia to be effective and finally that her treatment had been interrupted by her pregnancy and could not be resumed until the 'child' was born.[29] Therefore he held that the performance of a caesarean could be considered as treatment for her mental disorder. However, unlike B her refusal was not a consequence of her mental disorder, and unlike KB her refusal was not a symptom of her mental disorder, and it is difficult to see how a caesarean could be considered more closely linked to the treatment of schizophrenia than the amputation of a limb.

If, as is suggested, a caesarean could not be performed under the auspices of s.63 of the Act, such an operation could only be declared lawful if CH were to be considered incompetent and her best interests deemed to require the performance of a caesarean. Having determined that CH lacked the necessary competence to refuse consent, Wall J accepted the opinions of the consultant obstetrician and gynaecologist and consultant psychiatrist regarding CH's best interests, stating that it was 'plainly in the defendant's interests to give birth to a live baby'.[30] In considering the defendant's best interests, emphasis was placed on the fact that she felt medical staff were a threat to the foetus and that, according to the consultant psychiatrist, were the foetus to die, CH would blame the medical staff and would be unlikely to cooperate with them in the future. Although the doctors accepted that CH would not take kindly to being forcibly restrained whilst a caesarean was performed, *they* felt that her antagonism would be short-lived and that *they* would be able to cope with this. Thus a large proportion of the decision was based on how the doctors thought that they could best maintain a reasonably good relationship with CH, such a relationship being said to constitute her best interests.

Unlike Sir Stephen Brown P in *Re S*, Wall J did recognise that a competent woman's refusal should be respected. He held that competence should be determined by the application of the *Re C* test[31] – that is, the cumulative test whereby the patient must be able to comprehend and retain treatment information, must believe it and must be able to weigh it in the balance to arrive at a choice.[32] In cases where the patient is incompetent, Wall J held that treatment may lawfully be provided where the treatment is 'necessary to save the life or preserve or prevent a deterioration in the physical or mental health of the patient and in the patient's best interests', providing that 'the treatment is not contrary to the known competent previously expressed decision of the patient'.[33] Thus in this case Wall J held

29 *Tameside and Glossop Acute Services Trust v CH* (note 22), at 773.
30 Ibid., at 771.
31 Ibid., at 769.
32 *Re C* (note 23), at 33.
33 *Tameside and Glossop Acute Services Trust v CH* (note 22), at 769.

that the treatment (a caesarean) would be necessary to safeguard CH's mental health, because if the foetus were to die, her mental health would deteriorate due to the likelihood that it would undermine her trust in the psychiatric services. Moreover, her best interests were construed as requiring the maintenance of as amicable a relationship as possible with the healthcare professionals, a relationship which, according to the doctors, might suffer a temporary setback were she to be forced to undergo a caesarean, but which would be more likely to improve than if the foetus were to die.

c. Indirectly safeguarding the foetus via a finding of incompetence and a determination of best interests requiring the safe delivery of the foetus

In *Tameside and Glossop Acute Services Trust v CH* Wall J held that the Mental Health Act 1983 would allow the use of reasonable force as a necessary incidence of treatment, although he left the question of whether such a power existed at common law to be determined by a future case. Such a case arose in *Norfolk and Norwich Healthcare (NHS) Trust v W.*[34] W had gone to the hospital's Accident and Emergency department where she was found to be in a state of arrested labour. Nevertheless, throughout the day she continued to insist that she was not pregnant. The hospital sought a declaration that it would not be unlawful to attempt a forceps delivery, or, if necessary, to perform a caesarean section, and that it would be permissible to restrain W in order to do so. The Trust argued that the caesarean was necessary to preserve the life of the foetus, which was in danger of suffocating, and also to avoid the risk of the patient's earlier caesarean scars reopening and so endangering the life of the foetus. There was also a risk to W's own life. Whilst W had a history of mental illness, she was found not to be suffering from a mental disorder in the terms of the 1983 Act. The consultant psychiatrist stated that he was unsure whether she satisfied steps one and two of the *Re C* test – that is, the ability to comprehend and retain treatment information, and to believe that information. However, he said that she was certainly not able to weigh the information in the balance to arrive at a choice (the third step), although he did consider that W would be capable of instructing a solicitor!

Johnson J held that W was incompetent as she failed the *Re C* test. He stated that:

> She lacked the mental competence to make a decision about the treatment that was proposed because she was incapable of weighing up the considerations that were involved. She was called upon to make that decision at a time of acute emotional stress and physical pain in the ordinary course of labour, made even more difficult for her because of her own particular mental history.[35]

This conclusion is particularly disturbing as there is at least a suggestion that any woman in labour may be considered to be incompetent because of the very fact

34 [1996] 2 FLR 613.
35 Ibid., at 616.

that she is in labour, due to the stress and pain involved. A preferable, albeit only marginally so, interpretation of this statement is that W's own mental history exacerbated the customary pain and stress to such an extent that she became incompetent, albeit only with respect to the ability to refuse consent to medical intervention to deliver the foetus.

Having established that W was incompetent, Johnson J held that it would be in the best interests of the patient to terminate labour either by a forceps delivery or a caesarean because that would bring an end to the pain and stress of her labour and avoid the likelihood of harm to her physical health, and also it would avoid her 'feeling any guilt in the future were she, by her refusal of consent, to cause the death of the foetus'.[36] Johnson J adopted Goff LJ's test set out in *Re F (Mental Patient: Sterilisation)*,[37] holding that because the action would be in W's best interests and it was necessary to act, the court had a power at common law to authorise the use of reasonable force.

Therefore, the courts in England and Wales have held that there is the power under both the Mental Health Act[38] and at common law to use reasonable force to enforce medical treatment declared lawful by the courts in these circumstances. It will be remembered that May LJ described the use of force in such circumstances as unthinkable.[39] Nevertheless, enforcement of such orders can only be accomplished in the face of the woman's objection by physical force – for example, by tying the woman to the operating table and by forcibly anaesthetising her – and, in the circumstances, holding the woman to be in contempt of court is of little use. As was accepted by the District of Columbia Court of Appeals in *re AC*, 'Such actions would surely give one pause in a civilized society, especially when [the woman] had done no wrong'.[40] However, as Johnson J made clear in the *Norfolk and Norwich* case, the courts in England and Wales will be prepared to declare it lawful to perform a caesarean against the wishes of the incompetent pregnant woman and to allow the use of force if necessary to ensure the performance of the operation.

Unlike Sir Stephen Brown P's judgment in *Re S*,[41] Johnson J did stress that his concern was for W herself, rather than for her viable foetus, emphasising this to be the case notwithstanding the fact that 'the foetus was a fully formed child, capable of normal life if only it could be delivered from the mother'. Therefore, at least ostensibly, the decision focused upon the woman herself, but it was based upon the paternalistic notions of saving her life and saving her from her own guilt, with the safe delivery of the foetus playing a central role in the determination of her best interests.

During the hearing of *Norfolk and Norwich Healthcare (NHS) Trust v W*, Johnson J also made a declaration in *Rochdale Healthcare NHS Trust* v *C*.[42] In

36 Ibid.
37 *Re F (Mental Patient: Sterilisation)* [1990] 2 AC 1, at 75.
38 *Tameside and Glossop Acute Services Trust v CH* (note 22).
39 *Re F (in utero)* (note 7), at 196.
40 *Re AC* (note 1), at 1244.
41 *Re S* (note 11).
42 [1997] 1 FCR 274.

this case there was a risk to the life of the foetus and the health of C that could be avoided by the performance of a caesarean. C had undergone a caesarean previously and said that she 'would rather die than have one again'. Her life was not at risk, but in answer to the obstetrician's question of who would care for her daughter if she died, she said her mother and that she was prepared to die if the only alternative was to have another caesarean. The consultant obstetrician had no doubt that she was fully competent.

The hearing was extremely brief. Johnson J interrupted the hearing of the *Norfolk and Norwich* application at 5.15pm and granted the declaration sought within a matter of minutes, having been advised that the operation needed to be performed by 5.30pm in order to save the foetus's life and avoid harm to the woman's health. It had not been possible to obtain a psychiatric evaluation of C in the time available, but Johnson J felt able to disagree with the obstetrician's view that C was competent without seeing or speaking to her. Johnson J applied the *Re C* test and found that she was incompetent because she failed the third stage of the test – that is, that she was incapable of weighing up the information given to her. He stated:

> The patient was in the throes of labour with all that is involved in terms of pain and emotional stress. I concluded that a patient who could, in those circumstances, speak in terms which seemed to accept the inevitability of her own death, was not a patient who was able properly to weigh-up the considerations that arose so as to make any valid decision, about anything of even the most trivial kind, still one which involved her own life.[43]

Johnson J granted the declaration sought. As in *Norfolk and Norwich Healthcare (NHS) Trust v W*, it would appear that Johnson J suggested that the incidence of labour 'with all that is involved in terms of pain and emotional stress' could render a competent woman incompetent, regardless of whether the woman had any history of mental illness. Having determined that C lacked the capacity to make a valid decision, he held that it would be in her best interests for the caesarean to be performed. He did not set out details of how her best interests would be served by a caesarean, referring only to the reasons he had given in the *Norfolk* case,[44] namely that the caesarean would end the pain and stress of her labour, avoid the risk of harm to her physical health and avoid the risk of her feeling guilty if the foetus died as a result of her refusal.[45]

As recognised by Butler-Sloss LJ in the later case of *Re MB*,[46] it is questionable how Johnson J concluded that C was incompetent without psychiatric evidence and in the face of her obstetrician's view that she was competent. If C was competent, and there is no evidence to suggest that she was not, her best interests

43 Ibid., at 275.
44 Ibid.
45 *Norfolk and Norwich Healthcare Trust v W* (note 34), at 616.
46 [1997] 2 FLR 426, at 435.

were irrelevant and she was entitled to refuse to consent to a caesarean and to expect that refusal to have been respected, regardless of whether she might later regret that decision. C had already had a caesarean in a previous pregnancy and was adamant that she did not wish to have another. There was no threat to her own life, but there was a threat to the foetus and so she was deemed to be incapable of weighing the information given to her on the basis of the reason she gave for refusing treatment ('I'd rather die') and because of the context in which she made the decision (during labour).

In his judgment Johnson J noted that C changed her mind so that the caesarean was in fact performed with her consent, but the question remains how a woman who was found to be incompetent for the purpose of refusing consent could be considered competent to give consent to the same operation whilst still 'in the throes of labour with all that is involved in terms of pain and emotional stress'. It is well accepted that capacity is decision-specific and that some decisions will require a higher degree of capacity than others, with refusals leading to a risk of death arguably requiring the highest possible levels of capacity. However, Johnson J had stated that C was incapable of making 'any valid decision, about anything of even the most trivial kind' in the context of her refusal to consent. This case clearly demonstrates the shortcomings of the assessment of capacity, an assessment which often will be triggered by the mere fact that the patient is not prepared to comply with medical advice. The judge accepted the doctor's opinion of what treatment C required, showing complete disregard for the woman's autonomy and demonstrating how flexible a tool the assessment of capacity is. There is at least a suggestion that a finding of incapacity/incompetence depends in reality upon the existence of a therapeutic alliance between the doctor and patient – in other words, upon the patient accepting that the doctor knows best and consenting accordingly!

The issue of whether a court could grant a declaration authorising a caesarean in the case of women suffering from a phobia of needles arose in both *Re L*[47] and *Re MB*.[48] L had been in labour for some time, but labour had been obstructed for eight hours and the performance of a caesarean was medically indicated to save the life of the foetus. L suffered from a phobia of needles. In principle she was prepared to agree to the performance of a caesarean; however, due to her phobia she could not consent to the administration of the anaesthetic by injection. She was willing to consent to anaesthesia by gas inhalation, so that the intravenous drip could be inserted once she was unconscious, but the consultant anaesthetist was unwilling to proceed in this manner due to the risk of gastric inhalation and subsequent risk to her life. Thus an impasse had been reached. The Trust sought a declaration that it would not be unlawful to insert needles for the purpose of anaesthetising L and to perform an emergency caesarean.

The consultant obstetrician testified that L was capable of understanding and retaining information, believing it and weighing such information in the balance

47 *Re L (Patient: non-consensual treatment)* [1997] 2 FLR 837.
48 *Re MB* (note 46).

to make a choice, subject to her needle phobia. It was also suggested that the gas and air (entonox) that L was receiving for pain relief had resulted in her becoming confused. The effect of entonox is quick but short-lived, and so any confusion caused can have been of only very limited duration; certainly, it is difficult to believe that it could render a woman incompetent and that it would operate to render her incapable of making a valid decision in the gap between contractions where she would not have used the gas. Kirkwood J did not consider the impact of the analgesic upon L's competence, holding instead that 'her extreme needle phobia amounted to an involuntary compulsion', rendering her unable to weigh the information in order to make a choice, and thus that she was incompetent.[49] He then held that it would be in L's best interests if she were anaesthetised by injection and a caesarean carried out, as 'Her desire to be safely delivered of her child would be fulfilled. She would be spared the inevitably profound distress of losing her child. The risk to her own health and well-being would be reduced to a minimal risk'.[50] Kirkwood J granted the declaration sought.

At the end of his judgment Kirkwood J noted that the defendant had apologised for the trouble that she had caused to so many people,[51] perhaps as an added justification for his decision to grant the declaration. Certainly, in a number of the English cases the impression is given that, at least after the event, the women were grateful that their refusal had been overridden, a suggestion that is used to demonstrate that the women's refusals were misguided, silly or, at best, ill thought through. This framing of the women as incapable is important as the narratives provided seek to show women refusing to comply with medical advice to be victims of their own foolishness, in need of assistance and guidance from doctors or judges. This portrayal seeks to validate the necessity of treating women, without recognising foetal interests *per se*, and echoes the approach adopted to regulating abortion whereby women are deemed incapable of making a decision to terminate a pregnancy without the levelling support of two doctors,[52] or, in the case of Germany, a counsellor deemed necessary to ensure the woman makes a responsible decision.[53]

d. Appellate consideration of the issue: the emphasis of the woman's right to autonomy, provided that she is adjudged competent

The Court of Appeal had to consider a case very similar to that of *Re L* in *Re MB*.[54] The foetus was in the breech position and the practice of the hospital concerned was to deliver all such presentations by caesarean section; although vaginal delivery is possible in such circumstances, a caesarean delivery is considered to be safer for the foetus. The problem was that, just like L, MB had a severe needle phobia. Like L, MB was anxious that the foetus should be safely delivered;

49 *Re L* (note 47), at 839.
50 Ibid., at 840.
51 Ibid.
52 Abortion Act 1967, s.1(1).
53 §§ 218a I, 219 StGB.
54 *Re MB (Medical Treatment)* (note 46).

however, whilst she accepted the need for a caesarean, she could not endure the injection of anaesthetic. She had agreed to be anaesthetised by gas and the anaesthetist was prepared to provide initial anaesthesia by inhalation, prior to the introduction of intravenous anaesthesia, allowing the caesarean to be performed. However, MB panicked at the sight of the mask. Over the course of four days she consented to the performance of a caesarean a number of times, but withdrew her consent due to her phobia of needles. A consultant psychiatrist assessed her and formed the view that 'She is a naïve, not very bright, frightened young woman but is not exhibiting a psychiatric disorder'.[55] He believed that, just as in the case of L, MB had the capacity to consent according to the *Re C* test, apart from the fact that her phobia prevented her from balancing the information. Thus in both cases it was said that the needle phobia induced a panic that overshadowed everything else, rendering the women incapable of making any decision at all. The gynaecologist stated that the risk posed by vaginal delivery to the foetus was 50 per cent, but that there was little physical danger to the woman. At first instance Hollis J granted the declaration that a caesarean could be performed with reasonable force if necessary. MB instructed her solicitors to appeal, but did consent to the anaesthetic and caesarean on the following day after hearing that her appeal had been dismissed.

The Court of Appeal stressed that there is a rebuttable presumption that every person is competent to consent or refuse medical treatment and that a competent woman

> May for religious reasons, other reasons, for rational or irrational reasons or for no reason at all, choose not to have medical intervention, even though … the consequence may be the death or serious handicap of the child she bears, or her own death.[56]

This means that S's refusal of consent to a caesarean based upon her religious beliefs[57] would now appear to have been perfectly acceptable and indeed that any competent woman can refuse medical treatment regardless of whether that treatment might safeguard her life or health, or that of the foetus. Moreover, it was stressed that the fact that a woman may later regret her refusal of consent to treatment did not mean that her wishes should be overridden. Thus the Court of Appeal accepted that pregnant women should be able to make mistakes, just like any other patient, and Butler-Sloss LJ emphasised that 'The position in English law appears to be clear and contrary to the view expressed by Lord Donaldson [in *Re T*] and by the President [in *Re S*]',[58] namely that there is no exception to the requirement of consent in the case of a pregnant woman with capacity. However, the needle phobia was held to render MB incompetent, albeit temporarily, and so

55 Ibid., at 430.
56 Ibid., *per* Butler-Sloss LJ, at 436–7.
57 *Re S* (note 11).
58 Ibid., at 440.

it was held that she should be treated as required by her best interests. Butler-Sloss LJ emphasised that best interests are not limited to best medical interests and that, as both the woman and her partner wanted the child to be born alive and healthy, medical intervention would serve her best interests. Moreover, the Court of Appeal held that the use of reasonable force to compel treatment required by the patient's best interests was acceptable.

Therefore, in *Re MB* the Court of Appeal accepted the then current advice offered by the Royal College of Obstetricians and Gynaecologists[59] as reflecting the current law – that is, that faced with a woman's refusal of consent to treatment, the only course of action open to the doctor is to seek to persuade the woman to change her mind. The Royal College considers that to seek a court order to try to override the competent woman's refusal would be detrimental to the doctor–patient relationship. This must surely be so – as the Appeal Court recognised in *re AC*,[60] if women feel that their wishes will not be respected, they are less likely to seek medical advice or treatment, which would, of course, do little to protect the foetus or further its welfare. Indeed, the consequences of such a proactive approach to protecting the foetus are well illustrated by the case of *Raleigh Fitkin–Paul Morgan Memorial Hospital v Anderson*,[61] where Mrs Anderson discharged herself from the hospital and went into hiding, rather than face the prospect of a court-ordered blood transfusion. Mrs Anderson did in fact give birth without medical assistance. Her story had a happy ending – both she and her baby were fine – but surely it would have been better if she had felt that she could ask for medical help if she needed it, without fear that her autonomy would be entirely disregarded.

Echoing reasoning set out by the Illinois Appellate Court in *Baby Boy Doe* and *Brown*,[62] Butler-Sloss LJ emphasised that the interests of the foetus are irrelevant and that no exercise of balancing its interests against those of the women should be undertaken, questioning the correctness of the decision in *Re S*[63] where the interests of the foetus prevailed over the autonomy of the woman. Thus at first glance the Court of Appeal's decision in *Re MB* seems to be very positive; it appears to accept that concern for the foetus cannot outweigh a competent woman's autonomy. However, having said that a competent patient can refuse consent for whatever reason, the Court of Appeal went on to say that:

> Panic, indecisiveness and irrationality in themselves do not as such amount to incompetence, but they may be symptoms or evidence of incompetence. The

59 Royal College of Obstretricians and Gynaecologists, *A Consideration of The Law and Ethics in Relation to Court-Authorised Obstetric Intervention* (1994), revised 1996. A second edition updating and revising this guidance was published in 2006.

60 *Re AC* (note 40).

61 *Raleigh Fitkin–Paul Morgan Memorial Hospital v Anderson* 201 A 2d 537 (1964).

62 *In re Brown* 689 N.E.2d 397 (1997) and *re Baby Boy Doe* 632 North Eastern Reporter 2d Series 32y (1994).

63 *Re S* (note 11).

> graver the consequences of the decision, the commensurately greater the level of competence is required to take the decision.[64]

In this case MB's needle phobia meant that she was incapable of making any decision and thus was temporarily incompetent, but it is unclear whether a non-phobic fear of having an operation would have similarly rendered her incompetent. Moreover, there are worrying echoes of Johnson J's suggestion that the pain and emotional stress inherent in labour may render a woman incompetent; Butler-Sloss LJ recognised that fatigue, pain or drugs – all common factors in labour – may completely erode capacity. As the Court of Appeal stressed, women – even pregnant women – may make valid irrational decisions; however, irrationality may be a symptom of incompetence. The fact that the woman is refusing to consent to treatment that has the potential to save her life and/or that of her foetus is liable to be seen as irrational and as a strong indication of incompetence; if the woman is in labour, that indication may be even more compelling. Therefore this approach maximises the potential to find the woman to be incompetent, albeit temporarily. In all of the cases that preceded *MB* except *Re S*, all the women refusing treatment were held to be incompetent; it therefore seems a rather hollow victory to say that a competent woman may refuse treatment given the unlikelihood of a woman refusing treatment necessary to save the foetal life being adjudged competent. Following a finding of incompetence, the woman must be treated in accordance with her best interests, which thus far have always required the performance of a caesarean. As Butler-Sloss LJ stated, 'It must be in the best interests of a woman carrying a full-term child whom she wants to be born alive and healthy that such a result should if possible be achieved'.[65]

Butler-Sloss LJ provided some procedural guidelines to be followed in future cases.[66] These included the requirement that hearings should be *inter partes*, with the woman being represented, and that potential problems should be identified as early as possible so that the woman would be able to obtain legal advice and be represented. This is a significant improvement as in all of the English cases discussed above, with the exception of *Re MB*, the woman was unrepresented. Moreover, the early detection of possible problems should prevent at least some of the emergency decisions that take place with incomplete evidence being available and perhaps hasty decisions being taken. For example, in *Re S* the application was made at 1.30pm, the hearing started just before 2.00pm and the declaration was granted at 2.18pm – that is, less than an hour after the application was made. In *Re L* the declaration was granted within 25 minutes of the application being made, and in *Rochdale* the declaration was granted after a two-minute hearing. However, it will not suffice to identify problems early on in the pregnancy; rather, decisions must be taken wherever possible whilst there can be no doubts about the woman's capacity. In the case of MB, she had consistently refused all medical care

64 *Re MB* (note 46), at 437.
65 Ibid., at 439.
66 Ibid., at 445.

involving the use of needles, including the taking of blood for the blood tests that are routinely performed throughout pregnancy. Thus it was clear from the first time that she presented for antenatal care, at 33 weeks, that her needle phobia could cause problems should intervention be necessary at the time of birth. The panic and the consequences thereof that she endured may well have been prevented had she been offered behavioural therapy to manage her phobia during her pregnancy. At the very least, she should have discussed the potential problem with her doctors and been encouraged to clarify her wishes for the event that intervention became necessary through her birth plan, drafted at a time when her capacity was not in doubt.

The most recent appellate decision concerning court-ordered caesareans in England and Wales was rendered in *St George's Healthcare NHS Trust* v *S; R* v *Collins and others, ex parte S*,[67] although the first instance decision was handed down only months after the decision in *Tameside and Glossop Acute Services NHS Trust v CH*.[68] S was 28 years old and 36 weeks pregnant. When she tried to register as a new patient with a local GP, she had not received any previous antenatal care. She was diagnosed as being 'moderately depressed' and as suffering from severe pre-eclampsia, for which the doctor advised her to go into hospital and be induced to avoid the risks to the health and life of both herself and the foetus. She fully understood the potential risks involved but wanted her child to be born 'naturally'. A social worker, Collins, saw her and, following the advice of the duty psychiatrist that S was 'probably depressed', successfully applied for her to be compulsorily detained for assessment under the Mental Health Act 1983 s.2(2). This provision allows an individual to be detained for the purpose of assessment where he or she is suffering from mental disorder of a nature or degree which warrants detention in hospital for assessment *and* where it is felt that detention is necessary to safeguard the interests of that person's health and safety or in order to protect other persons. Under s.2(2) MHA the condition that must warrant detention is the mental disorder, not pregnancy, and it is difficult to comprehend how moderate depression might be classified as a disorder of a nature or degree that warrants detention in a hospital for assessment. Moreover, even if that disorder were to be considered sufficient to require the detention of the patient for assessment, it would have to be shown that there was a need to protect either the patient's own health and safety or that of other persons. The law in England and Wales is very clear: the foetus is not a person,[69] and so the only person that detention could serve to protect was S herself.

Within a few hours of her detention S was transferred, against her will, from the psychiatric hospital to St George's Hospital and the following day she was again examined by a psychiatrist, who concluded that she fully understood the proposed interventions, the reasons for them and the consequences of her refusal to consent to these interventions. The psychiatrist found S's capacity to consent to be intact

67 [1999] Fam. 26.
68 *Tameside and Glossop Acute Services NHS Trust v CH* (note 22).
69 *Re F* (note 7); *Paton v British Pregnancy Advisory Service Trustees* (note 7).

and unaffected by her mental state. S wrote a letter setting out her reasons for refusing the proposed interventions and spoke to a solicitor. However, at around the same time an *ex parte* application was made on behalf of the hospital seeking a declaration that a caesarean section could be performed despite her continued refusal of consent. Hogg J was (mis)informed that S had been in labour for 24 hours and that both her life and that of the foetus was in danger. Without specifically considering S's competence, Hogg J granted the declaration sought, saying, 'If the mother wishes to appeal this case it means that it has worked', presumably meaning that at least S would have survived. S was shown a copy of the order and continued to refuse her consent to a caesarean, although she did not actively resist the operation, believing active resistance to be undignified. A caesarean section was performed and S was safely delivered of a baby girl before being returned to the psychiatric hospital. Her detention under s.2(2) of the Act was terminated two days later, without her receiving treatment for any mental disorder.

S appealed against the declaration dispensing with her consent to treatment and applied for judicial review of her admission and detention in the mental hospital, her transfer, detention and treatment at the second hospital and her return to the mental hospital. The Court of Appeal rejected the submission that S lacked the capacity to consent and considered that the three principles relevant to its judgment were: autonomy, the status of the foetus and the application of the Mental Health Act 1983. It was held that S's detention in both hospitals had been unlawful, but that even if she had been lawfully detained under the Mental Health Act 1983, she could not have been 'forced into medical procedures unconnected with her mental condition unless her capacity to consent to such treatment [was] diminished'.[70] In fact, as in the case of *Re S*,[71] the pregnant woman's competence was not considered by Hogg J and, as Judge LJ makes clear, her competence was never really in question.[72]

In recognising the competent adult's right to autonomy and the lack of independent existence or legal recognition of the foetus as a person (including as a person in need of protection under s.2(2)(b) of the 1983 Act), the Court concluded that:

> While pregnancy increases the personal responsibilities of a woman it does not diminish her entitlement to decide whether or not to undergo medical treatment ... [An unborn child's] need for medical assistance does not prevail over her rights. She is entitled not to be forced to submit to an invasion of her body against her will, whether her own life or that of her unborn child depends on it. Her right is not reduced or diminished merely because her decision to exercise it may appear morally repugnant. The infringement of the

70 *St George's Healthcare NHS Trust* v *S; R* v *Collins and others, ex parte S* (note 67), at 52, *per* Judge LJ; cf. *Tameside and Glossop Acute Services Trust v CH* (note 22).

71 *Re S* (note 11).

72 *St George's Healthcare NHS Trust* v *S; R* v *Collins and others, ex parte S* (note 67), at 42–3.

> mother's autonomy could not, therefore, be justified by the perceived needs of the foetus.[73]

The Court of Appeal recognised the dichotomy between law and morality in *Re MB*,[74] and similarly in *St George's* the court stressed that there was no *legal* obligation to consent to medical treatment for the benefit of the foetus. However, the Court of Appeal clearly disapproved of S's behaviour, stating that 'no normal mother-to-be could think' like she did, that her refusal was 'morally repugnant' and that her bizarre thinking was 'contrary to the views of the overwhelming majority of the community at large'.[75] In fact, Judge LJ praised the courage of the social worker, Ms Collins, and accepted that both she and the doctors had acted in accordance with a genuine desire to do what was best for S and the foetus,[76] despite the fact that they had abused the Mental Health Act and unlawfully subjected S to major surgery.

The importance of *St George's* really lies in that fact that it confirmed the central holding of *Re MB*, namely that a competent pregnant woman does not belong to a special category of persons and that she is able to refuse to consent to medical treatment that would benefit her foetus. Nevertheless, although it was accepted that S had been competent, and thus that the caesarean performed against her will constituted a battery, it is questionable whether such a decision would have been reached had she still been pregnant and there still been a risk to the foetus. As discussed above, any woman refusing medical treatment in such circumstances is likely to be perceived as being irrational. This is well illustrated by Judge LJ in his discussion of the 'prohibited reasoning' that might lead to the misapplication of the Mental Health Act:

> Here is an intelligent woman. She knows perfectly well that if she persists with this course against medical advice she is likely to cause serious harm, and possibly death, to her baby and to herself. No normal mother-to-be could possibly think like that... . Her bizarre thinking represents a danger to their safety and health. It therefore follows that she must be mentally disordered and detained in hospital in her own interests and those of her baby. The short answer is that she may be perfectly rational and quite outside the ambit of the Act, and will remain so notwithstanding her eccentric thought process.

It is suggested that such circumstances would be likely suffice to found a finding of incompetence were the case to be heard in an emergency situation with the life of the foetus and health of the woman hanging in the balance.

73 Ibid., at 50.

74 *Re MB (Medical Treatment)* (note 46), *per* Butler-Sloss LJ, at 440.

75 *St George's Healthcare NHS Trust* v*S; R* v*Collins and others, ex parte S* (note 67), at 51.

76 Ibid., at 52–3.

e. The aftermath of St George's*: the calm before the storm*

In the decade following the Court of Appeal's ruling in *St George's*, only one case was reported, *Bolton Hospitals NHS Trust v O*,[77] as in all the other cases the woman was found to be incompetent and therefore a caesarean was authorised as being in her best interests. O was 39 weeks pregnant, in this her fifth pregnancy. Her previous four pregnancies had each ended in a caesarean delivery and following the fourth caesarean she experienced problems recovering from the anaesthetic and suffered flashbacks of the operation. Her obstetrician advised that a caesarean delivery would be necessary and estimated that there was only a 5 per cent chance of a successful vaginal delivery due to the risk of uterine rupture.

O was willing to consent to the performance of the caesarean, but, like *MB*, in the operating theatre she withdrew her consent. Over the period of a week, four attempts had been made to perform the caesarean with her consent, but on each occasion she had panicked and refused to go ahead with the operation. On the third occasion a consultant psychiatrist was present in the operating theatre and he formed the opinion that she had the capacity to refuse and to request a delay in the performance of the caesarean. From the report it appears that he did not fully comprehend the circumstances of the case and that he thought he was being asked to consider whether she should be sectioned under the Mental Health Act. On the next day, having again refused to go ahead with the operation, she was interviewed by another doctor who formed the opinion that O was suffering from post-traumatic stress disorder. She said that O temporarily lacked capacity at the point of going for the operation due to the overwhelming psychological fear and anxiety she experienced. Unlike many of the previous cases, the judge actually spoke to the woman concerned, discussing the matter with her over the telephone. Dame Butler-Sloss P formed the opinion that O had the requisite capacity to make her own decisions at that time, but that her panic rendered her incapable of making a decision at the operative time, as in the cases of *Re L* and *Re MB*. She once again stressed that everyone has the right to refuse treatment, even without good reason, but that

> There is a point at which that refusal and irrationality, as others might see it, tips the usually competent person over into a situation where the person, for however long or short a period, is actually unable to see through the consequences of the act, because that capacity to see through those consequences is inhibited by the panic situation in which the patient finds himself, or more particularly in this line of cases, herself.[78]

Dame Butler-Sloss P took pains to explain that O wanted the operation to be performed, not wanting herself or the 'baby' to die. However, she held that the overwhelming psychological fear and anxiety O suffered were such that she

77 [2002] EWHC 2871, [2003] 1 FLR 824.
78 Ibid., at 827.

temporarily lacked the capacity to make the decision and granted the declaration sought. She did recognise that the consultant psychiatrist present at the third attempt (18 December) had found O to have capacity to refuse the operation and to request a delay until the next day, but suggested that this meant he did not appreciate the full circumstances of the case, particularly that this was the third time O had withdrawn her consent to the operation.[79] However, in common with the other cases, this was heard as a case requiring great urgency and a report from the consultant was not available – Dame Butler-Sloss did not even know his name! She accepted the view of the second consultant, that O's capacity was temporarily impaired by a post-traumatic stress disorder, against the background that the hospital felt that the day of the hearing (20 December) was the last day on which an elective caesarean could be performed, before a crisis situation might be caused by O going into labour.

This case shares many of the same features that characterised *Re MB*, the urgent application to avoid a crisis situation being one of those particularly undesirable features. Clearly, it is regrettable that time could not be found to further investigate the differing opinions expressed by the consultants within only one day of another; however, it is suggested that it is extremely unlikely that a court would consider a woman in such a situation to have the capacity to refuse consent. Nevertheless, this case once again illustrates the need to identify potential problems during the pregnancy and to confront those problems at a time when the woman's capacity is undiminished. The second consultant, whose evidence was regarded as much more pertinent, stated that O was 'keen to pursue a psychiatric assessment and psychological treatment'.[80] Such an assessment and treatment could usefully have been provided earlier in the pregnancy, with the aim of avoiding the crisis situation that arose, where an urgent reference had to be made to the court in the face of a woman refusing to consent and with incomplete evidence from the medical professionals about her capacity. Whilst a finding of temporary incapacity may be unavoidable in those circumstances, where the refusal of consent results from a needle phobia or post-traumatic stress disorder, action must be taken to empower women, to enable them to overcome such problems and to facilitate their ability to make autonomous decisions, rather than forcing them to accept medical treatment in the face of their fears, knowing that this is likely to result in postnatal depression, as the second consultant in this case admitted.

f. The impact of the Mental Capacity Act 2005

In relation to court-authorised obstetric intervention, the Mental Capacity Act 2005 (MCA) largely codified the applicable common law, setting out a presumption of capacity (s.1(2) MCA), so that a pregnant woman should be presumed to have capacity to make decisions for herself. If she is found to lack capacity, treatment

79 Ibid., at 825.
80 Ibid., at 826.

may only be given in accordance with her best interests (s.1(5) MCA). To that end s.5 MCA provides protection from liability where a doctor takes reasonable steps to establish that the woman lacks capacity to decide the issue, and provides treatment on the basis of a reasonable belief both that she lacks capacity and that the treatment is in her best interests. Thus, under the Mental Capacity Act a determination of incapacity will continue to act as a device to enable the woman to be treated in accordance with her best interests, which remain the subject of a largely objective assessment and appear to be dominated by the need to ensure the safe delivery of the baby, as discussed below.

Capacity is most likely to be questioned where there is a disagreement between the woman and her obstetrician about treatment. However, in addition to the rebuttable presumption of capacity (s.1(2) MCA), the Act confirms the common law position and further demonstrates the priority to be given to autonomous decision-making in s.1(4) MCA by expressly providing that 'a person is not to be treated as unable to make a decision merely because he makes an unwise decision'.[81] The Act institutes a two-stage capacity test (s.2(1) MCA). The diagnostic criterion calls for the assessment of whether or not the individual has 'an impairment of, or disturbance in the functioning of, the mind or brain'. Thereafter, the functional threshold requires the determination of whether the impairment or disturbance renders the individual incapable of making the decision in question. The cumulative test of incompetence set out by Thorpe J in *Re C (refusal of medical treatment)*[82] is largely enshrined in s.3(1) MCA, providing that the person will be unable to make the decision for herself if she cannot understand, retain and use or weigh the information relevant to the decision, or communicate her decision.[83] The two limbs of the capacity test must both be satisfied; thus, as Holman J stressed in *Re SB*, the finding that the diagnostic test is satisfied 'is the beginning not the end of the enquiry; for the relevant test and requirement under section 2 of the Mental Capacity Act 2005 … is that because of such an impairment or disturbance the person "at the material time … is unable to make a decision for himself."'[84] Significantly, the introduction of the diagnostic threshold into the determination of capacity does mean, for example, that Johnson J could no longer authorise the performance of a caesarean on C, who said she would rather die than have another caesarean. It will be remembered that she was not found to be suffering from a mental disorder in the terms of the 1983 Act and her obstetrician considered her to have the capacity to refuse consent.[85] Absent an impairment of, or

81 Cf. *Re T* (note 4), *per* Lord Donaldson MR, at 113; *Re MB* (note 46), *per* Butler-Sloss LJ, at 436–7.
82 [1994] 1 FLR 31.
83 Unlike the common law, s.3 MCA 2005 does not expressly state that the individual must believe the information given, although the courts have held that this is an implicit requirement in s.3, *Local Authority X v MM and KM* [2007] EWHC 2003 (Fam), *per* Munby J, arguing that the specific requirement of belief had in fact been 'in the more general requirements of understanding and of ability to use and weigh information' in *Re MB* (note 46), at [82].
84 [2013] EWCOP 1417, at [37].
85 *Rochdale Healthcare NHS Trust v C* (note 42).

disturbance in, the functioning of the mind or brain, C's capacity would remain intact, despite Johnson J's view that someone in labour who could accept the inevitability of her own death was incompetent to make even a trivial decision.[86] In such a situation there is no scope to consider whether a caesarean would further her best interests and to so order. Similarly, in cases such as *Re MB* and *L*, where women suffer from a needle phobia, it will have to be established that the phobia amounts to 'an impairment of, or disturbance in the functioning of, the mind or brain'. A phobia may satisfy the diagnostic criterion, but thereafter it will still need to be shown that the phobia is so debilitating as to render the woman incapable of making the decision for herself.

The underlying philosophy of the Mental Capacity Act is that individuals should be empowered to take decisions for themselves wherever possible, and therefore s.1(3) MCA requires that all practical steps be taken to enable the individual to take the decision for herself without success before she is deemed to lack the capacity to decide for herself. This requirement is likely to be particularly important in relation to non-consensual caesareans, as the case law prior to the enactment of the Mental Capacity Act often raises the question of whether more could have been done to enable the women to take decisions for themselves. For example, in the cases of *Re MB*[87] and *Bolton Hospitals NHS Trust v O*[88] the women were known to be suffering from needle phobia and post-traumatic stress disorder, both conditions having been raised with healthcare professionals earlier in the pregnancy. In both cases psychological intervention at an earlier point in the pregnancy, for example, might have put the women in a position to be able to take decisions for themselves; instead, no action was taken to empower or facilitate the decisional capabilities of the women and, with the onset of labour imminent, recourse was had to court orders to compel the performance of a caesarean on the basis that they were unable to make the necessary decision for themselves.

Where an individual is found to lack capacity, the Court of Protection may make an order relating to her welfare (s.16 MCA), and such an order can include consent or refusal of consent to medical treatment.[89] In making the order, the court must consider whether the purpose can be achieved in a manner less restrictive of her rights and freedom of action (s.1(6) MCA). Again, there is some concern that in the earlier case law the least restrictive approach was not adopted. Thus, for example in the case of *Re MB*,[90] greater consideration should, it is suggested, have been given to the alternative of vaginal delivery. The consultant's practice was to deliver all footling breech births by caesarean, but, as he recognised, he had previously delivered a baby in a footling breach presentation vaginally. It is generally possible to deliver a breech presentation without recourse to a caesarean; therefore, at least a trial labour, with the potential to intervene if an emergency

86 Ibid., at 275.
87 *Re MB* (note 46).
88 *Bolton Hospitals NHS Trust v O* (note 77).
89 S.17 (1)(d) MCA 2005.
90 *Re MB* (note 46).

caesarean became necessary, would appear to have been the least restrictive approach, an issue that will be considered further below.

In making an order, the court must also act in the individual's best interests (s.1 (5) MCA), applying the section 4 principles that govern the determination of best interests. Central to the determination of an individual's best interests will be the individual's known wishes and feelings, the critical interests that make the individual the person she is. Prior to the Mental Capacity Act the courts paid only scant attention to the incompetent patient's contemporaneous and anticipatory wishes, generally only giving effect to those wishes when they supported, or at least did not conflict with, the patient's clinical best interests. Thus, for example, in *Re SS (Medical Treatment: Late Termination)*,[91] despite the woman's repeated request for a termination of pregnancy over a period of two months, Wall J held that it would not be in her best interests to allow an abortion to be performed, even though the expert evidence was very finely balanced. The Mental Capacity Act is based upon the Law Commission's report on Mental Incapacity (1995)[92] which recommended that the best interests criterion should encompass 'a strong element of "substituted judgment"',[93] so that in determining the individual's best interests 'regard should be had to the ascertainable past and present wishes and feelings of the person concerned, and the factors that person would consider if able to do so'.[94] This recommendation was incorporated into the Act, together with a requirement that 'the beliefs and values that would be likely to influence his decision if he had capacity' be considered (s.4 (6) MCA). Thus, the individual's views are an important component in the assessment of her best interests, as Lady Hale recognised in *Aintree University Hospitals NHS Foundation Trust v James and others*:[95]

> In so far as it is possible to ascertain the patient's wishes and feelings, his beliefs and values or the things which were important to him, it is those which should be taken into account because they are a component in making the choice which is right for him as an individual human being.

However, as the case law both prior to and after the introduction of the Mental Capacity Act demonstrates, whilst the individual's wishes may be an important element of the best interests assessment, they are not determinative thereof.

Following the enactment of the Mental Capacity Act, the position remains that if the woman has the capacity to decide how she wants her baby to be delivered, that decision is hers alone; she cannot be compelled to have a caesarean or other obstetric intervention for the sake of the foetus, no matter how unwise or immoral her decision may appear. However, if the woman is found to lack capacity, a

91 [2002] 1 F.L.R. 445.
92 Law Commission, *Mental Incapacity* (Law Com No. 231, 1995).
93 Ibid., at 3.25.
94 Ibid., at 3.28.
95 [2013] UKSC 67; [2014] AC 591, at 608–9, [45].

decision must be made in her best interests. Best interests have long been acknowledged to encompass much more than clinical interests,[96] but, worryingly, the most recent cases would appear to demonstrate the enduring nature of the view that the safe delivery of her baby will constitute one of the most significant considerations in the assessment of a pregnant woman's best interests,[97] a factor that will almost inevitably lead to the authorisation of an obstetric intervention, regardless of the woman's known wishes.

g. The re-emergence of the issue: court orders pertaining to women suffering from a mental health disorder

Re AA (Mental Capacity: Enforced Caesarean)[98] is the first reported case of court-authorised obstetric intervention since the Mental Capacity Act 2005 came into force and marks a new chapter in the case law concerning such intervention. Since 2012 a significant number of orders have been granted authorising the performance of a caesarean; in the majority of these cases the woman was suffering from a mental disorder and some of the women had been compulsorily detained under the Mental Health Act 1983. In each case where doctors considered that the woman lacked capacity, the judge confirmed that finding and proceeded to consider the woman's best interests which were determined to require the safe delivery of the baby and therefore obstetric intervention. Thus in each case a caesarean was authorised by the court. Given the large number of decisions reported since December 2013, it seems unlikely that such decisions are exceptional. Instead, it is suggested that the increased reporting of such decisions is attributable to the widespread condemnation in the media of a decision to authorise a caesarean upon a woman detained under the Mental Health Act (MHA) in *Re AA*.[99]

The judgment in *Re AA* was not published for over a year after the caesarean had been performed,[100] it only being reported after sensational articles had appeared in the national and international press suggesting that an Italian woman (Alessandra Pacchieri) had been subjected to a caesarean against her will in order

96 *Re A (Medical Treatment: Male Sterilisation)* [2000] 1 FLR 549; see also *Aintree University Hospitals NHS Trust v James* [2013] UKSC 67, [2014] AC 591, at 607, *per* Hale LJ.
97 Cf. *Re MB* (note 46), *per* Butler Sloss LJ, at 439.
98 [2012] EWHC 4378 (COP), [2014] 2 FLR 237.
99 Ibid. In *Re P (a child)* [2013] EWHC 4048 (Fam) the president of the Family Division, Sir James Munby, recognised that there is a 'pressing need for radical changes in the way in which both the family courts and the Court of Protection approach … transparency. Many more judgments must be published', at [45]. He went on to issue guidance on the publication of judgments in both the family courts and the Court of Protection: Practice guidance: transparency in the family courts, publication of judgments, 16/01/2014, and Practice guidance: transparency in the Court of Protection, publication of judgments, 16/01/2014.
100 Mostyn J delivered his judgment *ex tempore* on 24 August 2012; a transcript was released on 4 December 2013.

to enable social workers to take the child into care.[101] The woman was detained under the Mental Health Act 1983 and had previously had two caesarean sections; there was said to be a 1 per cent risk of uterine rupture if she were to give birth vaginally. Both her existing children had been taken into care due to neglect and the local authority intended to invite the police to exercise their powers under s.46 Children Act 1989 to take the child into police protection once it had been born. In an *ex tempore* judgment Mostyn J granted a declaration that it would be in AA's best interests for her baby to be delivered by caesarean section, with the use of reasonable restraint if necessary and appropriate.

There are a number of concerning features about this case, not least that it was not reported until media reporting that highlighted the lack of transparency in Court of Protection cases made the continued failure to publish the judgment untenable. The transcript of proceedings raises real concerns about the way in which AA was found to lack capacity to make decisions concerning the delivery of her baby. In a telling exchange, the question of AA's capacity was dismissed without any scrutiny of the assessment provided by the psychiatrist caring for AA, with no independent assessment being sought. Mr Lock, counsel for the Official Solicitor, stated:

> The question is: does she have capacity? She plainly does not, because there is evidence of delusional beliefs. We have thought carefully as to whether we ought to ask your Lordship to adjourn this so that we can get further into capacity, but given that this is the treating psychiatrist and she has been in his care since at least June of this year, there appears to be evidence, therefore, based on a fair amount of background information; not like a psychiatrist who has seen a patient on one occasion and just gives a view where there is always a concern that there may be some background that the psychiatrist was not fully aware of. This appears to be a reasoned report based on a good knowledge of the patient. Therefore we do not propose to ask your Lordship to adjourn.[102]

Somewhat surprisingly, Mostyn J responded to this rather cursory examination of AA's capacity saying, 'I am struggling to envisage a circumstance where a patient detained under section 3 as an inpatient with a diagnosed mental illness has got capacity'.[103] However, the Mental Capacity Act 2005 utilises a two-stage capacity test (s.2(1) MCA), and it is important to note that both the diagnostic and the functional criteria must each be satisfied; an individual cannot be classified as lacking capacity upon fulfilment of the diagnostic requirement alone.

101 The first report was made by Christopher Booker in The *Telegraph* under the headline 'Operate on this mother so that we can take her baby', The *Telegraph*, 30 November 2013.

102 *Re AA (Mental Capacity: Enforced Caesarean)* (note 98), transcript of proceedings, at 4, Mr Lock.

103 Ibid., at 4 Mostyn J.

AA was compulsorily detained under the Mental Health Act, although there was no clarity about the nature of the disorder from which she was suffering – at the hearing it was described as a 'schizophrenic disorder which is psychotic in nature',[104] with no further details being available to the court. By contrast, in the subsequent adoption proceedings Newton J described the woman as suffering from a bipolar affective disorder[105] – an entirely different condition. Detention under the Mental Health Act is not proof in itself of incapacity; although the diagnostic threshold will generally be satisfied, it is perfectly possible for someone detained under the Act to retain capacity to consent/refuse consent to treatment, because the second limb, the functional criterion, remains unsatisfied. Thus, in a case predating the introduction of the Mental Capacity Act 2005, the court held that C, a schizophrenic detained under the Act, had the ability to give a valid refusal of consent to the amputation of his gangrenous leg.[106] This position was confirmed after the Act had come into force in *Re SB* where Holman J held that SB (a bipolar disorder sufferer, detained under s.2 MHA 1983) had the requisite capacity to decide to elect a termination of pregnancy.[107]

The fact that there was no detailed consideration of AA's capacity represents a significant shortcoming in the decision. Whilst there is no doubt that she was suffering from a mental disorder such that could cause an impairment or disturbance in the functioning of her brain, it is less clear that she lacked the ability to make the decision for herself, being unable to understand, retain and weigh the information relevant to the decision and communicate her decision (s.3 MCA). The view of the treating psychiatrist was accepted without further consideration or scrutiny. However, as Baker J observed in *CC v KK*,[108] the court and the expert have distinct roles:

> The court must consider all the evidence, not merely the views of the independent expert. In many cases, perhaps most cases, the opinion of the expert will be confirmed by the other evidence, but inevitably there will be cases where the court reaches a different conclusion… . Whilst acknowledging the important role for expert evidence, the assessment is ultimately a matter for the court.

Nevertheless, in *Re AA* the court relied entirely upon the assessment of capacity provided by a single psychiatrist, a psychiatrist who was not independent but had been treating AA for six weeks. As Judge LJ emphasised in *St George's*:

> [I]n serious or complex cases involving difficult issues about the future health and well-being or even the life of the patient, the issue of capacity should be

104 Ibid., at 2, Ms Burnham opening.
105 *Re P (a child)* [2013] EW Misc 20 (CC), at [3].
106 *Re C (refusal of medical treatment)* [1994] 1 FLR 31.
107 *Re SB (A patient; capacity to consent to termination)* [2013] EWHC 1417 (COP); [2013] 3 F.C.R. 384.
108 [2012] EWHC 2136 (COP), at [24].

> examined by an independent psychiatrist, ideally one approved under section 12(2) of the Mental Health Act 1983.[109]

Unfortunately, this recommendation was not followed in the case of AA, despite the fact that this was an extremely serious case of the very nature Judge LJ described. Moreover, the judge did not have the benefit of speaking to AA himself, a factor that recent cases have demonstrated to be of great significance if the judge is to form an independent view of the individual's capacity.[110] Thus, for example, in *Re SB* Holman J rejected the psychiatrist's assessment that SB (a woman suffering from bipolar disorder and detained under s.2 MHA) lacked the capacity to decide to have an abortion. He stressed the importance of personal presence, stating, 'My assessment of this case has been enormously illuminated by her attendance and by the considerable oral evidence which she has given'.[111]

Significantly, no attention was given to whether, or how, AA could be assisted to make a decision. Once the question of whether she had capacity had been cursorily dismissed, the court considered her best interests, prioritising the obstetric and psychiatric evidence. AA was not present at the hearing and was represented by the Official Solicitor who did not oppose the application. A considerable problem in these cases is that nobody appears to argue against the performance of a caesarean; the judge, the Official Solicitor and the Trust's barrister each argued that a caesarean would be in AA's best interests, but nobody put forward the opposing view. In the circumstances, that is extremely regrettable. AA was not in labour, her own views were not reported – we do not even know if her wishes were known – and the risk of uterine rupture due to previous caesareans, if a caesarean were not performed, was set at only 1 per cent. Given the extremely invasive nature of the intervention and the risks posed to the woman by the procedure, it is essential that the court's assessment of her best interests is well informed, thorough and entirely transparent. A caesarean delivery, particularly a planned caesarean delivery of which AA was to be given no notice, can hardly be considered conducive to securing her longer-term mental health best interests, it being unlikely to promote confidence in her healthcare professionals. Moreover, it is not clear that a caesarean served AA's physical health best interests, given the small risk of uterine rupture attached to a vaginal delivery and the lack of a current need to intervene.

The Trust's barrister advised the court that AA's doctors were concerned that she would not tell them that she was in labour, and that if she dissembled or refused to cooperate, it would be impossible to monitor labour and so to intervene if it became necessary. This was reported to be a real risk as she feared that the child would be removed after birth, as indeed was the case. Thus it was argued by the Official Solicitor that a planned caesarean would best further AA's best

109 *St George's Healthcare NHS Trust* v*S; R* v*Collins and others, ex parte S* (note 67), *per* Judge LJ, at 64.

110 See, for example, *Re SB* (note 107), *A Local Authority v TZ* [2013] EWCOP 2322.

111 *Re SB* (note 107), at [29].

interests as it would be possible to ensure that the correct staff, in sufficient numbers, were available to support her.[112] Arguably, medical professionals closely observing a woman should be able to tell that she is in labour (she was compulsorily detained at the time) and there should have been sufficient time to gather the requisite staff to support her during the birth, or indeed to perform an emergency caesarean if that became necessary. Certainly, a planned caesarean would facilitate planning for the Trust, but the sole consideration for the court should be the woman's best interests and those do not include the convenience of the Trust's staff or indeed the Trust's staffing arrangements. Moreover, whilst the judge stressed that he could not take account of the foetal interests,[113] he suggested that AA's mental health best interests required the safe delivery of her child and that it not be exposed to risk during the birth.[114] If a pregnant woman's best interests are formulated in such a manner, particularly absent any consideration of her own known wishes, the authorisation of obstetric intervention would appear inevitable whenever the woman is found to lack capacity.

The judge referred to the proposed procedure as an 'elective caesarean', a telling reference as the mode of delivery was being elected by the medical professionals, without current medical necessity; there is no indication that the woman would have elected to undergo caesarean delivery. The Mental Capacity Act requires use to be made of supported decision-making (s.4(4) MCA), obligating the person determining the best interests to permit and encourage the individual concerned to participate, or to improve her ability to participate as fully as possible. In this case the woman was not aware of the application, there was no possibility for her to participate and her wishes were not referred to, despite the fact that the assessment of her best wishes should have included a consideration of her past and present wishes and feelings (s.4(6)(a) MCA). We cannot know what her wishes were; however, the fact that she had previously had two caesareans cannot be taken as evidence that she would have desired a caesarean in this her third pregnancy. Crucially, the court did not consider her wishes at all. The court's declaration concerned an invasive procedure, which would appear not even to have been discussed with the pregnant woman, despite the fact that she had been in the care of the Trust's psychiatrist and obstetrician for at least six weeks. Indeed, the declaration was granted subject to the order that the woman not be told of its contents until after the operation was carried out. This appears to be contrary to what was decided in *St George's*, namely that women should always be notified that an application for such a declaration has been made, never mind a declaration itself.[115]

Moreover, s.1(6) MCA requires that the least restrictive means be utilised to achieve the purpose sought. For this reason Cobb J refused to authorise the

112 *Re AA (Mental Capacity: Enforced Caesarean)* (note 98), transcript of proceedings, at 5.
113 *Re AA (Mental Capacity: Enforced Caesarean)* (note 98), at 239.
114 Ibid.
115 *St George's Healthcare NHS Trust* v *S; R* v *Collins and others, ex parte S* (note 67), *per* Law LJ, at 64.

sterilisation of a woman with Down's syndrome and learning difficulties in *A Local Authority v K*,[116] stating, 'Plainly risk management is better than invasive treatment. It is less restrictive'.[117] In the case of AA, the purpose was clearly the safe delivery of the child; however, it is not clear that a caesarean was proportionate to that aim. The risk of uterine rupture due to previous caesareans, if a caesarean were not performed, was set at only 1 per cent. Mostyn J described this as 'a significant risk',[118] but this is a relatively low level of risk; even in view of the consequences of uterine rupture, that would not normally justify a caesarean as being in her best interests. In fact, the National Institute for Health and Care Excellence (NICE) guidelines (not cited in court) state that women who have had four caesareans (two more than AA had undergone) should be informed that 'the risk of uterine rupture, although higher for planned vaginal birth, is rare'.[119] In this case the least restrictive approach would have been to permit AA to go into labour naturally and to intervene if it became necessary. However, as discussed above, Mostyn J accepted that her best interests required that a planned caesarean be performed, noting that where the proportionate response does not comply with the individual's best interests, her best interests will take precedence.

In this case it would appear that neither the capacity nor the best interests assessments were properly informed, and it is extremely regrettable that AA was not in a position to take part in the decision-making. It seems likely that AA did lack capacity to consent to a caesarean and that such an intervention may have served her best interests; however, it is imperative that such declarations are only granted upon clear and convincing evidence that the woman lacks capacity on the basis of not only the diagnostic but also the functional criteria, and that all possible steps have been taken to assist her to make a decision, or at least to participate in the decision-making process. Similarly, a much more detailed, holistic consideration of her best interests should have been undertaken, with much greater consideration being given to less invasive means of safeguarding her best interests.

Moreover, procedurally this case is extremely worrying. The safeguards set out in *St George's* and *Re MB* appear to have been circumvented. One of the recommendations made by the Court of Appeal in *Re MB* was that emergency applications should be avoided wherever possible.[120] This was not an emergency application; however, the judge termed it 'urgent'[121] and said that he was 'not going to give an extensive judgment because time is of the essence',[122] and the barrister representing the Trust in applying for the declaration apologised for the incomplete documentation submitted, explaining that the bundles had of necessity

116 [2013] EWHC 242 (COP).
117 Ibid., at [33].
118 *Re AA (Mental Capacity: Enforced Caesarean)* (note 98), at 239.
119 National Institute for Health and Clinical Excellence, *Caesarean Section: NICE Clinical Guideline 132*, 2012, at 1.8.2.
120 *Re MB* (note 46), *per* Butler-Sloss LJ, at 445.
121 *Re AA (Mental Capacity: Enforced Caesarean)* (note 98), *per* Mostyn J, at 238.
122 Ibid.

been prepared in haste.[123] Reading the transcript of the proceedings that led to the granting of the declaration, it is difficult to escape the view that they were extremely rushed and ill-prepared, surprisingly so given the circumstances. This was not an emergency application, nor was it so urgent that a fuller, more considered hearing could not have taken place. AA was detained under s.2 and subsequently s.3 Mental Health Act 1983 and had been so detained since 13 June 2012 – that is, for six weeks at the time of the application. She was not in labour, although she was 39 weeks pregnant and her due date was two days after the application date, and therefore it was reasonable to anticipate that she would go into labour within the next few weeks. However, this could not have come as a surprise to the Trust: she was clearly pregnant and was under the care of both a consultant psychiatrist and obstetrician, and therefore it is surprising that a care plan had not been developed to include the mode of delivery at an earlier point during her detention.

In *Re P*[124] the court was once again confronted with the issue of whether to issue a declaration that an obstetric intervention could lawfully take place in relation to a woman detained under the Mental Health Act. The case was heard in the wake of the media furore concerning *Re AA*, and the criticism levelled at the perceived secrecy of such decisions led Peter Jackson J to issue a stinging rebuke to the press:

> Those members of the media who are present have followed the proceedings and are in a position to inform the public in whatever way they think best. I cannot envisage circumstances in which an important matter of this kind would be dealt with in any other way. The court's only concern is that the interests of incapable or vulnerable people are not needlessly sacrificed. The time will surely come when responsible commentators will realise that attending hearings or making inquiries of the court as to how, and why, the decision has been reached will almost always lead to a fuller understanding and that it will no longer be respectable to fail to make basic inquiries and then to caricature the process as having somehow been closed or secretive.[125]

Nevertheless, his judgment only became publicly available three months after it was delivered. He followed this commentary with a significantly more detailed consideration of P's capacity and best interests than had occurred in *Re AA*. P was 36 weeks pregnant and suffered from type 2 diabetes, which impacted upon her pregnancy. She had been compulsorily detained under the Mental Health Act for almost a month and was reported to be suffering from paranoid schizophrenia and to have not reliably followed her medication regime. Whilst there was disagreement between the four psychiatrists who had assessed P, they agreed that she lacked capacity, merely disagreeing about the degree of incapacity suffered. Peter Jackson J accepted that P lacked the requisite capacity to make decisions concerning the

123 *Re AA (Mental Capacity: Enforced Caesarean)* (note 98), transcript p.1, Ms Burnham opening.
124 [2013] EWHC 4581 (COP).
125 Ibid., at [7].

delivery of her baby. Despite the fact that labour was not imminent, the Trust sought a declaration that it would be lawful to induce labour and to effect an instrumental delivery or a caesarean if necessary. Peter Jackson J reiterated the mantra that a woman with capacity can decide as she wishes for good, bad or no particular reason,[126] but, accepting the psychiatric evidence that P lacked capacity, found that she should be treated in accordance with her best interests.

This was P's fourth pregnancy; her first two children were delivered vaginally and the third was delivered by caesarean. The eldest two children had been taken into care; the youngest lives overseas. P was described as being 'very opposed' to the performance of a caesarean section, but 'relatively calm and accepting of the idea of being induced'.[127] Her obstetrician advised that labour should be induced due to her diabetes and argued that this planned induction would enable the best possible support to be given to P during delivery. He suggested that a caesarean be performed if it became necessary. Adopting a balance sheet approach, Peter Jackson J considered the risks associated with a caesarean, but offset them with the 'small, but not insignificant, risk that she would develop serious bleeding' due to scar dehiscence, which could be life-threatening.[128] He also emphasised that her best interests required that the baby be safely delivered, stressing that it would have an 'extremely adverse effect on Mrs P if unnecessarily her child was not born safely or was born with some avoidable disability as a result of a lack of obstetric care which might have been given'.[129] Thus once again, despite her clear and expressed desire for a vaginal delivery, her best interests were found to justify intervention to ensure the safest possible delivery of the baby. That being the case, Peter Jackson J held that P could be induced immediately and an instrumental delivery be effected if necessary. Furthermore, he held that a caesarean could be performed if the consultant considered it necessary to 'avoid significant bleeding as a result of scar dehiscence *or to avoid foetal distress*, or any similar significant threat to Mrs P's health for her to have a Caesarean section'.[130] The reference to avoiding foetal distress is a reflection of the weight given to securing the safe delivery of the baby within the assessment of the woman's best interests. Indeed, it would appear that consideration of this factor, together with the woman's physical health interests, will dominate the assessment, leaving little scope for considering the more subjective elements highlighted in s.4 MCA.

h. The use of the inherent jurisdiction to authorise a caesarean upon a woman detained under the Mental Health Act

Whilst the consideration of P's best interests was significantly more detailed, it is somewhat surprising that Peter Jackson J, like Mostyn J in the case of *AA*, failed

126 Ibid., at [10].
127 Ibid., at [15] and [4].
128 Ibid., at [16].
129 Ibid., at [17].
130 Ibid., at [3].

to consider whether an order authorising a caesarean in the case of a woman detained under the Mental Health Act might constitute a deprivation of liberty and thus fall outside the scope of the jurisdiction of the Court of Protection to make an order under s.16 MCA, necessitating the exercise of the inherent jurisdiction of the High Court. The determination of whether a deprivation of liberty exists within the meaning of Art. 5 of the European Convention on Human Rights (ECHR) will depend upon consideration of three elements: the objective element (the confinement of the individual in a limited space for a not negligible time),[131] the subjective element (that the individual has not validly consented to the confinement)[132] and finally the state must be responsible for the deprivation of liberty.[133] In both cases these elements are clearly present. Although *AA* predates Baker J's decision in *An NHS Trust v Dr A*,[134] the failure to consider this aspect is regrettable, particularly as the non-emergency setting of these cases should have permitted a comprehensive consideration of the issues.

Following the decision in *An NHS Trust v Dr A*,[135] it is clear that where a woman is detained under the Mental Health Act any application for a declaration that it would not be unlawful to perform a caesarean should be made under the inherent jurisdiction of the High Court and not as a welfare order by the Court of Protection. Amendments made to the Mental Capacity Act 2005 by the Mental Health Act 2007 following *HL v UK*[136] provide that the Court of Protection cannot authorise a deprivation of liberty in a welfare order if a person is ineligible to be so deprived under the Act.[137] This means that welfare orders cannot be made authorising treatment under s.16 MCA when the woman is subject to a hospital treatment regime (within the meaning of para 8(1) Schedule 1A MCA 2005) and detained in a hospital under that regime, as was the case in *Re AA* and *Re P*. Therefore, until such time as Parliament acts to close the gap created by s.16A MCA, in such cases treatment other than that for a mental disorder can only be authorised in line with the patient's best interests by the High Court exercising its inherent jurisdiction. This is significant because, as discussed above, a caesarean will rarely (if ever) be integral to the treatment of a mental disorder so that the patient's consent can be dispensed with under s.63 MHA.[138] Although Wall J's expansive interpretation of treatment 'for the mental disorder from which he is suffering' has been the subject of significant criticism, that decision has not been overturned. Nevertheless, in *St George's* the Court of Appeal took a much narrower approach, Judge LJ stressing that:

> [S] was neither offered nor did she refuse treatment for mental disorder ... In the final analysis a woman detained under the Act for mental disorder cannot

131 *Storck v Germany* (2005) 43 EHRR 96, at [74].
132 Ibid.
133 Ibid., at [89].
134 [2013] EWHC 2442 (COP); [2014] 2 W.L.R. 607.
135 Ibid.
136 (2004) ECHR 471.
137 S.16A(1) MCA 2005.
138 See above, text accompanying note 22ff.

> be forced into medical procedures unconnected with her mental condition unless her capacity to consent to such treatment is diminished.[139]

Similarly, in *Dr A* Baker J accepted the view of the patient's psychiatrists that force-feeding could not constitute treatment for the purposes of s.63 MHA as it was not directed towards his mental disorder (paranoia and a delusional disorder), but rather treatment for a physical disorder, starvation and dehydration,[140] distinguishing both *Ex P Brady*[141] and *B. v Croydon Health Authority*.[142] It is suggested that just as the amputation of a gangrenous leg was not treatment for C's schizophrenia, and force-feeding was not treatment for Dr A's paranoia or delusions, so too a caesarean cannot be treatment for a mental disorder and therefore such treatment cannot be compelled under s.63 MHA. It is suggested that the only possible scenario in which a caesarean might be considered treatment for a mental disorder would be where it is imperative that the pregnancy be brought to an end in order to enable the effective treatment of the woman's mental disorder. Such a situation will, it is suggested, be extremely rare.

There is a real question about the nature of the inherent jurisdiction and whether it is appropriate that it has continued, despite the introduction of the Mental Capacity Act.[143] In the context of court-authorised obstetric intervention, performed without the consent of a woman detained under the Mental Health Act, the use of the inherent jurisdiction is extremely problematic, bypassing the procedural safeguards built into both the Mental Health Act and the Mental Capacity Act. In such cases the inherent jurisdiction is utilised to enable treatment to take place that cannot be authorised under either Act, circumventing, for example, the procedural and substantive requirements set out in s.4 MCA for the determination of best interests in favour of the comparatively unfettered discretion to determine best interests using the balance sheet approach of the inherent jurisdiction.[144] Moreover, where a deprivation of liberty occurs, Article 5 requires that the woman be told of and have the ability to challenge the order, which was certainly not the case in *Re AA* where AA was not told of the application, the order or the intention to remove the child at birth.

In *Great Western Hospitals NHS Foundation Trust v AA, BB, CC & DD*[145] Hayden J recognised that it would be necessary to utilise the inherent jurisdiction

139 *St George's Healthcare NHS Trust* v*S; R* v*Collins and others, ex parte S* (note 67), at 52.
140 *An NHS Trust v Dr A* (note 134), at 635.
141 *R v Collins ex parte Brady* [2000] Lloyd's Rep Med 355.
142 *B. v Croydon Health Authority* (note 24).
143 A detailed consideration of the appropriate role of the inherent jurisdiction following the enactment of the Mental Capacity Act falls outside the scope of this work, but it is clear there are substantial difficulties with the use of the inherent jurisdiction to ease this new 'Bournewood' Gap following the insertion of the Deprivation of Liberty Safeguards.
144 It is worth noting that the 'balance sheet' approach has also been utilised by the court in determining best interests under s.4 MCA, but alongside the s.4 principles. See, for example, *A London Authority v JH and MH* [2011] EWHC 2420 (COP).
145 [2014] EWHC 132 (Fam).

to grant an order authorising a caesarean to be performed upon a woman detained under the Mental Health Act and lacking capacity. AA was 38 weeks pregnant; her membranes had ruptured on the morning of 26 January 2014, but she had not gone into labour two days later. She suffered from bipolar affective disorder and although she had complied with the antenatal care she had been offered, she had not been taking her medicine. On admission to hospital she was agitated and disorientated. She was assessed by a psychiatrist as suffering from hypomania and puerperal psychosis (although she had not yet gone into labour) and compulsorily detained under the Mental Health Act. Due to the fact that labour had not started spontaneously, there was a risk of infection to both AA and her foetus. In the normal course of events, induction of labour would be indicated; however, AA was in a state of high agitation and the healthcare professionals were concerned that she would not cooperate with the proposed induction, which would necessitate the intravenous administration of Syntocinon and foetal monitoring, both of which would only be achievable by ongoing physical restraint. The team felt that this was undesirable and the Trust made an emergency application for an order authorising the performance of a caesarean section. Due to the lack of notice, the Official Solicitor was unable to act and thus AA was unrepresented, leading Moor J to adjourn the hearing, granting only an interim order authorising a caesarean if AA went into labour and it became necessary, or if she began to exhibit signs of infection.[146]

The next morning, at the full hearing, Hayden J started by considering AA's best interests, prioritising her clinical interests. He reviewed the evidence concerning the relative merits of the induction of labour and the performance of a caesarean, adopting a balance sheet approach and finding that the weight of the evidence supported a caesarean delivery as the safest option for AA. Throughout this exercise he took pains to stress that his concern was for the AA, saying:

> I have addressed here the disadvantages to the mother in this process conducting a balance of the positives and negatives in the competing alternatives. I do so because I am not in this application concerned with the welfare of the foetus. It must be said however that the alternative to the elective caesarean plainly carries significant risks to the foetus or to the baby and the real clinical prospect of foetal distress.[147]

Having concluded that both AA and the foetus's clinical interests would demonstrably be best served by a caesarean, Hayden J did briefly address the subjective elements of the best interests assessment, noting that this was a wanted baby and that AA's partner (BB) believed that she would have followed the recommendation of the doctors, had she been able to consider her situation objectively.[148]

146 [2014] EWHC 1666 (Fam), at [17–18].
147 *Great Western Hospitals NHS Foundation Trust v AA, BB, CC & DD* (note 145), at [15].
148 Ibid., at [16].

An indication of AA's perceived self-evident lack of capacity is given by the fact that Hayden J only considered her ability to make a decision relating to the delivery after having concluded that a caesarean would serve her best interests. A bipolar affective disorder will satisfy the diagnostic limb of the capacity test, and AA's belief that she could only give birth on or around her due date, more specifically on her own birthday, together with the high level of agitation she was experiencing, prevented her from being able to comply with the functional limb of the test. Unsurprisingly, given the weight of the psychiatric evidence presented and the testimony of AA's father about her condition, Hayden J found AA to lack the requisite capacity to make the decision for herself.

It was clear that the performance of a caesarean would require a facilitative deprivation of liberty, and this case is important because it is the first time that a judge addressed this issue in the context of obstetric intervention. If the caesarean could be classified as integral to the treatment of her mental disorder, AA's consent would not be necessary (s.63 MHA). However, her treatment team took the unequivocal view that a caesarean was physical treatment, not treatment for her bipolar affective disorder, and therefore could not be provided under the auspices of the Mental Health Act. As she was detained under s.2 MHA, she was ineligible to be deprived of her liberty under paragraph 17 of Schedule A1 MCA,[149] and therefore the Court had no power to make welfare orders under the Mental Capacity Act 2005, s.16A. Endorsing Baker J's decision in *A NHS Trust v Dr A*,[150] Hayden J therefore held that the inherent jurisdiction should be utilised to authorise the treatment in AA's best interest and granted the declaration sought.

i. Court orders pertaining to women suffering from mental illness, but not detained under the Mental Health Act

Three days after granting the declaration sought by Great Western Hospitals NHS Trust, Hayden J again authorised the performance of a caesarean on another woman suffering from mental health problems, *Royal Free NHS Foundation Trust v AB*.[151] This case concerned a woman described as suffering from 'a serious enduring psychotic mental illness … [but without an] extant diagnosis available to the court'. She does not appear to have been compulsorily detained under the Mental Health Act, although she had spent almost one month on a maternity ward following an attempt to commit suicide by an overdose of insulin. Her pregnancy was complicated by type 2 diabetes mellitus, and at the time of the hearing she had not eaten or drunk anything for 24 hours, with serious consequences for her blood sugar levels. Her treating obstetrician considered that a caesarean should be performed urgently, despite the fact that AB's pregnancy was only in its 32nd week, due to the need to effectively treat, assess and manage her

149 AA fell within case A of paragraph 2 Schedule 1A, MCA, being both subject to and detained under a hospital treatment regime.

150 *An NHS Trust v Dr A* (note 134).

151 Unreported, 31 January 2014.

psychotic illness which could only be achieved if she was no longer pregnant. AB had earlier agreed to the proposed caesarean delivery, but during the hearing it was reported that she had refused a caesarean. Unfortunately, the consultant psychiatrist who had assessed her capacity failed to consider her capacity to consent to a caesarean and therefore an additional assessment had to be conducted. All the professionals involved agreed that AB lacked the requisite capacity. Hayden J accepted that her best clinical interests required that a caesarean be performed, but he stressed that 'the assessment of best interests involves to some degree having an understanding of the individual'.[152] As noted above, the best interests assessment under the Mental Capacity Act incorporates a subjective element, necessitating consideration of the woman's wishes and feelings, the beliefs and values that would influence her decision if she had capacity and any other factors that would have been influential if she were able to consider them (s.4(6) MCA). He stressed that AB is an intelligent individual, able to understand and manage her diabetes when stable, and concluded that 'if she was rationally able to put herself in this position AB would want an elective caesarean section'. Thus again the expectation was voiced that the rational woman would follow medical advice and undergo a caesarean. Hayden noted that compelled obstetric intervention is extremely draconian in nature and found that there was insufficient evidence to support an order for the use of force, although he did grant a declaration that it would be lawful to sedate AB. He granted the declaration sought that AB lacked the capacity to consent to a caesarean, regulate her diabetes medication and monitor her food and water intake, finding that her best interests required that a caesarean be performed and that medication for her diabetes and artificial nutrition and hydration be administered to her.

During the course of April 2014 the Court of Protection considered two further proposed non-consensual caesareans to be performed on women with mental health problems. In the first, on an application by City Hospitals Sunderland NHS Foundation Trust, Hayden J again granted a declaration that a caesarean could be performed upon a woman suffering from mental illness, but not compulsorily detained under the Act. No transcript or judgment is available for this case, but press reports refer to the woman suffering from an undefined, intermittent mental health problem, similar to schizophrenia. She also had a liver condition that rendered a vaginal delivery dangerous for both her and the foetus.[153] It was reported to be unclear whether the woman was refusing to consent to a caesarean, but the intervention was supported by her father and Hayden J stated:

> There is compelling evidence that (the woman) at this point lacks capacity to evaluate the medical advice that she is being given … There is equally compelling evidence that (the woman) would, if well, put the needs of the baby

152 Personal communication, a note taken by one of the solicitors and approved by the judge.

153 *Daily Mail*, 29.04.2014, BBC News, available at www.bbc.co.uk/news/uk-england-tyne-27211135 (accessed 13 August 2015).

> even before her own and that she would therefore follow the course recommended.[154]

Given that no transcript or judgment is available for this case, care must be taken in drawing conclusions from the decision. However, it is clear that although the judge found the woman to currently lack capacity, he stressed that she was an intelligent woman with a successful career and that her capacity did fluctuate. Therefore it is regrettable that her views concerning a caesarean were not ascertained at a time when she was able to make the decision for herself, rather than a decision having to be taken on her behalf. It is unclear what factors were accorded priority in the assessment of her best interests, but once again reference was made to the needs of the 'baby', again illustrating the permeability of the boundary between the woman's best interests and those of the foetus in the assessment of a pregnant woman's best interests.

In *North Somerset Council v LW and others*[155] the issue of whether LW should be subjected to a caesarean, and indeed whether she had the capacity to consent, arose during proceedings under the inherent jurisdiction where the local authority sought an order not to disclose to LW the care plan to remove the baby at birth. LW suffers from hebephrenic schizophrenia, but was not detained under the Mental Health Act. The foetus was in the breech position and the healthcare professionals treating her believed that she would require either an elective cervical inversion (ECI) or a caesarean. During the subsequent Court of Protection hearing a significant amount of time was taken up with the attempt to obtain an assessment of LW's capacity to consent to medical intervention. Despite an adjournment, no such assessment was conducted before the recommencement of the hearing on 16 April, and at the hearing the consultant obstetrician gave evidence that she was unsure whether LW had capacity to consent to a caesarean, but nevertheless invited the court to authorise the interventions.[156] The hearing was again adjourned to await the outcome of the capacity assessment and, to the surprise of the professionals involved, LW was found to have the requisite capacity! She refused an ECI but consented to a caesarean section. Thus she was prepared to accept medical advice; given the surprising finding of capacity, however, questions must surely remain as to whether she would have been adjudged to have the capacity to make a decision not endorsed by the professionals – that is, to refuse both forms of intervention. The professionals involved appear to have been extremely disorganised in this case, a case dominated by the need to ensure the child's safety after birth. It is particularly worrying that the consultant obstetrician requested that the court make a declaration, without a finding of incapacity, suggesting that more needs to be done to educate healthcare professionals about the importance of facilitating decision-making by women with mental health problems, the

154 http://grayfords.co.uk/judge-permits-caesarean-section-pregnant-woman-mental-health-problems/ (accessed 13 August 2015).
155 [2014] EWCOP 3.
156 Ibid., [19].

importance of treating such women as having capacity, unless and until they are found to lack capacity, and also the need to respect the autonomy of women with capacity who suffer from mental illness.

j. Guidance pertaining to women who lack the capacity to make decisions about perinatal care due to a diagnosed psychiatric illness

The final case reported in this wave of cases concerning non-consensual obstetric intervention involving women who are mentally ill was *NHS Trust and others v FG*.[157] Like *LW*, this case was not primarily about court authorisation for obstetric intervention; rather, the issue of such authorisation arose during the hearing to consider the County Council's application for permission not to disclose the care plan (removal of the child at birth) to FG and for a reporting restrictions order. During the proceedings the Official Solicitor voiced concern that no order was being sought in relation to the treatment to be given to FG, despite the fact that FG was considered to lack capacity to make treatment decisions. Despite taking an initial position that Court of Protection proceedings in this matter were not necessary, the Trusts did seek permission for the restraint and such medical treatment (including induction of labour, instrumental or caesarean delivery) as might become necessary in the view of the attending clinicians. FG had expressed a clear wish for a vaginal delivery and the hope was that this would be possible; the order sought was therefore seen as being a permissive order that would authorise intervention should it become necessary.

FG had been detained under the Mental Health Act for three months and was suffering from a schizoaffective disorder with paranoid delusions. She regarded the healthcare professionals as a threat to both her and her foetus. A consultant psychiatrist gave evidence that the safe delivery of the baby would serve her best interests by avoiding her attributing any harm suffered to the healthcare professionals and thus underlining her persecutory beliefs and making them harder to treat. Moreover, he suggested that any harm to the foetus could result in her becoming depressed or feeling inadequate.[158] He also suggested that FG's best interests would not be served by being informed of the proceedings, saying that if FG thought the state was colluding with the healthcare professionals whom she already saw as a threat, that would have a negative impact upon her relationship with both the psychiatric and obstetric teams, and reduce the likelihood of her complying with the labour plan. Moreover, he also suggested that FG should not be told of the decision, or of the proceedings, even after delivery, arguing that such information should only be given to her in a controlled and therapeutic environment at some point in the future and not during a period of ill health, in order to maintain what trust she had in the health services.[159]

157 [2014] EWCOP 30.
158 Ibid., at [47].
159 Ibid., at [48].

Keehan J accepted the expert evidence offered that FG lacked capacity and regarding her best interests, and he granted the permissive orders sought, noting, however, that they should only be implemented in extreme circumstances and as a last resort. FG gave birth a week later without the need for intervention and cooperated fully with the obstetric team. At the invitation of the Official Solicitor, Keehan J provided guidance for the steps to be taken when a pregnant woman lacks the capacity to make decisions about her perinatal care due to a diagnosed psychiatric illness.[160] He took pains to emphasise that the presumption of capacity applies to those detained under the Mental Health Act and that in the majority of cases involving pregnant women with a diagnosed mental illness there would be no need for an application to the court.[161] The guidance is intended to fulfil two purposes, namely to limit the use of applications to the out-of-hours judge to the rare cases of genuine medical emergency and to prevent Trusts from inappropriately relying on s.5 MCA.[162]

Keehan J confirmed that obstetric care may be provided under s.63 MHA without the consent of the pregnant woman, using proportionate and necessary restraint only if the primary purpose is to alleviate or prevent a worsening in the psychiatric illness or its symptoms. That might be the case where delivery is effected to enable treatment of a severe mental illness,[163] but, as discussed above, in general a caesarean will not constitute treatment capable of being provided under s.63 MHA.[164] Instead, as his Lordship recognised, in the vast majority of cases involving pregnant women lacking capacity as a result of a diagnosed psychiatric illness, obstetric care will be provided under the auspices of the Mental Capacity Act.[165] Treatment may be given without court authorisation under s.5 MCA which permits a person (D) to treat someone whom they reasonably believe to lack capacity in accordance with what D reasonably believes to be in her best interests. Thus, where the doctor reasonably believes that the woman lacks capacity and that a caesarean would be in her best interests, she can perform the caesarean without fear of liability.

Although Keehan J recognised that s.5 MCA would facilitate the provision of treatment in the majority of cases, he did recognise that 'the potential use of restraint complicates matters',[166] which, it is suggested, rather understates its significance. Restraint used in the course of providing treatment under s.5 must be both necessary (s.6(2) MCA) and proportionate (s.6(3) MCA), but may not amount to a deprivation of liberty (s.4A(1) MCA). As Keehan J noted, upon consideration of Lady Hale's 'acid test', set out in *P v Cheshire West and others*,[167] it is apparent that restraint used in order to facilitate an obstetric intervention is

160 Ibid., at [81].
161 Ibid., at [82].
162 Ibid., at [83].
163 Ibid., at [84–6].
164 See above text accompanying note 22ff. and 138ff.
165 *NHS Trust and others v FG* (note 157), at [88].
166 Ibid., at [92].
167 [2014] UKSC 19, at [49].

likely to amount to a deprivation of liberty; the woman will be subject to continuous supervision and control because obstetric and midwifery staff will be present throughout the labour and delivery and will take decisions on her behalf as she lacks capacity to make her own decisions; she will also not be free to leave the delivery suite.[168]

Having stressed that Trusts must ensure that any deprivation of liberty is lawful,[169] Keehan J went on to set out four categories of cases in which Trusts should seek permissive orders relating to the woman's obstetric care:

- Category 1: Where 'the interventions proposed by the Trust(s) probably amount to serious medical treatment (SMT) within the meaning of COP Practice Direction 9E, irrespective of whether it is contemplated that the obstetric treatment would otherwise be provided under the MCA or MHA'.[170]

His lordship stressed that delivery of a baby *per se*[171] and an uncomplicated planned caesarean[172] will not amount to a SMT within the meaning of the Practice Direction. However, he suggested that a proposed caesarean might become a SMT and therefore should be the subject of an application to the court if either the woman's medical history is such that there is greater risk of complications (PD9E paras 3 and 4) or because the use of force will be necessary.[173]

Moreover, Keehan J recognised that the categorisation of a proposed intervention as a SMT would need to be assessed on an individual basis and emphasised that 'A decision to compel a mother, who would otherwise wish to have as natural a birth as possible, to undergo treatment which amounts to SMT is a very serious interference with her human rights as protected by the ECHR'.[174] That being the case, his lordship recognised that an application to the court should be made whenever it is proposed to perform a caesarean upon a woman who wanted a vaginal delivery, regardless of whether such an intervention could be justified by reference to the broad authority set out in s.5 MCA or be categorised as treatment for her mental disorder under s.63 MHA.

- Category 2: Where there is a real risk that more than transient forcible restraint will be required in order to perform the intervention, due to the

168 *NHS Trust and others v FG* (note 157), at [96].

169 The deprivation of liberty will be lawful if it is authorised in accordance with Schedule A1 MCA, is justified by the common law doctrine of necessity, or pursuant to s.4B (2)–(5) whereby it is necessary in order to provide life-sustaining treatment or prevent a serious deterioration in the woman's condition whilst a decision is being sought from the court; in all other cases authorisation by the court will be necessary.

170 *NHS Trust and others v FG* (note157), at [103].

171 Ibid., at [107].

172 Ibid., at [110].

173 Ibid., at [111].

174 Ibid., at [113].

grave interference with her rights under Articles 3, 5 and 8 ECHR that such restraint will constitute.[175]

- Category 3: Where a serious dispute about the obstetric care that would be in P's best interests exists, either between the healthcare professionals or between the professionals and P or her family.

In such cases Keehan J suggested that the court's determination of her best interests would provide the Trusts with 'unequivocal legal authority to carry out the procedure irrespective of the dispute ... [and] to provide reassurance to the clinicians and, in due course, P, that the course adopted was the most appropriate'.[176]

- Category 4: Where the deprivation of liberty would be unlawful absent authorisation by the court exercising its inherent jurisdiction.[177]

Although his lordship stated that in each of these four scenarios an application should be made to the court, he stressed that in cases falling outside the four categories Trusts could continue to make applications where necessary.[178] Keehan J's emphasis upon the need for Trusts to plan effectively and at an earlier stage in the pregnancy is to be welcomed; indeed, it is suggested that the guidance does not go far enough in requiring healthcare professionals to proactively plan together with the woman for the management of her labour and delivery at an early enough stage to maximise the possibility of her participation, considered further below. Thus, whilst the need to avoid urgent applications absent a genuine medical emergency underpins the guidance, it is suggested that the expectation should be that applications be made by the end of the second trimester, rather than no later than four weeks before the expected date of delivery as set out in the guidance.

k. The granting of a declaration in the case of a woman with learning difficulties

The situation in *The Mental Health Trust, The Acute Trust & The Council v DD & BC*[179] was rather different to the foregoing cases. DD was not detained under the Mental Health Act, but suffers from an autistic spectrum disorder and has a mild-to-borderline learning disability. Her complex obstetric history gave significant cause for concern and led to an application for a declaration that it would be in her best interests to remove her (forcibly if necessary) from her home, to take her to hospital and for a caesarean section to be performed against her wishes. This is clearly a very different scenario to those discussed above and it is hard to

175 Ibid., at [114–20].
176 Ibid., at [122].
177 Ibid., at [124–8].
178 Ibid., at [129].
179 [2014] EWCOP 11 (COP).

imagine a more invasive deprivation of liberty. Labour was not imminent and therefore Cobb J was able to give thorough consideration to the issues involved and a lengthy, comprehensive hearing took place, albeit without DD taking part in proceedings, with the decision being rendered six weeks after the application was made. He concluded that DD lacked the capacity to decide where and how her baby should be delivered and granted the declaration sought. Thus this decision is of a very different ilk to those that preceded it, with pre-emptive action being taken to forcibly take a woman to hospital and perform a caesarean against her wishes, with no immediate risk to either the woman or the foetus.

DD had an extremely complex obstetric history. This was her sixth pregnancy; three of her children had been delivered by caesarean and she had delivered two babies vaginally at home, without medical assistance. Her first child was delivered by emergency caesarean; thereafter on each occasion DD had denied being pregnant and actively tried to conceal her pregnancy from healthcare and social workers. Her second child was delivered by elective caesarean being in a breech position; the third child was born at home in secret, her partner (BC) having apparently assisted the delivery with the use of barbecue tongs. Following the birth of her third child, DD became mentally ill, suffering from a delusional disorder. During her fourth pregnancy DD was discovered fitting and unconscious due to an intracerebral embolism; an emergency caesarean was performed to enable her to be treated and because the foetus was in distress. As a consequence of the embolism, future pregnancies carry an increased risk of stroke and haemorrhage. Nevertheless, the following year DD again became pregnant and sought to conceal her pregnancy from healthcare and social workers. Her fifth child was born at home without medical assistance. Four of her existing children had been adopted; the other child was in care. Whilst the proceedings concerned the proposed caesarean, the council did indicate that it intended to seek an order under Part IV of the Children Act in respect of the baby following the birth. It is highly likely that such an order will be granted. Whilst the judge emphasised that he had 'no jurisdiction in relation to the unborn baby',[180] the granting of the declaration clearly makes it easier for the council to commence proceedings once the baby is born than would be the case if DD were to give birth at home or outside the local area.

The psychiatric evidence offered concluded that DD's autism constituted an impairment of the mind which resulted in her inability to make healthcare decisions, fulfilling the two limbs of s.2(1) MCA. However, unlike previous, more rushed decisions, Cobb J took significant pains to fully consider DD's capacity. He pointed out that she was able to understand and retain the relevant information relating to making a decision to litigate and relating to the mode of delivery, and that she was able to communicate her decision, but that there was considerable doubt as to whether she could weigh the information to make the relevant decisions.[181] Significantly, DD had been judged to have the capacity to litigate in the care and placement order proceedings, the most recent of which had taken place in 2012,

180 Ibid., at [161].
181 Ibid., at [61].

and she had previously been considered to have the requisite capacity to take healthcare decisions for herself.[182] Nevertheless, after an in-depth review of the issues, Cobb J found that DD lacked the capacity to litigate and to determine how she should give birth. He stressed that all practicable steps had been taken to enable DD to make her own decision, but without success, and that her decision-making was not merely unwise but failed to satisfy the functionality test, as she was unable to weigh the information relevant to the decisions.[183]

Having determined that DD lacked the ability to take the relevant decisions for herself, Cobb J considered her best interests. The applicants proposed that DD should be removed from her home (following forcible entry if necessary) and taken to hospital a few weeks before her due date. Once there, she should be given a preoperative assessment, steroids (required in order to prepare the foetal lungs due to the planned premature delivery) and an anaesthetic assessment. The next day a caesarean would be performed and DD would be kept in hospital for four days after the operation, prior to being allowed to go home again. Although DD had refused to engage with the proceedings, it was clear that this plan did not accord with DD's or her partner's wishes – they had clearly and consistently stated that they wanted a home birth with no involvement from health or social care professionals.

Cobb J conducted a risk–benefit analysis of all the delivery options[184] – spontaneous vaginal delivery at home or in hospital; induced vaginal delivery or a caesarean section, both of which would need to take place in hospital. A consultant obstetrician and gynaecologist advised that a spontaneous vaginal delivery in a consultant-led obstetric unit would best further DD's best interests and accord with her wishes. However, it was felt that she was unlikely to cooperate, comply or acquiesce to the degree necessary to make such a delivery possible. Whilst there were clear benefits to this mode of delivery, it not requiring a general anaesthetic and being associated with fewer complications, if an emergency caesarean were to become necessary, the risks to DD would be significantly higher than those associated with a planned caesarean. Given DD's complicated obstetric history, this was a real possibility. An induced VBAC (vaginal birth after caesarean) in hospital would increase the risk of scar rupture and it was felt that DD would resist monitoring which could necessitate the use of restraint or sedation. Significant risks would be associated with a spontaneous home birth and there was real concern that neither DD nor her partner BC would seek medical assistance were it to become necessary, posing a risk to DD's life. By contrast with previous cases, Cobb J did set out in some detail the risks associated with a caesarean section (including the short- and long-term impact upon her mental health in the light of her opposition to a caesarean section), but found that a planned caesarean section would be the safest mode of delivery. He stated: 'Planned intervention by a specialist and well-briefed team in fulfilment of a carefully crafted plan enables DD to

182 Ibid., at [66].
183 Ibid., at [85–6].
184 Ibid., at [97–120].

benefit from an optimal environment in which to deliver the baby with the least risk of harm to DD'.[185] However, this 'planned intervention' in an 'optimal environment' was precisely what DD had consistently rejected.

Significantly, the Official Solicitor was less willing to find that a caesarean best furthered the woman's best interests in this case; although he accepted that DD lacked capacity to make the decision regarding the mode of delivery, he did not make a recommendation about whether a vaginal delivery or caesarean would best serve her best interests, and opposed the proposed assessment of her capacity to make decisions about future contraception. Nevertheless, as in the other cases, nobody actually advocated that DD should be permitted to give birth at home, or even in hospital without additional intervention. Unlike many of the previous cases, the woman's wishes concerning the mode of delivery were well known and reported. DD was strongly opposed to a caesarean birth, wishing to give birth at home with her partner and without assistance from health or social care professionals. Whilst the individual's views are an important component in the assessment of her best interests, as Lady Hale recognised in *Aintree University Hospitals NHS Foundation Trust v James and others*:[186]

> The purpose of the best interests test is to consider matters from the patient's point of view. That is not to say that his wishes must prevail, any more than those of a fully capable patient must prevail. We cannot always have what we want.

As Mary Donnelly argues:

> At a practical level, the participation requirement should, at a minimum, necessitate the acknowledgement … that the person lacking capacity has an alternative preference. This in turn should lead to a rigorous scrutiny of the evidence presented in favour of the argument that the decision-maker should act against this preference. It cannot be enough for a decision-maker simply to acknowledge the views of the person lacking capacity before reaching a decision which takes no account of these views.[187]

Despite there being clear evidence of DD's wishes, Cobb J took the view that her best interests demanded that her wishes be overridden. At the start of his judgment detailing best interests, he noted: 'It must be in the best interests of any woman carrying a full-term child whom she wants to be born alive and healthy that such a result should if possible be achieved'.[188] Whilst he took significant care to examine the alternatives to a compelled caesarean, he took a very cautious, therapeutic outcome-orientated approach, prioritising risk management and the

185 Ibid., at [119].

186 Note 95, at 608–9, [45].

187 M. Donnelly, 'Best Interests, Patient Participation and the Mental Capacity Act 2005' (2009) 17 *Medical Law Review* 1, at 20.

188 *The Mental Health Trust, The Acute Trust & The Council v DD & BC* (note 179), at [97].

safe delivery of the baby over DD's wishes, as has occurred in each of the other cases discussed above.

This decision exhibits a level of intrusion not previously reported in the English case law and is clearly not compliant with the United Nations Convention on the Rights of Persons with Disabilities (CRPD), given that a decision was taken about treatment that should be performed on DD that was entirely contrary to her consistently expressed wishes. However, health and social care professionals made significant attempts to engage with DD and BC to no avail; the couple also refused to take part in the court proceedings. Therefore, although DD made her wishes concerning the delivery very clear, she consistently refused to engage with the authorities and it is difficult to see how an alternative decision could have been reached in the circumstances.

4. Interim conclusion

Whilst there is a clear dichotomy evident in the American jurisprudence between those states where the courts have recognised the state's interest in the foetus and sought to balance that interest against the woman's right and those that have recognised the woman's right to autonomy, the courts in England and Wales have consistently[189] confirmed that a woman with capacity may refuse any treatment, including that necessary to protect, or even preserve, a foetus.[190] Similarly, unlike the position under German law, a pregnant woman does not owe a duty to protect her foetus. Instead, the English case law has steadfastly maintained that the foetus has no legal rights capable of protection and purports to recognise a woman's autonomy, unrestricted by pregnancy. Nevertheless, in reality it is difficult to conceive of circumstances in which a woman's refusal of treatment necessary for the benefit of the foetus will be upheld. The Court of Appeal decisions in both *Re MB* and *St George's* recognised the woman's autonomy, albeit with some disapproval of the woman who exercises that autonomy in such a way as to endanger a foetus. However, both decisions were rendered after the caesareans had taken place, at a time when the life of a viable foetus was not at stake. The acid test will be when another pregnant woman not suffering from a panic attack induced by a phobia or post-traumatic stress disorder refuses to consent to a caesarean and by so doing puts the life of the foetus at risk. The courts in England and Wales retain a very broad discretion to classify any woman refusing to consent to follow medical advice as lacking the capacity to decide, thus preventing these women from being able to realise their autonomy. As Brenda Hale recognised, 'One has to question whether the concept of capacity is yet strong enough to bear the weight which the law lays upon it'.[191]

189 With the exception of *Re S* (note 11).

190 *Re MB* (note 46), *per* Butler-Sloss LJ, at 436–7; *St George's Healthcare NHS Trust* v *S; R* v *Collins and others, ex parte S* (note 67), *per* Judge LJ, at 50.

191 B. Hale, 'A Pretty Pass: When Is There a Right to Die?' (2003) 32 *Common Law World Review* 1.

In *CC v KK & ST*[192] (a case that concerned the living arrangements of an elderly woman) Baker J recognised the risk of paternalistic capacity assessments being made, stating:

> In cases of vulnerable adults, there is a risk that all professionals involved with treating and helping that person – including, of course, a judge in the Court of Protection – may feel drawn towards an outcome that is more protective of the adult and thus, in certain circumstances, fail to carry out an assessment of capacity that is detached and objective.[193]

It is suggested that this risk is equally present in the case of a pregnant woman refusing obstetric treatment required for the benefit of the foetus, a situation where the professionals involved, including the judge in the Court of Protection, may adopt a very paternalistic view of the woman's capacity and best interests, at least indirectly seeking to protect the foetus from avoidable harm.

It is suggested that the concept of capacity is inherently malleable, that it is too easy to find that a woman lacks the requisite capacity to decide for herself how her child should be delivered and what level of intervention she is willing to undergo for the benefit of the foetus. In each of the English cases discussed above where capacity was considered, the women were found to lack the requisite capacity, with the one exception of LW who consented to a caesarean, the course of action endorsed by the professionals.[194] It will be remembered that in *Norfolk and Norwich v W* and *Rochdale Healthcare NHS Trust v C* Johnson J suggested that any woman in labour would lack the capacity to determine whether or not to consent to a caesarean whilst in the throes of labour, with all that involves in terms of stress and pain.[195] Thus Johnson J appeared to suggest that any woman could be considered to lack capacity whilst in labour. Following the enactment of the Mental Capacity Act it is clear that the diagnostic limb of the capacity assessment must also be satisfied; it will not suffice to find that the woman is unable to comply with the functional aspect of capacity, and thus it is suggested that he could not now find C to lack capacity in the circumstances of the case. However, the concern remains that it is simply too easy to find that a woman lacks capacity. As Jane Bryan argues:

> It becomes a game: medicine gives judges the means, the evidence of incompetency, by which they can achieve their objective, the protection of the foetus, whilst maintaining the law's position of neutrality and whilst refusing to acknowledge that the woman's right to self-determination has been ignored.[196]

192 [2012] EWCOP 2136.

193 Ibid., at [25].

194 *North Somerset Council v LW and others* (note 155).

195 *Norfolk and Norwich v W* (note 34), at 616; *Rochdale Healthcare NHS Trust v C* (note 42), at 275.

196 J. Bryan, 'Reading Beyond the Ratio: Searching for the Subtext in the "Enforced Caesarean" Cases' in D. Carpi (ed.) *Bioethics and Biolaw through Literature*, Berlin: Walter de Gruyter, 2011, 115 ff, at 120–1.

The advantage of the reliance upon capacity is that it allows the legal principle to be maintained that the foetus has no interests prior to birth capable of protection by the court in considering whether to authorise obstetric intervention,[197] but simultaneously permits protection to be afforded to the foetus without the need to engage with the question of foetal rights. Thus the use of capacity facilitates and maintains the pretence that pregnant women are not being treated differently from other patients, be they male or female. As Kristin Savell argues, it '[subverts] the personhood of the woman to benefit the foetus, while maintaining the commitment to unitary personhood',[198] producing what Jane Bryan describes as 'A win-win situation: the law maintains its apparent respect for the woman's autonomy and the foetus is saved'.[199]

Following the enactment of the Mental Capacity Act, it is suggested that the legal landscape of court-authorised obstetric intervention has changed little; rather, the battle lines have been redrawn to focus upon women who are mentally ill. Nevertheless, it remains likely that women not suffering from a psychiatric disorder are also being found to lack capacity and thereafter being treated in accordance with their best interests, with doctors being protected from liability by virtue of s.5 MCA, provided that they have formed a reasonable belief that the woman lacks capacity and believe that the intervention is in her best interests. Thus it is suggested that capacity continues to operate as a device, opening the way to an assessment of best interests that will enable others to determine what should be done in the name of those interests and subjecting vulnerable women to caesareans against their wishes.

Writing prior to the enactment of the Mental Capacity Act, Thorpe LJ stated:

> It is unnecessary to dwell on best interests in the context of cases involving Caesarean section. Obviously if the patient lacks capacity, the obstetrician proceeds towards the goal of successful delivery in the exercise of his clinical judgment. However, if the consultant is faced with a clinical choice between two possible procedures, in making that choice he should have regard to the circumstances and the patient's stated or presumed preference.[200]

He regarded it as self-evident that the successful delivery would be the determining factor in the woman's best interests, with the woman's wishes being accorded little weight. Whilst the Act adopts a participative approach, the cases demonstrate that the central focus of the best interests determination continues to be the woman's physical health and the welfare of the foetus, often cloaked in references to the

197 *Re MB* (note 46), *per* Butler-Sloss LJ, at 444.

198 K. Savell, 'The Mother of the Legal Person' in S. James and S. Palmer (eds) *Visible Women: Essays on Feminist Legal Theory and Political Philosophy*, Oxford: Hart, 29 ff, at 51.

199 J. Bryan (note 196), at 120–1.

200 M. A. Thorpe, 'Consent for Caesarean Section: Part 2 – Autonomy, Capacity, Best Interests, Reasonable Force and Procedural Guidelines' (1999) 5 *Clinical Risk* 209, at 210.

impact that harm suffered by the foetus/baby would have upon her mental health. In cases unconnected to obstetric intervention, the courts have demonstrated the relatively limited importance of an individual's wishes where that individual's life is at stake, adopting the maxim *in dubio pro vita* and prioritising the safeguarding of life, even when contrary to the patient's wishes, as being required by her best interests.[201] In cases of refusal of obstetric intervention the life of the foetus may be at stake. However, in the latest tranche of cases there has generally not been a threat to the life of the woman, or even an immediate risk to the life of the child, but rather there has been a perceived need to ensure that the child is born in supervised, controlled circumstances in order to ensure the safe delivery of the baby, optimum care for the woman and the availability of protection for the child from birth.

Therefore, the cases concerning obstetric intervention demonstrate the immense flexibility of the best interests standard, allowing the indirect protection of the foetus. By contrast, little weight has been attached to the impact that non-consensual caesareans are likely to have upon the woman following the intervention. A number of cases note the gratitude of the women who have been subjected to such an intervention. Thus, for example, Kirkwood J noted L's apologies for the trouble she had caused (by refusing to consent to a caesarean due to a needle phobia);[202] similarly, Hayden J noted that AB hugged the obstetrician who performed the caesarean.[203] However, not all women subjected to a caesarean without their consent will react so positively. In *Rochdale Healthcare (NHS) Trust v C* Johnson J concluded his judgment by reporting that C had in fact changed her mind whilst the application was being heard, and that she had consented to a caesarean.[204] In the circumstances, it seems unlikely that this could be categorised as anything more than acquiescence, and following the delivery C was granted legal aid to challenge the decision.[205] She was certainly not grateful that she had been compelled to have a caesarean. Quite apart from the obvious physical impact that a caesarean delivery will have upon the woman, it may have far-reaching effects upon the woman's mental health, effects that should form a part of the best interests assessment. For example, in *Bolton Hospitals NHS Trust v O*[206] it was recognised that a compelled caesarean might lead to postnatal depression; in the case of DD[207] it was clear that any remaining trust between DD and her health and social care professionals would be severely impacted, if not eradicated, as a result of her forcible removal from her home, detention and the performance of a caesarean against her wishes. It is suggested that the determination of a woman's best interests must take much greater account of such factors, factors that may

201 See, for example, *Re E (Medical treatment: Anorexia)* [2012] EWCOP 1639 and *W v M & Ors* [2011] EWHC 2443 (Fam), [2011] Fam Law 1330.
202 *Re L* (note 47).
203 *Royal Free NHS Foundation Trust v AB* (note 151).
204 *Rochdale Healthcare (NHS) Trust v C* (note 42).
205 C. Dyer, 'Mother vs Big Brother' *Guardian*, 19.12.1996, T4.
206 *Bolton Hospitals NHS Trust v O* (note 77).
207 *The Mental Health Trust, The Acute Trust & The Council v DD & BC* (note 179).

have a substantial, ongoing impact upon the woman's mental and physical health for a long period of time after the intervention has taken place. The safe delivery of a baby will not be the end of the matter for the women concerned; the severity of the intervention requires a much more thorough assessment of the risks it poses to the woman and that those risks be fully considered in the assessment of her best interests.

Although the English case law repeatedly emphasises the woman's rights and best interests as the courts' sole concern, the fact remains that if the woman is found to lack capacity, there is unlikely to be anyone who will champion her right to refuse a caesarean. The Official Solicitor's role is not to act as her advocate, demanding that her voice be heard, but rather to represent her best interests. As these cases demonstrate, the Official Solicitor has consistently argued that the women lacked capacity to make the decision for themselves, and has argued in favour of a caesarean as best fitting her best interests even where less restrictive options appear to have been available, with the sole exception of DD where he failed to take a view on which mode of delivery would best serve her best interests.[208] Moreover, despite the participative approach adopted by the Mental Capacity Act, the courts and doctors concerned have consistently diminished the value of the woman's known wishes, demonstrating the low level of importance generally attributed to the subjective elements of the best interests determination. Whilst the courts in the latest tranche of cases often made little attempt to discover the woman's wishes with regard to delivery, in some cases there was some consideration of what the woman would have wanted, had she been in a position to decide for herself.[209] In each instance Hayden J suggested that the woman would have followed medical advice, should she have been in a position to give a valid consent. Such references can be seen as promoting compliance with the socially constructed view of motherhood which requires women to act altruistically, doing whatever is necessary for the foetus. There is an expectation that pregnant women will act altruistically, setting aside their own wishes and values for the sake of the foetus. In the case of a woman with capacity, she may refuse to accede to such expectations, but in the case of a woman lacking capacity, compulsion may be used to ensure that she complies with this expectation by focusing upon the need to deliver the foetus safely in determining her best interests.

As the cases discussed above illustrate, the English courts, like their US counterparts, are very unwilling to reject medical evidence; although in the case of *Rochdale Healthcare (NHS) Trust v C*[210] Johnson J did not accept the obstetrician's assessment of C's competence, he did accept the necessity of the caesarean being performed. It is submitted that the finding of incapacity is merely a means to an

208 Ibid., at [14].

209 See, for example, comments made by Hayden J in *Great Western NHS Foundation Trust v AA, BB, CC & DD* (note 145), at [16]; in *Royal Free NHS Foundation Trust v AB* (note 151); and in the unreported decision made on the application by City Hospitals Sunderland NHS Foundation Trust (note 154).

210 *Rochdale Healthcare (NHS) Trust v C* (note 42).

end – that is, the safe delivery of the foetus by caesarean section. The predominantly unquestioning acceptance of medical opinion, both in relation to the assessment of capacity and the best course of action, does little to reassure women that their wishes will be respected. Indeed, a woman's capacity will in practice only be at issue where she disagrees with medical advice,[211] so it may be suggested that a finding of incapacity is at least partly the result of disagreements about medical treatment between the pregnant woman and her doctors. The particularly risk-averse conceptualisation of best interests, with the emphasis upon the importance of ensuring the safe delivery of the baby in the assessment of the best interests of the pregnant woman, means that it is almost unthinkable that obstetric intervention will not be authorised when the woman is deemed to lack the capacity to decide for herself and her clinicians are advocating intervention; the protection of the woman (and thereby the protection of the foetus) are prioritised over her autonomy.

The latest tranche of cases illustrate that more needs to be done to enable women to take decisions for themselves. The much vaunted finding that the foetus has no rights capable of protection prior to birth and that the focus of the decision is upon the woman herself is insufficient. Representation by the Official Solicitor is not enough. The woman needs an opportunity to be heard, to make her own decision. She needs to be *enabled* to make her own decision, to be *supported* in making her own decision – for example, by means of a birth plan. The latest cases clearly demonstrate that there is the potential for problems to arise where the woman suffers from a mental health disorder and there is a risk that she will lack capacity to make decisions for herself in the later stages of pregnancy. These problems reflect the difficulty in achieving an appropriate balance between treating the woman's disorder and protecting the embryo and foetus from harm, given that no psychotropic drugs are licensed for use during pregnancy. The drugs used to treat serious mental health disorders such as schizophrenia and bipolar affective disorder can be teratogenic; however, discontinuation of medication can lead to relapse. Thus the National Institute for Health and Care advises that the potential teratogenic and neurodevelopmental risks to the foetus need to be balanced carefully against the risks of not treating the mental health problems and the likely benefits of treatment.[212] Such a balance needs to be sought on an individual basis and will often be extremely difficult to achieve, resulting in higher relapse rates than usual and increasing the likelihood that the affected women will be considered no longer to have the capacity to make decisions for themselves. The cases suggest that more thought needs to be given to how such cases can best be managed, in

211 In *St George's Healthcare NHS Trust* v*S; R* v*Collins and others, ex parte S* (note 67), Collins (the social worker) informed MS that if she would agree to be induced she would not be detained under the Mental Health Act.

212 National Institute for Health and Clinical Excellence, *Clinical Guideline 45: Antenatal and Postnatal Mental Health: Clinical Management and Service Guidance*, 2007, at 15–16; National Institute for Health and Clinical Excellence, *National Clinical Guideline 192: Antenatal and postnatal Mental Health: Clinical Management and Service Guidance*, 2014, at 32–3.

such a way as to facilitate the woman's ability to make decisions. The most obvious way to do this is through an advance directive – a birth plan. However, in England and Wales advance decisions may only refuse specific treatments; they do not bind healthcare professionals in a positive sense by providing consent to a particular procedure.[213] Thus, although a birth plan might say that the woman wishes a caesarean to be performed, or that she wishes to be induced in specified circumstances, if she lacks the capacity to give contemporaneous consent, the advance decision has no legal standing; it deserves consideration, but has no binding effect, falling merely to be considered as an expression of her past wishes under the assessment of her best interests. Nevertheless, it is suggested that positive steps should be taken to facilitate anticipatory decision-making in all women who have a serious psychiatric disorder, or who have a history of severe mental illness. As Andrew Kent argues, such women 'are likely to benefit from specialist mental health review and care planning early on in the course of pregnancy'.[214] Care planning should lead to the agreement of a perinatal mental health plan between the woman and the various healthcare professionals treating her, bringing together care planning in relation to both the woman's mental health and her obstetric needs. This plan should include her treatment preferences and should be formulated at a time when the woman has the capacity to take decisions for herself. Thereafter, should a conflict arise between that which was agreed in the care plan and the views of those treating the woman who no longer has capacity, her treatment preferences should be accorded great weight in the determination of her best interests, with any proposal that they be disregarded being subjected to rigorous scrutiny.

As the case law demonstrates, whilst maintaining the right of a woman with capacity to refuse medical treatment, including that necessary to safeguard the foetus, the courts in England and Wales have demonstrated a considerable willingness to prioritise the protection of foetal welfare over a woman's autonomy. It is likely that the degree of capacity required to refuse treatment deemed necessary for the foetus will be so high as to be unattainable; as the cases demonstrate, once the woman is found to lack capacity her best interests have invariably been dominated by the need to ensure the safe delivery of the foetus. Thus, it is argued that what is really maintained is medical freedom with the appearance of legal control; the determination of both capacity and best interests are dominated by medical evidence which is not subjected to rigorous external audit – indeed, it is suggested that the court's treatment of medical evidence goes beyond what might be termed professional courtesy, exhibiting undue deference. As Margaret Brazier wrote in 1997, by focusing upon capacity,

213 S.24 MCA, *R (Burke) v General Medical Council* [2005] EWCA 1003. Cf. § 1901a I BGB which provides for anticipatory consent or refusal of consent to medical treatments, clinical investigations or medical interventions.

214 A. Kent, 'Psychiatric Disorders in Pregnancy' (2011) 21(11) *Obstetrics, Gynaecology and Reproductive Medicine* 317, at 317.

> The way is left open to establish in a great many cases where women and doctors disagree about childbirth that the woman was incompetent so that what others consider her interests and her child's interests require can lawfully be done.[215]

It is suggested that almost 20 years later this assessment remains true. The advent of the Mental Capacity Act has changed the language used, but has not changed the way in which decisions are taken to compel obstetric intervention for the benefit of the foetus.

215 M. Brazier, 'Hard Cases Make Bad Law?' (1997) 23 *Journal of Medical Ethics* 341, at 343.

III. The imposition of a duty to protect the foetus upon a pregnant woman and her doctor in Germany

1. Introduction: the very different context of the German debate

As the foregoing chapters make clear, a significant number of the American courts have demonstrated a considerable willingness to adopt a broad-based interpretation of the state's interest in potential life, mandating obstetric intervention to benefit the foetus in a number of cases.[1] By contrast, the English courts have recognised that a woman's autonomy is not diminished by pregnancy and that the foetus has no rights capable of protection in this scenario. Nevertheless, they have consistently found women to lack the necessary capacity to give a valid refusal of consent to a caesarean viewed as necessary for the protection of the foetus. Thereafter the courts have adopted an expansive interpretation of the woman's best interests to encompass the course of action judged by doctors to offer the best outcome for both the foetus and the woman, masking foetal protection with findings of incapacity. Thus the law's response in the USA has focused upon controlling women in the name of protecting the state's interest in potential life; in England and Wales the focus has been upon ensuring compliance with medical advice, where necessary by finding the woman refusing treatment to lack capacity and then assessing her best interests in the light of that medical advice, ensuring that the foetus is protected, without recognising any foetal interest capable of protection *per se*.

By contrast, there are no reported cases of German courts ordering obstetric intervention against the wishes of a pregnant woman. Nevertheless, the German law pertaining to this topic is of particular interest for a number of reasons. First, unlike the American and English courts, the *Bundesverfassungsgericht* (the German constitutional court) has held that the constitutional guarantee of human dignity, and the right to life, apply to the foetus in and of itself,[2] describing pregnancy as involving a *Zweiheit in Einheit* (duality in unity), rather than merely a pregnant

1 But cf. *In re Brown* 689 N.E.2d 397 (1997) and *In re Baby Boy Doe, a Fetus v Mother Doe* 632 N.E. 2d 326 (1994), discussed above, B I.

2 Abortion I: *BVerfGE* 39, 1, at 1, headnote 1; Abortion II: *BVerfGE* 88, 203, at 252. Cf. *Roe v Wade* 410 US 113 (1973), *per* Blackmum J at 158; *Paton v British Pregnancy Advisory Service Trustees* [1979] QB 276, *per* George Baker P, at 279.

woman.[3] Second, the German crime of *Schwangerschaftsabbruch* (termination of pregnancy) is much more broadly conceived than its Anglo-American counterparts, encompassing not only the typical medical or surgical abortions, but also any act, or even in some cases an omission, intentionally causing the death of a foetus. This will include the situation where treatment necessary to maintain the pregnancy, or save the life of the foetus, is withheld, contrary to a duty to act. As will be considered below, in contrast to Anglo-American law, German law recognises a much greater duty to rescue, so that where a foetus dies for want of an indicated caesarean, for example, both the doctor and the woman may incur liability for homicide or termination of pregnancy by omission. Nevertheless, there is no suggestion that the law could be used to compel 'good motherhood' or appropriate antenatal behaviour as in the United States. Instead, should the woman fail to comply with the duty to actively protect the foetus, and the foetus dies as a result, she may be guilty of a crime, subject to imprisonment or a fine; she will not, however, be subject to forcible anaesthesia and surgery.

In its abortion decisions the *Bundesverfassungsgericht* recognised that the pregnant woman's rights to life and bodily integrity, to personality and her dignity are engaged, but found that her rights must be curtailed to the extent necessary to protect the foetus, unless her choice to terminate the pregnancy (or, in the case of an omission, her decision to allow the foetus to die) can be justified. As the *Bundesverfassungsgericht* stressed, in all but the most serious situations a woman's failure to continue the pregnancy will not be capable of justification and therefore will be unlawful.[4] Thus the court stressed that a pregnant woman owes a duty to her foetus, a duty to continue the pregnancy to full term.[5] This duty is, however, not limited to simply refraining from having an abortion; rather, it requires the pregnant woman to take positive action to avert dangers to the life of the foetus. Whilst the typical form of abortion involves an intervention to terminate a pregnancy, the subject of this book involves the termination of pregnancy through the failure to intervene to maintain the pregnancy or save the life of the foetus.

In Germany both the foetus's and the woman's interests are protected by the constitution. At least on the face of it, it would appear that the foetus is given significantly more protection by German law than its counterpart in England and Wales or the United States of America, and that the woman's autonomy will be of limited relevance in the face of a threat to the life of the foetus. That being the case, it is important to consider why there are no reported cases of court-ordered obstetric intervention in Germany. Despite giving the appearance of valuing foetal life, it will be argued that the protection afforded is really rather limited due to the concurrent protection of the woman's rights and the minimum standard applied to the state's duty to protect prenatal life, at least in the traditional abortion context. Thus the recognition that foetal life is protected by both the guarantee of

3 *BVerfGE* 88, 203, at 253; cf. *BVerfGE* 39, 1 at 42, stressing the separateness of the foetus and the pregnant woman.

4 *BVerfGE* 39, 1, at 48ff.; 88, 203, at 255ff.

5 *BVerfGE* 39, 1, at 44; 88, 203, at 253.

human dignity (Art. 1 I GG) and the right to life (Art. 2 II GG) is intended to give the appearance of a duty to protect prenatal life, rather than to ensure the realisation of comprehensive protection. Nevertheless, the German approach is particularly instructive in the manner in which it seeks to reconcile the woman's fundamental rights and those of the foetus, adopting a facilitative rather than adversarial approach to managing these problematic cases of women refusing treatment necessary to secure the welfare, or life, of the foetus.

This chapter will outline the constitutional background that impacts upon this topic, considering the protection of human dignity, the right to life and the right to self-determination, and how these rights can be reconciled in cases where the woman refuses obstetric intervention beneficial to the foetus. It will then move on to consider the circumstances in which both a doctor and a woman may be held to be under a duty to protect the life of the foetus and analyse the extent of those duties, considering whether the refusal of consent to obstetric intervention deemed necessary for the survival of the foetus may constitute a termination of pregnancy, or even homicide, by omission, rendering both the pregnant woman and her doctor criminally liable.

2. The constitutional guarantees of life, human dignity, bodily integrity and self-determination

a. Introduction

The principal fundamental rights engaged by compelled obstetric intervention are the liberty rights enshrined in Art. 2 GG – the rights to life, bodily integrity and free development of personality. Additionally, the *Bundesverfassungsgericht* has stressed that the guaranteed protection of human dignity (Art. 1 I GG), the primary value of the constitution, is applicable to both pre- and postnatal life, ascribing it a key role in resolving the conflicting interests of the pregnant woman and the foetus.[6] Whilst a detailed examination of these constitutional guarantees falls outside the scope of this book, the following is intended to provide an overview of the relevant constitutional backdrop to compelled obstetric intervention and the way in which the conflicting fundamental rights may be reconciled.[7] Central to this analysis are the two *Bundesverfassungsgericht* abortion decisions, 1975 and 1993,[8] where the *Bundesverfassungsgericht* addressed the conflict between the constitutionally protected interests of the foetus and the pregnant woman, examining the extent to which protection of foetal life should prevail over the woman's fundamental rights. In both cases the court struck down legislation regulating abortion

6 *BVerfGE* 39, 1, at 43; *BVerfGE* 88, 203, at 251ff.

7 A comprehensive consideration of the applicable constitutional law and the literature pertaining to it can be found in R. Müller-Terpitz, *Der Schutz des pränatalen Lebens: eine verfassungs-, völker- und gemeinschaftsrechtliche Statusbetrachtung an der Schwelle zum biomedizinischen Zeitalter*, Tübingen: Mohr Siebeck, 2007; and A. B. Dolderer, *Menschenwürde und Spätabbruch*, Berlin: Springer, 2012, chapter 4.

8 Abortion I: *BVerfGE* 39, 1; Abortion II: *BVerfGE* 88, 203.

on the basis that it did not sufficiently satisfy the state's duty to protect the life of the foetus.

b. The **Bundesverfassungsgericht's** *abortion decisions*

This section analyses some of the key features of the *Bundesverfassungsgericht's* abortion jurisprudence. The court's decisions were and remain extremely controversial, not least due to the internal inconsistencies within the decisions. The *Bundesverfassungsgericht's* abortion decisions were given shortly after the US Supreme Court had considered the question of abortion in *Roe v Wade* (1973)[9] and *Planned Parenthood v Casey* (1992).[10] It is worth noting from the outset that there is a clear difference between the German and the American abortion jurisprudence:[11] the *Bundesverfassungsgericht* focused upon the state's positive duty to take affirmative action to protect and promote foetal life throughout pregnancy, whilst the US Supreme Court set out the state's duty in negative terms, namely that the state is not under an obligation to intervene to protect foetal life (the foetus not being a person within the meaning of the constitution),[12] and that it may only intervene to protect its interest in prenatal life if in doing so it does not impose an undue burden upon the woman's right to elect a pre-viability abortion.[13] As will be apparent from the discussion below, this divergence is indicative of the very different constitutional philosophies followed by the two jurisdictions.

The *Grundgesetz* (the German constitution, the Basic Law), as interpreted by the *Bundesverfasungsgericht*, promotes communitarianism, recognising not only freedoms from state interference in the enumerated rights (the subjective rights

9 *Roe v Wade* (note 2).

10 *Planned Parenthood of Southeastern Pennsylvania v Casey* cf. 505 US 833 (1992).

11 In England and Wales there is no recognition of a foetal right to life or a woman's right to choose an abortion; instead, the Abortion Act 1967 classifies abortion as a medical matter, with doctors performing a gate-keeping function in determining access to abortion in accordance with the social, medical and embryopathic indications (s.1 (1)). The courts have refused to supervise the operation of the Act, holding that 'The great social responsibility is firmly placed by the law upon the shoulders of the medical profession', *Paton v British Pregnancy Advisory Service Trustees* (note 2), *per* George Baker P at 281; *R* v. *Smith (John)* [1973] 1 W.L.R. 1510, *per* Scarman LJ at 1512. S.1(2) Human Rights Act 1998 gives effect to the convention rights; however, the European Court of Human Rights has yet to determine when, if ever, the right to life (Art. 2 ECHR) might apply to the foetus, but it has made it clear that a broad margin of appreciation applies (see, for example, *Vo v France* (2005) 40 E.H.R.R. 12; *Evans v United Kingdom* (2008) 46 E.H.R.R. 34; *A, B, and C v Ireland* (2011) 53 E.H.R.R. 13). Similarly, although abortion clearly engages Art. 8 ECHR (the right to respect for private life), the European Court of Human Rights has not held that the right encompasses a right to elect an abortion: *Tysiac v Poland* (2007) 45 E.H.R.R. 42, para 107; *Brüggermann and Scheuten v Germany* (1977) 3 E.H.R.R. 244; *A, B, C v Ireland* (2011).

12 *Roe v Wade* (note 2), at 157.

13 *Planned Parenthood v Casey* (note 10).

that can be asserted by the individual against the state) but also more broadly based public values and obligations. The resulting objective normative framework can be considered to express the core values and commitments of the state and stands in stark contrast to the individualistic conceptualisation of rights adopted by the US Supreme Court. Whilst *Grundrechte* (the fundamental rights set out in Art. 2–19 GG) are generally regarded as defensive rights, held by individuals to protect themselves against state interference, with regard to a foetus it is not the state that poses a threat to its continued existence. Therefore, in its first abortion decision the *Bundesverfassungsgericht* emphasised the duty to protect life as part of the objective values of the state, saying that the fundamental rights embody the objective values binding upon all areas of law.[14] It stressed that the constitution does not merely protect individual rights against the state, but that it also imposes a protective function upon the state, requiring it to take positive action to protect and realise the underlying objective values.[15] The court held:

> The state's duty to protect is comprehensive. Self-evidently it does not only prohibit direct state interference in the developing life, but also requires the state to take a stance protecting and promoting this life, ... above all, to protect it from unlawful interference from others.[16]

Thus the state is required to take affirmative action to protect foetal life, including from threats posed by the pregnant woman.

In Abortion I the *Bundesverfassungsgericht* expressly left the question open as to whether the foetus is a rights-holder in and of itself, holding that the objective normative framework of the constitution requires the protection of foetal life.[17] The court stressed that the protection of human life would be incomplete if Art. 2 II GG did not also encompass prenatal life.[18] Recognising the uniqueness of the relationship between the pregnant woman and the foetus, the court emphasised that the foetus is not merely a part of the woman, but that it is an individual and protected in its own right, even against the pregnant woman.[19] At the same time it acknowledged that pregnancy impacts upon the woman's private sphere, protected by Art. 2 I GG and Art. 1 I GG.[20] The court recognised that the woman's right to freedom of action, including the freedom to choose whether or not to

14 *BVerfGE* 39, 1, at 41.
15 For an excellent analysis of the protective function in this and other contexts, see V. MacDonnell and J. Hughes, 'The German Abortion Decisions and the Protective Function in German and Canadian Constitutional Law' (2013) 50(4) *Osgoode Hall Law Journal* 999; and V. MacDonnell, 'The Protective Function and Section 7 of the Canadian Charter of Rights and Freedoms' (2012) 17(1) *Review of Constitutional Studies* 53.
16 *BVerfGE* 39, 1, at 42.
17 *BVerfGE* 39, 1, at 41.
18 *BVerfGE* 39, 1, at 37.
19 *BVerfGE* 39, 1, at 42.
20 *BVerfGE* 39, 1, at 42.

continue the pregnancy (based on Art. 2 I GG), must be acknowledged and protected, but that this freedom was not absolute.[21]

The protection of human dignity (Art. 1 I GG) played only a supporting role in the first abortion decision; the court held that the duty to protect foetal life was grounded directly in Art. 2 II s.1 GG, but that it also results from the express provision of Art. 1 I s.2 GG that the state is under a duty to respect and protect human dignity

> because the developing life participates in the protection of human dignity afforded by Art. 1 I GG. Where human life exists, human dignity is present; whether the bearer is aware of this dignity and knows how to preserve it himself is not decisive. The potential capabilities present from the beginning of human existence suffice to establish human dignity.[22]

The court did not articulate the relationship between these two sources of protection, saying: 'Human life is, as need not be further explained, an ultimate value within the constitutional order, it is the living foundation of human dignity and the prerequisite of all other fundamental rights'.[23] However, it attributed a pivotal role to the protection of human dignity in the weighing of the 'maternal' and foetal interests. Concluding that a balance between the protection of foetal life and the pregnant woman's freedom to have an abortion could not be achieved, because abortion always entails the destruction of foetal life, it found that the weighing of the competing constitutional interests must take account of their relationship with the protection of human dignity (Art. 1 I GG) and that this would necessarily mean that the foetal right to life had to be prioritised over the woman's right to self-determination.[24]

Moreover, it held that foetal life must take priority throughout the pregnancy, from implantation onwards,[25] and that only in cases where it would not be reasonable to expect the woman to continue the pregnancy (in the case of a risk to the woman's life or health, for example) could the duty to do so be not imposed and thus a termination of pregnancy be justified.[26] In a particularly paternalistic recognition of the impact pregnancy may have upon a woman's life both during and after the pregnancy, the *Bundesverfassungsgericht* recognised that the burdens imposed upon women by pregnancy may not always be offset by the 'new fulfilment in her role as mother' that it considered a woman will experience following the birth of her child. Therefore it indicated that an unreasonable expectation might be found in other, less extreme, situations, where the continuation of the pregnancy would require the woman to sacrifice her own values, although it

21 *BVerfGE* 39, 1, at 43.
22 *BVerfGE* 39, 1, at 41.
23 *BVerfGE* 39, 1, at 42.
24 *BVerfGE* 39, 1, at 43.
25 *BVerfGE* 39, 1, at 43.
26 *BVerfGE* 39, 1, at 48.

stressed that this would not be the case in relation to the burdens normally associated with pregnancy.[27]

In Abortion II the *Bundesverfassungsgericht* categorised the relationship between the pregnant woman (referred to as the mother) as one of *Zweiheit in Einheit* (duality in unity), and found that the state's duty to protect the foetus from the pregnant woman required the fundamental prohibition of abortion and the imposition of a duty to continue the pregnancy to full term.[28] It accepted that the duty to protect life is not absolute (Art. 2 II s.3 GG), but found that the scope of protection required consideration of the conflicting interests, both in terms of their significance and their need for protection.[29] Thus it ranged the protection of foetal life against the woman's claims to protection and respect for her human dignity (Art. 1 I GG), her right to life and bodily integrity (Art. 2 II GG) and her right to personality (*Persönlichkeitsrecht*, Art. 2 I GG).[30] It stressed that the degree of protection is unrelated to gestational development, and thus that termination of pregnancy must be regarded as unlawful throughout pregnancy.[31] This meant that abortion must be forbidden even during the early stages of pregnancy; the state could not abdicate responsibility for protecting the foetus by arguing that the woman had the right to make a decision about whether to continue the pregnancy, based upon her human dignity.[32]

In the second abortion decision the rather more enlightened court avoided references to the natural role of women and the fulfilment associated with being a mother, but whilst the court accepted that the woman's fundamental rights must be protected, it found that they did not generally outweigh the duty to continue the pregnancy to full term.[33] As in Abortion I, it accepted that in exceptional circumstances such a duty could not be imposed where it would be unreasonable to do so (*unzumutbar*), cautioning that an unreasonable expectation could not be found in the normal pregnancy, but rather that it would be based on burdens requiring a significant sacrifice of the woman's core values.[34] The court made it very clear that the question of whether the pregnant woman could reasonably be expected to continue the pregnancy is not a question for the woman herself; instead, a neutral, objective arbiter (a doctor) should determine whether or not an indication exists that would permit the woman to choose a termination of pregnancy.[35] Therefore the court emphasised that abortion cannot be justified on the basis of a woman's autonomous choice to terminate her pregnancy. Instead, it is the unreasonable expectation, as verified by a third party, that can justify the woman's failure to continue the pregnancy to full term.

27 *BVerfGE* 39, 1, at 48.
28 *BVerfGE* 88, 203, at 253.
29 *BVerfGE* 88, 203, at 253–4.
30 *BVerfGE* 88, 203, at 254.
31 *BVerfGE* 88, 203, at 254.
32 *BVerfGE* 88, 203, at 255.
33 *BVerfGE* 88, 203, at 255.
34 *BVerfGE* 88, 203, at 257.
35 *BVerfGE* 88, 203, at 255.

In contrast to the first decision, in Abortion II the *Bundesverfassungsgericht* did not refer to objective values; instead, in an important shift in reasoning from its first decision, it emphasised the link between Art. 1 I and 2 II GG, grounding the state's duty to protect foetal life in the protection of human dignity (Art. 1 I GG), but referring to Art. 2 II GG (the right to life) to determine the scope of that protection.[36] The *Bundesverfassungsgericht* failed to address the question of whether the foetus is a rights-holder with subjective rights, or is merely protected by objective norms, preferring instead to emphasise the link between human dignity, found to exist in prenatal life, and the consequent duty to protect foetal life.[37] It held that the duty is not dependent upon the agreement of the pregnant woman and her willingness to continue the pregnancy, that 'where human life exists, human dignity is accorded to it'.[38] Holding that the right to life is accorded to the foetus by virtue of its very existence, the court described it 'as the most elementary and inalienable right derived from human dignity',[39] and emphasised that 'The duty to protect prenatal life is based upon individual life, not just on human life in general. Compliance [with the duty] is a fundamental condition of orderly cohabitation in the state'.[40]

Therefore, in its abortion decisions the *Bundesverfassungsgericht* recognised that the state has an affirmative duty to protect foetal life that requires it to refrain from direct interference with prenatal life, but also requires the state to protect the foetus from third parties, including the pregnant woman herself.[41] The basis for this holding is not consistent in the two abortion decisions; similarly, there is no definitive statement about the status of the foetus. Nevertheless, for the purposes of this book it is not necessary to analyse this debate further, or to draw a conclusion as to whether the foetus is a bearer of constitutional rights or merely protected by the objective normative framework, as the level of protection demanded would appear to be the same.[42] Similarly, it is clear that foetal life derives protection from both the guarantees of human dignity and life, both of which will be considered below. In the context of obstetric intervention, the crucial question will be to what extent the protective duty will override other fundamental rights held by the pregnant woman.

c. The right to life and bodily integrity as applied to the foetus, the differentiation between a person extant and the foetus

aa. The application of Art. 2 II GG to prenatal life

Art. 2 II GG states: 'Everyone has the right to life and bodily integrity. The liberty of the person is inviolable. Interference with these rights may only occur in

36 *BVerfGE* 88, 203, at 251.
37 *BVerfGE* 88, 203, at 251ff.
38 *BVerfGE* 88, 203, at 252.
39 *BVerfGE* 88, 203, at 252.
40 *BVerfGE* 88, 203, at 252.
41 *BVerfGE* 39, 1, at 42; 88, 203, at 255.
42 See also R. Müller-Terpitz (note 7), at 271.

accordance with an Act'. Thus the right to life is guaranteed by Art. 2 II s.1 GG, protecting the physical-biological existence of human beings,[43] although the parameters of that right are not set out in the constitution, leading to debate about when protection might start and indeed when it might end.[44] The right to life has consistently been classified as a supreme constitutional value by the *Bundesverfassungsgericht*.[45] Unlike the Irish constitution,[46] the German constitution does not state that the right to life expressly applies to prenatal life, although there is some precedent for this; for example, the Prussian General Code (*Allgemeines Landrecht für die Preußischen Staaten*) 1794 recognised that 'The general rights of man also apply to unborn children from the time of conception'.[47] The legislative history of the *Grundgesetz* demonstrates that the legislature intended the right to life to apply prior to birth[48] and the judges in each of the abortion decisions were unanimous in holding that the right to life is not limited to life extant. As Rupp-v.-Brünneck and Simon JJ point out in their dissenting opinion, the question is not *whether* but *how* the right applies to the foetus.[49]

In Abortion I and II the *Bundesverfassungsgericht* recognised that the right to life applies to prenatal life, holding that the foetus is an independent legally protected value (*Rechtsgut*) that 'does not develop into a human being, but as a human being'.[50] It held:

> 'Everyone' in the sense of Art. 2. II s.1 GG is 'everyone living', or put another way: every human individual possessing life; 'everyone' is therefore also the as yet unborn human entity. ... The protection of human existence from state interference would be incomplete if it did not include the preliminary stage of 'completed life', prenatal life.[51]

43 H. Schulze-Fielitz, in *Dreier*, Art. 2 II, Rn. 25.
44 See U. Di Fabio, in *Maunz/Dürig*, Art. 2 II s.1, Rn. 21–2.
45 See, for example, *BVerfGE* 39, 1, at 42; 45, 187, at 254; 49, 24, at 53.
46 Art. 40.3.3 Irish constitution states: 'The State acknowledges the right to life of the unborn and, with due regard to the equal right to life of the mother, guarantees in its laws to respect, and, as far as practicable, by its laws to defend and vindicate that right'. Noticeably, the only conflicting right relevant in the Irish context is the woman's own right to life; her right to self-determination cannot be weighed against the foetal right to life, *Attorney General v X* [1992] ILRM 401. Significantly, the Health Service Executive's *National Consent Policy*, 2013, states: 'The consent of a pregnant woman is required for all health and social care interventions. However, because of the constitutional provisions on the right to life of the "unborn", there is significant legal uncertainty regarding the extent of a pregnant woman's right to refuse treatment in circumstances in which the refusal would put the life of a viable foetus at serious risk. In such circumstances, legal advice should be sought as to whether an application to the High Court is necessary'. Para. 7.7.1, at 41.
47 § 10 I s.1 ALR.
48 For a comprehensive account of the parliamentary debates, see R. Beckmann, 'Der Parlamentarische Rat und das "keimende Leben"' (2008) 47(4) *Der Staat* 551.
49 *BVerfGE* 39, 1, at 68.
50 *BVerfGE* 88, 203, at 252; 39, 1, at 37.
51 *BVerfGE* 39, 1, at 37.

Thus there can be no doubt that the guaranteed protection of life set out in Art. 2 II s.1 GG applies to prenatal life, at least from implantation.[52]

In Abortion I the court explained the need to protect all life by drawing on the context within which Art. 2 II GG was drafted, namely as a reaction to the Nazi atrocities, particularly as a reaction to the destruction of life categorised as unworthy of life, in order to emphasise the fundamental value of *all* human life.[53] However, it is suggested that the mass destruction of human life by the state is inherently different to an abortion performed at the request of the woman concerned and that reference to the crimes committed by the state during the Third Reich contributes little to an analysis of the application of the right to life in the context of consensual abortion,[54] or indeed the context of a woman refusing treatment necessary to protect the foetus. Moreover, whilst it is true that the National Socialist state perpetrated the most appalling crimes against humanity, showing complete disregard for life it categorised as worthless, the lives destroyed were primarily born rather than unborn life. Generally, the Nazis treated prenatal life as worthy of protection, provided that it coincided with their conception of what constitutes a life worthy of life (that it was of 'Aryan' parentage and not disabled). They adopted a very different view of the role of women (primarily to provide children for the fatherland) and of the crime of abortion to the stance taken during the Weimar Republic, reintroducing the death penalty for abortion and actively prosecuting abortionists. Thus, a clear example of the pronatalist policies pursued by the Nazis can be seen in the Decree for the Protection of Marriage, Family and Motherhood 1943, which included the stipulation that all abortions performed by someone other than the woman herself were to be punished by hard labour, or, in cases of repeat offending considered to have damaged 'the life force of the German people', the defendant should be sentenced to death.[55] Against that background, the dissenting opinion is surely correct in suggesting that the lesson to be learnt from history is that restraint in the use of the criminal law is required, rather than that the constitution mandates the punishment of abortion.[56] As Anja Karnein argued:

> There is no obvious reason for why the answer to gross human rights violations is one of breadth – by including more instances of human life as potential addressees of human rights violations – rather than one of depth – by institutionally making sure that such abuses can no longer occur… . There is no obvious or necessary link between including embryos in the realm of those

52 H. Dreier, *Bioethik: Politik und Verfassung*, Tübingen: Mohr Siebeck, 2013, at 39; U. Di Fabio, in *Maunz/Dürig*, Art 2 II s.1, Rn. 24; *BVerfGE* 39, 1, at 37; 88, 203, at 251.

53 *BVerfGE* 39, 1, at 36.

54 See also *BVerfGE* 39, 1, *per* Rupp-v. Brünneck and Simon JJ (dissenting), at 76.

55 § 5 III *Verordnung zum Schutz von Ehe, Familie und Mutterschaft* 9.03.1943, RGbl. I 140.

56 *BVerfGE* 39, 1, at 77.

> who are constitutionally protected and ensuring greater safety from atrocious abuses of human rights.[57]

The second reason advanced by the court for applying the protective effect of the right to life to the foetus is much more compelling: namely that life exists, according to biological-physiological knowledge, from implantation and from that point the development from pre- to postnatal life is continuous. Thus the court held that:

> The protection of Art. 2 II s.1 GG cannot be limited to either 'complete' human beings after birth, nor to the independent, viable foetus ...[58]

It emphasised the comprehensive nature of the state's duty to protect prenatal life, holding that this duty

> self-evidently does not only prohibit direct state interference in the developing life, but also requires the state to take a stance protecting and promoting this life, ... above all, to protect it from unlawful interference from others.[59]

The quoted passage would suggest that the duty to protect foetal life is comprehensive, but the right to life is itself not absolute; Art. 2 II s.3 permits derogation pursuant to statute, although it is clear that the right may only be abrogated in exceptional circumstances. As the dissenting judgment pointed out, if the protection of the right to life were comprehensive, abortion could not be justified in any circumstance.[60] This highlights one of the inconsistencies in the majority's opinion, whereby having established the comprehensive nature of the protective duty owed, it recognised that abortion could be justified on the basis of an embryopathic, a medical or a social indication.[61] Thus it is suggested that the majority's statement about the comprehensive nature of the protection of prenatal life has more to do with creating the appearance of respecting life and affording all life protection than with the provision of such protection. The discrepancy in the level of protection owed to foetal life and that provided is also to be found in the second abortion decision. As Reinhard Merkel explains, having held that the state has a duty to protect foetal life (Art. 1I, 2 II GG) and that the termination of pregnancy is unlawful *per se*, the court also found that:

> All resistance towards the abortion categorised as unlawful earlier [in the judgment] is categorically excluded. The contract between the doctor and pregnant woman, according to the cited headnote an appointment to

57 A. Karnein, *The Theory of Unborn Life from Abortion to Genetic Manipulation*, Oxford: Oxford University Press, 2012, at 46.
58 *BVerfGE* 39, 1, at 37.
59 *BVerfGE* 39, 1, at 42.
60 *BVerfGE* 39, 1, at 79.
61 *BVerfGE* 39, 1, at 48ff.

unlawfully kill a person protected by the constitution, is declared to be valid. All emergency assistance for the unlawfully killed individual is forbidden. The pregnant woman is entitled to sickpay for the time spent on such an unlawful killing. And above all: the state that the first headnote obliges to protect every single embryonic life from unlawful killing is subsequently obliged to set up facilities nationwide in which the mass possibility of such unlawful killings should be secured.[62]

bb. Distinguishing life: when is a Mensch a Mensch?

In its second abortion decision the *Bundesverfassungsgericht* stated:

> If the dignity of a human being lies in its very existence, and if this also applies to prenatal life, there can be no differentiation in the protective duty on the basis of the age and developmental stage of this life, or the willingness of the woman to let it continue to live within her.[63]

In both its abortion decisions the court adopted the continuity theory, according to which life is to be viewed as a continuum from implantation to death and therefore any boundaries drawn within that continuum should be rejected as no more than arbitrary waypoints on the journey. Whilst the majority opinions in both abortion decisions held that the state has an extensive duty to protect foetal life, without regard to gestational development, that duty is of a very different nature and extent to that owed to persons extant. The suggestion that all life is inherently equal is at best disingenuous. Certainly, the state has a duty to protect life in its pre- and postnatal forms; however, the content and extent of that duty differs significantly and, it will be argued, is largely shaped by gestational development and consideration of the woman's interests.

Thus life created outside the human body (*in vitro*) is protected from conception by the Embryo Protection Law (*Embryonenschutzgesetz*), prohibiting, for example, the instrumentalisation of the embryo as a research object, whilst the *in vivo* embryo is entirely unprotected until implantation, whereupon it becomes the subject of the offence of termination of pregnancy (§ 218 StGB). This differential in protection demonstrates the relevance of both gestational development and the woman's interests – in the case of an embryo *in vitro* the protection of its life and dignity cannot conflict with the woman's rights to life, bodily integrity, self-determination and dignity, and is therefore accorded primacy. In the case of the *in vivo* embryo the potential for conflict exists from conception and protection is only afforded to the embryo from implantation, from the time at which the woman can be described as being 'with child' or 'carrying a child'. Up until that point her interests will prevail, enabling her to utilise 'emergency' contraception to prevent implantation occurring. Nevertheless, even after implantation has occurred, the embryo's life is afforded a significantly lower level of protection than a person extant.

62 R. Merkel, 'Rechte für Embryonen?' *Die Zeit* 25.01.2001, at 37.
63 *BVerfGE* 88, 203, at 267; see also 39, 1, at 37.

In Abortion I the only female judge on the panel (Rupp-v-Brünneck J, dissenting) argued in favour of a concept of protection based upon gestational development, maintaining that this would reflect the reality of pregnancy. She contended that a bond develops between the woman and the foetus as pregnancy progresses and that legal protection should similarly increase with increased gestation.[64] However, this argument fails to convince as it suggests that the level of protection afforded should be dependent upon the bond between the pregnant woman and the foetus, a bond that is inherently difficult to quantify and that may never develop, or that may be strong from the very start. Although the *Bundesverfassungsgericht* suggested that the level of protection afforded to the foetus was not dependent upon gestational development, in reality the protection afforded to prenatal life is not consistent throughout the pregnancy; rather, as Horst Dreier argues, the level of protection increases in parallel with gestational development,[65] although it does so independently of emotional ties between the woman and the foetus.

In its abortion decisions the *Bundesverfassungsgericht* sought to locate the foetus within the human family, to refute the argument that it is less deserving of protection than an already born human being. The court recognised that the fact that the state had an affirmative duty to protect foetal life did not require it to utilise the same criminal law measures to protect pre- and postnatal life.[66] Nevertheless, the pronouncements made by the court purporting to hold that the duty to protect should apply to all life equally[67] belie the reality to be found in the corpus of German law, where very different standards of protection apply to the person extant and prenatal life, and indeed to prenatal life at various stages. Anglo-American jurisprudence is clear that live birth marks the dividing line between the foetus and a person; by contrast, in its second abortion decision the *Bundesverfassungsgericht* emphasised that the foetus does not develop into a *Mensch* (a human being/person), but rather as a *Mensch*.[68] This argument has much merit: it recognises the artificiality of birth as a legal bright line, but it also suggests that the degree of protection afforded to human life, whatever its stage of development, should be the same. However, German law does not take a coherent, unified approach to when one becomes a person enjoying the full protection of the law; instead, a number of legal bright lines exist, delineating the protection afforded to persons, with the level of protection depending very much upon the stage reached on the continuum from conception to death, despite statements to the contrary by the *Bundesverfassungsgericht*. As will be argued below, some distinctions are necessary: a developing (not yet born) person is inherently different from a person extant and it is suggested that a woman should continue to enjoy full legal

64 *BVerfGE* 39, 1, at 80–1.

65 See, for example, H. Dreier (note 52), at 53ff.; H. Dreier, 'Stufungen des vorgeburtlichen Lebensschutzes' (2002) 35 (9) *Zeitschrift für Rechtspolitik* 377, at 378; H. Dreier, 'Grenzen des Tötungsverbotes – Teil 1' (2007) *Juristen Zeitung* 261, at 267ff.

66 *BVerfGE* 39, 1, at 45.

67 *BVerfGE* 39, 1, at 37; *BVerfGE* 88, 203, at 267.

68 *BVerfGE* 39, 1, at 37; *BVerfGE* 88, 203, at 252.

protection of her rights and interests notwithstanding that she is pregnant, even though the consequence may be the diminution of the protection available to unborn life.

As a matter of public law, the constitutional guarantees of the right to life (Art. 2 II s.1 GG) and human dignity (Art. 1 I GG) have been held to apply to the embryo from the point of implantation.[69] By contrast, at the other extreme end of the developmental scale, the acquisition of personhood in civil law is dependent upon live birth, § 1 BGB stipulating that a person's *Rechtsfähigkeit* (legal personality, or the capacity to possess legal rights and duties) begins upon the completion of live birth. This corresponds to the Anglo-American position, but, as Walter Gropp points out, the function of § 1 BGB is to recognise status rather than to protect a legal interest (*Rechtsgut*).[70] Generally, therefore, in civil law the foetus is incapable of possessing legal rights and duties, but its interests are protected in certain circumstances; for example, a guardian can be appointed for the foetus (§ 1912 I BGB) and inheritance rights are recognised contingent upon subsequent live birth (§ 1923 II BGB).[71]

The difference between persons extant and prenatal life on the one hand and between different stages of prenatal life on the other is highlighted by the Criminal Code (the *Strafgesetzbuch*). As Wilfried Küper points out, in the Criminal Code the homicide provisions (§§ 211ff., 222 StGB) refer to a '*Mensch*' (a human being), whilst the provisions relating to trespass to the person (§§ 223ff., 229 StGB) refer to a 'Person'. The two terms are used synonymously, but neither is used in § 218f. StGB in relation to the offence of termination of pregnancy; indeed, in contrast to the normal style of legislative drafting, that offence determines only the condition (pregnancy) that is ended, rather than the subject of protection.[72] Whilst persons extant enjoy comprehensive protection against both intentional and negligent injury and death, in the case of the foetus it is protected only against the intentional destruction of its life. As Horst Dreier has pointed out, were § 218 StGB to be repealed, the foetus would be entirely unprotected by the criminal law.[73] The very fact that the crime of termination of pregnancy exists serves to emphasise the different manner in which foetal life is protected and indeed the extent to which it is protected. Certainly, the state has a duty to protect the foetus, as the *Bundesverfassungsgericht* stated, but it is a very different duty to that which pertains to the lives of those already born and, as will be discussed, the level of protection is differentiated in accordance with gestational development and even takes account of the woman's willingness to allow the foetus continued residence within her uterus.

69 *BVerfGE* 39, 1, at 37; 88, 203, at 251.

70 W. Gropp, 'Strafrechtlicher Schutz des Lebens vor und nach der "Geburt"', in E. Schumann (ed.) *Verantwortungsbewusste Konfliktlösungen bei embryopathischem Befund*, Göttingen: Universitätsverlag Göttingen, 2008, 19 ff, at 32.

71 For further examples, see J. Schmitt, in *MüKo-BGB*, § 1, Rn. 26ff.

72 W. Küper, 'Mensch oder Embryo? Der Anfang des "Menschseins" nach neuem Strafrecht' (2001) *Goltdammer's Archiv für Strafrecht* 515, at 515.

73 H. Dreier, 'Stufungen des vorgeburtlichen Lebensschutzes' (note 65), at 378.

Whilst § 218 StGB is to be found within the part of the criminal code containing the provisions relating to the crimes against life, termination of pregnancy constitutes a separate offence; it is not part of the offence of aggravated murder (§ 211 StGB) or homicide (§ 212 StGB). Indeed, unlike the killing or injury of a person extant, which is proscribed by law and a crime whether committed negligently or with intent, the negligent killing and/or harming (even with intent) of a foetus is not a criminal offence. Moreover, the applicable punishment proscribed for these offences serves to underline the difference between a foetus and a person extant, even where a foetus is killed intentionally. The crime of abortion attracts a penalty of up to three years' imprisonment or a fine,[74] a significantly lesser sentence than that handed down for aggravated murder (life imprisonment) or homicide (from five years up to life imprisonment).[75] A further demonstration of the protection differential can be seen in the exculpatory and justificatory grounds applicable to abortion (§ 218a StGB), grounds that would be unimaginable in the case of a person extant.[76] Although the *Bundesverfassungsgericht* held that the state is under a duty to protect all life, it also accepted that the termination of pregnancy could be justified either on the basis of a threat to the life or a serious risk to the pregnant woman's health, thus giving the woman's life and health precedence over the life of the foetus.[77] On this basis the medico-social indication set out in § 218a II StGB acts as a justification for the termination, which is therefore classified as not unlawful. The same applies in the case of the criminological indication that justifies abortions performed within the first 12 weeks of pregnancy (§ 218a III StGB). In both instances the woman's interests will prevail over the state's duty to protect foetal life, although even in the case of rape the gestational development stage (approaching the end of the first trimester) will be crucial in determining whether or not the termination can be justified in accordance with the criminological indication.

Most abortions in Germany are performed pursuant to the counselling provision and not under either indication.[78] Such abortions are classified as unlawful, but will incur no criminal liability where the termination of pregnancy takes place at least three days after the mandatory pro-life counselling and within 12 weeks' gestation (§ 218a I StGB). It is clear that the woman's right to bodily integrity and her right to make the autonomous choice to have an abortion is limited to the first 12 weeks of pregnancy and even then is contingent upon her undergoing counselling designed to protect the life of the foetus (§ 219 StGB). In reality the counselling is the price exacted for the recognition of the woman's right to elect

74 § 218 StGB, but note in aggravated cases a sentence of up to five years' imprisonment may be imposed, whilst in the case of a termination by the pregnant woman the maximum sentence is one year.

75 See also H. Dreier, 'Grenzen des Tötungsverbotes – Teil 1' (note 65), at 267.

76 Ibid.

77 *BVerfGE* 39, 1, at 49; 88, 203, at 254.

78 During 2014, 96.4 per cent of all abortions performed were performed on the basis of the counselling provision, Statistisches Bundesamt, *Schwangerschaftsabbrüche 2014*, Fachserie 12, Reihe 3, Wiesbaden, 2015, Table 1.2.

an early abortion. It is described as 'serving the protection of unborn life' and as being intended to assist the woman 'to make a responsible and conscientious decision' (§ 219 StGB). Whilst much could be said about the negative view adopted of the woman's agency, this legislative compromise does at least accord primacy to the woman's decision to terminate a pregnancy within the first trimester, unlike in the UK where such a decision must be made by two doctors upon the request of the woman (s.1(1) Abortion Act 1967). Moreover, the widespread availability of abortion and counselling facilities ensures that abortion remains accessible, unlike in the USA where the much trumpeted right to elect a pre-viability abortion[79] has become largely theoretical with women experiencing severe difficulties in accessing even early abortion services. Therefore it is clear that the German law relating to termination of pregnancy does provide protection for the foetus that increases in parallel with gestation; the further the pregnancy develops, the greater the protection afforded to the foetus, with abortion after 12 weeks only being available on the basis of a threat to the woman's life or a grave danger to her health. It is thus clear that, contrary to the statements made by the *Bundesverfassungsgericht*,[80] both the woman's unwillingness to continue the pregnancy and the gestational developmental stage reached will impact upon the protective duty owed by the state.

Moreover, the boundary between the offence of termination of pregnancy and the other homicide offences is particularly instructive in considering the protection afforded to life in its various forms and, as will become clear, is of crucial importance in the context of obstetric intervention required for the benefit of the foetus. Whilst English law relies on the completion of live birth as the dividing line between abortion and murder, in German criminal law the homicide provisions have a much broader application, displacing the offence of termination of pregnancy, from the beginning of the birth process. One of the purposes of the English Infant Life Preservation Act 1929 was to close the gap in protection between s.58 Offences Against the Persons Act 1861 (procuration of a miscarriage) and murder, creating the offence of child destruction that would be committed in relation to a 'child capable of being born alive' (s.1) where that 'child capable of being born alive' was killed in the process of birth. In a similar manner the now repealed § 217 StGB[81] attributed personhood to the 'child' from the onset of the '*Eröffnungswehen*',[82] so that from this point onwards acts or omissions leading to the

79 *Roe v Wade* (note 2), *Planned Parenthood v Casey* (note 10).

80 *BVerfGE* 39, 1, at 37; 88, 203, at 267.

81 Repealed by the 6. *Strafreformgesetz* (6th Act to Reform Criminal Law), BGBl. I 1998, 164.

82 The *Eröffnungswehen* are a specific form of contractions, the contractions that dilate the cervix. Once the cervix has dilated to 3cm the woman is classified as being in the first stage of labour. *Eröffnungswehen* should be distinguished from the earlier occurring Braxton Hicks contractions and the later contractions of second stage labour designed to expel the foetus. In the case of surgical delivery, without the prior onset of birth, the application of the scalpel will constitute the beginning of birth and thus the transformational event, effecting the status change from foetus to person; see A. Eser, in *Schönke/Schröder*, Vorb. zu § 211, Rn. 13; W. Gropp (note 70), at 32.

death of the foetus will fall to be considered under the general homicide provisions, rather than as a termination of pregnancy.[83]

§ 217 StGB (repealed) prohibited infanticide, providing for a lesser penalty than that applicable to homicide in the case of a woman who killed her illegitimate child during or straight after the birth. Relying on this provision, the *Reichsgericht*, and later the *Bundesgerichtshof* (Supreme Court), adopted the beginning of the birth process as the demarcation line between the applicability of the provisions protecting a person's life and bodily integrity (§§ 211ff., 222; 223ff., 230 StGB) and that protecting the *Leibesfrucht*[84] (the foetus) from intentional destruction (§ 218 StGB).[85] Therefore, as the courts have consistently held, it is the onset of the birth process, not the completion of live birth, that is the legally relevant time, with the higher standard of protection being applicable to the foetus from that point, notwithstanding that it is still located within the woman's body. For that reason, the defendant who pushed a pregnant woman off a cliff, after the dilatory contractions had already begun, was convicted of murdering both the woman and the still unborn child.[86] By contrast, in the so-called Buscopan case doctors had treated a woman by providing pain relief for 'menstrual cramps', failing to recognise that she was nine months pregnant at the time. As a result of the treatment given, the birth was overlong and the foetus died as a result of oxygen deprivation, being stillborn three days after the woman was first prescribed the painkillers. The *Bundesgerichtshof* (Criminal Division) held that because it could not be determined with certainty that the process of birth (by virtue of the dilatory contractions) had commenced, the doctors could not be convicted of negligent homicide contrary to § 222 StGB. In such circumstances the doctors' negligence was not actionable; the foetus was only protected by § 218 StGB from the intentional termination of pregnancy.[87]

The general consensus is that the repeal of § 217 StGB has not changed the position in criminal law that the foetus becomes a person from the onset of birth.[88] However, a number of commentators have criticised this position; for

83 *RGSt* 1, 446, at 447; 9, 131; 26, 178; *BVerfGE* 88, 203, at 251; *BGHSt* 10, 5; 31, 348, at 350ff; 32, 194; *BGH* NStZ 2008, 393. For an excellent analysis of this case law, see W. Küper (note 72), at 520ff.

84 Literally, the fruit of the womb. Since the 5th Act for the Reform of Criminal Law 1974 (*Das Fünfte Gesetz zur Reform des Strafrechts*, 18.06.1974, BGBl. I S. 1297), § 218 StGB no longer refers to '*Leibesfrucht*', but it remains clear that the foetus is the subject of the protection afforded by § 218 StGB. A. Eser, in *Schönke/Schröder*, Vorb. zu den §§ 218 bis 219b, Rn. 9.

85 *RGSt* 1, 446, at 447; 9, 131; 26, 178; *BVerfGE* 88, 203, at 251; *BGHSt* 10, 5; 31, 348, at 350ff.; 32, 194; *BGH* NStZ 2008, 393.

86 *BGHSt* 32, 194.

87 *BGHSt* 31, 348.

88 See, for example, A. Eser, in *Schönke/Schröder*, Vorb. zu § 211, Rn. 13, vor § 218, Rn. 9; R. Merkel, *Früheuthanasie: rechtsethische und strafrechtliche Grundlagen ärztlicher Entscheidungen über Leben und Tod in der Neonatalmedizin*, Baden-Baden: Nomos, 2001, at 102; but see note 92 below; H. J. Hirsch, 'Die Grenze zwischen Schwangerschaftsabbruch und allgemeinen Tötungsdelikten nach der Streichung des Privilegierungstatbestands der Kindestötung (§ 217 StGB a.F.)' in J. Arnold, B. Burkhartd, W. Gropp et al. (eds) *Menschengerechtes Strafrecht: Festschrift für Albin Eser zum 70.*

example, Walter Gropp has argued that it may be extremely difficult to identify the precise point at which the foetus transformed into a child by the commencement of dilating contractions and that in reality the end of pregnancy flows into the beginning of life in a continuous process, with birth being no more than an episode in that process and thus being undeserving of the significance attributed to it.[89] Moreover, this somewhat artificial boundary is likely to pose problems in the case of premature labour where labour is successfully halted and the pregnancy maintained, or indeed in the case of foetal surgery, where the uterus is opened, only to be resealed following surgery, with no intention to deliver the foetus at the time of the intervention.[90] In such cases the foetus has already become a child by virtue of the commencement of the contractions, or the opening of the uterus, and will not revert to being a foetus. Instead, the foetus may remain a resident of the woman's uterus for some time – a person within a person, a living matryoshka – and protected by the full might of the criminal law.

In the context of obstetric intervention, the timing of the transformation from foetus to *Mensch* is significant, because if the onset of the birth process is adopted as the threshold of personhood and a 'child' dies as the result of the woman's refusal of treatment, she could face liability for homicide by omission. If birth is adopted as the demarcating feature, the same woman would face 'only' liability for termination of pregnancy by omission, which attracts a significantly lower penalty than that applicable to homicide. Moreover, in such cases the inherent uncertainty of what would have happened if the woman had consented to the intervention means that causation will be very difficult to establish to the requisite degree of a probability bordering upon certainty, so that any resulting liability is likely to be for an attempt; significantly, § 218 IV StGB excludes liability for attempted termination of pregnancy in the case of the woman. As will be recalled from the discussion of the English and American case law above,[91] many of the English and American cases involved women who were in labour and where, according to the dominant view of German law, the foetus had already metamorphosed into a child capable of being killed by omission.

A number of suggestions may be made regarding the appropriate boundary in the development from a foetus to a person. For example, Rolf and Annika Herzberg argue that the dividing line should mirror that in civil law – that is, from completed birth.[92] By contrast, Walter Gropp has argued that there is a need for

Geburtstag, München: C.H. Beck, 2005, 309 ff, at 314ff. But cf. W. Gropp, 'Der Embryo als Mensch: Überlegungen zum pränatalen Schutz des Lebens und der körperlichen Unversehrtheit' (2000) *Goltdammer's Archiv für Strafrecht* 1, at 10, arguing that the legislature inadvertently removed the demarcation line by repealing § 217 StGB; W. Küper (note 72), at 524ff.

89 W. Gropp (note 70), at 32.

90 Cf. N. Heinemann, *Frau und Fötus in der Prä- und Perinatalmedizin aus strafrechtlicher Sicht*, Baden-Baden: Nomos, 2000, at 162ff. arguing that the separation must be complete and permanent in order to effect a transition from foetus to person.

91 B I and II.

92 R. Herzberg and A. I. Herzberg, 'Der Beginn des Menschseins im Strafrecht: Die Vollendung der Geburt' (2001) 22 *Juristen Zeitung* 1106, at 1112; this position has

greater clarity and that this could be achieved by reference to a set gestational time – he suggests 22 weeks, reflecting viability.[93] Nevertheless, he does not argue that from that point the protection of foetal life should prevail in all circumstances; rather, he notes that, even after viability, feticide (which would then fall to be considered under the general homicide provisions, rather than § 218 StGB) could be justified in the case of a threat to the woman's life or health[94] and suggests that policy reasons require that women should be exempted from punishment for negligent homicide or personal injury.[95] These arguments are persuasive; they reflect the unique nature of the relationship between a woman and the foetus she carries and recognise that legal intrusion in that relationship must be extremely limited. I return to this theme below,[96] but for the moment it is important to note that such policy reasons have been found to justify the exclusion of liability for prenatal injuries and they would seem to be even more compelling in relation to liability for omissions in the context of obstetric interventions where the woman's dignity and her rights to both bodily integrity and self-determination are directly impacted to a significantly higher degree. For that reason it is suggested that gestational development should be an extremely important factor in determining what can reasonably be expected of the pregnant woman in the context of her duty to protect the foetus, but that birth should be regarded as the point at which the foetus becomes a person for the purposes of crimes against life (§ 211ff. StGB), at least in the case of the pregnant woman. This would provide certainty and bring consistency with the civil law position. More importantly, though, it would recognise the unique relationship between the pregnant woman and the foetus, which is reflected in the privileged position enjoyed by the pregnant woman in relation to the regulation of abortion. Significantly, such an approach would also recognise the unique impact that compelled obstetric intervention would have upon the pregnant woman, requiring her to sacrifice her own compelling interests for the benefit of the foetus.

d. Competing conceptions of dignity: human dignity as a protective mechanism applied to the foetus, human dignity as protective of the woman's identity (as opposed to reproductive capacity)

The concept of human dignity has become increasingly important, particularly in relation to medical treatment and the law at the beginning and end of life. As the European Court of Human Rights recognised in *Pretty v UK*, human dignity and

also been adopted by R. Merkel, in *NK-StGB*, § 218, Rn. 29ff., in contrast to his earlier position in favour of maintaining the beginning of birth as the demarcation point; see R. Merkel (note 88), at 102.

93 This time limit also reflects the statutory exclusion of punishment for the pregnant woman where a pregnancy has been terminated within 22 weeks, by a doctor, after counselling (§ 218a IV StGB).

94 W. Gropp (note 70), at 39; W. Gropp (note 88), at 7ff., 17.

95 W. Gropp (note 88), at 16f.

96 C III.

human freedom form 'the very essence of the Convention'.[97] However, despite frequent reference to the notion in international instruments[98] and in the German constitution (Art. 1 I GG), there is no consensus on what is meant by 'dignity' in this or other medical contexts, or indeed to whom the guarantee extends.[99] Recognising that it can be used as both a sword and a shield, Deryck Beyleveld and Roger Brownsword offer two constructions of dignity, namely dignity as empowerment and dignity as constraint.[100] Conceptualising dignity as empowerment recognises the manner in which it can be used to support choice, to reinforce autonomy. Whilst the European Court of Human Rights recognised the synthesis of dignity with autonomy in *Pretty* (dignity as empowerment), it has also recognised that dignity is engaged in the prenatal context. In *Vo v France* the court once again considered the application of Art. 2 European Convention on Human Rights (ECHR) to the foetus, on this occasion outside the abortion context. Although it failed to determine whether or not the foetus is a person for the purposes of the Art. 2 ECHR, the majority held: 'The potentiality of [the foetus] and its capacity to become a person … require protection in the name of human dignity, without making it a "person" with the "right to life" for the purposes of Article 2'.[101] Thus the European Court of Human Rights clearly anticipated that dignity could protect the foetus, and in doing so could restrict individual choice, illustrating Beyleveld and Brownsword's construction of human dignity as constraint. As will be discussed below, both constructions of dignity are evident in the judicial consideration of the regulation of abortion in Germany.

In its abortion jurisprudence the US Supreme Court has relied upon the concept of dignity to reject limitations upon the woman's right to choose an abortion prior to viability. Writing for the majority in *Casey*, O'Connor J expressed this notion in the following terms:

> These matters, involving the most intimate and personal choices a person may make in a lifetime, choices central to personal dignity and autonomy, are central to the liberty protected by the Fourteenth Amendment. At the heart of liberty is the right to define one's own concept of existence, of meaning, of the universe, and of the mystery of human life. Beliefs about these matters could not define the attributes of personhood were they formed under compulsion of the State.[102]

97 (2002) 35 EHRR 1, at para 65.

98 See, for example, the preamble to the Council of Europe's Convention on Human Rights and Biomedicine and Art. 1 United Nations Universal Declaration of Human Rights 1948.

99 See, for example, the multiple understandings of dignity adopted by contributors to E. D. Pellegrino et al. (eds) *Human Dignity and Bioethics*, Notre Dame: University of Notre Dame Press, 2009.

100 D. Beyleveld and R. Brownsword, *Human Dignity in Bioethics and Biolaw*, Oxford: Oxford University Press, 2001.

101 *Vo v France* (note 11), at para 84.

102 *Planned Parenthood of Southeastern Pennsylvania et al. v Casey* (note 10), at 851.

The plurality's formulation of dignity, based upon autonomy and the construction of personhood through choices, had the effect of empowering women, reinforcing a pregnant woman's claim to self-determination.[103] Similarly, the Hungarian Constitutional Court found that dignity was engaged in the regulation of abortion, holding: 'Among the rights to be weighed against the state's duty to give increased protection to foetal life, the mother's right to self-determination – as part of the right to human dignity – is the most important one'.[104] Thus both courts adopted a conception of dignity that focused upon personal choice and recognising women's agency. By contrast, in its abortion decisions the *Bundesverfassungsgericht* linked both the woman's right to self-determination and the foetal right to life to the protection of human dignity. Dignity is an inherently nebulous concept, open to multiple meanings, and the *Bundesverfassungsgericht*'s abortion jurisprudence demonstrates conflicting constructions of dignity, conceptualising it both as liberty (in the sense of decisional autonomy promoted in *Casey*) and constraint, in so far as it requires the woman's liberty interests to be restrained in order to protect the foetus.

Art. 1 I GG states: 'The dignity of human beings [*Menschen*] is inviolable. All state authority is under a duty to respect and protect it'. The guarantee plays a central role within the constitution, acting as a preamble to the fundamental rights that follow it and underpinning the constitution as a whole. It has been described by the *Bundesverfassungsgericht* as the 'highest legal value',[105] the 'primary constitutional principle',[106] the 'supreme value in the *Grundgesetz*'[107] and 'the root of all fundamental rights';[108] nevertheless, a definition of what the guarantee requires has proved elusive. Art. 1 I GG does not articulate a protective sphere; the first sentence is simply a statement asserting the dignity of man. It is suggested that the definition of human dignity is extremely malleable and ultimately context-specific. As the *Bundesverfassungsgericht* has recognised, 'The judgment of what constitutes human dignity can therefore only be based on our present understanding of it and makes no claim to timeless validity'.[109] Thus in Germany, as in other jurisdictions, the principle of human dignity has remained inherently vague, leading Wolfram

103 But note that in *Gonzales v Carhart* 127 S.Ct. 1610 (2007) Kennedy J stated that the Partial Birth Abortion Ban Act 'expresses respect for the dignity of human life', at 1633. Given that the Partial Birth Abortion Ban Act contains no exception safeguarding the health of the woman, it is suggested that Kennedy's understanding of dignity can at best be characterised as one-sided.

104 Decision 48/1998 (IX.23) AB, para 3(b), quoted in C. McCrudden, 'Human Dignity and Judicial Interpretation of Human Rights' (2008) 19(4) *EJIL* 655, at 689. For an excellent comparison of the use of dignity in relation to abortion by the German and Hungarian constitutional courts, see C. Dupré, *Importing the Law in Post-Communist Transitions: The Hungarian Constitutional Court and the Right to Human Dignity*, Oxford: Hart, 2003.

105 *BverfGE* 12, 45, at 53(1960, conscientious objection).

106 *BVerfGE* 6, 32, at 36 (1957, Elfes); 87, 209 at 228 (The Evil Dead).

107 *BVerfGE* 6, 32, at 41.

108 *BVerfGE* 93, 266, at 293 (1995, 'Soldiers are murderers').

109 45 *BVerfGE* 45, 187, at 229 (1977, life imprisonment).

Höfling to describe it as a constitutional principle of 'comprehensive generality'.[110] Similarly, Norbert Hoerster has criticised Art. 1 I GG as an empty formula,[111] both critics echoing Schopenhauer's sentiment that dignity is nothing more than 'the shibboleth of all emptyheaded moralists'.[112] Notwithstanding concerns about the content of the guarantee, there is widespread support for the principle of human dignity and, as the overarching principle of the *Grundgesetz*, it is arguably best seen as the lens through which all other constitutional guarantees must be viewed, with the fundamental rights and the guarantee of human dignity set in a relationship of mutual reinforcement. Despite being phrased in descriptive terms, it is clear that Art. 1 I GG imposes positive duties upon the state to both respect and protect human dignity. It is this element that is likely to be called into question in the context of obstetric intervention, where it must be determined how the state can respect and protect the dignity of both the woman and the foetus.

In both its abortion decisions the *Bundesverfassungsgericht* declared that foetal life is encompassed in the protection of human dignity. In Abortion I the court held that life is the 'living foundation of human dignity',[113] conceptualising the guarantee of human dignity as a parallel source of protection for prenatal life. Although the court determined that the guarantee of human dignity acts as a source of support for the primary duty of protection derived from Art. 2 II s.1 GG, it failed to clarify the nature of this support.[114] It held that the appropriate balance between protecting the woman's right to self-determination and the foetal right to life must be achieved by reference to the protection of human dignity.[115] However, there is little evidence of balance in the discussion that follows this key holding. Instead, the majority opinion concentrates upon the application of the guarantee of dignity to foetal life, with no detailed analysis of how the woman's dignity is to be protected. Thus the majority adopted a construction of dignity as constraint, recognising that it could require the woman's autonomy to be curtailed in order to protect foetal life throughout pregnancy.[116]

In an important shift, in Abortion II the *Bundesverfassungsgericht* held that the guarantee of human dignity is the basis of the state's duty to protect prenatal life, with the measure of that protection being derived from Art. 2 II s.1 GG.[117] As human dignity is stated to be inviolable, all interference therewith is prohibited, regardless of whether it emanates from the state or a private individual – in this context, the pregnant woman. Inevitably, this formulation of the state's protective duty will prioritise the protection of foetal life over the woman's liberty interests.

110 W. Höfling, in *Sachs*, Art. 1, Rn. 7.

111 N. Hoerster, *Ethik des Embryonenschutzes: Ein rechtsphilosophischer Essay*, Stuttgart: Reclam, 2002, at 24.

112 A. Schopenhauer, *Die beiden Grundprobleme der Ethik behandelt in zwei akademischen Preisschriften*, 2nd edn, Leipzig: Brockhaus, 1860, at 166.

113 *BVerfGE* 39, 1, at 41.

114 *BVerfGE* 39, 1, at 51.

115 *BVerfGE* 39, 1, at 43.

116 Ibid.

117 *BVerfGE* 88, 203, at 251.

However, in the second decision the *Bundesverfassungsgericht* did recognise that the woman's dignity and liberty interests must also be protected and that therefore a proportionate solution must be found that sufficiently protects foetal life without disproportionately restricting the woman's right to self-determination.[118]

Thus in both decisions the *Bundesverfassungsgericht* held that the foetus is protected by the guarantee of human dignity and adopted a duty-driven conception of dignity, imposing a duty to protect foetal life upon the state and a duty to carry the pregnancy to term upon the woman. The court stated: 'Where human life exists, it is accorded human dignity'.[119] However, it did not elucidate this finding in either decision, failing to explain why the existence of prenatal life will in and of itself automatically engage the protection of human dignity. As Horst Dreier argues, 'Life is the *condition sine qua non* not the *sine per quam* for the applicability of Art. 1 I GG'.[120]

The court's finding that the foetus benefits from the guarantee of human dignity remains controversial, particularly as it recognised that the foetus is not accorded human dignity merely because it is a member of the human race, but on the basis of its own existence.[121] As Horst Dreier points out, whilst the wording of Art. 2 II GG stipulates that the right to life belongs to 'everyone', the wording of Art. 1 I GG refers to dignity being possessed by 'human beings' (literally, 'The dignity of human beings is inviolable'). Whilst he supports the view that the foetus's life is protected by Art. 2 II GG, he argues that it is not self-evident that it should also be protected by the guarantee of human dignity, pointing out that whilst dignity cannot exist without life, the existence of life does not necessarily require that life to be protected by the guarantee of human dignity.[122] Therefore he argues that the protection of human dignity and of life should not be amalgamated, that the two guarantees should be viewed separately, with only the protection of life being applicable to the foetus.[123] Similarly, Jörn Ipsen argues that the foetus cannot be a holder of human dignity as that is the preserve of persons extant. Nevertheless, he suggests that the foetus is protected by the objective protection of human dignity in an analogous manner to the way in which the *Bundesverfassungsgericht* held that there is a post-mortem right to human dignity in its *Mephisto* decision.[124] It must be recognised that there is a significant difference between a dead person and a foetus: the deceased was a person with identifiable critical interests and as such enjoyed dignity whilst alive; the foetus has yet to become a person and thus only has a prospective dignity interest. Nonetheless, it is submitted that this prospective dignity interest will be worthy of protection and that Jörn Ipsen is correct to argue

118 *BVerfGE* 88, 203, at 254ff.
119 *BVerfGE* 39, 1, at 41; 88, 203, at 252.
120 H. Dreier, 'Menschenwürdegarantie und Schwangerschaftsabbruch' (1995) 24 *Die Öffentliche Verwaltung* 1036, at 1037.
121 *BVerfGE* 88, 203, at 252; *BVerfGE* 39, 1, at 41.
122 H. Dreier (note 120), at 1037; H. Dreier, in *Dreier*, Art. 1 I, Rn. 67.
123 H. Dreier, in *Dreier*, Art. 1 I, Rn. 67.
124 J. Ipsen, 'Der "verfassungsrechtliche Status" des Embryos in vitro: Anmerkungen zu einer aktuellen Debatte' (2001) *Juristen Zeitung* 989, at 992f.

that the foetus is protected by the guarantee of human dignity operating as an objective fundamental constitutional principle. Similarly, although the *Bundesverfassungsgericht* held that where there is life, there is dignity and that the protection afforded by Art. 1 I commences at implantation,[125] it is suggested that Jörn Ipsen is correct to argue that the scope of the state's protective duty will increase in parallel with foetal development, requiring greater protection as the foetus nears birth and that this graduated level of protection is consistent with the court's abortion decision that recognised that the state's duty to protect foetal life could be fulfilled during the first 12 weeks of pregnancy through the imposition of counselling designed to protect the foetus by encouraging the woman to continue the pregnancy.[126]

There is undoubtedly a fundamental association between the right to life and the human dignity guarantee,[127] but regardless of whether the protection of foetal life is subjective or objective in nature, it is important to note that human dignity will not require the preservation of life in all situations. As Art. 2 III GG makes clear, the right to life is not absolute; it may be breached in accordance with statute. Thus, in cases where interference with the right to life is justifiable (e.g. in the case of self-defence), it cannot be said to breach the protection of human dignity.[128] Similarly, it is well accepted that the protection of human dignity will not always require that life is protected or preserved. For example, the notion of dying with dignity will not require that the state protect life at the expense of requiring individuals to submit to life-prolonging treatment.[129] In the same way, termination of pregnancy *per se* is not necessarily contrary to human dignity. In order to establish a breach of Art. 1 I GG, it must be demonstrated that the extinguishing of foetal life is contrary to human dignity in the context in which it takes place. Thus, for example, an abortion performed on the basis of gender, for the purpose of family balancing rather than on the basis of a sound medical reason, could be found to be contrary to human dignity, but it is the motivating factor, rather than the termination of foetal life, that makes it so.[130] Therefore it is submitted that far from finding that all abortions will infringe human dignity, in recognising the symbiotic nature of the relationship between the right to life and the guarantee of human dignity, the *Bundesverfassungsgericht* underlined the significance of the right to life within the hierarchy of fundamental rights and the need for restraint in abrogating that right, even within the confines of Art. 2 III GG.[131]

125 *BVerfGE* 88, 203, at 252; 39, 1.
126 J. Ipsen (note 124), at 993f.
127 U. Di Fabio, in *Maunz/Dürig*, Art. 2 II s.1, Rn. 11.
128 See also U. Di Fabio, in *Maunz/Dürig*, Art. 2 II s.1, Rn. 15; H. Dreier (note 120), at 1037.
129 For a more detailed consideration of the application of the guarantee of human dignity at the end of life, see S. Halliday, 'Comparative Reflections upon the Assisted Dying Bill 2013: A Plea for a More European Approach' (2013) 13 *Medical Law International* 135, at 140ff.
130 See also M. Herdegen, in *Maunz/Dürig*, Art. 1 I, Rn. 112.
131 See also U. Steiner, *Der Schutz des Lebens durch das Grundgesetz*, Berlin: Walter de Gruyter, 1991, at 13.

Unlike the right to life, which may be infringed pursuant to statute (Art. 2 III GG), human dignity is guaranteed as inviolable (*unantastbar*); it is an absolute value and will remain so due to the eternity clause, Art. 79 III GG, which prohibits the amendment of Art. 1 GG. This marks a significant difference between the guarantee of human dignity and the fundamental rights set out in Art. 2–19 GG; although not every interference with a fundamental right will constitute a breach, an infringement of human dignity cannot be justified in any circumstance: dignity is absolutely inviolable.[132] It is submitted that by including the protection of foetal life within the protection of human dignity the court broadened the scope of available protection substantially, permitting itself significantly more leeway to determine that the abortion legislation in question[133] was unconstitutional.

If dignity is construed as life, it constitutes a trump card[134] in the armoury of those seeking to compel obstetric intervention, but claims that human dignity requires the preservation of foetal life must be treated with care. The *Bundesverfassungsgericht* stressed that 'the dignity of a human being lies in its very existence' and that it applies to prenatal life as well as life extant.[135] However, the significance of this second factor would appear to have been rather underplayed – the court held that the guarantee of human dignity applies to prenatal life *as well as*, rather than *instead of*, life extant. It is suggested that the very fact that dignity applies to life extant requires that women are treated as complete persons, not merely a uterine environment, and that in conceptualising dignity as life, great care must be taken not to devalue the status of pregnant women. In both abortion decisions the *Bundesverfassungsgericht* recognised that the foetus is accorded human dignity, that the state has a duty to respect and protect its dignity. That the foetus is not 'nothing', in the sense that it is demonstrably human and a living organism, is clear; however, it is equally clear that the pregnant woman is also the beneficiary of human dignity and that the state is equally obliged to respect and protect her dignity. Unlike the right to life, the protection of human dignity is not subject to exceptions; thus it is clear that pregnancy should not be taken to diminish the dignity of the woman *per se*.

The question remains: what is required of the state by its duty to promote and protect the dignity of women? In seeking to define the content of the guarantee, the negative aspects of the guaranteed respect for human dignity (Art. 1 I GG) are normally emphasised. Thus one of the leading definitions is that proposed by Günter Dürig, whereby human dignity is impinged 'whenever the actual human

132 H. Dreier, in *Dreier*, Art. 1 I, Rn. 44; but cf. M. Baldus, 'Menschenwürdegarantie und Absolutheitsthese Zwischenbericht zu einer zukunftsweisenden Debatte' (2011) 134(4) *Archiv des oeffentlichen Rechts* 529.

133 *Schwangeren- und Familienhilfegesetz* (Pregnant Woman and Family Assistance Act) 27.07.1992 BGBl. I S. 1398.

134 See also H. Dreier (note 52), at 25; J. Isensee, 'Menschenwürde: die säkulare Gesellschaft auf der Suche nach dem Absoluten' (2006) 131(2) *Archiv des öffentlichen Rechts* 173, at 194.

135 *BVerfGE* 88, 203, at 267.

being is degraded to an object, to a means to an end, to a replaceable value'.[136] This definition is clearly based upon Immanuel Kant's second categorical imperative, the principle that persons should not be instrumentalised, that they should be an end in themselves and not a means to an end.[137] Similarly, emphasising the conceptualisation of dignity as liberty, Joseph Raz wrote: 'Respecting human dignity entails treating humans as persons capable of planning and plotting their future. Thus respecting people's dignity includes respecting their autonomy, their right to control their future'.[138] In the context of compelled obstetric intervention, this would clearly support a woman's right to refuse medical treatment, even when such a refusal may lead to her own death and/or that of the foetus she carries. Whilst autonomy is not an enumerated right in the *Grundgesetz*, it is well accepted that every individual has a right to self-determination. Respect for human dignity requires the state to accept that the woman should be able to decide for herself what medical treatment she wishes to have, to exercise her own autonomy and thus preserve her bodily integrity, even if the cost of that respect is the loss of foetal life.

As the jurisprudence of the *Bundesverfassungsgericht* clearly demonstrates, what is meant by human dignity will vary depending upon the life phase of the subject of the protection and the situation she finds herself in; it will not always require the protection of life. A good example of this outside the abortion context is provided by the Aviation Security Act case, 2006. Reviewing the constitutionality of the Aviation Security Act,[139] the court found § 14 III LuftSiG to infringe the right to life in conjunction with human dignity (Art. 2 II s.1 and 1 I GG).[140] § 14 III LuftSiG is an example of a legislative provision that authorises an infringement of the right to life (in accordance with Art. 2 II s.3 GG); in this case the provision permitted the Minister of Defence to order the shooting down of a plane where the circumstances were such that it could be assumed that the plane was intended to be used against human life and armed force was the only means of averting the danger. It was intended to deal with situations such as the 9/11 bombings, where four planes were hijacked and crashed killing more than 3,000 people. As in its abortion decisions, the *Bundesverfassungsgericht* again stressed the link between the right to life and human dignity, stating that the provision authorising the infringement of Art. 2 II s.1 GG 'must be viewed in the light of [that] fundamental right and the closely associated guarantee of human dignity … Human life is the living basis of human dignity, the primary constitutional principle

136 G. Dürig, 'Der Grundsatz von der Menschenwürde' (1956) 81 *Archiv des öffentlichen Rechts* 117, at 127.

137 I. Kant, 'Grundlegung zur Metaphysik der Sitten' in J. Timmermann (ed.) *Sammlung Philosophie*, Göttingen: Vandenhoeck & Ruprecht, 2004, vol. 3, at 44, Rn. 49.

138 J. Raz, *The Authority of Law: Essays on Law and Morality*, 2nd edn, Oxford: Oxford University Press, 2009, at 221.

139 Luftsicherheitsgesetz (LuftSiG) 11.01.2005, BGBl. I S. 78.

140 For an excellent discussion of this case in English, see K. Moller, 'On Treating Persons as Ends: The German Aviation Security Act, Human Dignity, and the German Federal Constitutional Court' (2006) *Public Law* 457.

and supreme constitutional value'.[141] It considered the relationship between the right to life and the guarantee of human dignity, holding that whilst the state is required to protect all human life, particularly from third-party interference, it may not disrespect human dignity in so doing.[142]

Having thus opened the way to considering the matter under human dignity, the majority went on to outline what the guarantee of human dignity means, conceptualising dignity as both empowerment and restraint. In setting out what the guarantee of human dignity requires of the state, the court emphasised that the authors of the *Grundgesetz* had conceptualised both the liberty to decide for oneself and to develop freely on the one hand, together with the right to demand recognition as an equal and intrinsically valuable member of the community on the other, as inherent elements of personhood. The *Bundesverfassungsgericht* continued:

> Much more generally the duty to respect and protect human dignity excludes treating a human being as a mere object of the state. Therefore every dealing of a public authority with a person, that fundamentally questions her subjectivity, her status as a legal entity in that it fails to accord due respect to the value that every person is accorded in her own right, because of her own personhood, is clearly forbidden.[143]

The court held that the contested provision infringed Art. 1 I GG on the basis that the state would treat the innocent crew and passengers (but interestingly not the hijackers whose subjectivity was considered to be reinforced by the official response to their actions)[144] as mere objects, sacrificing them to save the lives of others.[145] The fact that the passengers would be killed anyway was irrelevant. The majority held that such action would fail to recognise those affected as subjects with dignity and inalienable rights. Killing the victims, who were themselves in need of protection, as a means to save others would reduce the victims to objects and simultaneously deprive them of their rights.[146]

As Bernhard Schlink has recognised, 'Objectifications, instrumentalisations and sacrifices are sometimes justified, but only sometimes, and then they are also compatible with the dignity of the sacrificed'.[147] In the present context there is a clear concern that failure to respect a woman's refusal of consent to obstetric intervention intended to benefit the foetus will instrumentalise her to the extent that she is reduced to the status of an 'incubator on legs', a foetal environment. Such objectification can no more be demanded of a pregnant woman for the

141 *BVerfGE* 115, 118 (2006, Aviation Security Act), at 152.
142 *BVerfGE* 115, 118, at 152.
143 *BVerfGE* 115, 118, at 153, internal references omitted.
144 *BVerfGE* 115, 118, at 161.
145 *BVerfGE* 115, 118, at 154.
146 *BVerfGE* 115, 118, at 154.
147 B. Schlink, *Aktuelle Fragen des pränatalen Lebensschutzes*, Berlin: Walter De Gruyter, 2002, at 11.

benefit of her foetus than it can be demanded of aircraft passengers for the benefit of others, despite the recognisable relationship between the woman and her foetus, a matter to which I return in Part C. However, as discussed above, dignity may also be construed as requiring the protection of unborn life, in this context by imposing a duty upon the woman to submit to obstetric treatment for the benefit of the foetus. Therefore in this, as in other matters, dignity is capable of supporting both sides of the argument. The inherent vagueness of the concept of human dignity leaves it open to criticism; as Josef Isensee notes, 'The suspicion arises that the fundamental constitutional principle is nothing more than a constitutional decoration'.[148] However, it is submitted that Art. 1 I GG should not be viewed in isolation, that it needs to be considered in conjunction with the other fundamental rights engaged, in this case the rights to life, bodily integrity and self-determination. So regarded, this flexible approach to the protection of dignity provides a useful mechanism that may be utilised to mitigate the effect of finding that the life of the foetus is protected under Art. 2 II GG; it functions as an aid to reconciling competing interests in an area where a balance cannot be achieved – either the woman's rights or those of the foetus must prevail.

In the Anglo-American obstetric intervention case law the foetus has generally been viable; therefore it is argued that the foetus should be granted a high level of protection. However, as the *Bundesverfassungsgericht* made clear in its second abortion decision, protection can be afforded through means other than the criminal law. All members of the court in both abortion decisions agreed that the foetus has a right to life; however, there was disagreement about how the state could fulfil its obligation to protect foetal life. The legislation at issue in both cases sought to decriminalise abortion in certain circumstances, but the *Bundesverfassungsgericht* held that as abortion terminates the life of the foetus, abortion can never be lawful. It can be justified (and therefore be classified as 'not unlawful') where it would not be reasonable to expect the woman to continue the pregnancy – for example, in the case of risk to life or health, or on the basis of an embryopathic or criminological indication – but all other abortions must continue to bear the stigma of being unlawful. In Abortion I the majority of the court held that such abortions must remain a criminal offence, that no other tool was available to the state capable of providing sufficient protection to foetal life. However, whilst the majority of the *Bundesverfassungsgericht* held that the use of criminal law was necessary to sufficiently protect the foetus, the dissenting judges argued that the best protection for the foetus comes from the woman herself and that other means could better persuade her to continue the pregnancy than criminal sanctions.[149] Indeed, one of the shifts evident between the decisions in Abortion I and Abortion II is that in Abortion II the majority accepted this argument, moving from a duty to protect the foetus that categorised the woman as an aggressor to a conception that framed her as a collaborator, as someone whose cooperation is essential in safeguarding the foetus.[150]

148 J. Isensee (note 134), at 182.
149 *BVerfGE* 39, 1, at 79.
150 *BVerfGE* 88, 203, at 266.

In the present context it is suggested that the state's duty to protect foetal life could be satisfied by seeking to persuade the woman to accept treatment for the benefit of the foetus and by supporting women throughout pregnancy in the hope of avoiding (as far as possible) the crisis situations that dominate the Anglo-American case law. Whilst the loss of foetal life due to the woman's refusal of treatment would be extremely regrettable, a one-sided consideration of human dignity cannot be permitted; it cannot be allowed to become what Norbert Hoerster termed a 'blank cheque for personal value judgements'.[151] The principle of human dignity thus demands that the recognition of the foetus as a beneficiary of human dignity should not eclipse respect for the woman's own dignity, dignity that requires that her autonomy, her bodily integrity and her life be respected. The imposition of a duty to protect the foetus will not in itself undermine the woman's dignity, provided that the scope of the duty imposed is consistent with maintaining the woman's own dignity. Thus the duty imposed must be both proportionate and reasonable. An absolute duty to protect the foetus would be incompatible with the woman's dignity and a proportionate solution must be found that sufficiently protects foetal life, without disproportionately restricting the woman's right to self-determination and bodily integrity. I return to the question of the scope of the woman's duty to protect the foetus below, but it is clear that the guarantee of human dignity plays a pivotal role in the assessment of that duty and it is suggested that all that doctors and state actors can do in the face of a woman's treatment refusal is to recognise her as an individual with her own beliefs and values and try to persuade her to accept treatment for the benefit of the foetus. Any positive action would infringe upon her dignity as well as constitute a battery.

e. The woman's right to self-determination and bodily integrity

In *Roe v Wade*[152] the US Supreme Court prioritised women's agency, holding that a woman's right to privacy encompasses the right to elect an abortion (in consultation with her doctor) during the first two trimesters of pregnancy, free of state control other than that designed to protect maternal health.[153] Faced with similar questions about the regulation of abortion two years later, the German *Bundesverfassungsgericht* emphasised that women have a duty to continue the pregnancy and that a woman's right to self-determination cannot trump the right to life.[154] As in Anglo-American law, German law recognises the right of an adult with capacity to refuse medical treatment, including life-sustaining medical treatment for any reason at all.[155] Art. 2 I GG protects both the right to life and the right to

151 N. Hoerster, 'Zur Bedeutung des Prinzips der Menschenwürde' (1983) *Juristische Schulung* 93, at 96.
152 *Roe v Wade* (note 2).
153 *Roe v Wade* (note 2), at 154, 163. Note, in *Planned Parenthood v Casey* (note 10) the US Supreme Court based the woman's right on the right to autonomy, and held that it included the woman's right to elect an abortion prior to viability.
154 *BVerfGE* 39, 1, at 43.
155 *BGHSt* 11, 111, at 114.

bodily integrity, and the fact that an individual with capacity can refuse life-sustaining treatment demonstrates clearly that the right to life will not necessarily outrank the right to bodily integrity. Similarly, it is well recognised that individuals, including pregnant women, have a constitutionally protected right to self-determination, although the right is not enumerated in the constitution and the basis upon which it is protected is the subject of significant debate.

Typically, the right to self-determination is viewed as being anchored in either the general right to personality (derived from a combination of Art. 2 I and Art. 1 I GG),[156] or the right to bodily integrity (Art. 2 II s.1 GG).[157] However, some commentators go further, founding the right to self-determination on a broader combination of constitutional protections. For example, Adolf Laufs argues that patient autonomy is based upon the guarantee of human dignity, together with the rights to personality, life and bodily integrity (Art. 1 I, 2 I and 2 II GG).[158] This broader, more inclusive view of self-determination has much to recommend it; the principle lies at the very heart of the rights and dignity guaranteed by Art. 1 and 2 GG and, as Friedhelm Hufen suggests, self-determination is the 'core of human dignity'.[159] Clearly, each of these protections are closely related and together they ensure that within the doctor–patient relationship the patient's will, rational or irrational, right or wrong, will determine whether or not medical treatment can be lawfully provided.[160] Although no consensus exists as to the basis of protection, it is clear that the right to self-determination is protected by the constitution. As Horst Dreier maintains, 'constitutional freedom entails self-determination of one's own life plan and its execution. And that applies to old and young, to the healthy and sick'.[161] This chapter will argue that it applies equally to pregnant women as well!

aa. Medical treatment as a trespass to the person

One expression of the woman's rights to self-determination and bodily integrity is the right to refuse medical treatment. As the *Bundesgerichtshof* stressed in 1957, a patient may refuse treatment, including life-sustaining treatment, for any reason.[162] Indeed, the courts have long recognised that medical treatment requires prior, informed consent, absent an emergency situation.[163] A refusal of consent to medical

156 *BVerfGE* 52, 131, at 168 (majority opinion).
157 *BVerfGE* 52, 131, at 174 (dissent).
158 A. Laufs, in A. Laufs and W. Uhlenbruck, *Handbuch des Arztrechts*, München: C.H. Beck, 3rd edn, 2002, § 61, Rn. 14.
159 F. Hufen, 'In dubio pro dignitate' (2001) *NJW* 849, at 851.
160 *BVerfGE* 89, 120, at 130.
161 H. Dreier, 'Die Freiheit des Andershandelnden', *Frankfurter Allgemeine Zeitung*, 30.08.2008, at 8.
162 *BGHSt* 11, 114.
163 See, for example, *RGSt* 25, 375, at 377; *RGSt* 38, 34; *RGZ* 68, 431, at 433; *BGHSt* 11, 111, at 112; 16, 309; 35, 246; *BGHZ* 29, 46, at 49; *BGHZ* 29, 176, at 179; *BVerfGE* 128, 282, at 302–3. The requirement of prior informed consent was recently inserted into the BGB as § 630 d BGB, *Gesetz zur Verbesserung der Rechte von Patientinnen und Patienten* (Act for the Improvement of Patient Rights), 20.02.2013, BGBl. I S.277.

treatment will bind the doctor, regardless of whether she agrees with it or regards it as irrational. As the *Bundesgerichtshof* categorically stated:

> The right to bodily integrity guaranteed in Art. 2 II s.1 GG demands respect even in the case of a person who refuses to sacrifice his bodily integrity where he would be saved from a life-threatening condition. Nobody may appoint herself as judge in the question of in which circumstances another should sensibly be prepared to sacrifice her bodily integrity in order to get better. This rule is also binding upon a doctor… . Even a patient whose life is in danger can have cogent reasons to refuse an operation, reasons that are both humanly and ethically respectable, even where she would be saved by the operation, and only by it, from her suffering.[164]

Treatment in contravention of a valid refusal will constitute a battery (§ 223 StGB).[165] For more than 120 years the German courts have conceptualised medical treatment as a battery requiring consent to justify it.[166] Thus in 1894 the *Reichsgericht* pointed out that the fact that a doctor considers herself better able to understand the true interests of a patient, and better able to foster her physical or mental well-being, than the person herself, does not entitle the doctor to treat a patient without consent.[167] From this decision onwards the courts have consistently prioritised the patient's right to self-determination over the doctor's ability to treat her, recognising that just because a doctor can treat somebody, she doesn't have a right to do so against the patient's will. Instead, the patient's consent will be required to justify the touching, even where the treatment is indicated, successful and performed in accordance with professional standards. In the case of an emergency, necessity (§ 34 StGB) will operate to justify treatment if the patient's wishes are not known, but treatment provided in contravention of the patient's refusal (contemporaneous, advance or presumed (*mutmaßlicher Wille*)) will not be justified, even in the case of life-sustaining treatment.[168]

§ 223 StGB defines battery as the physical abuse or injury to health of another person and, in contrast to the case law, the dominant view in the literature is that as medical treatment is intended to benefit the patient it will not fulfil this

164 *Myom* case, *BGHSt* 11, 111, at 113f.

165 § 229 StGB proscribes negligent personal injury. Whilst the majority of cases involving a doctor will ultimately be adjudged to be cases of negligent rather than intentional personal injury, it is suggested in this instance, where a doctor intentionally operates upon a woman against her will and for the benefit of a third party, the offence of intentional personal injury, § 223 StGB, will be made out.

166 *RGSt* 25, 375, at 378; *BGHSt* 11, 111, at 112; *BGHZ* 29, 46, at 49; *BGHZ* 106, 391, 397f.; 12, 379; 16, 309. For a detailed consideration of the categorisation of medical treatment as personal injury, see B. Tag, *Der Körperverletzungstatbestand im Spannungsfeld zwischen Patientenautonomie und Lex Artis: Eine arztstrafrechtliche Untersuchung*, Heidelberg: Springer, 2000.

167 Ibid., at 378.

168 *BGHSt* 11, 111, at 113f.

definition.[169] Some commentators adopt a result-orientated definition of battery, arguing that medical treatment cannot fulfil the statutory criteria if it is successful, on the basis that it is not the act of treatment but rather the consequence of treatment that is determinative. According to this view, if the treatment is successful, the patient's physical well-being is not negatively impacted, whilst if the treatment is unsuccessful, it will not improve the patient's well-being and will fulfil the objective element of the offence.[170] Other authors argue that only if the doctor fails to meet professional standards of practice will medical treatment be capable of constituting a battery.[171] Although the basis for the conclusion is debated, the consensus in the literature is that medical treatment will not normally satisfy the requirements of § 223 StGB.

The desire to avoid tarring medical treatment with the same brush as a stabbing is understandable; indeed, a scalpel when utilised by a doctor may not be considered a weapon or even a dangerous instrument within the meaning of § 224 I 2 StGB,[172] because, as the *Bundesgerichtshof* explained, medical instruments such as scalpels and syringes are utilised for the purpose of healing, not for attack or defence.[173] However, the social utility of medical treatment is less obvious in the case of coerced treatment, particularly where that treatment is intended to serve the good of another individual rather than the community at large.

The literature emphasises the benevolence of medical treatment, that the doctor's intention is to improve the patient's health, but, in the context of obstetric intervention to treat the foetal patient, the doctor must 'invade' the woman's body to obtain access to her patient. Such treatment is not intended to benefit the woman's health and, particularly in the case of more major interventions such as a

169 See, for example, P. Bockelmann, *Strafrecht des Arztes*, Stuttgart: Thieme, 1968, 66ff.; E. Schmidt, *Der Arzt im Strafrecht*, Leipzig: T. Weicher, 1939, 69ff.; H. Lilie, in *LK*, Vor § 223, Rn. 3ff.; A. Eser, in *Schönke/Schröder*, § 223, Rn. 30, with further references. Some of the more recent literature supports the position taken by the courts; see, for example, P. Cramer, 'Ein Sonderstraftatbestand für die eigenmächtige Heilbehandlung. Einige Bemerkungen zu §§ 229, 230 des Entwurfs eines 6. Gesetzes zur Reform des Strafrechts (6. StrRG)' in A. Eser et al. (eds) *Festschrift für Theodor Lenckner zum 70. Geburtstag*, München: C.H. Beck, 1998, 761, at 773f.; V. Krey and M. Heinrich, *Strafrecht Besonderer Teil: Band 1, Besonderer Teil ohne Vermögensdelikte*, 15th edn, Stuttgart: Kohlhammer, 2012, Rn. 219; G. Küpper, *Strafrecht Besonderer Teil I: Delikte gegen Rechtsgüter der Person und Gemeinschaft*, 3rd edn, Springer: Berlin, 2007, § 2, Rn. 13; W. Mitsch, *Strafrechtlicher Schutz gegen medizinische Behandlung. Zur Problematik des ärztlichen Heileingriffs*, Baden-Baden: Nomos, 2000, at 22.

170 P. Bockelmann, *Strafrecht des Arztes* (note 169), at 66ff.; P. Bockelmann, 'Der ärztliche Heileingriff in Beiträgen zur Zeitschrift für die gesamte Strafrechtswissenschaft im ersten Jahrhundert ihres Bestehens' (1981) 93 *Zeitschrift für die gesamte Strafrechtswissenschaft* 103, at 124ff.; W. Hardwig, 'Betrachtungen zur Frage des Heileingriffes' (1965) *Goltdammer's Archiv* 161, at 163.

171 K. Engisch, 'Ärztlicher Eingriff zu Heilzwecken und Einwilligung' (1939) 58 *Zeitschrift für die gesamte Strafrechtswissenschaft* 1, at 5; E. Schmidt, *Der Arzt im Strafrecht* (note 169), 1939, at 90.

172 Causing bodily injury by dangerous means.

173 *BGH* NJW 1978, 1206; NStZ 1987, 174; but cf. *BGH NJW* 2011, 1088, the so called '*Zitronensaftfall*' (lemon juice case), B. Hardtung, in *MüKo-StGB*, § 224, Rn. 42–3.

caesarean or instrumental delivery, is not without risk to the woman's physical health. Moreover, it is one thing to argue that treatment will not constitute a battery, and thus that there is no need for justification in the form of the patient's consent, but it is another thing entirely to argue that obstetric intervention can occur not merely without the consent of the woman but in the face of her refusal, as has occurred in cases in both the United States of America and England and Wales. Therefore, in the current context, if a woman refuses treatment, it would be inappropriate to view the obstetric intervention as anything other than a trespass to the person, and the approach of the courts is to be preferred, regardless of the ongoing broader debate about the categorisation of medical treatment as a trespass to the person.[174]

bb. The Bundesverfassungsgericht's conceptualisation of a woman's right to self-determination and bodily integrity in the context of abortion

The abortion slogan '*Mein Bauch gehört mir*'[175] gives voice to women's claims to bodily integrity, to their right to self-determination and indeed to their own dignity. However, the *Bundesverfassungsgericht* has taken a much narrower view of the woman's rights in the abortion context. In its first abortion decision the court's consideration of the woman's right to self-determination focused upon her right to personality, a catch-all right that acts as a fallback position where no other specific right provides the requisite protection.[176] The right encompasses both freedom of action and the protection of a private sphere of life. Therefore it acts as a sword in allowing the individual to do whatever she wants (subject to the rights of others, the constitutional order and morality) and as a shield by designating a protected private sphere into which the state may not encroach. Pregnancy undoubtedly falls within this protected private sphere and the court recognised that a woman's right to freedom of action encompasses the right to decide against parenthood and its duties, but stressed that the right is not unlimited and that it could never include the authority to destroy the life of another, especially as the woman bears a particular responsibility for the existence of the life in question.[177]

One of the key shifts between the two abortion decisions concerns the view of women adopted by the court. In Abortion I the court viewed pregnancy as part of the woman's natural role, referring to women rejecting pregnancy 'because they are not willing to accept the accompanying sacrifices and the natural maternal duties'.[178] The duty to continue a pregnancy to term, unless a justification for

174 Whilst it is possible that a doctor treating a patient against her will could incur liability under §§ 239, 240 StBG (unlawful imprisonment and the unlawful use of force or threats of harm to cause a person to suffer an act), it is unlikely that the offences will be made out due to the lack a suitable means of coercion – physical compulsion or threat of serious harm as required by § 240 StGB.

175 My stomach belongs to me.

176 *BVerfGE* 6, 32, at 37.

177 *BVerfGE* 39, 1, at 43.

178 *BVerfGE* 39, 1, at 55.

termination exists, was regarded as merely requiring women to fulfil their natural role; thus, in protecting life, the court viewed the state's role as being to attempt to reawaken the maternal protective instinct.[179] By contrast, in the German Democratic Republic (GDR) early abortion was freely available, lawful and without charge from 1972 when the Act relating to the interruption of pregnancy was passed. Three years before the *Bundesverfassungsgericht* delivered its first abortion decision, that Act's preamble emphasised that access to abortion is an integral part of women's equality and that the responsibility for the decision whether to continue a pregnancy or not must rest with the woman concerned, stating: 'The equality of women in education and career, marriage and family requires that the woman can decide herself about whether to continue a pregnancy to term'.[180]

In *Roe*, the US Supreme Court did not express itself in such paternalistic tones as the *Bundesverfassungsgericht*, but it did qualify the decision to abort as one to be exercised in conjunction with her doctor, despite it being a part of her right to privacy. Twenty years later, when the Supreme Court revisited the matter in *Casey*, the plurality opinion emphasised:

> The liberty of the woman is at stake in a sense unique to the human condition and so unique to the law. The mother who carries a child to full term is subject to anxieties, to physical constraints, to pain that only she must bear. That these sacrifices have from the beginning of the human race been endured by woman with a pride that ennobles her in the eyes of others and gives to the infant a bond of love cannot alone be grounds for the State to insist she make the sacrifice. Her suffering is too intimate and personal for the State to insist, without more, upon its own vision of the woman's role, however dominant that vision has been in the course of our history and our culture. The destiny of the woman must be shaped to a large extent on her own conception of her spiritual imperatives and her place in society.[181]

By contrast with the emphasis placed upon individualism in the American abortion jurisprudence[182] and the GDR's legislation, the *Bundesverfassungsgericht* stressed the social and relational aspects of pregnancy.[183] In Abortion I the court emphasised the objective values that ground the duty to protect human life,[184] whilst in Abortion II it adopted the position that the best way to protect the foetus is for the state to cooperate with the woman.[185] Highlighting the relationship between

179 *BVerfGE* 39, 1, at 45.

180 *Gesetz über die Unterbrechung der Schwangerschaft* of 9.3.1972, GBl DDR 1972 I, S.89.

181 *Planned Parenthood of Southeastern Pennsylvania v Casey* (note 10), at 852.

182 See, for example, *Planned Parenthood of Southeastern Pennsylvania v Casey* (note 10), at 852.

183 For an interesting analysis of the juxtaposition between the communitarian and individualist stances of the two courts, see C. McCrudden (note 104).

184 *BVerfGE* 39, 1, at 41.

185 *BVerfGE* 88, 203, at 266–7.

the pregnant woman and the foetus, the court found that rather than regarding the two entities as adversaries (with the foetal life being protected against the pregnant woman), the state should view the woman herself as a source of protection for the foetus and attempt to persuade her to continue the pregnancy. Although the court did not go as far as holding that the pregnant woman's right to self-determination will encompass a right to elect an abortion, it did accept that women would not incur criminal liability for having an abortion within 12 weeks of pregnancy, subject to undergoing compulsory pro-life counselling three days before the procedure. Importantly, such counselling-based abortions are not subject to a third-party determining that the woman has just cause to have an abortion. Therefore, whilst not wholeheartedly embracing the woman's right to self-determination as including a right to elect an early abortion, the *Bundesverfassungsgericht* did at least move some way in that direction, ostensibly retaining its commitment to the protection of foetal life throughout pregnancy by virtue of the compulsory counselling.

In its abortion decisions, the court expressed the limitations of a woman's right to self-determination in the abortion context, but an important distinction arises between the typical form of abortion (where a pregnancy is actively terminated) and the termination of pregnancy by omission which forms the focus of this book. Where a woman refuses treatment necessary to save the foetus, there can be no suggestion that she exercises her right to self-determination in order to terminate the pregnancy; rather, the termination of pregnancy will be the consequence of the woman's refusal of treatment in the exercise of her right to self-determination. This is clearly a crucial distinction and it is suggested that in the context of obstetric intervention a significantly higher weight will have to be accorded to the woman's right to self-determination than is the case in the typical termination of pregnancy.

f. Reconciling the rights and interests involved

As will be apparent from the discussion above, the rights and protection of the woman and foetus cannot be symmetrical; there are significant differences between the two and it is suggested that the key to navigating the conflict that arises between the rights and interests involved lies in the proper application of the protection of human dignity. In its first decision the *Bundesverfassungsgericht* recognised the unattainability of a compromise guaranteeing the protection of foetal life and the woman's freedom to terminate her pregnancy, given that abortion necessarily destroys the foetal life. It held that the conflicting constitutional values must be weighed by reference to their relationship with the protection of human dignity, the epicentre of the constitutional value system.[186] However, in weighing the conflicting interests, the impact of dignity was only discussed in relation to the foetus; there was no consideration of the impact of dignity on the weight to be accorded to the woman's right to self-determination. Instead, a one-dimensional

186 *BVerfGE* 39, 1, at 43, citing *BVerfGE* 35, 202, at 225.

view of dignity was promoted, with the court holding that the protection of dignity requires the protection of human life, and that such protection will outweigh the woman's right to self-determination throughout the pregnancy.[187] Thus in its first decision the *Bundesverfassungsgericht* adopted the formulation of dignity as restraint. In Abortion II the court derived the protection of human life not from objective constitutional norms, but rather from the protection of human dignity (Art. 1 I GG). It held that the object and scope of the protection were determined by the application of Art. 2 II GG. Thus conceived, it inevitably prioritised the protection of foetal life over the unrestricted self-determination of the woman. However, the court also recognised that the woman's dignity, bodily integrity (Art. 2 II) and right to personality (Art. 2 I GG) must be protected, decreeing that a proportionate solution must be devised by the legislature that breached neither the *Untermassverbot* (providing insufficient protection of foetal life) nor the *Übermassverbot*, disproportionately restricting the woman's right to self-determination.[188]

According to the *Übermassverbot*, fundamental rights may be limited for the purpose of protecting the rights of others, or even for the general good, but only to the extent necessary to achieve that aim. By contrast, the *Untermassverbot* requires that measures taken to protect a legal interest achieve at least the minimum level of protection necessary. Any restriction of the woman's rights must therefore be appropriate to achieve that protection and must also represent the least possible interference with the woman's rights; a duty that imposed unreasonable expectations upon the pregnant woman would exceed the *Übermassverbot* and would thus fail the proportionality test. In such cases – for example, where the continuance of the pregnancy poses a threat to the woman's life or health – a justification will exist, so that the duty need not be imposed, or perhaps even should not be imposed.

Recognising that cooperation with the pregnant woman presents the best opportunity to protect foetal life,[189] at least in the early stages of pregnancy where the existence of the embryo remains hidden from the outside world, the *Bundesverfassungsgericht* held that a proportionate response to the conflicting interests of the woman and the foetus would include permitting abortion in situations where it would be unreasonable to impose a duty to continue the pregnancy (where a medical, criminological or embryopathic indication would justify termination). This was consistent with its earlier decision, but the court went on to find that, absent a justificatory indication, a woman could still be free to make a choice to terminate the pregnancy throughout the first trimester, provided that she underwent counselling designed to encourage women to continue their pregnancies. It found that the state could provide the necessary minimum of protection of foetal life by requiring that the woman undergo counselling, by providing support (such as childcare facilities) for bringing up children, and by maintaining the position

187 *BVerfGE* 39, 1, at 43.
188 *BVerfGE* 88, 203, at 254ff.
189 *BVerfGE* 88, 203, at 266.

that non-justified abortion is unlawful throughout pregnancy. Nevertheless, it found that effective protection would not require the imposition of criminal penalties upon women having an abortion during the first trimester following counselling. In relation to the woman's rights, the court found that such counselling (which would not require the counsellor to approve the woman's reasons for wanting a termination, but merely to conduct the counselling) would comply with the duty to respect the woman's dignity.[190] Thus the prolife counselling now enshrined in § 219 StGB forms an integral part of the protection of foetal life.

The protection of human dignity requires that both the foetal life and the woman's autonomy and bodily integrity be protected, but, as the court's abortion jurisprudence demonstrates, that is possible. On the one hand, the foetal life is protected throughout pregnancy in the sense that a woman is never able to elect an abortion without any form of counterbalance to her right to self-determination. Where a threat to her life or health (broadly defined) exists, clearly her right to life (Art. 2 II GG) will outweigh that of the foetus; outside such a situation, she can only access abortion by undergoing pro-life counselling designed to encourage her to continue the pregnancy to term. However, provided that she undergoes the required counselling she is able to exercise her right to self-determination and elect an early abortion, albeit having been subjected to mandatory counselling designed to assist her to reach a 'responsible and conscientious' decision about terminating the pregnancy. Clearly, the imposition of such a requirement treats women as less able to make a responsible decision without external assistance, and it is regrettable that the *Bundesverfassungsgericht* held that abortions performed after counselling must continue to bear the stigma of being designated unlawful. As Mahrenholz and Sommer JJ (dissenting) pointed out, the label 'unlawful' contributes nothing to the state's protection of unborn life.[191] It is submitted that this is correct: there is little dignity in being forced to undergo compulsory pro-life counselling, to be told that the foetus has a right to life, and that if you go ahead with a termination, you will act unlawfully, but will not be punished. This suggests that women do have autonomy, but can only exercise it if they jump through hoops arrayed in front of them by the state and are then still treated as law-breakers. The stigma remains, and, of course, the practical impact is that the abortion will not be covered by healthcare insurance.

In the context of obstetric intervention, it is clear that the guarantee of human dignity, in combination with Art. 2 II GG will require that the foetal life is protected; however, when viewed against the backdrop of the object formula, it is clear that the woman's autonomy must be prioritised, to avoid the instrumentalisation of the woman, the reduction of her worth to her reproductive capacity. As will be suggested below, the state will be able to fulfil its duty to protect foetal life by engaging with the woman, by supporting her throughout the pregnancy and by requiring that she makes a conscientious decision to refuse treatment required

190 *BVerfGE* 88, 203, at 265ff.
191 *BVerfGE* 88, 203, at 348.

to safeguard the foetus. However, there can be no case for compelled treatment in order to protect the foetus.

3. Crimes against life committed by omission

By comparison with the law in England and Wales and the United States of America, German law recognises a much broader duty to rescue. The significance of criminal liability for omissions to rescue is particularly important in relation to the foetus, as both a pregnant woman and the doctor treating her may be held to have a duty to actively protect the life of the foetus. In the following section I analyse the extent of those duties, considering whether the refusal of consent to, or failure to undertake, obstetric intervention deemed necessary for the survival of the foetus may constitute a termination of pregnancy, or even homicide, by omission, rendering both the pregnant woman and her doctor criminally liable.

a. The tripartite structure of offences: Tatbestand, Rechtswidrigkeit *and* Schuldhaftigkeit

German criminal law is based upon a tripartite structure of offences requiring three elements to be satisfied for the imposition of criminal liability. The first element, *Tatbestandmäßigkeit*, requires consideration of whether the defendant has fulfilled the objective (*actus reus*) and subjective (*mens rea*) components of the offence. In the case of § 218 StGB the offence consists of intentionally terminating a pregnancy and thereby causing the death of the foetus. As discussed above, German law adopts a much broader conception of the crime of abortion than English and American law; thus the *actus reus* does not require the destruction of the foetus (the subject of the protection afforded by § 218 StGB) to result from a positive act, although that will typically be the case. Instead, liability may be based upon an omission to maintain the pregnancy, or preserve foetal life where the law imposes a duty to act to prevent harm to the foetus (the legally protected interest), the *Garantenstellung*. A doctor treating a pregnant woman will owe a duty of care towards the foetus, being categorised as a *Beschützergarantin* (protective guarantor) with a duty to protect its life. One example of a situation in which a doctor would be under a duty to act to protect foetal life is where a pregnancy has continued for more than 42 weeks, it being well recognised that there is a significant risk of stillbirth if pregnancy continues past that point. Therefore, induction of labour will be indicated in such cases and the doctor who fails to induce labour, where it was possible to do so, may face liability for termination of pregnancy if the foetus, or indeed the baby born, dies as a result of this omission (§§ 218, 13 StGB).[192] Similarly, a pregnant woman, also categorised as a protective guarantor owing a duty of care towards the foetus, may face liability if she refuses to consent to a medically indicated caesarean necessary to ensure the safe delivery of the foetus and the foetus dies as a result (§§ 218, 13 StGB).

192 See also R. Merkel, in *NK-StGB*, § 218, Rn. 116; P. Kröger, in *LK*, § 218, Rn. 24.

Therefore, whilst the typical case of termination of pregnancy will involve an active intervention, normally terminating the foetal life within the uterus, it is clear that the objective element of the crime may be satisfied by an omission where an individual (in this case both the pregnant woman and the doctor) has a legal duty of care to prevent the death of the foetus and it was possible to do so, but failure to act led to the death of the foetus. Causation will be established if active intervention by way of the provision or acceptance of medical treatment on the part of the guarantor would have prevented the foetus's death or prolonged its life.[193] The omission need not be the sole cause of death, but quasi-causation must be established, whereby it must be demonstrated with a probability bordering on certainty[194] that the foetus would not have died if the treatment had been given.[195] However, it should be recognised that in the case of omitted obstetric intervention it will be extremely difficult to prove causation due to the difficulties in discharging the evidential burden that, had treatment been provided, the foetus would have survived. Whilst medical evidence may suggest that the foetus would have been likely to survive if the treatment had been provided, that will not suffice; rather, the standard required is that of a probability bordering upon certainty. As a result of this high burden of proof, it is suggested that any liability incurred will be for an attempt, a crucial distinction given that liability for an attempted termination of pregnancy is excluded in the case of the pregnant woman (§ 218 IV StGB).[196]

As considered above, one of the distinctions between the protection afforded to the life and bodily integrity of persons, as opposed to the foetus, is that the subjective component of § 218 StGB requires intention; negligence will not suffice. Therefore it must be considered whether the doctor's failure to provide treatment or the woman's refusal of consent to treatment necessary for the preservation of the foetal life can amount to the intentional termination of pregnancy. Significantly, unlike England and Wales and the United States of America, German law does not recognise a separate category of recklessness; it distinguishes merely between intent and negligence. However, intention is much more broadly construed than in common law jurisdictions, encompassing three forms: *dolus directus* I, where the harmful consequence was directly intended by the defendant; *dolus directus II*, where the harmful consequence was not sought by the defendant, but she recognised that the consequences were almost inevitable); and *dolus eventualis*, or conditional intention, where the defendant recognised that the harmful outcome was possible (although not inevitable) and was positively disposed towards, or at least reconciled to, the outcome.

In the case of a typical termination of pregnancy the death of the foetus will be directly intended (*dolus directus* I), but in cases that do not involve a positive action – for example, where a woman refuses medical treatment required to preserve the foetal life – such intention is unlikely to be present. In such cases it is

193 P. Kröger, in *LK*, § 218, Rn. 18.

194 *Eine an Sicherheit grenzender Wahrscheinlichkeit, BGHSt* 43, 381, 397.

195 *BGH* NJW 2000, 2754, 2757; NJW 2010, 1087, 1090; NJW 2015, 96.

196 The exclusion of liability only applies to the pregnant woman herself; thus the question of liability for an attempt is still of relevance in the case of the doctor who fails to intervene.

irrelevant that the foetus was not the victim of a direct attack, that its death was not the desired outcome of the woman's refusal of treatment, but rather an undesired consequence of that decision. The woman must act *wissentlich* and *willentlich* – that is, with knowledge and volition. The knowledge that the foetus will die, or at least that it might die without the intervention, will fulfil the *Wissen* requirement, but a degree of volition is also required in order to establish intent. In the case of termination of pregnancy, intention may take the form of *dolus eventualis*,[197] so that if either the doctor or the pregnant woman fails to act, knowingly running the risk that the foetus will die, and being at least reconciled to that result, she will be taken to have the requisite intent. However, where, for example, the woman does not accept the risk that the foetus will die, but rather earnestly trusts that it will not, perhaps believing that God will intervene to save the foetus, she will lack the necessary intent, her mental state being categorised as non-culpable conscious negligence (*bewusste Fahrlässigkeit.*)

If the stipulated objective and subjective components of the offence are made out, *Rechtswidrigkeit* (unlawfulness) must be considered. The question of whether the defendant's conduct was unlawful requires consideration of whether or not her conduct may be justified, and therefore not unlawful; thus it must be considered whether self-defence (§ 32 StGB), necessity (§ 34 StGB) or one of the abortion-specific justifications (§ 218a II, III StGB) might justify the failure to act. In the absence of justification, *Schuldhaftigkeit* (culpability) falls to be considered, which will incorporate an assessment of whether an excusatory defence can be relied upon by the defendant. Only if each of the three elements of the statutory offence is satisfied will criminal liability be incurred.

b. Derivative crimes of omission

German law recognises that crimes, including the termination of pregnancy, can be committed both by a positive act or an omission in certain circumstances; thus § 13 I StGB imposes liability for an *unechtes Unterlassungsdelikt* (a derivative crime of omission).[198] However, such liability will only be imposed where an individual is under a legal duty to avert harm, where the aversion of harm would have been both possible and *zumutbar* (reasonable) had she acted in accordance with that duty, and where the omission is equivalent to the realisation of the offence through a positive act. In 'result crimes' the equivalence requirement will generally be uncontroversial; thus the offence of terminating a pregnancy (§ 218 StGB) is 'achieved' by the destruction of foetal life, whether by a positive act or an omission.

The imposition of liability for an omission depends upon an individual being categorised as a guarantor (a *Garant*) as a result of the imposition of duty of care (*Garantenstellung*); thus, in the context of obstetric intervention to preserve the

197 A. Eser, in *Schönke/Schröder*, § 218, Rn. 41; *BGH* NJW 1951, 412.

198 By contrast, in the case of an *echtes Unterlassen* (a genuine omission) the crime itself is based upon inactivity as, for example, in § 323c StGB, the crime of failing to effect an easy rescue, *unterlassene Hilfeleistung*.

life of the foetus, it must be considered whether the pregnant woman and her doctor are guarantors, responsible for ensuring the protection and even promotion of foetal welfare, and, if so, the ambit of their duty (*Garantenpflicht*). As will be argued below, in both cases a duty to avert danger to the foetal life will exist due to both the woman and her doctor being categorised as protective guarantors (*Beschützergaranten*). Therefore in cases where a blood transfusion or a caesarean is necessary to preserve the life of the foetus, yet the woman refuses to consent to the intervention, both the doctor and the pregnant woman may face criminal liability for not acting to protect the foetus. For liability to be imposed it must be established that the foetus died as a result of the omission, that it would have been possible and reasonable for the guarantor to act to avert the harm to the foetus, that she had the requisite intention and that neither justificatory nor excusatory defences apply. On the facts of the majority of the cases discussed above – including, for example, the American cases of *Re AC*[199] and *Samantha Burton*[200] and the English cases of *Re MB*[201] and *St George's Healthcare NHS Trust* v *S; R* v *Collins and others, ex parte S*[202] – had the courts not intervened to authorise the performance of a caesarean and the foetus died, any resulting liability would be for termination of pregnancy by omission (§§ 218, 13 I StGB). However, in cases such as *Pemberton*[203] and *Rochdale Healthcare NHS Trust* v *C*,[204] where the dilating contractions have commenced and the woman refuses consent to a caesarean necessary to preserve the life of the foetus, the foetus will be considered to have made the transition from *Leibesfrucht* to *Mensch* so that the doctor's omission to provide obstetric treatment required for the protection of the foetus or the woman's refusal of such treatment, resulting in foetal death, may lead to liability for manslaughter (§§ 212, 13 StGB) or negligent homicide (§§ 222, 13 StGB).

The *Garantenstellung* gives rise to a duty to do everything possible and reasonable to avert the criminalised result.[205] Thus the duty is not absolute; rather, it will depend upon the circumstances being such that it is possible for the guarantor to avert the harm caused by intervening and for the imposition of such a duty to be reasonable. If the guarantor is unable to act, or if her action would not have averted the harm anyway, the objective component of the crime is not satisfied.[206] For example, if the performance of a caesarean would not save the life of the foetus, the doctor will not be required to intervene in such a manner. Moreover, in the case of legal impossibility – for example, where the doctor's inability to intervene is due to the woman's refusal of consent – the doctor's duty to act will lapse. Even in cases where the aversion of harm is possible, the duty to act must

199 573 A.2d 1235 (1990).
200 *Samantha Burton v Florida* 39 So. 3d 263 (Fla. Dist. Ct. App. 2010).
201 [1997] 2 FLR 426.
202 [1999] Fam. 26.
203 *Pemberton v Tallahassee Memorial Regional Medical Center* 66 F.Supp.2d 1247 (N.D. Fla. 1999).
204 [1997] 1 FCR 274.
205 *BGHSt* 37, 106, at 119ff.
206 *Fischer*, § 13, Rn.78.

also be *zumutbar* (reasonable) – that is, it must be reasonable to expect the guarantor to act in such a way as to avoid the harm.

It is clear that fulfilment of the duty will be *unzumutbar* if it would significantly endanger the guarantor's own protected interests.[207] However, there is significant debate about whether a woman can reasonably be expected to endure treatment for the benefit of the foetus against her will. In the light of the *Bundesverfassungsgericht*'s abortion decisions, it is undoubtedly the case that the pregnant woman owes a duty of care towards the foetus, and it may be argued that the more advanced the pregnancy, the greater the scope of that which can be reasonably expected of the woman.[208] However, the duty to protect the foetus is not unlimited. In its second abortion decision the *Bundesverfassungsgericht* defined *Unzumutbarkeit* as entailing an unacceptable sacrifice of the woman's life values, those values that make her an individual,[209] and this would surely include religious beliefs such as those relied upon in *Jefferson*[210] and those personal values held by S in *St Georges*,[211] where she wanted a natural birth in a non-medical setting, yet was unlawfully subjected to a caesarean.

In the context of obstetric intervention for the benefit of the foetus, the woman's duty to act will inevitably require her to sacrifice her own interests to some degree, simply because treatment for the foetus can only be provided through her body with all the risks that entails. However, she is more than a mere vehicle for treating the foetus; in assessing the extent to which she can be expected to accept medical treatment for the benefit of the foetus, her own interests will need to be considered and a balance between the conflicting protected interests must be sought. The German courts have not yet been required to consider whether a woman should be forced to undergo obstetric intervention for the benefit of the foetus, or indeed whether she should be punished for a culpable refusal of treatment resulting in the death of or harm to the foetus/child. Therefore, there is little clarity about when and how a duty to rescue will apply in the obstetric context. What follows attempts to provide an analysis of how that duty might be applied to the two addressees of the duty of care – the pregnant woman and her obstetrician.

c. The pregnant woman as guarantor: the scope and nature of her duty towards the foetus

aa. The pregnant woman's guarantor status

§ 218 StGB prohibits the intentional termination of pregnancy and thereby the killing of the foetus; as a result crime, it may be committed by a positive act, or by

207 *Fischer*, § 13, Rn. 82; W. Stree and N. Bosch, in *Schönke/Schröder*, Vorb zu § 13, Rn. 156.

208 See, for example, A. Eser, in *Schönke/Schröder*, § 218a, Rn. 34; *Lackner/Kühl*, § 218a, Rn. 13, P. Kröger, in *LK*, § 218, Rn. 53; R. Merkel, in *NK-StGB*, § 218, Rn. 107.

209 *BVerfGE* 88, 203, at 257.

210 *Jefferson v Griffin Spalding County Hospital Authority* 274 SE 2d 457 (1981).

211 *St George's Healthcare NHS Trust* v *S*; *R* v *Collins and others, ex parte S* (note 202).

an omission. However, there is no general obligation to actively maintain the life of the foetus; any such duty can only arise from a *Garantenstellung*, and in the case of a termination of foetal life for want of obstetric intervention there are two possible addressees of such a duty – the pregnant woman and her obstetrician. If it can be demonstrated that a duty to avert the death of the foetus existed, that it was possible and reasonable to expect the guarantor to act, liability for termination of pregnancy, or indeed another crime against life, may be incurred, provided that the failure to act led to the death of the foetus and that the defendant had the requisite intent.

The dominant view in the literature is that the natural connection between the woman and the foetus she carries will suffice to found a protective duty of care towards the foetus,[212] but Reinhard Merkel argues that the *Garantenpflicht* is better explained by analogy to the duty imposed upon parents to their children extant, arguing that the duty to act is based on the fact that, outwith rape cases, the woman has created the dangerous situation by becoming pregnant.[213] Whilst Merkel is undoubtedly correct to argue that if the woman were not pregnant, the foetus would not be imperilled by her failure to accept medical treatment (of course, if she had not become pregnant, the foetus would not exist!), it is suggested that the approach adopted by the majority of commentators is to be preferred. The foundation of the duty (the close natural bond between the woman and the foetus) better reflects the relationship between the woman and the foetus, a relationship described as a duality in unity by the *Bundesverfassungsgericht*,[214] emphasising the close bond between the two and the need to enlist the pregnant woman in the promotion of foetal welfare and indeed protection of life.[215] The scope for such cooperation is reduced significantly if the woman and the foetus are framed as antagonists, with the act of conception being categorised as the creation of a dangerous situation.

bb. The scope of the duty owed

Whilst there is no doubt that a woman is a *Garantin* (guarantor) with regard to the foetus she carries and the *Bundesverfassungsgericht* has made it clear that a woman has a duty to continue her pregnancy to full term,[216] there is little clarity about the scope of the duty imposed upon her to actively protect the foetus in terms of accepting medical intervention intended to safeguard the foetus. Thus it is unclear whether that duty – a duty to refrain from terminating the pregnancy – should extend as far as to require the woman to take positive action to ensure the continued welfare of the foetus – for example, by consenting to a blood

212 See, for example, W. Gropp, in *MüKo-StGB*, § 218, Rn. 50, 54; P. Kröger, in *LK*, § 218, Rn. 36; A. Eser, in *Schönke/Schröder*, § 218, Rn. 31; *Fischer*, § 218, Rn. 7.
213 See R. Merkel, in *NK-StGB*, § 218, Rn. 96ff.
214 *BVerfGE* 88, 203, at 253.
215 *BVerfGE* 88, 203, at 266.
216 *BVerfGE* 39 1, 44; 88 203, 253.

transfusion necessary to save its life. Perdita Kröger argues that the woman's duty will include the duty to avert dangers to foetal life, and that this may include a duty to undergo medical treatment for the benefit of the foetus.[217] However, she accepts that a duty to acquiesce to obstetric intervention for the benefit of the foetus, reinforced by criminal sanctions should the woman refuse, cannot be derived from the abortion decisions of the *Bundesverfassungsgericht* as such a duty would render her a mere object.[218] This analysis must be correct. It is one thing for the court to hold that the woman has a duty to continue the pregnancy to term, but it is another thing entirely to argue that she must accept medical intervention to preserve or protect the foetal life, regardless of how that will impact upon her own life, health or even values. The *Garantenstellung* does not define the content or the boundaries of the duty owed; the mere identification of the woman as a guarantor will not suffice to require her to undergo any and all treatment intended to benefit the foetus. Thus, in determining the scope of the duty, the question is not what *could* a guarantor do, but rather what *must* a guarantor do? Certainly, it would be nice of a woman to undergo any treatment necessary for the foetus, and one might convincingly argue that she has a moral duty to do so, but in order for her to incur liability for a crime against life by omission, it must be shown that she was under a legal duty to accept medical treatment necessary to save the life of the foetus. Key to that determination will be the question of *Zumutbarkeit*: what could reasonably be expected of the woman?

cc. Zumutbarkeit*: reasonable expectations*

The criterion of *Zumutbarkeit* recognises the unique relationship between the woman and the foetus she carries, acknowledging that there must be a balancing of the interests engaged and that the protection of foetal life cannot prevail over the woman's conflicting rights in all circumstances. In its second abortion decision the *Bundesverfassungsgericht* held that a woman could not be required to continue her pregnancy where that would subject her to such burdens as to require the sacrifice of her own values to such an extent as cannot reasonably be expected of her.[219] That being the case, it explicitly recognised that in certain circumstances it would not be reasonable to expect the pregnant woman to continue the pregnancy due to the severity of the conflict with her own interests, the typical examples being where to do so would pose a threat to her life or health, or, much more controversially, where the child, if born, would be disabled.[220] Indeed, the current text of § 218a StGB acknowledges that a woman's rights will prevail over the protection of foetal life by the incorporation of both a medical and a criminological indication.[221] Significantly, the embryopathic indication (present in the

217 P. Kröger, in *LK*, § 218, Rn. 20, 21.
218 P. Kröger, in *LK*, § 218, Rn. 21.
219 *BVerfGE* 88, 203, at 257.
220 Ibid.
221 § 218a II and III StGB.

previous incarnation of § 218a StGB) has been subsumed within the medical indication (§ 218a II StGB), clearly expressing the priority to be afforded to the woman's rights and (future) interests, over the protection of (disabled) foetal life.

In cases such as *In re Brown*,[222] where a blood transfusion is necessary to save the life of the foetus, the likely consequence of a woman being able to refuse treatment is clear, but there is less clarity about whether she can reasonably be expected to endure treatment contrary to her wishes and/or beliefs for the sake of the foetus. The American case of *McFall v Shimp*[223] clearly demonstrates the Anglo-American position that nobody is required to donate an organ or indeed blood for the sake of another person, even if that will result in the death of a close relative. Similarly, the German textbook blood donation case[224] demonstrates that individuals can lawfully refuse to donate blood required for the survival of another person. The scenario envisages a patient with a very rare blood group being admitted to hospital in need of a blood transfusion, without which he will die. In the hospital there just happens to be a patient with the same blood group (Patient 1), but he refuses to donate blood to save the incoming patient. Thus the question arises whether an individual has a duty to endure treatment, or in this case to donate blood, against her wishes to save the life of another.[225]

In the blood donation case it is clear that a strong argument can be made that the life of the person requiring a blood transfusion weighs significantly more heavily than the potential donor's interest in bodily integrity. Nevertheless, the overwhelming majority of commentators believe that there is no legal duty to donate, nor would it be permissible to extract blood against the wishes of a potential blood donor, concluding that the interests of the potential donor in bodily integrity, self-determination and dignity outweigh the interest in the victim's life.[226] There is no place for compelled solidarity or generosity if that requires such a high level of sacrifice; indeed, as Walter Perron argues, substantial further support is provided for the recognition of the potential donor's right to refuse to donate by the public interest in maintaining respect for private autonomy as a fundamental legal principle.[227] Applied to the obstetric context, this would suggest that doctors should not be able to compel treatment for the benefit of a third party, the foetus, and that the woman will not be under a duty to endure treatment against her wishes for the benefit of the foetus. However, the key difference between the two scenarios is that the foetus is not a stranger; the woman is a

222 *In re Brown* (note 1).

223 *McFall v Shimp* 10 PaD. & C. 3d 90 (1978).

224 See, for example, W. Gallas, 'Pflichtenkollision als Schuldausschliessungsgrund' in K. Engisch and R. Maurach (eds) *Festschrift für Edmund Mezger zum 70. Geburtstag am 15.10.1954*, München: C.H. Beck, 1954, 311ff.; W. Gropp, *Strafrecht Allgemeiner Teil*, 4th edn, Berlin: Springer, 2015, § 6, Rn. 143.

225 The related question of whether a doctor can override the patient's refusal and extract blood to save another patient is addressed below, at B III 3 d (dd)ff.

226 See, for example, W. Gropp, *AT* (note 224), § 6, Rn. 144; W. Gallas (note 224), at 326; W. Perron, in *Schönke/Schröder*, § 34, Rn. 41e, with further references.

227 W. Perron, in *Schönke/Schröder*, § 34, Rn. 47.

guarantor and thus subject to an enhanced duty to act to protect the foetus. In discussing the blood donation case, Johannes Wessels et al. argue that a duty to donate blood could exist in some circumstances, giving the following as examples: between spouses, parents and children, and possibly also amongst soldiers on the frontline. Even in such cases, however, they suggest that the duty to donate blood is not absolute, but rather depends upon it being the only means of saving life and it not posing a serious risk to the donor's health.[228]

As Walter Gropp emphasises, whilst the *Garantenstellung* (the imposition of a duty of care) requires that the guarantor act to avert harm, it does not require that harm to be averted in a particular way and it does not impose a *special* duty to endure or even suffer upon the addressee.[229] Instead, where there is no other way of safeguarding the foetus, the key question will be whether it would be reasonable to expect the woman to endure obstetric intervention for the sake of the foetus. *Zumutbarkeit* – the assessment of what can reasonably be expected of the guarantor – will depend upon the individual circumstances of the case, but, as the *Bundesverfassungsgericht* made clear in its abortion decisions, a finding of *Unzumutbarkeit* (unreasonableness) will require more than the usual burdens associated with pregnancy.[230] Obstetric intervention, whether it takes the form of a surgical or instrumental delivery, a blood transfusion or indeed a corticosteroid injection, is not a usual part of pregnancy and labour. Although none of these examples of obstetric intervention are rare, they each constitute an additional burden upon the woman, going beyond those usual burdens associated with pregnancy. Moreover, whilst the usual burdens of pregnancy are naturally occurring and imposed by the condition itself, in this context the burdens under consideration would be imposed by law, rather than nature – a very different matter.

The doctor–patient relationship has evolved during the last 50 years, moving from a medical paternalism paradigm to one that emphasises the overriding importance of patient autonomy and adopts a model of shared decision-making. Within this model, doctors play a pivotal role in providing information and expertise to enable patients to make effective choices about the medical care and treatment they receive. This shift in perspective from 'doctor knows best' to patient autonomy is reflected in the requirement of consent to medical treatment (§ 630d BGB). Thus the gold standard in medical law has become the prioritisation of patient choice, recognising that patients should make choices in accordance with their own values and interests. Although a second(ary) patient is affected by the woman's choices, it is clear that her right to autonomy must weigh heavily against the imposition of a duty to acquiesce and to accept all treatment intended to benefit the foetus.

228 J. Wessels, W. Beulke and H. Satzger, *Strafrecht Allgemeiner Teil: Die Straftat und ihr Aufbau*, 44th edn, Heidelberg: C. F. Müller, 2014, at 132. See also J. Hruschka, *Strafrecht nach logisch-analytischer Methode: Systematisch entwickelte Fälle mit Lösungen zum Allgemeinen Teil*, 2nd edn, Berlin: De Gruyter, 1988, at 147.

229 W. Gropp, 'Atypische rechtmäßige Schwangerschaftsabbrüche' in K. Amelung et al. (eds) *Strafrecht, Biorecht, Rechsphilosophie: FS für Hans-Ludwig Schreiber zum 70. Geburtstag am 10.Mai 2003*, Heidelberg: C. F. Müller, 2003, 113 ff, at 126.

230 *BVerfGE* 39, 1, at 48; 88, 203, at 257.

Recognising that the weight accorded to the woman's interests and that the requirement of proportionality exclude the possibility of compelled treatment being justified by § 34 StGB, Walter Gropp argues that the requirement of consent to treatment demonstrates that a woman is not required to accept medical treatment against her will, even when the consequence of her refusal will be the death of the foetus.[231] Thus he argues that even where there is no alternative to surgery a woman's interest in bodily integrity will outweigh the foetal interests and that her refusal to endure the surgery will be justified by necessity (§ 34 StGB).[232]

As noted above, Reinhard Merkel maintains that the woman has a *prima facie* duty to act to protect the foetus, arguing that by becoming pregnant she creates a situation of dependence, a dangerous situation in which the foetus is dependent upon her body for survival.[233] He is very critical of Walter Gropp's argument that the requirement of consent demonstrates that the woman's duty cannot extend to a duty to accept any treatment required by, or for, the foetus, arguing that the existence of a duty cannot depend upon the addressee's capriciousness. Nevertheless, just as Gropp prioritises the woman's rights to bodily integrity, to self-determination and her dignity, Merkel recognises that her omission may be justified by the existence of sufficiently weighty grounds for her refusal of treatment.[234] The evaluation of such grounds will in turn require an assessment of the impact of treatment upon the woman's bodily integrity, her right to self-determination and her dignity, each of which is reflected in the requirement of consent to medical treatment.

Zumutbarkeit may operate at the *Tatbestand*, illegality or culpability level. Walter Gropp argues that the device operates at the level of *Rechtswidrigkeit* (illegality), on the basis that the question of whether or not the guarantor's omission (in this context the failure to prevent foetal death) is lawful will depend upon whether it can be justified or not.[235] Just as a father may refuse to donate a kidney for his son,[236] so too may a woman refuse consent to treatment for the benefit of the foetus. In doing so she is exercising her right to refuse consent and thus her omission is justified. As Gropp points out, there is a conflict of interests in the sense of the justification of necessity (§ 34 StGB) and therefore, if accepting the treatment would entail the wholesale sacrifice of her own interests, or even if her interests outweigh those of the foetus to a lesser degree, her omission will be justified.[237] By contrast, Regine Kiesecker argues that the subjective nature of the woman's failure to comply with the duty to protect the foetus will require that *Unzumutbarkeit* be considered exculpatory.[238] Nevertheless, the dominant view

231 W. Gropp, in *MüKo-StGB*, § 218, Rn. 54; W. Gropp (note 229), at 125–6.
232 W. Gropp, in *MüKo-StGB*, § 218, Rn. 54.
233 R. Merkel, in *NK-StGB*, § 218, Rn. 97; see above, text accompanying note 213.
234 R. Merkel, in *NK-StGB*, § 218, Rn. 104.
235 W. Gropp, *AT* (note 224), § 11, Rn. 50ff.
236 W. Gropp, *AT* (note 224), § 11, Rn. 52ff.
237 W. Gropp (note 229), at 124f.
238 R. Kiesecker, *Die Schwangerschaft einer Toten: Strafrecht an der Grenze von Leben und Tod – der Erlanger und der Stuttgarter Baby-Fall*, Frankfurt am Main: Peter Lang, 1996, at 269.

in the literature is that in the case of a derivative crime of omission the question of reasonableness is to be considered at the *Tatbestand* level, so that if the guarantor cannot reasonably be expected to act, the duty is limited in exactly the same way as it would be by impossibility and thus the objective element of the crime will not be satisfied.[239]

Walter Gropp argues that the woman's refusal of consent to the proposed intervention can be conceptualised as an attack upon the foetus, but that the (unlawful) attack can be justified by § 34 StGB (defensive necessity).[240] By contrast, Merkel argues that the question of whether the woman could be expected to endure treatment against her will arises at the *Tatbestand* level; if it were not reasonable to expect her to accept the treatment against her wishes (due to the sufficiency of the reasons justifying her refusal), the duty itself would lapse.[241] Thus both commentators accept that the woman is *prima facie* subject to a duty to protect the foetus, but differ in their view of how an unreasonable expectation will impact upon the duty. A detailed consideration of the level at which *Zumutbarkeit* should operate falls outside the scope of this book, but it is clear that, operating at any level, the question of what can reasonably be expected of the woman is key to determining whether or not she will incur liability for refusing medical treatment for the benefit of the foetus; it will obviate the duty to act or either justify or excuse non-performance. The much more significant consideration is what can reasonably be expected of the pregnant woman where medical treatment is indicated to save the life, or protect the welfare, of the foetus.

There can be no suggestion that a woman has a duty to create the optimal environment for the developing foetus, or indeed to undergo all possible treatment for its benefit, no matter how invasive and dangerous such treatment might be; instead, the concept of *Unzumutbarkeit* will limit the duty owed. Although the *Bundesverfassungsgericht* stressed that foetal life is protected at all stages of development, emphasising that the foetus 'does not develop into a human being, but as a human being',[242] the protection afforded undoubtedly reflects gestational development, with a greater degree of protection being given to the foetus as it nears birth.[243] Thus it is argued that the more advanced the pregnancy, the

239 See, for example, E. Hilgendorf, 'Zwischen Humanexperiment und Rettung ungeborenen Lebens – Der Erlanger Schwangerschaftsfall' (1993) *Juristische Schulung* 97, at 99; *Fischer*, § 13, Rn. 81; W. Stree and N. Bosch, in *Schönke/Schröder*, Vorb. zu den §§ 13ff., Rn. 155, with further references. Substantial support for this position is derived from the fact that *Zumutbarkeit* forms part of the *Tatbestand* of § 323c StGB, the crime of omitting to effect an easy rescue (a true crime of omission), W. Stree and N. Bosch, in *Schönke/Schröder*, Vorb. zu den §§ 13ff., Rn. 155.

240 W. Gropp, in *MüKo-StGB*, § 218, Rn. 54.

241 R. Merkel, in *NK-StGB*, § 218, Rn. 113.

242 *BVerfGE* 39, 1, at 37; 88, 203, at 252.

243 See also H. Dreier, *Bioethik: Politik und Verfassung* (note 52), at 53ff.; H. Dreier, 'Stufungen des vorgeburtlichen Lebensschutzes' (note 65); H. Dreier, 'Grenzen des Tötungsverbotes – Teil 1' (note 65), at 267ff.; A. Eser, in *Schönke/Schröder*, Vorb zu § 218, Rn. 9; W. Gropp (note 70), at 38f.; R. Merkel, in *NK-StGB*, § 218, Rn. 67.

greater the scope of that which can reasonably be expected of the woman.[244] In the majority of cases where obstetric intervention is mooted for the benefit of the foetus, the foetus will have achieved viability and thus have the capacity for independent life.[245] It is suggested that prior to viability there can be no question of a woman being under a duty to accept treatment for the benefit of the foetus. Once the foetus achieves viability, the question of whether the woman is obligated to accept treatment will arise for consideration, but whilst gestational development will impact upon the weight to be accorded to the foetal interests, in assessing the *Zumutbarkeit* of such an obligation a balance will need to be sought between the protection of the foetal interests and those of the woman. Even in cases where the foetus is viable, account will need to be taken of a low probability of survival following treatment, and of whether the foetus will have suffered such harm as would justify the termination of pregnancy under § 218a II StGB. The existence of either factor will weigh heavily against it being considered reasonable to expect the woman to undergo treatment.

(I) THE IMPACT OF LOW LEVELS OF RISK AND INVASIVENESS

Although it might be argued that the right to life is inevitably more stringent than any other interest, it is clear from the *Bundesverfassungsgericht*'s abortion jurisprudence that a woman's interests can outweigh the protection of foetal life. In order to constitute an unreasonable expectation, the woman's own protected interests must be impaired to such an extent as would be considered disproportionate to the avoidance of the threatened harm. The more serious the consequences of the omission, the more that can be expected of a guarantor, but the guarantor will not be required to expose herself to a risk to her life or even to the risk of serious injury.[246] As the cases discussed above demonstrate, one of the most frequent interventions ordered is a caesarean. Caesareans are now comparatively common, accounting for approximately one-third of all deliveries in Germany each year,[247] but they pose a greater risk to the woman's health and future pregnancies than vaginal delivery. A caesarean constitutes major abdominal surgery, requires an anaesthetic and entails a lengthy recovery period; the maternal mortality rate associated with a caesarean is higher than that associated with vaginal delivery and complications such as damage to the ureter and bladder may occur. The level of risk involved in a caesarean, albeit relatively low, clearly excludes the possibility that a woman could be under a duty to undergo such an operation against her wishes, even if the foetus is at risk. In considering the scope of the woman's duty,

244 See also A. Eser, in *Schönke/Schröder*, § 218a, Rn. 34; *Lackner/Kühl*, § 218a, Rn. 13, P. Kröger, in *LK*, § 218, Rn. 53; R. Merkel, in *NK-StGB*, § 218, Rn. 107.

245 Only one of the reported American cases involved a foetus that was not viable, *In re Jamaica Hospital* 491 N.Y.S.2d 898 (1985). None of the reported cases from England and Wales has involved a non-viable foetus.

246 W. Stree and N. Bosch, in *Schönke/Schröder*, Vorb. zu den §§ 13ff., Rn. 156.

247 Statistisches Bundesamt, *Gesundheit: Grunddaten der Krankenhäuser 2013*, Fachserie 12, Reihe 6.1.1, Wiesbaden, 2014, Table 2.15.

a number of commentators have sought to distinguish between different levels of risks. For example, whilst Walter Gropp argues that a woman's refusal of consent to surgery can be justified under § 34 StGB, he suggests that the position would be rather different in the case of a more minor intervention, arguing that such a differentiation reflects the wording of the medical indication (§ 218a II StGB) that sets out the justification for a termination of pregnancy in the case of a threat to the woman's life or of serious injury to her physical or mental health.[248] Reinhard Merkel makes a similar suggestion, and goes even further by suggesting that the scope of the duty to act will also depend upon whether the risk to the foetus emanates from the woman's body or is an external threat, suggesting that in the former the duty to act will be much more extensive.[249] It is difficult to sustain this particular argument, given that the risk to the foetus is not actively caused by the pregnant woman (unlike, for example, in the case where she abuses drugs), but rather results from what will often be a naturally occurring condition over which she has no influence – for example, placenta previa. Indeed, it is suggested that such a distinction, differentiating between risk emanating from the foetus or from the woman herself, would be inconsistent with § 218a II StGB (the medical indication) which draws no such distinction.[250] The medical indication that operates to justify a termination of pregnancy requires only a risk to the woman's life, or a risk of grave injury, that cannot be avoided by a reasonable alternative; thus it is suggested that the fact that the risk emanates from her body will not impact upon the scope of the woman's duty.

There is considerable support for the argument that a woman can be expected to endure minimally invasive treatment provided that it does not pose a risk to her life or health and that it is likely to be successful in saving the foetus.[251] Reinhard Merkel provides a good example of such a case by considering the position of a pregnant woman with APC resistance Factor V Leiden, a haemostatic disorder where regular heparin injections are indicated for the benefit of both the woman and the foetus. The treatment is minimally invasive (a daily injection), without risk to the woman and offers great benefit to both the woman and the foetus, protecting against thrombosis, miscarriage and in utero death. In such a situation if the pregnant woman refuses to accept the daily injections, Merkel argues that she will be in breach of her duty to act it would be reasonable to expect her to accept such a minor intervention and possible for her to do so.[252] In common with Walter Gropp, Reinhard Merkel suggests that the failure to accept less invasive interventions (within which both would include injections) will be unlawful. Nevertheless, both conclude that it would be inappropriate for a doctor to compel the woman to accept the treatment; all that she can do is inform the woman of the

248 W. Gropp (note 229), at 125.
249 R. Merkel, in *NK-StGB*, § 218, Rn. 98ff.
250 See also W. Gropp (note 229), at 126.
251 See, for example, W. Kapp, 'Der Fötus als Patient' (1986) 5 *Medizinrecht 276*, at 278; L.-M. Bleiler, *Strafbarkeitsrisiken des Arztes bei religiös motiviertem Behandlungsveto*, Heidelberg: Springer, 2010, at 203ff.; R. Merkel, in *NK-StGB*, § 218, Rn. 103ff.
252 R. Merkel, in *NK-StGB*, § 218, Rn. 107.

benefits of the treatment and try to persuade the pregnant woman to cooperate.[253]

The question of what will constitute minimally invasive treatment is controversial. Both Gropp and Merkel suggest that an injection (in Merkel's example, a daily injection) will be only minimally invasive. In *In re Baby Boy Doe* the Appellate Court of Illinois drew a similar distinction between invasive treatment (such as a caesarean) and relatively non-invasive, relatively risk-free procedures (such as a blood transfusion), saying that the question of whether a woman could be required to submit to the latter for the benefit of the foetus should be considered at a later date.[254] This question was resolved by the Illinois Supreme Court in *In re Brown*[255] where it was held that a pregnant woman may refuse any medical treatment, including a blood transfusion, regardless of whether that refusal might lead to the foetus suffering harm or indeed death. The court stressed that a blood transfusion is not a minimally invasive procedure,[256] and it is suggested that the risks of a blood transfusion, whilst low, remain risks that cannot be imposed upon a pregnant woman against her wishes. Even in the case of treatment delivered orally, without an invasive procedure, the risks and impact of the treatment may render it unreasonable to expect a woman to accept the treatment. A good example would be the case of antiretroviral therapy (ART). Pregnant women with HIV infection are strongly recommended to take antiretrovirals (ARV) to reduce the risk of transmission to the child (with treatment the risk is less than 1 per cent; without treatment the risk is around 25 per cent);[257] however, ART can have side effects and some women may be reluctant to take the drugs. The fact that the drugs are in tablet form means that the invasion of the woman's body is minimal; however, the severity of the side effects and the length of time that they would impact upon her necessarily mean that such treatment would not be a minor intrusion upon her bodily integrity and that it could not reasonably be expected that she would take the drugs against her will.

It is undoubtedly true that 'minor' risks are only ever those risks incurred by other people, in the same way that 'minor' procedures are those undergone by others, but ultimately even a single injection will breach the woman's bodily integrity and constitute a battery if administered against her wishes. There is a significant difference between advising pregnant women not to eat soft cheese and drink alcohol (a minimal intrusion) and requiring that she submit to (daily) injections against her will. Moreover, it is important to recognise that in this discussion about the level of risk and degree of invasive treatment the pregnant woman can be expected to bear, and thus about the limiting effect that these factors have upon the scope of her duty to endure treatment for the benefit of the foetus, the focus is upon limiting the risks and degree of invasion to which she may be

253 W. Gropp (note 229), at 125; R. Merkel, in *NK-StGB*, § 218, Rn. 107.

254 *In re Baby Boy Doe, a Fetus v Mother Doe* (note 1), at 333.

255 *In re Brown* (note 1).

256 Ibid., at 405.

257 C. L. Townsend et al., 'Earlier Initiation of ART and Further Decline in Mother-to-child HIV Transmission Rates, 2000–2011' (2014) 28 *AIDS* 1049, at 1049, 1051.

subjected, rather than upon promoting her autonomy and respect for her as a person with her own values, beliefs and priorities. Whilst most women will do anything and everything possible to safeguard the foetus, that cannot be the default expectation transposed into a legal obligation and applied to all women. It is submitted that creating such an adversarial situation is unhelpful. The pregnant woman cannot be treated as a vehicle for delivering treatment to the foetus; instead, her rights to self-determination, dignity and bodily integrity demand that her wishes and values are determinative regardless of the level of risk and invasion of her body involved.

(II) THE COMPATIBILITY OF A DUTY TO ACCEPT TREATMENT WITH THE GUARANTEE OF HUMAN DIGNITY

Whilst Perdita Kröger argues that a duty to accept treatment would be contrary to the woman's dignity, treating her merely as a means to an end,[258] Reinhard Merkel suggests that requiring a woman to accept treatment is not degrading to her dignity and that any degradation would result from the force used to compel her to accept treatment rather than the duty to accept treatment. He utilises an interesting example to illustrate his point, arguing that a father's duty to exert himself to save his son if he falls into water cannot be conceptualised as degrading, as reducing the man to a mere means to rescue his child.[259] However, there is a key difference between the drowning son and the foetus in the woman's uterus: the drowning son is not located within his father's body; the father's bodily integrity is not breached by leaping into the lake as is the case in which a pregnant woman is obliged to acquiesce to obstetric intervention for her unborn child. A better analogy would be with a father who is the only known match for his son suffering from leukaemia. Despite the fact that his son is dependent upon a bone marrow transplant for survival, the father refuses to consent. In such circumstances nobody would doubt that the father would have a moral duty to donate some bone marrow, a moral duty to act, but the imposition of a legal duty to act in such circumstances would be unreasonable. The father will be a guarantor in exactly the same way as the pregnant woman: he is in a position to save his son's life by undergoing a medical procedure and knows that he is the only person who can do so; the only significant differences appear to be that his son is a person extant and is not located within the father's body.

As the archetypal blood donor case demonstrates, there is no duty to save the life of another by consenting to the invasion of one's bodily integrity;[260] even in the case of a guarantor, the duty to act will be dependent upon it being reasonable

258 P. Kröger, in *LK*, § 218, Rn. 21.

259 R. Merkel, in *NK-StGB*, § 218, Rn. 104.

260 See, for example, W. Gropp, *AT* (note 224), § 6, Rn. 144; W. Gallas (note 224), at 326; W. Perron, in *Schönke/Schröder*, § 34, Rn. 41e, with further references; but cf. C. Roxin, *Strafrecht Allgemeiner Teil: Grundlagen. Der Aufbau der Verbrechenslehre*, Band I, 4th edn, München: C.H. Beck, 2005, § 16, Rn. 48f., arguing that as blood may be taken compulsorily by force in the resolution of minor crimes (§ 81a I 2

to expect the guarantor to act. Considering this issue, Nicola Heinemann makes an excellent point, referring to the nature of the duty imposed upon a father to rescue his children from a burning attic. In this well-known case[261] the man and his young children were trapped in a burning attic. On the ground below, bystanders called to the man to throw his children down to them, but fearing they would not survive the drop he did not do so. At the last moment he jumped from the window himself, leaving his children in the burning attic where they died. This is an interesting case because, as Heinemann points out, the father was criticised because he didn't throw the children out of the window; he failed to take action to save them, but he was not criticised for failing to jump from the window with his children, using his own body to break their fall.[262] Such a sacrifice could clearly not be expected of him; it would diminish him to a means of saving his children. Similarly, compelling the father to donate bone marrow would be to treat him as an object, as a mere source of cells required by his son. In exactly the same way that such a duty to acquiesce is unthinkable in the case of the father, so too the subjection of women to a duty to have treatment for the benefit of the foetus diminishes her dignity, reducing her status to that of a foetal support system. Reinhard Merkel is quite correct in his argument that the use of coercion cannot be justified and that it would be harmful to the medical profession to allow doctors to forcibly treat pregnant women against their wishes.[263] The suggestion that the use of physical force would be degrading is beyond refute, but it is not merely the use of force that is degrading; rather, it is the imposition of a duty to endure treatment, rendering the woman no more than a uterine environment, a living incubator, that undermines her dignity, treating her as a means to an end.

(III) REFUSALS BASED UPON RELIGIOUS BELIEFS

Whilst the majority of commentators agree that the woman has a duty to protect the foetus, the consensus appears to be that the duty will not require her to accept treatment against her wishes, unless that treatment is minimally invasive, poses only minimal risks to the woman and has a high likelihood of success. By contrast, Lisa-Marie Bleiler argues that it will be reasonable to expect the woman to accept treatment in almost all cases, arguing that in comparison with the risk to foetal life, the risks to the woman's health and life are of a significantly lower magnitude, even in cases of surgical intervention.[264] Similarly, she argues that the woman's religious freedom and self-determination must yield to the prevailing need to protect foetal life and that her dignity is not diminished by requiring her to accept medical intervention for the benefit of the foetus.[265] Whilst Bleiler is undoubtedly

StPO) it must be permissible for a doctor to compel a blood donation to save the life of another.

261 *BGH*, JZ 1973, 173f.

262 N. Heinemann (note 90), at 329.

263 R. Merkel, in *NK-StGB*, § 218 StGB, Rn. 104f.

264 L.-M. Bleiler (note 251), at 203ff.

265 Ibid., at 205.

correct to argue that the foetal life should be protected, it is submitted that much greater account needs to be taken of the woman's own interests and the protection thereof. Just as a patient cannot be compelled to donate blood to save the life of another patient, so too the fact that the foetus will die if the woman fails to accept the proposed medical treatment will not suffice to require her to accept treatment against her will. The *Bundesverfassungsgericht* made it clear in its abortion decisions that the protection of foetal life will not always prevail; were that not the case, a woman would not be entitled to terminate a pregnancy in the case of medical or criminological indications. Thus a much more nuanced weighing of the interests will be required. In this context it is submitted that the woman's values and religious beliefs must be accorded very great weight in the assessment of what can reasonably be expected of the woman as they constitute what Ronald Dworkin termed her critical interests[266] and define her as an individual.

The first reported case in England and Wales (*Re S*)[267] and a number of the American cases discussed above involved treatment refusals motivated by religious beliefs, both in relation to blood transfusions and caesareans. The German constitution protects the right to religious freedom (Art. 4 GG) and in a landmark decision, the *Gesundbeter* case,[268] the *Bundesverfassungsgericht* held that court decisions finding a man guilty of failing to provide assistance to his wife (§ 323c StGB) had interfered with his Article 4 I GG right to religious freedom.[269] The complainant and his late wife were members of the Evangelical Brethren and believed in the healing power of prayer. Following a difficult home birth the woman's husband called a doctor to examine her. The doctor diagnosed anaemia, treated her and, as her condition worsened, advised that she be admitted to hospital for a blood transfusion, warning that without a transfusion she could die. Earlier, the complainant's wife had told the attending midwife that she would not go to hospital for any reason and her husband informed the doctor that with faith and God's help she would recover without hospital treatment. Whilst making it clear that he was opposed to the proposed hospitalisation, the complainant told his wife that it was her decision and she could go to hospital for treatment if she so desired, although the Brethren preached that if someone is ill, an elder should be called to pray for their recovery. His wife refused to go to hospital and requested that one of the elders be brought to pray with them; shortly afterwards she died, having remained conscious and able to express her own wishes throughout.

It was accepted that the woman had possessed the capacity to refuse treatment and that she had been able to make her own decision without undue influence from her husband. However, it was argued that it would have been reasonable to expect him to try to persuade his wife to follow medical advice. The *Bundesverfassungsgericht* stressed that the freedom of conscience embodied by Art. 4 GG is

266 R. Dworkin, *Life's Dominion: An Argument about Abortion, Euthanasia, and Individual Freedom*, London: Harper Collins, 1993, 199ff.

267 [1993] Fam 123.

268 The faith healing case.

269 *BVerfGE* 32, 98.

more than mere religious tolerance, but encompasses the right of the individual to act in accordance with her beliefs and live her life accordingly.[270] It held that in cases where acting, or refraining to act, as dictated by her conscience brings the individual into conflict with the criminal law, it should be considered whether in the circumstances punishment would be consistent with the functions of criminal law. In such a situation the individual has not acted criminally through a disregard of the law, but due to a conflict of conscience, feeling that she has no choice but to disobey the law and follow the dictates of her faith. The court pointed out that even if the individual's decision is inconsistent with general social values, it may not be so blameworthy as to justify the use of criminal law (society's harshest weapon) against the perpetrator. Thus it concluded that the state's duty to respect deeply held beliefs to the greatest extent possible under Art. 4 I GG may require that the application of criminal law be suspended in cases where the legal duty and dictates of faith conflict and the stigmatisation of the individual as a criminal would be disproportionate and would undermine her dignity.[271]

This is a relatively old decision from 1971. Now it is suggested that the court would approach this case on the basis of the woman's right to self-determination, accepting that it was not reasonable to expect the man to seek to change his wife's mind, or even to take her to hospital after she had refused treatment; however, the recognition of the impact of religious beliefs is particularly important in the context of obstetric intervention. Thus it is suggested that the firmly held religious belief that it would be a sin to undergo a blood transfusion, or that God will heal her body, will render a duty to act to preserve the foetal life in contravention of those beliefs unreasonable. By acting in accordance with her beliefs the woman will come into conflict with the criminal law, but there can be no suggestion that § 218 StGB was ever intended to compel women to have medical treatment for the sake of the foetus; its purpose is to criminalise intentional terminations of pregnancy – the typical abortion. This is clearly demonstrated by the fact that despite it being accepted that the offence may be committed by omission, legislative and judicial consideration of the criminal offence of termination of pregnancy has been limited to its active variant. Whilst the woman's refusal of treatment may lead to the death of the foetus, her intention is not to cause its death but rather to refuse treatment incompatible with her beliefs, and it is suggested that the use of the criminal law in such a context will be inappropriate and that punishment would be disproportionate and would serve only to undermine her dignity.

However, in discussing this case Lisa-Marie Bleiler suggests that the decision rests upon the fact that the woman's decision would not directly imperil anyone else's life, unlike the scenario of a pregnant woman whose refusal will impact upon the foetus. She points out that the court emphasised that the man and his wife shared the same belief in the healing power of faith, that they both believed that the best thing to do in the circumstances was to pray,[272] whilst the foetus cannot

270 *BVerfGE* 32, at 106.
271 *BVerfGE* 32, at 108–9.
272 *BVerfGE* 32, at 110.

be said to share the woman's beliefs. In this way she argues that a duty to accept medical treatment for the benefit of the foetus cannot be an unreasonable expectation in view of the woman's beliefs and the impact they will have upon a third party, the foetus, who does not share those same beliefs and who, unlike the woman in this case, has not personally refused treatment.[273] Certainly, in the case of a child, its parents cannot impose their religious views, or the consequences thereof, upon the child by refusing to allow her to have a life-saving blood transfusion; in such cases the parental refusal will be overridden, either by the family court exercising its powers under § 1666 BGB or in an emergency by doctors relying on § 32 StGB (self-defence) or § 34 StGB (necessity).[274] I return below to the question of the applicability of § 1666 BGB to a foetus and the potential for a doctor being able to rely upon a defence if she treats a patient without consent,[275] but Bleiler's conclusion clearly contradicts the general consensus that it would be unreasonable to expect a woman to accept medical treatment against her religious convictions.

The obstetric context is significantly different to that which pertains in the case of a child extant: the foetus is not an independent being; it is encased within the woman's body and therefore cannot be treated without that treatment impacting upon her bodily integrity. As the *Bundesgerichtshof* recognised in the context of a claim for prenatal injuries, the woman's consent to medical procedures during birth is given on behalf of both herself and the foetus; she is the person with the responsibility for making decisions about treatment during birth due to the fact that birth impacts upon her person as well as the foetus and therefore she should be regarded as the natural trustee for the foetus.[276] That being the case, it would seem unreasonable to expect the woman to abandon her religious convictions in order to rescue the foetus when presented with the choice of being stigmatised as making an attack upon the foetus (by not permitting the treatment to be administered) or losing all hope of an eternal life (by accepting the treatment proscribed by her religious beliefs). In any event, it is clear that whilst the woman's refusal of consent could be considered an attack in the sense of § 32 StGB, it will not be an unlawful attack and therefore cannot excuse a doctor intervening forcibly to treat the foetus.[277]

In summary, it is clear that the question of what can reasonably be expected of the woman (*Zumutbarkeit*) will determine the scope of her duty towards the foetus, and that in all cases, except perhaps those involving a truly minimal invasion, the woman will not be required to accept treatment for the benefit of the foetus. In the case of a duty to refrain from action, *Unzumutbarkeit* will generally be relevant at the *Schuld* (culpability) level, but in this context, where there is a duty to act to avert risk to the foetus, it will be most relevant at either the *Tatbestand* or

273 L.-M. Bleiler (note 251), at 206–7.

274 *OLG Hamm*, NJW 1968, 212; *BayObLG*, FamRZ 1976, 43; *OLG Celle*, NJW 1995, 79; *AG Nordenham*, Med R 2008, 225.

275 See below, B III 3 d.

276 *BGHZ* 106, 153, at 157.

277 W. Gropp, in *MüKo-StGB*, § 218, Rn. 54.

the illegality level. As previously mentioned, the dominant view in the literature is that in the case of a derivative crime of omission *Zumutbarkeit* will operate at the *Tatbestand* level.[278] If, as Stree suggests,[279] it operates at this level, it will negative the existence of a duty to undergo medical treatment for the benefit of the foetus where that could not reasonably be expected of the woman due to the consequential sacrifice of her own protected interests. Alternatively, Gropp has cogently argued that *Zumutbarkeit* operates at the level of *Rechtswidrigkeit* (illegality), leaving the duty to act intact, but justifying the omission to act where a weighing of the interests finds that the woman's compromised interests significantly outweigh those interests protected by the duty to act.[280]

In the case of termination of pregnancy, § 218a II and III StGB provide two justifications specific to the abortion context, namely the medical and the criminological indications. The standard position is that these offence-specific justifications exclude recourse to the general necessity justification set out in § 34 StGB.[281] However, in the same way that § 218a I StGB will not be relevant to the termination of pregnancy by omission,[282] not least due to the lack of counselling, it is difficult to conceive of a situation where either of the statutory justifications for termination of pregnancy could apply to a woman's refusal of treatment necessary to save the foetal life because the woman will not be seeking to terminate a pregnancy that results from a sexual offence or to terminate in order to avert a threat to her life or health.[283] An argument can be made that the refusal of a blood transfusion due to religious reasons may well accord with averting a risk to the woman's future health, as Jehovah's Witnesses who are subjected to non-consensual blood transfusions report feelings of violation and suicidal ideation. However, as Lisa-Marie Bleiler correctly notes, a termination of pregnancy by omission resulting from the failure to perform a blood transfusion does not avert a risk to the woman's health posed by her pregnancy as required by the indication; instead, the risk averted is that posed by a compelled blood transfusion.[284]

That the offence-specific justifications are ill-suited to termination of pregnancy by omission is hardly surprising. As Nicola Heinemann points out, the consideration of abortion at both the judicial and the legislative levels has focused upon the boundaries of permissible abortion resulting from a positive act intended to terminate a pregnancy.[285] However, in the context of refused obstetric intervention

278 See, for example, E. Hilgendorf, 'Zwischen Humanexperiment und Rettung ungeborenen Lebens – Der Erlanger Schwangerschaftsfall' (1993) *Juristische Schulung* 97, at 99; *Fischer*, § 13, Rn. 81; W. Stree and N. Bosch, in *Schönke/Schröder*, Vorb. zu den §§ 13ff., Rn. 155, with further references.

279 W. Stree, in *Schönke/Schröder*, Vorb. zu § 13, Rn. 155.

280 W. Gropp (note 229), at 123f.; see also N. Heinemann (note 90), at 319, 324ff.

281 See, for example, A. Eser, in *Schönke/Schröder*, Vorb. Zu § 218, Rn. 37; W. Gropp, in *MüKo-StGB*, § 218, Rn. 29; L.-M. Bleiler (note 251), at 204.

282 § 218a I StGB excludes punishment for abortions performed within the first 12 weeks of pregnancy, following pro-life counselling, § 219 StGB.

283 See also W. Gropp (note 229), at 119.

284 L.-M. Bleiler (note 251), at 204.

285 N. Heinemann (note 90), at 318.

the pregnant woman does not make a choice to terminate a pregnancy; rather, she elects to refuse obstetric intervention in the knowledge that such a refusal is likely to lead to the death of the foetus and quite possibly her own death. Thus, whilst it is clear that the general justification of necessity set out in § 34 StGB will not normally apply in the abortion context, due to the existence of the abortion-specific justifications set out in § 218a StGB, this situation falls outside the standard application of that provision and the justifications set out therein are inapplicable. As Eric Hilgendorf points out, where the context differs from the class of cases considered by the legislature, the priority accorded to the special justification ceases to apply.[286]

§ 34 StGB, the general justification of necessity, requires the existence of a current unavoidable danger to a protected legal interest. Such a danger is clearly present in the obstetric intervention context when the woman is unwilling to undergo the indicated treatment for the benefit of the foetus and therefore it is necessary to weigh the danger posed to the woman's interests by a duty to act against the foetal interests protected by such a duty. Thus the woman's rights to bodily integrity, self-determination and dignity must be weighed against the foetal right to life and bodily integrity. The foetal interest in life and bodily integrity are clearly important, but suggestions that § 34 StGB cannot justify the termination of life are clearly misplaced; were that not the case, it would never be justifiable to terminate a pregnancy even to avert a risk to the woman's life. In order to justify her omission to act, it will be necessary to show that the woman's interests *considerably* outweigh those that would have been protected had she complied with the duty to act.[287] In fact, it is suggested that in all but the most minor forms of treatment, requiring only minimal invasion of the woman's bodily integrity and posing no risk to her health, the woman's refusal will be considered justified due to the fact that a duty to act would require the sacrifice of her own interests, interests that are supported by public policy considerations.

§ 34 StGB requires that the omission constitutes an adequate and proportionate means to avert the risk. This will entail consideration of whether the omission is consistent with socio-ethical values and it is suggested that in this context the public interest in patient autonomy, bodily integrity and human dignity will be of significant importance, lending substantial additional weight to the woman's interests. Moreover, other public policy considerations will also support the woman's right to refuse treatment, including, for example, the importance of maintaining trust in the doctor–patient relationship and ensuring that pregnant women feel confident in accessing medical care during pregnancy – if women fear that their needs and interests will be subjugated to those of the foetus, they are unlikely to seek prenatal care, depriving healthcare professionals of the opportunity to try to help the

286 E. Hilgendorf (note 239), at 100.

287 Cf. N. Heinemann (note 90) suggesting that in the case of an omission, the balancing of interests required by § 34 StGB should be conducted on the basis that the woman will only be required to act in cases where the foetal interests significantly outweigh her own, at 321.

women themselves and the foetus. As will be argued in more detail in Part C below, there is little scope to influence a woman's decision if an adversarial rather than cooperative approach is adopted towards antenatal care. Therefore there are strong public policy reasons to support a woman's autonomy, even where the cost of that support may be the death of a foetus.

dd. Interim conclusion on the scope and nature of the woman's duty as guarantor

The pregnant woman clearly is a guarantor, owing a duty to act to safeguard the foetus's life and well-being. Nevertheless, there is a fundamental difference between requiring a woman to continue the pregnancy to term by allowing the foetus to remain in her uterus and requiring the woman to undergo medical treatment for the benefit of the foetus, entailing the sacrifice of her own interests and values. It has been argued that whilst the pregnant woman has a duty to protect the foetus, the ambit of that duty is dependent upon the gestational development of the foetus, the invasiveness of the proposed protective measure and the risks posed by it to the woman and, most especially, the requirement that the woman's dignity be respected. On the facts of all of the American and English cases discussed above, under German law it is suggested that the balancing of the woman's interests against those protected by a duty to act would have been resolved in favour of the woman's right to lawfully refuse treatment, even if that resulted in the death of a viable foetus. Only in the case of treatment that is necessary for the foetus and carries a high likelihood of success, whilst posing no or truly minimal risks to the pregnant woman, may there be a reasonable expectation that she will be under a duty to accept that treatment. It is suggested that this potential exception should be interpreted extremely narrowly and will only apply to the case of medication required on an infrequent basis.

In cases where a duty to accept treatment would be *zumutbar*, if the woman survives and her refusal of treatment led to the death of the foetus, there is the potential that the woman could face criminal liability for termination of pregnancy (§§ 218, 13 StGB). In theory there is the potential for liability for manslaughter (§§ 212, 13 StGB) or negligent homicide (§§ 222, 13 StGB) if the dilating contractions had already started at the time of the woman's refusal, transforming the foetus into a *Mensch* for the purposes of criminal law. However, it is suggested that after the commencement of the dilating contractions any proposed intervention will be more than minimally invasive (typically involving surgical or instrumental delivery, or a blood transfusion) and therefore will be *unzumutbar* as discussed above, obviating the duty to accept the treatment or justifying the woman's omission to accept treatment.[288]

Whilst the potential for liability for termination of pregnancy by omission (§ 218, 13 StGB) exists, it is extremely limited due to a number of factors. First, even if the foetus dies and the woman survives to be prosecuted, it is unlikely to

288 Liability under § 323c StGB would be excluded due to *Unzumutbarkeit.*

be possible to demonstrate that the woman's omission – her refusal of treatment – led to the death of the foetus with a probability bordering upon certainty. Moreover, as the 'mother', liability for attempted termination of pregnancy is excluded (§ 218 IV StGB). Even if the woman's refusal to consent to treatment can be shown to be (quasi) causal for the death of the foetus, the subjective element of the *Tatbestand* of abortion by omission remains to be satisfied. The pregnant woman must have intentionally caused the death of the foetus, typically regarded as requiring the defendant to act with both knowledge and volition. Conditional intention will suffice[289] and in the context of obstetric intervention there will generally be no question as to the satisfaction of the cognitive element (the pregnant woman will know that the likely result of her refusal of consent is the death of the foetus), but the required volition is likely to be significantly more difficult to ascertain. In each of the cases in England and Wales and America, the women concerned did not want the foetus to die and so cannot be said to have directly intended such a consequence, despite knowing that it was likely. In the cases where women refused treatment on the basis of religious beliefs, believing that God would heal their bodies, the voluntary element would not be satisfied, because the women, whilst appreciating the danger that the foetus would die, did not want that to happen and did not acquiesce, trusting in God that the foetus would be saved. In such a case there can be no liability for termination of pregnancy, as § 218 StGB requires intent; negligence will not suffice. The same principle will apply where women refused intervention earnestly believing that it was not necessary, as, for example, in the case of *Re Madyun*[290] – Mrs Madyun was not reconciled to the prospect of her child dying; rather, she firmly believed that it was not yet necessary to undergo a caesarean. On the other hand, in cases where the woman acquiesced, resignedly accepting that the foetus would die as a consequence (albeit undesired) of her refusal, the requirements of conditional intent (*bedingter Vorsatz/dolus eventualis*) could be satisfied.

Therefore, it is extremely unlikely that the woman will incur criminal liability for her refusal to accept treatment, but if the foetus dies, causation and the necessary intent are proven and her omission can be neither justified nor excused, she could face imprisonment of up to one year, or a fine (§ 218 III StGB). Ultimately, it must be recognised that the criminal law is of limited utility in this situation; it is simply too blunt an instrument. It is highly unlikely that punishment would be consistent with the purposes of criminal law, given that the woman's refusal is not motivated by a disregard for the law but rather by the dictates of her own value system. There is no suggestion that force could be used in order to compel

289 *Bedingter Vorsatz* will suffice, *BGH* NJW 51, 412; A. Eser, in *Schönke/Schröder*, Vorb. zu § 218, Rn. 45. There is significant debate about the content of the volition requirement. For a detailed consideration of the requirement of volition, see D. Sternberg-Lieben and F.Schuster, in *Schönke/Schröder*, § 15, Rn. 80ff. and the literature referred to therein.

290 573 A 2d 1259 (DC, 1990). 114 Daily Wash Law Rptr. 2233 (D.C. Super.Ct. July 26, 1986). Published as appendix to *Re A.C.*, 573 A.2d 1235, 1262 (D.C.App. 1990).

treatment, even in such cases where the duty to accept treatment would be considered *zumutbar*. Recognising this, Lisa-Marie Bleiler argues that doctors could use the potential for criminal liability in order to 'encourage' women to accept medical treatment for the benefit of the foetus;[291] similarly, Kapp refers to legal proceedings having a warning function.[292] However, neither of these functions is consistent with the *Bundesverfassungsgericht*'s second abortion decision, where the court recognised that the protection of unborn life does not always require the imposition of criminal sanctions and that the foetus is best protected by cooperation with the pregnant woman.

It has been argued that the pregnant woman's interests in dignity, self-determination and bodily integrity will outweigh the foetal interests in bodily integrity and life in all but the most minor forms of obstetric intervention because a duty to accept treatment for the benefit of the foetus would require the sacrifice of her own protected interests such as cannot be reasonably be expected of her. The state is enjoined to protect and promote developing life and, as the counselling-based abortion demonstrates (§ 218a StGB), may do so without recourse to criminal penalties.[293] Thus it is suggested that, rather than a duty to accept treatment, the woman's duty will require that she consciously consider the foetus and the impact of her decision upon it. Such a duty could require that outwith emergency situations the woman undergo counselling similar to that mandated by § 218a StGB. Thus it should be designed to ensure that her refusal is informed and entirely voluntary and that she has taken full account of the impact it will have upon the foetus, stressing that the foetus also has a right to life and bodily integrity.[294] Such counselling would mirror the use of counselling in § 218a StGB, but a duty to take up such counselling should not be limited to those cases where it would be reasonable to expect the woman to accept treatment, but rather would also apply to non-emergency cases where the woman's refusal will be *unzumutbar*, including, for example, a religious-based refusal. Moreover, the state will bear responsibility for ensuring that resources are available to support women during pregnancy, so that they can be assisted to overcome needle phobias, for example, but also to ensure that alternatives to blood are available should the need for a transfusion arise. There is also a need to discuss potential problems before they develop to try to avert conflict arising in an emergency setting. Many of the cases that have arisen in the United States of America and England and Wales have been foreseeable and problems could have been averted, or at least minimised, if better care planning had been undertaken.

291 L.-M. Bleiler (note 251), at 212ff.
292 W. Kapp (note 251), at 280.
293 *BVerfGE* 88, 203, at 272.
294 A similar suggestion is made by C. Robben, although she envisages the counselling being limited to such cases where the health risk posed by the intervention to the woman is low and the intervention would benefit the foetus, *Pränatale Schädigungen mit postnatalen Folgen: Überlegungen zu einem neuen Schutz- und Haftungskonzept unter Berücksichtigung der US-amerikanischen Rechtslage*, Frankfurt am Main: Peter Lang, 2014, at 253.

Ultimately, strong public policy reasons exist for not imposing a duty upon pregnant women to accept medical treatment for the benefit of the foetus. Therefore it is essential that healthcare professionals cooperate with the pregnant woman, supporting and encouraging her to provide the best possible environment for the foetus to develop and to enable the best possible antenatal care to be provided. Threats and punishment are inimical to such an environment, and therefore references to the use of legal proceedings as a warning and the criminal law as a tool to assist doctors in persuading women seem misplaced, belonging as they do to a confrontational approach.

d. The doctor as guarantor: the scope and nature of her duty towards the pregnant woman and the foetus

In taking on the treatment of the pregnant woman, the doctor assumes the role of protective guarantor, and thus is required to act to avert dangers to her life and health. However, by treating the woman, knowing her to be pregnant, the doctor also assumes a responsibility towards the foetus, so that she will owe a duty of care to both the woman and the foetus.[295] As the *Bundesärztekammer*'s[296] *Guidelines on prenatal diagnosis* point out, 'By taking on the care of an early pregnancy a treatment contract is formed between the pregnant woman and the doctor. This includes, as well as the care of the mother, also that of the unborn'.[297] Thus the doctor is *Garant* for both the foetus and the woman separately.

aa. The doctor's duty towards the pregnant woman

The doctor–patient relationship forms the basis for the imposition of a duty of care (the *Garantenstellung*) towards the pregnant woman. However, if the woman refuses medical treatment, including life-sustaining medical treatment, the doctor will be released from her duty to act to avert dangers to her patient's life and health.[298] Therefore, a doctor who respects a refusal of consent will not incur liability for manslaughter (*Totschlag*, §§ 212, 13 StGB) or negligent homicide (*fahrlässige Tötung*, §§ 222, 13 StGB) in respect of the woman's death because the woman's effective refusal absolves the doctor of her duty as guarantor towards the woman. Similarly, the patient's refusal will exclude liability under § 323c StGB.

295 W. Gropp, in *MüKo-StGB*, § 218, Rn. 50; W. Stree/N. Bosch, in *Schönke/Schröder*, § 13 StGB, Rn. 28a; P. Kröger, in *LK*, § 218, Rn. 38; R. Merkel in *NK-StGB*, § 218, Rn. 99, 115; R. Kiesecker (note 238), at 242f. But cf. E. Hilgendorf (note 239), at 99 who argues that the duty arises by virtue of the protective effect for third parties of the contract between the woman and the doctor.

296 The Federal Medical Association.

297 Bundesärztekammer, *Richtlinien zur pränatalen Diagnostik von Krankheiten und Krankheitsdispositionen* [Guidelines on prenatal diagnosis of diseases and predisposition towards disease] (1998) 95 (50) *Deutsches Ärzteblatt* A-3236 p. 69.

298 A. Eser, in *Schönke/Schröder*, Vorb. zu § 211, Rn. 28; R. Merkel, in *NK-StGB*, § 218, Rn. 116, OLG München, NJW 1987, 2943.

The woman's refusal of treatment will bind the doctor; should the doctor treat the woman, or indeed invade her body in order to treat the foetus, she will commit a battery contrary to § 223 StGB. However, the doctor's duty towards the foetus is undiminished by the woman's refusal of consent and will survive the death of the pregnant woman. Therefore, until the woman dies, the doctor must respect her refusal of consent; however, after her death the foetal right to life will take priority and the doctor will be justified in intervening to save it – for example, by performing a caesarean *in mortua*.[299]

bb. The scope and nature of the doctor's duty towards the foetus

There is no doubt that the doctor owes a separate duty of care as a guarantor towards the foetus, requiring that she act to avert harm to the foetus's life and bodily integrity whenever it would be possible and reasonable to do so. The failure to intervene in cases where treatment is medically indicated could result in liability for termination of pregnancy by omission (§§ 218, 13 StGB), or, if the dilatory contractions have commenced, another crime against life – homicide (*Totschlag* §§ 212, 13 StGB) or negligent homicide (*fahrlässige Tötung*, §§ 222, 13 StGB); alternatively, in the case of an accident, liability could arise under § 323c StGB (the crime of omitting to effect an easy rescue). In order for liability to be imposed it would have to be demonstrated that the doctor's failure to treat the pregnant woman caused the death of the foetus, despite the fact that it was reasonable and possible to avert this happening, and that she knew the woman was pregnant and had at least *dolus eventualis*.

Importantly, as Merkel points out, the doctor's duty is clearly limited to medical matters;[300] thus she is not required to act to ensure that a pregnant woman has stopped working, or even smoking, on medical advice. The DGGG[301] guidance recognises this, stating that 'It is not the doctor's task to investigate and monitor the pregnant woman's lifestyle', although it does recommend that if the doctor knows that the woman uses drugs, alcohol or nicotine, or engages in other risky behaviour, she should point out the risk to the woman and document that she has done so.[302] As the treating doctor, she has a duty to provide medically indicated treatment to the foetus and, although the doctor's duty towards the pregnant woman will lapse as a result of her refusal of treatment, her duty towards the foetus remains unaffected by that refusal. Nevertheless, the doctor's ability to fulfil that duty towards the foetus will largely depend upon her ability to convince the pregnant woman to cooperate in the treatment.

299 W. Gropp, in *MüKo-StGB*, § 218, Rn. 9.
300 R. Merkel, in *NK-StGB*, § 218, Rn. 115.
301 German Association for Gynaecology and Obstetrics.
302 Deutsche Gesellschaft für Gynäkologie und Geburtshilfe (DGGG), Arbeitsgemeinschaft Medizinrecht (AG MedR) *Empfehlungen zu den ärztlichen Beratungs- und Aufklärungspflichten während der Schwangerenbetreuung und bei der Geburtshilfe*, 1996, confirmed 2010, at § 1.2.

cc. The application of § 1666 BGB

The woman's right to self-determination enables her to consent, or refuse consent, to the proposed intervention on her own behalf; however, as the mother-to-be, she is also the person with the right to consent, or refuse consent, to treatment on behalf of the foetus.[303] § 1912 BGB regulates the guardianship of the foetus, stating that where necessary a guardian is responsible for protecting the foetus's future rights, but that the parents are responsible for its welfare as they would be if the child had already been born. Thus § 1912 II BGB suggests that parental responsibility will precede birth, and clearly refers to the parents. Nevertheless, in the case of obstetric intervention, the only access to the foetus is via the woman's body and so it would clearly be inappropriate for the father-to-be to consent to treatment of the foetus, in just the same way that a man cannot veto or consent to the invasion of the woman's body for the purpose of the performance of an abortion.[304] Thus the woman's decision will be determinative.

Whilst the woman is at liberty to refuse treatment on her own behalf, her ability to refuse indicated treatment required to preserve the foetus's life or health is much more circumscribed because parental responsibility must be exercised consistently with the child's welfare (Art. 6 GG, § 1666 BGB). According to § 1666 I BGB, where a child's physical, mental or emotional welfare is endangered and the parents are unwilling, or unable, to avert the danger, the family court can intervene, adopting the measures necessary to avert the danger. This may include overriding a refusal of consent to medical treatment given by a holder of parental responsibility. However, the applicability of § 1666 BGB to the foetus is controversial. On the one hand, § 1912 II BGB suggests that parental responsibility will precede birth, but the wording specifically limits its application to the preservation of future rights.[305] On the other hand, the existence of § 1912 BGB, restricted as it is to the protection of foetal rights, and the fact that § 1666 I BGB refers specifically to 'child' endangerment, would suggest that § 1666 BGB cannot be applied to the foetus and that the court may only intervene to prevent harm to a child extant. Nevertheless, in a landmark decision the Celle district court held that '"child" in the sense of § 1666 BGB includes the conceived, but not yet born life'.[306] The dominant view in the literature reflects this position. As Dirk Olzen argues, the foetus is protected by various provisions of civil and criminal law, but most significantly the *Bundesverfassungsgericht* has recognised that the foetal life is

303 *BGHZ* 106, 153, at 157.

304 *Paton v UK* (1980) 3 E.H.R.R. 408; A. Eser, in *Schönke/Schröder*, § 218, Rn. 62; Heinemann (note 90) at 127ff., 153. But note that the location of the foetus is crucial. In the case of a frozen embryo, the potential father retains the right to refuse consent to implantation, *Evans v United Kingdom* (2008) 46 E.H.R.R. 34.

305 But cf. M. Coester, in *Staudinger*, § 1666, Rn. 26, arguing that following the *Bundesverfassungsgericht*'s second abortion decision, the future rights of the foetus should be extended to include its current rights.

306 *AG Celle*, NJW 1987, 2307, at 2308.

to be protected from implantation.[307] Thus, it is suggested that § 1666 BGB is at least *prima facie* applicable in the context of 'foetal' endangerment.[308]

The question arises as to whether the woman's refusal of consent to medical treatment could constitute child endangerment in the context of § 1666 I BGB. § 1666 BGB does not require wrongdoing on the part of the parent; indeed, as Michael Coester makes clear, court involvement under § 1666 BGB is not intended to ensure optimal conditions for the child's welfare, but rather to prevent specific risks to the child.[309] In the context of the foetus this necessarily means that recourse cannot be had to § 1666 BGB in order to require women to provide the optimal foetal environment by taking vitamin supplements and avoiding soft cheese. Instead, it is suggested that the same principle will apply as in the case of a child extant – namely that where the proposed treatment is medically indicated, there is no reasonable alternative and a failure to provide the treatment poses a serious threat to the foetus's life or health, the doctor should make an application to the family court for the woman's refusal of consent to be set aside and for the court to substitute its own decision in accordance with § 1666 III BGB.[310] In such circumstances it is likely that the woman's refusal will constitute a threat to the foetus's welfare, justifying court intervention to override her refusal of consent.[311] However, there must be a clear and present danger to the foetus; the fact that a woman *might* refuse treatment, should it become necessary, will not justify court involvement,[312] nor would treatment that might improve the foetus's health be justified absent a clear and present danger. This contrasts starkly with a number of the English cases where pre-emptive orders were made authorising caesareans in the event that the woman were to refuse consent, albeit that these cases were ostensibly determined on the basis of the woman's best interests.[313]

Whilst the court may be prepared to override the woman's refusal of consent to the foetus being treated, it is likely to grant pregnant women a significant degree of latitude in determining what will constitute an actionable threat to the foetal welfare.[314] In the case of existing children, the courts have recognised that parents have significant latitude with respect to their own private sphere. For example,

307 *BVerfGE* 39, 1, at 37; 88, 203, at 251.
308 See also D. Olzen, in *MüKo-BGB*, § 1666 I, Rn. 40; I. Rakete-Dombek, in *NK-BGB*, § 1666 I, Rn. 4.
309 M. Coester, 'Kinderschutz: Übersicht zu den typischen Gefährdungslagen und aktuellen Problemen' (2009) *Famile Partnerschaft Recht* 549, at 549.
310 In relation to a child extant, see G. Wagner, in *MüKo-BGB*, § 823 BGB, Rn. 736.
311 For analogous cases involving parents refusing blood transfusions for children extant, see OLG Hamm, NJW 1968, 212; OLG Celle, NJW 1995, 792, at 793; M. Coester, in *Staudinger*, § 1666 BGB, Rn. 102; D. Olzen, in *MüKo-BGB*, § 1666 BGB, Rn. 80.
312 *BayObLG* FamRZ 1976, 43, 46; *OLG Oldenburg* NJW 1997, 2962; *OLG Saarbrücken* FamRZ 1996, 561; M. Coester, in *Staudinger*, § 1666 BGB, Rn. 102.
313 See, for example, *Tameside and Glossop Acute Services Trust v CH* [1996] 1 FLR 762; *Re AA (Mental Capacity: Enforced Caesarean)* [2012] EWHC 4378 (COP), [2014] 2 FLR 237.
314 See also D. Olzen, in *MüKo-BGB*, § 1666, Rn. 41; M. Coester, in *Staudinger*, § 1666, Rn. 24.

although passive smoking represents a clear risk to children, the courts have not recognised that a parent's smoking in the presence of her (already born) child can constitute endangerment of that child's welfare. Rejecting an appeal against the refusal to grant an order prohibiting a mother and stepfather from smoking in the presence of their daughters, in the family home, the Bavarian appeal court stressed that a court order on the basis of § 1666 BGB could only be justified if the passive smoking represented a specific risk to the child – for example, because of illness; the generally recognised risk of passive smoking would not suffice.[315] A similar reluctance to intervene in the private sphere of pregnant women underlies the report of the Federal Ministry of Justice's working group, reporting on family court measures to counter threats to child welfare under § 1666 BGB, which concluded that no provision should be adopted for the use of § 1666 BGB in the case of a foetus. Instead, it recommended that an explicit offer of help for pregnant women and parents-to-be should be included in the assistance catalogue contained in the *Sozialgesetzbuch* VIII[316] providing for advice and help during pregnancy.[317] In reaching this conclusion the working group stressed that the function of § 1666 BGB is to enable the court to act to avert danger to the foetus, rather than to control the woman in order to ensure the optimal pregnancy for the foetus.[318] Therefore, like the *Bundesverfassungsgericht*, the working group regarded cooperation with the pregnant woman and the provision of assistance to be much more likely to safeguard the foetus. It is suggested that this approach is correct and that considerable restraint is required in the application of § 1666 BGB to the context of obstetric intervention. Although an application to the court may be justified where a woman refuses treatment, posing a serious threat to the foetus's welfare, it is suggested that a court will be unlikely to intervene to compel 'proper' antenatal behaviour absent an immediate and identifiable risk to life or health.

Nevertheless, the court could set aside the woman's refusal of consent to the foetus being treated. Whilst the courts have overridden parental vetoes to blood transfusions in the case of existing children, the administration of those transfusions did not impact upon the parent's own bodily integrity. By contrast, the foetus is located within the woman's body, and thus any treatment afforded to the foetus against her wishes will violate the woman's constitutional rights. This is a key distinction: whilst the court's intervention may justify the doctor's treatment of the foetus, it will not justify the infliction of bodily harm to the woman that will be an inherent part of treating the foetus. Thus the granting of such an order will have little more than symbolic significance. It will not authorise the use of force to administer treatment through the woman's body, although, as Lisa-Marie Bleiler points out, there is the potential for a fine to be issued if the woman refuses to

315 *BayObLG*, FamRZ 1993, 1350, at 1351.

316 Social Code part VIII, concerning support for children and adolescents.

317 Bundesministerium der Justiz Arbeitsgruppe (Federal Ministry of Justice Working Party) Familiengerichtliche Maßnahmen bei Gefährdung des Kindeswohls – § 1666 BGB, *Abschlussbericht*, 14 July 2009, at 32.

318 Ibid., at 37f.

allow the treatment to be provided.[319] Together with Wolfgang Kapp, she sees the involvement of the court as having a warning function that may 'encourage' the woman to consent to treatment on behalf of her foetus.[320] As detailed above, it is suggested that court involvement and the threat of penalties, be they criminal or civil in nature, are unlikely to persuade the woman to allow treatment and the threat of such intervention may lead to the situation where women fail to seek medical advice for fear that they might be coerced into accepting treatment against their will.

dd. The performance of obstetric intervention without the woman's consent

As a guarantor, the woman may have a duty to accept treatment for the benefit of the foetus. However, as shown above, it will almost always be unreasonable to expect a woman to accept treatment against her wishes for the benefit of the foetus, the only possible exception being where the intervention does not involve a significant invasion of her bodily integrity, has a high likelihood of success in protecting the foetal life or bodily integrity and does not pose anything more than a minor risk to the woman. Such a situation is only likely to arise in relation to medicinal treatment. However, even if it would be reasonable to expect the woman to accept treatment, a doctor cannot compel treatment against her wishes. As the DGGG points out, the doctor must respect a woman's right to self-determination even if she regards the woman's decision as irrational[321] and even though obstetric intervention is the only means of safeguarding the foetus's life and health.[322] In such cases the doctor is not entitled to disregard the woman's wishes; instead, she must point out the dangers with the requisite forcefulness in order to change the woman's mind.[323] In the DGGG's view, the only exception would be where the woman's decision is manifestly wrong and she lacks the capacity to make it.[324] This reflects the positions taken by the DGGG's British and American counterparts that the refusal of a woman with capacity must be respected,[325] but the reference to a manifestly wrong decision suggests that a refusal of indicated treatment will trigger a capacity assessment. It is suggested that the issue of whether a woman has the capacity to make the decision is distinct from that of whether the doctor regards

319 L.-M. Bleiler (note 251), at 212.

320 Ibid.; W. Kapp (note 251), at 280.

321 DGGG, *Absolute und relative Indikationen zur Sectio caesarea*, 2001, revised 2008, currently under revision, at § 3.4.

322 DGGG, *Absolute und relative Indikationen zur Sectio caesarea*, 2001, revised 2008, currently under revision, at § 4.2.1.

323 Ibid.

324 DGGG,*Empfehlungen zu den ärztlichen Beratungs- und Aufklärungspflichten während der Schwangerenbetreuung und bei der Geburtshilfe*, 1996, confirmed 2010, at § 2.2.

325 American College of Obstetricians and Gynecologists Committee on Ethics, *Committee Opinion No. 321: Maternal Decision Making, Ethics, and the Law* (2005), at 9; Royal College of Obstetricians and Gynaecologists, *A Consideration of the Law and Ethics in Relation to Court-Authorised Obstetric Intervention* 2nd edn, London, 2006, at 7.

her decision as correct. As the discussion of the English case law demonstrates, there is significant scope for the determination of capacity to be used to undermine a pregnant woman's autonomy in this manner. In German law, if a woman is found to lack capacity, it is not her best interests but rather her known or presumed will that will be determinative. If the woman has refused treatment, either orally or in an advance directive, the fact that she now lacks capacity should not undermine her refusal, manifestly wrong or not.[326] However, where no such refusal exists, the decision will depend upon her presumed will (*mutmaßlicher Wille*). Initially, this will require a subjective assessment, considering the woman's earlier oral and written statements, her religious faith, other personal values and her life expectancy.[327] Should the subjective assessment prove inconclusive, an objective assessment will be necessary, but there will be considerable pressure to find that the woman would have wanted treatment for the benefit of the foetus as the default position.

The doctor owes a duty to protect the foetal life and health as far as it is possible and reasonable for her to do so. As the pregnant woman's refusal of consent will render it impossible for the doctor to treat the foetus, the doctor's duty towards the foetus will be discharged by making the woman aware of the danger to the foetus and trying to persuade the woman to consent to treatment; she will incur no liability for failing to actively intervene to save it.[328] Therefore, where a doctor respects the pregnant woman's refusal of consent to the proposed obstetric intervention, she will not incur criminal liability. However, it is less clear whether she may be able to justify her actions, or have a defence, should she treat the pregnant woman without her consent in order to prevent harm to the foetus. In one of the most recent cases reported from the United States of America, the hospital's director of maternal and foetal medicine is reported to have written on Rinat Dray's notes: 'I have decided to override her refusal to have a C-section'.[329] There is no suggestion that Mrs Dray lacked capacity; rather, in what appears to be an astonishing display of arrogance, the doctor ignored her valid refusal and performed a caesarean against her express wishes. Were the same to happen in

326 It is argued that a valid advance directive will continue to have effect throughout pregnancy; see S. Halliday, 'Legislating to Give Effect to Precedent Autonomy: Comparative Reflections on Legislative Incompetence' (2011) 11 *Medical Law International* 127; but cf. A. Spickhoff, 'Rechtssicherheit kraft Gesetzes durch sog. Patientenverfügungen?' (2009) *FamRZ* 1949, at 1951; P. Balz, *Lebenserhaltung als Haftungsgrund*, Berlin: Springer, 2010, at 67. I return to this issue below, C III 2 a.

327 § 1901a II BGB, *BGHSt* 40, 257, at 261f. For a detailed consideration of the presumed will and best interests approaches in the context of the refusal of life-sustaining treatment, see S. Halliday and L. Witteck (2002) 'Die Regelung von Nichtaufnahme und Abbruch einer medizinischen Behandlung am Lebensende in Deutschland und England' (2002) 15 *Juristen Zeitung* 752.

328 E. Schmidt, 'Das Reichsgericht und der "übergesetzliche Notstand"' (1929) 49 *Zeitschrift für die gesamte Strafrechtswissenschaft* 350, at 403; W. Gropp, in *MüKo-StGB*, § 218, Rn. 55.

329 A. Hartocollis, 'Mother Accuses Doctors of Forcing a C-Section', *New York Times*, 16.05.2014, A18.

Germany, it would certainly amount to a battery (§ 223 StGB), but it must be considered whether the doctor's actions could be justified or excused. Whilst the family court can override the woman's refusal of consent to treatment for the foetus (§ 1666 III BGB), such an order will not justify the invasion of the woman's bodily integrity without her consent and thus in practice the doctor will not be able to lawfully treat the foetus.

ee. The availability of a justificatory defence to the doctor

In order to justify subjecting a woman to treatment without consent, the doctors may claim self-defence or necessity. The justification of self-defence set out in § 32 StGB is unlikely to justify the doctor's actions in the context of obstetric intervention. According to § 32 II StGB, self-defence is a defensive act necessary to avert a current unlawful attack upon oneself or another. There is some debate as to whether an omission may constitute an attack, but the dominant view is that it can be an attack where there is a duty to act. In this context the woman's omission may constitute an unlawful attack within the meaning of § 32 II StGB if she could reasonably be expected to accept treatment necessary for the foetus, but outside such exceptional circumstances her omission will not be unlawful precluding any defence of the foetus.[330] The 'attack' is directed towards another (the foetus); therefore, if there were no other way to avert the threat to the foetus, the doctor may be able to justify overriding her consent. However, it is the act of defence, not the result, that must be necessary and proportionate, requiring that the least intrusive means be used that will suffice to halt the attack. In the case of obstetric intervention there are other possibilities open to the doctor, such as discussion of any alternatives, ensuring that the woman fully understands the consequences of her refusal and attempting to persuade her to change her mind; compelled treatment is unlikely to be considered proportionate. Moreover, the act of self-defence must be *geboten* (§ 32 I StGB) – that is, required and appropriate. As Merkel argues, forcibly subjecting a woman to invasive treatment against her will cannot fall within the duties of an obstetrician and thus it cannot be categorised as *geboten*.[331] Therefore § 32 StGB will not justify compelled treatment.

§ 34 StGB – the justification of necessity – justifies an unlawful act when the act is committed in order to avert a present, otherwise unavoidable danger to life, body, freedom and other protected interests, if upon a balancing of the conflicting interests the affected interests and degree of danger to them significantly outweigh the protected interests. The act must be a proportionate means to avert the danger. As discussed above, the foetal interests in life and bodily integrity will need to be weighed against the woman's rights to bodily integrity and self-determination. In order to justify compelled treatment, the foetal interests affected by the woman's omission would need to significantly outweigh the woman's protected

330 W. Gropp, in *MüKo-StGB*, § 218, Rn. 54.

331 R. Merkel, in *NK-StGB*, § 218, Rn. 107. See also W. Gropp, in *MüKo-StGB*, § 218, Rn. 54.

interests, but just as in the case of the blood donor that will not be the case. Whilst the dominant view is that a doctor cannot justify taking blood from one individual in order to save the life of another, Claus Roxin argues that as blood may be taken by force in the resolution of minor delicts, it must be permissible to save the life of another.[332] As Roxin suggests, there is some precedent for the law requiring invasion of an individual's bodily integrity; thus, for example, § 81a I 2 StPO permits the taking of blood samples from a suspect in the course of a criminal investigation. However, such samples are not taken from someone unconnected with the investigation; for example, they are generally taken to establish blood alcohol levels following a road traffic offence – a very different prospect to someone being compelled to donate blood. Moreover, the amount taken is significantly less than that required to transfuse another and the individual's dignity is not undermined in that she is not treated like a walking blood bank. Thus, as Nicola Heinemann argues, the compelled donation of blood is very different to the taking of a blood sample as a matter of criminal procedure or indeed the duty to be vaccinated that serves both the good of the individual and the community of which they are part.[333]

In the context of obstetric intervention, the treatment is not intended to benefit the woman or the community at large, but rather a specific individual – the foetus. Unlike the classic blood donor scenario, a clear relationship does exist between the woman and the foetus; however, that relationship, and indeed her status as guarantor, cannot justify a doctor overriding her refusal of consent and treating her as a mere conduit for the treatment of the foetus. Instead, the guarantee of human dignity requires that her bodily integrity and her right to determine what should happen to her own body must take precedence over the foetal interests.[334] Moreover, the adequacy/proportionality requirement (§ 34 II StGB), which necessitates a consideration of the positive legal order and general legal principles, will bolster the weight given to the woman's interests, requiring that the woman's autonomy and bodily integrity be respected and protected. The public interest in respecting women's equality, in ensuring that all individuals are able to maintain bodily integrity and not be subjected to treatment for the benefit of others, and the interest in encouraging women to engage with healthcare professionals and thus promote 'maternal' and foetal health throughout the pregnancy are powerful reasons that mitigate against compelled treatment. Thus necessity will not justify the doctor overriding the woman's consent and invading her body in order to treat the foetus.

Furthermore, although the doctor faced with the woman's refusal to permit indicated treatment to be performed is undoubtedly faced with a conflict of duties, her intervention will not be capable of justification under the unwritten collision of duties justification, due to the lack of two conflicting duties to act or two

332 C. Roxin, *AT I* (note 260), § 16, Rn 48f.

333 N. Heinemann (note 90), at 326. See also W. Gropp (note 229), at 126.

334 Cf. L.-M. Bleiler (note 251), arguing that the foetal interest in life will outrank the woman's rights, at 214.

conflicting duties to refrain from acting. The doctor has a duty to act to save the foetus and a duty to respect the woman's right to self-determination (an omission). Therefore there will be no scope for justification if the doctor decides to take matters into her own hands, overriding a woman's consent and invading her body in order to treat the foetus.

ff. The availability of an exculpatory defence to the doctor

Although compelled treatment cannot be justified, it must be considered whether the doctor's treatment of the pregnant woman could be excused. Duress may excuse unlawful acts, according to § 35 StGB. In circumstances where a person commits an unlawful act in order to avert a present, not otherwise avoidable danger to the life, body or personal liberty of herself, her family or another person close to her, that unlawful act can be excused. Thus, even where the interests of the woman outweigh those of the foetus, excluding justification under § 34 StGB, the exculpatory defence of duress may apply. Whilst foetal life may be capable of protection in the sense of § 35 StGB,[335] the foetus is not a relative or other close person and thus falls outside of the class of individuals who may be protected by the doctor. Moreover, although § 35 StGB does not require a weighing of the conflicting interests, it does require that the act be proportionate. As discussed above, that is extremely unlikely to be the case where a doctor subjects a patient to treatment against her will. Thus the doctor will not be able to rely on § 35 StGB to excuse her actions. Furthermore, it is suggested that there is no scope for the doctor's action being excused by supra-legal duress. Although the doctor's intervention is intended to save the life of the foetus and this is a truly exceptional situation, it is not comparable with that in which the euthanasia doctors found themselves during the Third Reich – the classic example of how supra-legal duress may act as an exculpatory defence.[336]

gg. Interim conclusion on the scope and nature of the doctor's duty as guarantor

Therefore, no matter how hard it may be for a doctor to watch the woman and/or the foetus die for lack of treatment, it is clear that if she decides to override the woman's refusal of consent, she will commit a battery and will be unable to rely upon any defence. The doctor's freedom of action is limited by the (primary) patient's right to self-determination. Thus, even if the woman's refusal of consent on behalf of the foetus is overridden in accordance with § 1666 BGB, her refusal to allow access to the foetus through her body will render it impossible for the doctor to treat the foetus. Therefore, where a woman refuses to consent to

335 The dominant view is that foetal life does not constitute life in this context; see, for example, B. Müssig, in *MüKo-StGB*, § 35, Rn. 13; C. Roxin, AT I (note 260), § 22, Rn. 24; *Fischer*, § 35, Rn. 3; but cf. W. Perron, in *Schönke/Schröder*, § 35, Rn. 5.

336 See also L.-M. Bleiler (note 251), at 215.

treatment, the doctor's duties to both the woman and the foetus will lapse and she will incur no liability for failing to act to safeguard the life and welfare of either the foetus or the woman. In such circumstances the only option open to the doctor is to seek to persuade the woman to consent to the indicated treatment; there is no scope for coerced cooperation.

4. Interim conclusion

At the outset of this chapter it was noted that German law is distinctive by virtue of the fact that it recognises both that the foetus's life is protected by the constitution and the duty to rescue. However, as has been demonstrated, the German law provides significantly more protection for the woman's autonomy and respect for her dignity than has been generally shown by the courts in England and Wales and the United States of America when confronted with the need to protect a foetus in face of the woman's refusal of consent to medical treatment. In order for a woman to be subject to a duty to accept medical treatment for the benefit of the foetus, it must be reasonable to expect her to do so. Thus the primary question where treatment is clinically indicated is not what does the foetus need, but rather what can reasonably be asked of the woman. This approach emphasises that the foetus is not a separate, free-floating entity that can be treated as its clinical best interests require, but rather that any treatment given to the foetus will impact upon the pregnant woman. That impact goes beyond the physical impact of invading her body, simultaneously impacting upon her very being, her values and beliefs – those very elements that make her an individual. Moreover, the requirement that the duty be *zumutbar* ensures that the woman remains not only the focus of the decision-making but also the decision-maker. Whilst commentators such as Wolfgang Kapp have suggested that a duty to accept treatment will exist where the intervention is necessary for the foetus and involves only a low level of invasiveness and no more than a minimal risk to the pregnant woman,[337] here it has been argued that this approach is fundamentally flawed. It treats her autonomy as irrelevant, focusing upon a third party's determination of whether or not the risks are sufficiently low to subject her to a duty to accept treatment.

Instead, it has been argued that respect for dignity is the key to resolving the conflict between the interests of the woman and those of the foetus. On the one hand dignity requires that the woman is not treated as a mere conduit enabling treatment of the foetal patient, whilst on the other hand dignity requires that the foetal life is given an appropriate level of protection. In the context of obstetric intervention, the state can best fulfil its duty to protect unborn life by supporting women, by trying to persuade women to act in the best interests of the foetus, but fundamentally by recognising that women have to be enabled to make decisions for themselves. This means that people suffering from phobias, for example, should be supported and that a treatment plan should be developed early in pregnancy to ensure that agreed strategies exist if a crisis situation does develop.

337 W. Kapp (note 251), at 278.

Ultimately, strong public policy reasons exist for not imposing a duty upon the pregnant woman to accept medical treatment for the benefit of the foetus. As the *Bundesverfassungsgericht* accepted in its second abortion decision, the protection of the foetus is likely to be much more successful where the state and, particularly in this context, healthcare professionals cooperate with the pregnant woman, supporting her and enabling her to provide the best possible environment for the developing foetus and enabling her to access the best possible antenatal care without fear, rather than punishing her for failing to meet the ideal standard.

Whilst there is a potential for criminal liability for an omission on the part of either the pregnant woman or the doctor leading to the death of the foetus, primarily pursuant to §§ 218, 13 StGB, as has been shown, there is no scope for compelled treatment of the pregnant woman. In all but the most minimal forms of obstetric intervention, it will be unreasonable to expect the woman to accept the proposed medical treatment against her wishes. The *Unzumutbarkeit* will justify her omission, or alternatively exclude the duty to accept the treatment at the *Tatbestand* level. Although the distinction is of little practical importance, it is argued that *Unzumutbarkeit* is best regarded as operating at the *Tatbestand* level, excluding a duty to act, in accordance with the dominant position in the literature. This position recognises the dichotomy that exists between social expectations that assume a woman will undergo all treatment expected to benefit the foetus and the lack of a corresponding legal obligation in view of the fact that the woman's duty to protect the foetus is limited to the extent that the woman cannot be expected to sacrifice her own countervailing interests in bodily integrity, self-determination and dignity. As is suggested above, rather than a duty to accept treatment, the woman's duty to protect the foetus will require that she consciously consider the foetus and the impact of her decision upon it. Absent an emergency situation where the woman will die without treatment, and thus where it would be inappropriate to impose counselling upon the woman, the woman should undergo counselling similar to that mandated by § 218a StGB. The counselling should be designed to ensure that her refusal is informed and entirely voluntary, and that she has taken full account of the impact it will have upon the foetus, stressing that the foetus also has a right to life and bodily integrity.

Even in circumstances where the woman can be expected to accept medical treatment for the benefit of the foetus, there is no scope for compulsion as has occurred both in the United States and in England and Wales. Should she refuse to accept the medical treatment and the foetus dies, there is a (remote) possibility that she may incur criminal liability. Moreover, where the woman refuses treatment either on behalf of the foetus, or herself, thus inhibiting access to the foetus, the doctor's duty towards the foetus will lapse due to impossibility. The doctor's duty towards the pregnant woman will lapse by virtue of the woman's effective treatment refusal. Should a doctor override the woman's refusal of treatment, she will commit a battery contrary to § 223 StGB and no defence will be available to her. The only conceivable situation in which a doctor could act to save the foetus despite the woman's refusal of treatment would be by performing a caesarean after death, a so-called *sectio in mortua*. After the woman has died, although her personality right will survive death, it will be accorded significantly less weight and thus the duty to protect the foetus's life will outweigh the respect due to the woman's refusal.[338]

The strength of the German law lies in its ability to navigate the conflict between 'maternal' and foetal interests. It demonstrates that the foetus does not have to be regarded as nothing in order to protect and recognise women's rights; rather, the foetus can be accorded value and protection, to the extent that it can be considered to have a right to life, even as against the pregnant woman, without extinguishing or even diluting the woman's rights, provided that that right to life is set within the context of respect for the woman's rights and interests. In its first abortion decision the *Bundesverfassungsgericht* rejected the view that the foetus is merely part of the 'maternal organism'.[339] Whilst Abortion I stressed the separateness of the woman and foetus, the second abortion decision emphasised their connectedness, conceptualising the relationship as one of duality in unity.[340] Ultimately, the key to protecting the foetus and promoting its welfare depends upon cooperation between the woman and her doctors, and such cooperation relies on trust, not compulsion. It is well recognised that the only instances of lawful compelled medical treatment are those where the interests of society collide with and outweigh those of the affected individual – for example, through the duty to vaccinate and treatment for a mental health disorder. In the present context the interests of society will support the need for the woman to retain autonomy over her own body, and for her to be recognised as an equal member of society, with her own rights and interests that are undiminished by pregnancy, to ensure that she is not reduced to the status of reproducer or even an incubator on legs.

338 See also W. Gropp, in *MüKo-StGB*, § 218, Rn. 9; A. Eser, in *Schönke/Schröder*, § 218, Rn. 27.

339 *BVerfGE* 39, 1, at 42ff.

340 *BVerfGE* 88, 203, at 253.

C. Comparative analysis of the legal responses to a woman's refusal of medical treatment required for the benefit of the foetus

I. The medicalisation of pregnancy and creation of the foetal patient

As the preceding chapters have made clear, medical technology and increased medical knowledge about reproduction, particularly the ways in which the woman's lifestyle and medical choices impact upon the foetus, have had a huge impact upon the way in which we perceive pregnancy and the way in which women experience it. The medicalisation of pregnancy continues: technology is now an inherent part of all pregnancies, routinely utilised even in those pregnancies with no risk factors, from the use of ultrasounds to date the pregnancy, to the standard use of electronic foetal monitoring during labour. At the other end of the spectrum, improvements in technology and knowledge mean that pregnancies can be maintained even after brain death in the woman, and that the foetus can be treated prior to birth through foetal therapy or even surgery.

Technology has, however, proven itself to be a double-edged sword. That same technology that gives us our first glimpses of our 'baby' can also be utilised as a surveillance tool, used to ensure that the pregnancy is progressing as healthcare professionals would wish, and to identify needs that may be met, through medical intervention, to benefit the foetus. In the same way that the ultrasound image is commonly posted on social media websites and shown to friends and family, constructing the foetus as an individual in social terms, it also frames the foetus as a patient, an independent focus for the obstetrician's attention. As Susan Mattingly has convincingly argued, technology has not changed the biological relationship between a woman and the foetus, but

> the medical model of that relationship has shifted emphasis from unity to duality. Clinicians no longer look to the maternal host for diagnostic data and a therapeutic medium; they look through her to the fetal organism and regard it as a distinct patient in its own right.[1]

1 S. S. Mattingly, 'The Maternal-Fetal Dyad: Exploring the Two-Patient Obstetric Model' (1992) 22(1) *Hastings Center Report* 13, at 13.

It is noticeable that in the cases considered above the courts have not treated the foetus as a secondary patient, but rather as a second patient, often with equal or even superior status to the pregnant woman herself. Significantly, however, it is a patient with a difference as it can only be accessed for treatment through the body of the pregnant woman. Ultrasound images encourage the view that the foetus is separate from the pregnant woman,[2] but, as Anne Lyerly and Mary Mahowald point out, the foetus is never separated from the pregnant woman; if the connection between the two is severed, it ceases to be a foetus and instead becomes variously an abortus, a newborn or a stillbirth.[3] Nevertheless, rather than the word 'patient' being applied to the foetus in a purely descriptive manner, it has been imbued with normative connotations – the fact that the foetus *can* be treated has led to suggestions that the foetus *has a right* to be treated, regardless of the wishes of the pregnant woman, or indeed of the risks and burdens that the treatment might impose upon her.

A reading of the cases discussed in the preceding chapters suggests that in reality this second patient is being treated as the primary patient, subordinating the woman and her care to its welfare. The dystopia portrayed by Margaret Atwood in *The Handmaid's Tale* appears all too real when one considers cases such as *Jefferson*[4] and *Re S.*[5] In both cases the women were treated as little more than a walking uterus, reminiscent of the way Offred explains the function of the handmaids: 'We are for breeding purposes ... we are two-legged wombs, that's all: sacred vessels, ambulatory chalices'.[6] Despite pronouncements that the pregnant woman's autonomy is to be respected, the case law would appear to suggest that this dystopian vision has become the reality for women in England and Wales and the USA who are unable, or unwilling, to consent to treatment deemed necessary for the foetus, at least in cases involving women less able to defend themselves against social and professional expectations of pregnant women. Indeed, it is significant that Veronica Kolder's study of the early US cases of court-ordered obstetric intervention found that 81 per cent of those subjected to compelled obstetric intervention were black, Asian or Hispanic, and that 24 per cent involved women whose first language was not English.[7] Similarly, the latest tranche of cases in England and Wales also disproportionately affected women from minority groups, women who might be regarded as different because they suffered mental illness or had learning difficulties, who were often non-white and not born in the UK. They were 'other', outsiders who could be distinguished from the 'good' expectant

2 For an excellent analysis of how ultrasound has rendered the uterus and its contents visible, see R. P. Petchesky, 'Fetal Images: The Power of Visual Culture in the Politics of Reproduction' (1987) 13 *Feminist Studies* 263.

3 A. D. Lyerly and M. B. Mahowald, 'Maternal-Fetal Surgery for Treatment of Myelomeningocele' (2003) 31(1) *Clinics in Perinatology* 155, at 156.

4 *Jefferson v Griffin Spalding County Hospital Authority* 274 SE 2d 457 (1981).

5 *Re S* [1993] Fam 123.

6 Margaret Atwood, *The Handmaid's Tale*, Boston: Houghton Mifflin, 1986, at 136.

7 V. E. B. Kolder, J. Gallagher and M. T. Parsons, 'Court-ordered Obstetrical Interventions' (1987) 316 *New England Journal of Medicine* 1192.

mothers and who, having been found to lack capacity to decide for themselves, could be treated in line with how judges and doctors believed a 'normal', altruistic expectant mother would want to be treated, such treatment being considered to serve her best interests.

II. Law's attempts to navigate the triadic conflict between the pregnant woman, (the state's interest in) the foetus and medical authority

The courts in both England and Wales and the United States of America have shown themselves to be willing to authorise, or even order, obstetric intervention to safeguard the foetus, despite the pregnant woman's refusal of consent. In the US such intervention has been justified by the state's interest in potential life, whilst in England and Wales the courts have sought to avoid considering the impact of viability and foetal personhood by addressing this issue as a question of whether the woman has the requisite capacity to make the decision.[8] Importantly, whilst some courts in the US have found the pregnant woman to have the requisite capacity,[9] the English courts have yet to uphold a woman's refusal of consent when a foetus is at risk, as opposed to retrospectively finding that the woman was competent and that the intervention constituted a battery after the baby has been safely delivered.[10] Instead, having found the women to lack the necessary capacity, the courts have gone on to authorise the procedure, the woman's best interests apparently always requiring the safe delivery of the foetus. In this manner the proprieties have been observed; the courts have stressed that pregnant women have a right to refuse treatment and that the foetus has no interests capable of being taken into account by the court, but have been able to save the foetus by declaring the women in question to lack capacity to make the decision herself, albeit only temporarily.

A key difference in the positions adopted by the US and Germany on the one hand and the English response to the question of compelled obstetric intervention on the other is that English law has not accepted any possible limitation upon a woman's autonomy by virtue of pregnancy. Thus the courts have avoided the need to engage with the question of foetal rights or even the state's interest in the foetus, suggesting that pregnant women are not treated differently from other patients, be they male or female. Provided she is judged to have capacity, her autonomy will remain intact; it is not set off against the state's interest in the foetus as in some American states, and it is not dependent upon whether or not it would be reasonable to expect her to accept the recommended treatment in view

8 Only the now discredited *Re S* (note 5) overtly considered the interests of the foetus and failed to consider the woman's capacity to refuse treatment. In *St George's Healthcare NHS Trust v S; R v Collins and others, ex parte S* [1999] Fam. 26, Hogg J decided to follow *Re S*; the woman's capacity to refuse does not appear to have been in doubt.

9 See, for example, *In re Baby Boy Doe, a Fetus v Mother Doe* 632 N.E. 2d 326 (1994).

10 *St George's Healthcare NHS Trust v S; R v Collins and others, ex parte S* (note 8).

of the countervailing duty to protect foetal life as in Germany. In practice, however, reliance upon capacity merely serves to highlight just how unique pregnant women really are. The pregnant woman's autonomy is compromised precisely because she deviates from societal expectations of pregnant women, of what is considered good, or even adequate, antenatal behaviour. In fact, as the case law demonstrates, non-compliance with medical advice tends to be regarded as deviant and requires explanation, displacing the presumption of capacity and opening the way to find that the woman lacks capacity and thus should be treated in accordance with her best interests.

Capacity is decision-specific, requiring a commensurately greater degree of capacity the graver the decision to be taken,[11] and few decisions will be graver than the decision to refuse treatment which may lead to the woman and/or the foetus dying or being injured unnecessarily. Therefore, it is suggested that this risk-related standard ensures that the degree of capacity required to refuse treatment will prove unattainable and that reference to capacity is merely a way to disguise intervention for the benefit of the foetus; by focusing on capacity, the courts are able to pay lip service to the rhetoric of patient autonomy whilst still protecting foetal life in practice. In this regard the majority of the US case law has at least the advantage of honesty, acknowledging as it does the state's interest in the foetus as the basis for compelled interventions.

In the light of the appellate decisions in both England and Wales and the US, it might be argued that the pendulum has now swung, that instead of focusing upon the need to protect the foetus, the courts in both jurisdictions will now also stress the need to respect the woman's autonomy regardless of whether or not the court approves of the choices she makes. However, as the most recent cases from the US demonstrate, such an approach has not found favour throughout the US; indeed, even in states such as Illinois, as in England and Wales, a woman's treatment refusal will only be valid where she is found to have capacity, a requirement that can be seen to introduce a high degree of uncertainty with great potential for her refusal to be overridden. Moreover, in the case of decisions taken in advance of incapacity and documented in an advance directive, treatment refusals will be invalidated for the duration of her pregnancy in much of the US, or at the very least will require consideration of their continuing validity in Germany and England and Wales.

In reality the difference between the approaches adopted in the case law is often no more than a difference in the way in which the argument is framed. In the cases that prioritise the woman's autonomy, generally leading to a finding of incapacity, the legal basis for intervention is found in promoting the woman's best interests, which are extremely broadly defined so as to include protecting her from making a decision that it is assumed she will later regret, rather than in acting to safeguard the foetus *per se*. The focus of protection shifts under the alternative approach, so that it is the overt protection of the foetus that takes precedence;

11 *Re MB (Medical Treatment)* [1997] 2 FLR 426; *Re T (An Adult) (Consent to Medical Treatment)* [1993] Fam 95.

there is an expectation that the woman will choose to do whatever is necessary for the foetus's welfare and, should she fail to do so, the state will step in to ensure that its interest in potential life is protected. A similar expectation, transposed into a legal duty, is (at least theoretically) imposed upon the pregnant woman in Germany, although there are no reported cases of compelled obstetric intervention in Germany and, as argued above, it will be unreasonable to expect a woman to sacrifice her own rights to bodily integrity and self-determination, so that the duty to accept treatment for the benefit of the foetus will lapse in the case of all but the most minimal of interventions. Even in those exceptional cases where it would be reasonable to expect the woman to accept intervention to protect the foetal life and welfare, there is no effective means to enforce compliance, other than the imposition of a fine for contempt,[12] which would appear unlikely to induce the woman to comply in circumstances where she continues to refuse treatment despite the fact that the life of her foetus and often her own life lie in the balance. There is no scope for the woman to be subjected to forcible treatment as has occurred in both England and Wales and the United States of America.

Common to each of the approaches evident in the case law is the portrayal of the woman either as in need of guidance or as deviant and a direct threat to the foetus. Cases such as *Re L*,[13] *Re MB*[14] and *Bolton Hospitals NHS Trust v O*[15] fall into the first category. In each case the woman was prevented by an intervening needle phobia or PTSD-induced panic from consenting to the caesarean they each desired. In each of these cases doctors and judges adopted the role of protector, stepping in to relieve the women concerned of the responsibility and, more crucially, the ability to refuse consent to the caesarean required to ensure the safe delivery of the foetus. In these cases the women were regarded as deserving sympathy; they were to be treated with respect. By contrast, in a number of other cases women who refused to consent due to their own desire for a vaginal delivery, or for religious reasons, have been denigrated as dangerous and the courts have been willing to intervene to compel 'proper' behaviour – that is, to authorise intervention for the benefit of the foetus. Such an approach can be seen in the English case of *Rochdale Healthcare NHS Trust* v *C*[16] and American cases such as *Pemberton*,[17] *Jefferson*[18] and *Burton*.[19] In such cases judges adopt the role of liberator of the foetus, rather than mentor to the pregnant woman. One judge even went as far as to explain that the matter was so important that he had interrupted dressing for dinner in order to determine the case where a woman's religious-based refusal of consent to a blood transfusion put the life of a non-viable foetus at

12 § 1666 BGB together with § 35 FamFG.
13 [1997] FLR 837.
14 *Re MB (Medical Treatment)* (note 11).
15 [2002] EWHC 2871; [2003] 1 FLR 824.
16 [1997] 1 FCR 274.
17 *Pemberton v Tallahassee Memorial Regional Medical Center* 66 F.Supp.2d 1247 (N.D. Fla. 1999).
18 *Jefferson v Griffin Spalding County Hospital Authority* (note 4).
19 *Samantha Burton v Florida* 39 So. 3d 263 (Fla. Dist. Ct. App. 2010).

risk.[20] In this category the woman is clearly viewed by the judges and medical professionals alike not as a woman in trouble but rather as the source of the trouble. She is the villain of the piece, the intruder who prevents the doctor accessing her patient, jeopardising the foetal life on a capricious whim or an irrational fear. Thus Hinkle J described Laura Pemberton (the dehydrated woman who was refused fluids unless she consented to a caesarean) as 'surreptitiously' leaving the hospital against hospital advice.[21] Even in those cases where the courts have stressed that the woman has a right to refuse medical treatment, a right undiminished by pregnancy, the same courts have gone on to condemn the women for exercising that choice and disregarding their moral obligations to the foetus.[22] Common to both categories is the conclusion that the woman is an inappropriate decision-maker, that someone else, normally the attending doctor, should determine whether or not a caesarean or other intervention should take place.[23]

The cases are framed in terms of conflict – either a direct conflict between the woman and the foetus or a conflict between the woman and her healthcare professionals who seek to protect the foetus from her decisions and in some cases to protect her from her own decisions as well. Typically, this conflict is described as dyadic – the maternal–foetal dyad; however, this description fails to appreciate the way that technology enables others to 'participate', or at least observe the progress of a pregnancy, and thus overlooks the increasingly central role played by healthcare professionals throughout pregnancy. If the approach taken emphasises the state's interest in (US) or duty to protect (Germany) potential life, the express focus of the consideration will be upon the conflict between the woman and the foetus. By contrast, in cases that centre upon the woman's capacity (England and Wales and some US states) any consideration of the foetus is limited to an expression of regret that it has no interests capable of protection by the court. Instead, the woman is ranged against medical professionals and, just as in the case of abortion, the woman is portrayed as incapable of making a responsible decision on her own without a doctor's guiding hand.[24] Just as doctors have been given the role of gate-keeper, controlling access to abortion, they also hold significant influence in determining what medical treatment the woman will be required to accept during pregnancy and at birth. The same doctor who offers her advice as to the need to act for the benefit of the foetus will be required to consider whether or not the woman has the capacity to make a decision to reject the treatment she advises as

20 *In re Jamaica Hospital* 491 N.Y.S.2d 898 (1985), at 898.

21 *Pemberton v Tallahassee Memorial Regional Medical Center* (note 17), at 1249.

22 See, for example, Judge LJ's condemnation of S in *St George's Healthcare NHS Trust v S; R v Collins and others, ex parte S* (note 8), at 50.

23 See also Jane Bryan, 'Reading Beyond the Ratio: Searching for the Subtext in the "Enforced Caesarean" Cases' in D. Carpi (ed.) *Bioethics and Biolaw through Literature*, Berlin: Walter de Gruyter, 2011, 115 ff, at 124.

24 For an excellent analysis of the framing of abortion as a medical matter and the role of the doctor in England and Wales, see S. Sheldon, 'Who is the Mother to Make the Judgement? The Construction of Woman in English Abortion Law' (1993) 1(1) *Feminist Legal Studies* 3, at 17; S. Sheldon, *Beyond Control: Medical Power and Abortion Law*, London: Pluto Press, 1997.

necessary! She will then advise the court on the necessity to act, prior to performing the caesarean authorised by the court. Thus the doctor is not a neutral observer, or even an expert witness; instead, she has become a participant in the decision-making or, perhaps more aptly, the management of pregnancy and labour.

In fact, the conflict under each approach may best be viewed as triadic in nature: the woman is set against the foetus and medical authority, often portrayed as having common interests. This is well illustrated by the fact that the Marlowes' foetus was a co-applicant in the action against Amber Marlowe, applying for the hospital to be appointed its guardian and for an injunction restraining her from refusing to consent to a caesarean if it were considered necessary by the attending doctors.[25] This chapter will consider the triadic relationship in two halves – that of the woman and the foetus on the one hand, and the relationship between the woman and her doctor on the other. It will consider the ways in which compelled obstetric intervention may be justified and suggest that the best hope for protecting and promoting both women's and foetal well-being lies in creating an atmosphere of trust, safety and cooperation between the pregnant woman and healthcare professionals. I argue that a change in focus is required: that instead of viewing pregnancy and particularly labour as a technology-driven process, it should be conceptualised as a life stage where technology and medical advice can support the pregnant woman's autonomy, rather than seek to enforce conformity with ideals of maternity. I conclude that whilst there is a public interest in protecting foetal welfare, there is an even greater public interest in maintaining the protection of human dignity and the principle of patient autonomy for all individuals, regardless of their pregnant status.

III. Constructing the 'maternal'–foetal relationship

It was suggested in the introduction that technology has been used to endow the foetus with patient status. Early gynaecological texts of the 17th and 18th centuries portrayed the foetus as a homunculus, a perfectly formed and fully developed miniature man, merely housed in its mother's uterus from which it will emerge fully grown. Similarly, ultrasound has been used to suggest that the foetus is a baby, or at the very least should be treated as a baby, showing and indeed emphasising the separateness of the foetus and the pregnant woman. In Lennart Nilsson's celebrated photos 'The Drama of Life Before Birth',[26] the foetus takes centre stage. The woman is invisible; only the umbilical cord can be seen, suggesting that the foetus is tethered to the woman, but capable of independence if set free from its 'prison'. Images such as these have been used to found a narrative of severability rather than dependence, inviting judges, doctors and society at large to view the foetus as an individual capable of protection and the uterus as a

25 *WVHCS-Hosp., Inc. v. Doe*, No. 3-E-2004, 1–2 (Pa. Ct. Com. Pl. Jan. 14, 2004), unreported.

26 'The Drama of Life before Birth,' *Life*, April 1965.

potentially hostile environment. They have played a great role in increasing public awareness of, and, indeed, interest in, the development of life before birth, an interest reflected in the fact that we live in a society where foetuses talk in films and even try to sell us cars, asking us to consider 'Is something inside you telling you to buy a Volvo?'![27] In this way foetal well-being has become a public matter, an issue of social concern, to be set against the private issue of the woman's personal preference in medical treatment.

In each of the jurisdictions the courts have referred to the foetus as an 'unborn child', a 'child' or a 'baby', stressing the individuality of the foetus and recognising that its welfare and interests may not coincide with those of the pregnant woman. However, by equating the foetus with a child, the courts have marginalised the pregnant women, raising the prospect that, alongside the physiological changes brought by pregnancy, there is also a corresponding loss of personhood, at least for the duration of the pregnancy. In authorising obstetric intervention, the courts' focus has been upon the foetus, as distinct from the pregnant woman, albeit sometimes couched in terms of protecting the woman from her own guilt.[28] However, no matter how interested we may be in the foetus, it must be remembered that the foetus is not a baby, that our reaction to the ultrasound image is an emotional rather than scientific or legal response. The fact that a foetus enjoys the potential to become a baby, following birth, does not mean that it should be treated as already enjoying the rights and protection that are accorded on live birth. Similarly, the 'vessel' in which it is located is not an inanimate machine to be tinkered with to produce the best product; rather, the woman is and remains a person, despite her impending maternity, a person who already enjoys rights that should be upheld rather than negated or circumvented by the courts.

In approaching these cases, the problem lies in determining how to categorise the relationship between the woman and the foetus. In *Attorney General's Reference (No. 3 of 1994)* Lord Mustill held that 'The foetus does not have the attributes which make it a "person"',[29] a statement that reflects the law in each of the jurisdictions under consideration. However, despite the lack of personhood, it is common ground that the foetus is not worthless, as Judge LJ acknowledged in *St George's*: 'Whatever else it may be a 36-week foetus is not nothing: if viable it is not lifeless and it is certainly human'.[30] Whilst the courts in the United States and England and Wales have not gone as far as the German *Bundesverfassungsgericht* in recognising that the foetus is protected by the right to life, all three jurisdictions recognise that the foetus has value and that that value increases with increased gestation.

27 J. S. Taylor, 'The Public Fetus and the Family Car: From Abortion Politics to a Volvo Advertisement' (1992) 4 *Public Culture* 67.

28 See, for example, *Norfolk and Norwich Healthcare (NHS) Trust v W* [1996] 2 FLR 613, at 616.

29 *Attorney General's Reference (No. 3 of 1994)* [1998] AC 245, at 256.

30 *St George's Healthcare NHS Trust v S; R v Collins and others, ex parte S* (note 8), at 45.

1. Three models of pregnancy

A number of models of pregnancy may be suggested, each of which adopts a different approach to framing the relationship between the woman and the foetus.[31] Each model will be assessed, before moving on to consider the woman's status and rights and those of the foetus with regard to medical treatment.

a. The separate entities model

This model lies at the centre of the compelled obstetric intervention cases and can be seen as the basis of the maternal/foetal conflict. It regards the pregnant woman and the foetus as distinct entities; in the words of Barbara Katz Rothman, it portrays 'mother and fetus as separate beings, like nesting Russian dolls, one inside the other'.[32] Significant weight has been given to this model of pregnancy by ultrasound imaging. As Julie Palmer convincingly argues:

> The foetus, centre frame, is depicted as if disconnected from the pregnant body and pregnant subjectivity. Women are literally and discursively erased from pregnant pictures, allowing the foetus to appear as an autonomous individual, as patient and as citizen. Separated in this way, the rights of women and foetuses are often set in opposition.[33]

As considered above, medical technology has promoted this model of pregnancy, suggesting that two separate patients exist. Indeed, the terms 'foetal medicine unit', 'foetal surgery' and 'foetal therapy' explicitly recognise the patient status of the foetus; the impact upon the woman is left unspoken, with no reference to the surgery she will endure in order to grant access to the foetus. This access requirement leads to the woman's abdominal wall being conceptualised as a barrier to be breached in order to save the foetus.

There is significant support for this model of pregnancy in the United States. For example, the State Child Health Insurance Programme (S-CHIP) defines a foetus as a child from the point of conception for the purposes of the state-sponsored health insurance;[34] significantly, however, only services directly affecting the foetus are covered so that care required by the woman in connection with pregnancy may not be reimbursed, including postnatal care required after a caesarean. Similarly, the separate entity model has been enshrined in the form of a federal statute in the Unborn Victims of Violence Act (UVVA) 2004,[35] which makes it a crime to

31 See, generally, J. Seymour, *Childbirth and the Law*, Oxford: Oxford University Press, 2000, chapter 9.

32 B. K. Rothman, *Recreating Motherhood*, New Brunswick, NJ: Rutgers University Press, 2000, 2nd edition reprint, at 109.

33 J. Palmer, 'Seeing and Knowing: Ultrasound Images in the Contemporary Abortion Debate' (2009) 10(2) *Feminist Theory* 173, at 174, internal references omitted.

34 42 Code of Federal Regulations (CFR) 457, § 457.10.

35 18 U.S.C. § 1841 (2011).

injure or cause the death of a foetus (at any stage of the pregnancy) whilst committing a federal offence – that is, a separate crime to that committed by injuring the pregnant woman carrying the foetus. Clearly, the fact that the crime can only be committed during the commission of a federal offence limits the scope of this provision, but its significance, like the definition of 'child' adopted by the S-CHIP, lies in the recognition that the foetus is not a mere part of the woman's body but a separate entity with the capacity to be a victim in its own right.

Moreover, the separate entities model has also been adopted by some of the courts in the USA (e.g. in *Pemberton*[36]) but rejected by others – thus, for example, in *In re Baby Boy Doe* the court held that the rights of the foetus should not be balanced against those of the woman.[37] Consideration of these two cases makes it clear precisely how misconceived the separate entities model is. Neither Laura Pemberton nor Tabita Bricci wanted to harm the foetuses they were carrying. Both were willingly pregnant and wanted their babies to be born safely; they simply did not accept medical advice that a caesarean was necessary in order to achieve that result. Nevertheless, in both cases those seeking a court order to force the women to have a caesarean did so on the basis that the women posed a threat to the foetuses by their refusal to consent to the indicated treatment. Refusing the order, the Appellate Court of Illinois stressed that:

> A woman's right to refuse invasive medical treatment, derived from her rights to privacy, bodily integrity, and religious liberty, is not diminished during pregnancy. The woman retains the same right to refuse invasive treatment, even of lifesaving or other beneficial nature, that she can exercise when she is not pregnant. The potential impact upon the fetus is not legally relevant; to the contrary, the Stallman court explicitly rejected the view that the woman's rights can be subordinated to fetal rights.[38]

The court specifically noted that a caesarean section poses additional risks to the woman's health and relied on *Thornburgh* in finding that 'any degree of increased risk to the woman's health is unacceptable'.[39] By contrast, in *Pemberton* the court was not prepared to allow the woman to give birth in the manner she desired, imposing the risks of a caesarean upon Laura Pemberton rather than allowing her to put the foetus at risk by failing to acquiesce to medical advice. In fact, Laura Pemberton went on to deliver four children vaginally in subsequent pregnancies, demonstrating that the 'clear and uncontradicted' medical evidence preferred by the court, that the interests of the foetus required a caesarean section in order to avert the serious threat to its life, was perhaps not as compelling as Hinkle J assumed.[40]

36 *Pemberton v Tallahassee Memorial Regional Medical Center* (note 17).
37 *In re Baby Boy Doe, a Fetus v Mother Doe* (note 9), at 333.
38 Ibid., at 332.
39 Ibid., at 333, citing *Thornburgh v. American College of Obstetricians and Gynecologists* (1986), 476 U.S. 747, at 769.
40 *Pemberton v Tallahassee Memorial Regional Medical Center* (note 17), at 1253.

As the case law demonstrates, it is not necessarily the woman herself who is perceived as being hostile towards the foetus; instead, it may be her body that is considered to be toxic, as in the case of Angela Carder,[41] the woman with cancer who was unwilling to undergo a caesarean that she knew would hasten her own death until the 28th week of pregnancy when she believed her foetus had a better chance of survival. It is difficult to see Angela Carder as the foetus's adversary, as hostile to the much wanted 'child' within her body; nevertheless, counsel was appointed for the foetus – separate counsel to that appointed to represent Angela Carder, emphasising the severability of their relationship. Thus the separate entity model supports an illusion of equality between the foetus and the pregnant woman, suggesting that doctors and courts have equal duties in respect of each; it fails to take account of the fact that only one person, as opposed to a potential person, is engaged in the relationship. As the most recent American case law, together with Sir Stephen Brown P's decision in *Re S*,[42] makes clear, foetal interests have all too often been recognised at the cost of a corresponding diminution in the woman's autonomy.

With the exception of the now discredited decision in *Re* S,[43] the English courts have rejected the separate entities model on the basis that the foetus 'up to the moment of birth does not have any separate interests capable of being taken into account when a court has to consider an application for a declaration in respect of a caesarean section operation'.[44] In *St George's* Judge LJ recognised that the interests of the foetus may be distinct from those of the pregnant woman and that the two sets of interests may conflict, but emphasised that:

> While pregnancy increases the personal responsibilities of a woman it does not diminish her entitlement to decide whether or not to undergo medical treatment… . An unborn child is not a separate person from its mother. Its need for medical assistance does not prevail over her rights. She is entitled not to be forced to submit to an invasion of her body against her will, whether her own life or that of her unborn child depends on it. Her right is not reduced or diminished merely because her decision to exercise it may appear morally repugnant.[45]

In emphasising the severability of the foetus and the woman, this model acknowledges that the foetus is not simply a part of the woman, in the sense of being analogous to one of her organs; it is within her body, but not part of her body and ultimately will be expelled from her body to become a person in its own right. However, in emphasising the separateness of the woman and the foetus, the model fails to recognise the interconnectedness of the foetus and the pregnant

41 *Re AC* 537 A 2d 1235 (1990).
42 [1993] Fam 123.
43 Ibid.
44 *Re MB (Medical Treatment)* (note 11), *per* Butler Sloss LJ, at 444.
45 *St George's Healthcare NHS Trust v S; R v Collins and others, ex parte S* (note 8), at 50.

woman, a connection that is more than a tie that binds in the form of an umbilical cord. As the European Commission of Human Rights recognised in *Paton v United Kingdom*, 'the "life" of the foetus is intimately connected with, and cannot be regarded in isolation from, the life of the pregnant woman'.[46] Thus the separate entities model is problematic for a number of reasons. Apart from the connection between the woman and the foetus that might best be described as an emotional bond, there is also a very physical bond between the two – as a matter of geography the foetus is clearly not separate from the pregnant woman. However, this model reduces the status of the woman to that of a foetal container, rejuvenating the Aristotelian view of pregnancy whereby the woman's role in reproduction is reduced to that of functioning as a plant pot into which a man would plant his seed, from which the foetus would fruit. This conceptualisation of the woman as a passive receptacle containing an animated foetus is graphically illustrated in William Liley's seminal article 'The foetus as a personality', where he argues:

> Far from being an inert passenger in a pregnant mother, the foetus is very much in command of the pregnancy. It is the foetus who ... induces all manner of changes in maternal physiology to make her a suitable host.[47]

In the article he refers to the woman's uterus as the foetus's 'warm and humid microclimate',[48] clearly delimiting the foetus and 'his host' as separate entities, and contrasting the woman's passive role of incubating the foetus, with foetal dynamism up until the point of separation, concluding: 'When our cords were cut, we were not severed from our mothers but from our own organs – our placentae – which were appropriate to our old environment but unnecessary in our new one'.

The framing of the woman and the foetus as separate marginalises women and makes conflict between the two almost inevitable. Upon reading the judgments discussed above, it is difficult to avoid the conclusion that the foetus has been accorded the starring role, sharing centre stage with the doctor who is trying to save it, whilst the pregnant woman is banished to the wings as the courts focus upon the doctors' assessment of the foetus's needs and how they may be met. Despite judicial pronouncements to the contrary, it is impossible to overlook the fact that women are rendered invisible in the recounting of the tale. At best they are viewed as a foetal support system in need of expert guidance; at worst, a toxic influence, providing a malfunctioning environment and perniciously jeopardising the foetus that only the doctor can save. Yet, as Catherine MacKinnon points out, 'the pregnant woman is more than a location for gestation';[49] her role in this production should not be limited to that of a passive incubator or villain.

46 (1980) 3 E.H.R.R 408, at 415.
47 A. W. Liley, 'The Foetus as a Personality' (1972) 6 *Australian and New Zealand Journal of Psychiatry* 99, at 100.
48 Ibid.
49 C. A. MacKinnon, 'Reflections on Sex Equality under Law' (1991) 100 *Yale Law Journal* 1281 at 1316.

b. The single entity model of pregnancy

It has been noted that the distinction between a baby and the viable foetus is simply one of geography. As Levie J stated in *Re Madyun*: 'All that stood between the Madyun fetus and its independent existence, separate from its mother, was, put simply, a doctor's scalpel. In these circumstances, the life of the infant inside its mother's womb was entitled to be protected'.[50]

This argument, however, demonstrates the key distinction between the baby and the foetus – a foetus is located within the woman's body, unlike a baby who is a person in her own right, separate from the woman.[51] That being so, can the foetus be categorised as a part of the woman, mere tissue that she can treat as she wishes?

The single entity model of pregnancy is a one-dimensional model which views the foetus as part of the woman; it has no separate identity and is regarded as equivalent to one of her limbs. Adopting this model of pregnancy in 1900, the *Reichsgericht* held: 'The embryo is not an independent being, but rather forms a part of the uterus'.[52] This model dominated the jurisprudence in the common law jurisdictions during the twentieth century, and continues to be adopted in Canada where the Supreme Court applied it in *Winnipeg Child and Family Services (Northwest Area) v G*, describing the foetus as 'one part of a legal and physical entity',[53] the pregnant woman. Giving the judgment for the majority, McLachlin J stated:

> To permit an unborn child to sue its pregnant mother-to-be would introduce a radically new conception into the law; the unborn child and its mother as separate juristic persons in a mutually separable and antagonistic relation. Such a legal conception, moreover, is belied by the reality of the physical situation; for practical purposes, the unborn child and its mother-to-be are bonded in a union separable only by birth.[54]

Adherence to this unitary model of pregnancy led the American courts to exclude the possibility of recovery for prenatal injuries until 1946. The classic statement of the law was set out by in *Dietrich v Northampton*, where Oliver Wendell Holmes J held that there was no cause of action for wrongful death as the foetus 'was a part of the mother at the time of the injury'.[55] Similarly, in England and Wales, when the Court of Appeal considered whether the death of a child as a result of injuries

50 Re *Madyun*, published as appendix to *Re A.C.*, 573 A.2d 1235, 1262 (D.C.App. 1990), at 1262.
51 C. Overall, 'Mother/Fetus/State Conflicts' (1988) *Health Law in Canada* 101, at 102.
52 *Reichsgericht, GA* 1900, 286.
53 *Winnipeg Child and Family Services (Northwest Area) v G* (1997) 152 DLR (4th) 193, at para 27.
54 Ibid., at para 29.
55 138 Mass. 14 (1884), at 17.

sustained in utero could constitute murder or manslaughter, it adopted the conventional model, holding that:

> In the eyes of the law the foetus is taken to be a part of the mother until it has an existence independent of the mother. Thus an intention to cause serious bodily injury to the foetus is an intention to cause serious bodily injury to a part of the mother just as an intention to injure her arm or leg would be so viewed.[56]

Conceptualising the foetus as a part of the woman, the Court of Appeal applied the doctrine of transferred malice, holding that thereby a defendant could commit murder by causing prenatal injuries that led to death after the child was born. On appeal, the House of Lords rejected this application of the doctrine, holding that the requisite double transfer of malice, from the woman to the foetus and then from the foetus to the child, was one legal fiction too many.[57] Moreover, their Lordships, whilst accepting that the foetus is not a person, refused to accept that it was a mere body part.

Whilst there are obvious advantages to conceptualising the woman and the foetus as separate entities in cases involving prenatal injuries caused by a third party, it is suggested that such an approach is inappropriate where the source of harm is the pregnant woman herself, pitting as it does the woman against the entity resident (albeit temporarily) in her uterus. Thus, within the context of medical treatment, the single entity model applied by the Court of Appeal offers substantial benefits from the perspective of those wishing to maintain the woman's autonomy – it clearly recognises the pregnant woman as the sole patient and thus supports her right to determine what medical treatment to have without regard to foetal interests. Nevertheless, the unitary model fails to fully capture the relationship between the woman and the foetus, not least because it lacks any appreciation of the significant difference between a foetus and a leg! Indeed, as Catherine MacKinnon recognises, 'No other body part gets up and walks away on its own eventually'.[58]

Although the foetus is carried within the woman's body for the duration of the pregnancy, it will become independent at a reasonably predictable point of time in the future, unlike other tissue within the woman's body which lacks any capacity for independence. Similarly, the foetus can be differentiated from the woman's tissue by virtue of the genetic difference between the woman and the foetus. The foetus has its own genetic make-up, drawing upon the genetic heritage of both its parents-to-be. In that sense it is not merely part of the woman; rather, as Catherine MacKinnon suggests, it is more akin to a parasite:

> Physically, no body part takes as much and contributes as little. The fetus does not exist to serve the woman as her body parts do. The relation is more the

56 *Attorney General's Reference (No. 3 of 1994)* [1996] 2 Q.B. 581 (Court of Appeal), *per* Taylor LCJ, at 593.

57 *Attorney General's Reference (No. 3 of 1994)* (note 29), *per* Lord Mustill, at 261–2.

58 C. MacKinnon (note 49), at 1315.

> other way around; on the biological level, the fetus is more like a parasite than a part.[59]

A recognition of the biological realities led the American Supreme Court to reverse the central holding of *Dietrich v Northampton* in *Bonbrest v. Kotz* (1946), where the court drew on medical evidence to dispute the finding that the foetus was always a part of the mother and held that from viability, if born alive, recovery would be permitted for prenatal injuries. As McGuire J explained, from viability the foetus

> is in the womb, but it is capable now of extra-uterine life – and while dependent for its continued development on sustenance derived from its peculiar relationship to its mother, it is not a 'part' of the mother in the sense of a constituent element... . It has ... its own bodily form and members, manifests all of the anatomical characteristics of individuality, possesses its own circulatory, vascular and excretory systems and is capable now of being ushered into the visible world.[60]

In rejecting the single entity model, McGuire J referred to the foetus's 'peculiar relationship to its mother', defining the relationship in biological terms, but it is suggested that the woman is much more than a food source, and that to diminish the relationship between the woman and the foetus in such a way ignores the symbiotic nature of that relationship. Whilst the single entity model obviates the potential for conflict between the woman and the foetus, it is fundamentally flawed in that it fails to take any account of the foetus. In doing so, the model does not reflect the way that many pregnant women view their pregnancy, neglecting as it does the social relational context of pregnancy. Barbara Katz Rothman alludes to this 'special relationship' in her defence of what she calls the 'woman-centred model of pregnancy':

> The baby is not planted within the mother, but flesh of her flesh, part of her. Maybe, as very early in an unwanted pregnancy, a part of her like the ovum itself was part of her, an expendable or even threatening part, or maybe, as is most often the case by the end of a wanted pregnancy, an essential part of her, a treasured aspect of her being. If one thinks of pregnancy this way, then the rights argument is an absurdity. It is not the rights of one autonomous being set against the rights of another, but the profound alienation of the woman set against part of herself.[61]

Just as the separate entities model fails to recognise the subtleties of the relationship between a woman and the foetus she carries, treating them as severable

59 Ibid., at 1314.
60 *Bonbrest v Katz* 65 F. Supp. 138 (1946), at 140–1.
61 B. K. Rothman (note 32), at 109.

adversaries, the single entity model entirely disregards the foetal interests and indeed the wider societal interest in the foetus. Thus this model has been subject to much criticism and is similarly inadequate in conceptualising the nature of the relationship between the pregnant woman and the foetus. In England and Wales it was finally rejected by the House of Lords in *Attorney General's Reference (No. 3 of 1994)* where Lord Hope posited that the embryo is 'a separate organism from the mother from the moment of its conception'.[62] It is suggested that such pronouncements should be treated with great care. Just because the foetus is a separate organism, it is not, and should not be treated as, a separate entity with rights capable of protection and enforcement against the pregnant woman. To do so would create an adversarial relationship between the woman and the foetus, a possibility recognised by Cunningham J in *Stallman v Youngquist* who cautioned against treating the foetus as an entirely separate entity, stating:

> A legal right of a fetus to begin life with a sound mind and body assertable against a mother would make a pregnant woman the guarantor of the mind and body of her child at birth ... Mother and child would be legal adversaries from the moment of conception until birth. The error that a fetus cannot be harmed in a legally cognizable way when the woman who is its mother is injured has been corrected; the law will no longer treat the fetus as only a part of its mother. The law will not now make an error of a different sort, one with enormous implications for all women who have been, are, may be, or might become pregnant: the law will not treat a fetus as an entity which is entirely separate from its mother.[63]

For this reason it is suggested that Lord Mustill best captured the nature of the relationship in *Attorney-General's Reference (No. 3 of 1994)*. He considered the relationship between the woman and the foetus at some length and recognised that there are both physical and emotional bonds between the two. In terms of a physical bond, the foetus is entirely dependent upon the woman for the nutrients and oxygen it needs, and there is also a very special emotional bond, but he stressed:

> The relationship [is] one of bond, not identity. The mother and the foetus [a]re two distinct organisms living symbiotically, not a single organism with two aspects... . The foetus is neither [a person nor an adjunct of the mother]. It is a unique organism.[64]

c. *The 'not one, but not two' model*

The courts in each of the three jurisdictions under consideration largely appear to have adopted the third model of pregnancy averred to by Lord Mustill – that

62 *Attorney General's Reference (No. 3 of 1994)* (note 29), at 267.
63 *Stallman v Youngquist* 125 Ill.2d 267 (1988), at 276–7.
64 *Attorney General's Reference (No. 3 of 1994)* (note 29), at 255–6.

referred to as the 'not one, but not two' model by Isabel Karpin.[65] This model recognises the interdependence of the relationship between a pregnant woman and the foetus. It recognises that they are not antagonists, but that the foetus is more than simply a part of the woman's body; in what is now rather quaint language, the woman is 'with child'. Thus in *Attorney-General's Reference (No. 3 of 1994)* Lord Mustill recognised that the foetus is 'a unique organism', describing it as 'an organism *sui generis* lacking at this stage the entire range of characteristics both of the mother to which it is physically linked and of the complete human being which it will later become'.[66] Similarly, in its second abortion ruling (*Schwangerschaftsabbruch II*) the *Bundesverfassungsgericht* characterised the relationship between the pregnant woman and the foetus as a *Zweiheit in Einheit*[67] – duality in unity – distancing itself from its first abortion decision where it had emphasised the separateness of the foetus and the pregnant woman.[68] In Abortion II the *Bundesverfassungsgericht* stressed that pregnancy involves a unique constitutional situation. It concluded that the concept of duality in unity best represents the relationship as it encompasses recognition that the woman and the foetus are both separately and severally protected by the guarantee of human dignity and the right to life,[69] and that both the woman and the state have a duty to protect foetal life in so far as it is reasonable to do so. Moreover, the term often used in the literature to refer to the foetus, '*Leibesfrucht*' (literally, fruit of the womb), encapsulates the connectedness between the woman and the foetus, the fact that it grows within her body, that it is of her, but not her, and in no way comparable to a body part.[70] Just like the apple will fall from the tree, the foetus will become physically separate from the woman.

As the American case law demonstrates, no single model of pregnancy has been adopted throughout the country, although the Supreme Court has categorically stated that the foetus is not a person.[71] Whilst many of the American courts have treated the foetus as a separate entity, the Appellate Court[72] and Supreme Court of Illinois appear to subscribe to this indivisibly linked model. Thus the Illinois Supreme Court recognised the special nature of the relationship in *Stallman v Youngquist*, holding that the relationship between the woman and the foetus within her is 'unlike the relationship between any other plaintiff and defendant' and that

65 I. Karpin, 'Legislating the Female Body: Reproductive Technology and the Reconstructed Woman' (1992) 3 *Columbia Journal of Gender and Law* 325, at 329.
66 *Attorney General's Reference (No. 3 of 1994)* (note 29), at 256, 255.
67 *BVerfGE* 88, 203, at 253.
68 *BVerfGE* 39, 1, at 42.
69 Art. 1 I and Art. 2 II GG.
70 See also N. Heinemann, *Frau und Fötus in der Prä- und Perinatalmedizin aus strafrechtlicher Sicht*, Baden-Baden: Nomos, 2000, at 11. Since the 5th Act for the Reform of Criminal Law 1974 (*Das Fünfte Gesetz zur Reform des Strafrechts*, 18.06.1974, BGBl. I S. 1297) § 218 StGB no longer refers to 'Leibesfrucht', but it remains clear that the foetus is the subject of the protection afforded by that provision.
71 *Roe v Wade* 410 U.S. 113 (1973), at 158.
72 *In re Baby Boy Doe, a Fetus v Mother Doe* (note 9); *In re Brown*, 689 N.E.2d 397 (1997).

whilst 'the law will no longer treat the fetus as only a part of its mother ... the law will not treat a fetus as an entity which is entirely separate from its mother'.[73]

In addition to the approval with which this model has been met in the courts, it has also been well received by academics and is regarded as providing a more measured response to the need to categorise the relationship between the woman and the foetus. Thus Catherine MacKinnon has described the foetus as

> More than a body part but less than a person, where it is, is largely what it is. From the standpoint of the pregnant woman, it is both me and not me. It 'is' the pregnant woman in the sense that it is in her and of her and is hers more than anyone's. It 'is not' her in the sense that she is not all that is there.[74]

The key advantage of the 'not one, but not two' model is that it recognises the organic value of the woman and the foetus, circumventing the potential for 'maternal'/foetal conflict, whilst still enabling the state to protect the foetus from third parties. This more nuanced approach recognises that the woman and foetus are connected to each other, that there is more than a mere physical bond between them, but also that this is not a symmetrical relationship of equals with equal rights. Thus it recognises the inherent value of the foetus, without requiring the sacrifice of the pregnant woman's autonomy and reducing her to little more than a machine, the sole purpose of which is to provide life support to the foetus.

2. *Reconciling the rights and interests of the woman and the foetus*

It is suggested that the 'not one, but not two' model of pregnancy provides the most appropriate basis for considering intervention against the wishes of the pregnant woman for the benefit of her foetus, but the question remains how the woman's rights and the interests of the foetus can be reconciled within that context. However, as Janet Gallagher argued, 'Given the very geography of pregnancy, questions as to the status of the fetus must follow, not precede, an examination of the rights of the woman within whose body and life the fetus exists'.[75]

a. Anticipatory decision-making

It is well recognised that generally in each of the jurisdictions under consideration every patient with the requisite capacity has the right to refuse medical treatment, even that which may save her life.[76] The question is, however, whether an

73 *Stallman v Youngquist* (note 63), at 279, 277.

74 C. MacKinnon (note 49), at 1316.

75 J. Gallagher, 'Fetus as Patient' in S. Cohen and N. Taub (eds) *Reproductive Laws for the 1990s*, New Brunswick, NJ: Rutgers University Press, 1989, at 187–8.

76 *Re T (An Adult) (Consent to Medical Treatment)* (note 11); *Airedale NHS Trust v Bland* [1993] 1 All ER 821; *Re MB (Medical Treatment)* (note 11); *Ms B v An NHS Hospital Trust* [2002] EWHC 429 (Fam); *BGHSt* 11, 111 at 113; *BGHZ* 154, 205; *BGHZ* 163, 195; *Cruzan v Director, Missouri Dept of Health* 111 L ed 2d 224 (1990).

exception to this general principle exists such that a pregnant woman's consent is not necessary for treatment intended to benefit the foetus. In the context of anticipatory decision-making such an exception has considerable support in each of the jurisdictions. In the case of advance directives, legislation in the US and guidance in England and Wales and Germany suggest that advance refusals of treatment should not be applicable or should be of limited applicability in the case of a pregnant woman.[77] Whilst that is expressly provided for in the relevant legislation of many US states,[78] in the case of England and Wales and Germany it is only a factor that must be considered in assessing the applicability and validity of the advance decision.

In both Germany and England and Wales the legislation relating to advance decisions makes provision for an advance directive to be invalidated by a change of circumstance indicating that the directive no longer represents the patient's fixed decision.[79] In *HE v A Hospital NHS Trust, AE* Munby J suggested that marrying or having children might create a materially changed circumstance, such as to give rise to sufficient doubt as to override the clear and otherwise valid and applicable advance directive.[80] Similarly, assessing the German law, Andreas Spickhoff [81] and Petra Balz[82] have argued that founding a family after drafting a directive might suffice to cast doubt upon the continuing validity of the directive. Certainly, becoming pregnant and having a child are life-changing events; however, particularly in the case of a religious-based objection, such a change in circumstances is unlikely to affect the patient's refusal of treatment. In other cases the impact of overriding her anticipatory refusal will need to be carefully assessed in the circumstances; if the patient is unlikely to regain capacity and the terms of the directive are fulfilled, serious questions should be asked about whether the fact that the woman is pregnant creates sufficient doubt about the validity of her express wishes to justify applying the preference for life and overriding her advance refusal of treatment.

Given that doubts concerning the continuing validity of an advance directive arise after the woman has been found to lack capacity – that is, at a time when she

77 *Mental Capacity Act 2005: Code of Practice, 2007*, at paras 9.16 and 9.43; BMA, *Advance decisions and proxy decision-making in medical treatment and research: Guidance from the BMA's Medical Ethics Department*, 2007, at 6; GMC,*Treatment and care towards the end of life: good practice in decision-making*, 2010; German Medical Association guidelines, 'BÄK Empfehlungen der Bundesärztekammer und der Zentralen Ethikkommission bei der Bundesärztekammer zum Umgang mit Vorsorgevollmacht und Patientenverfügung in der ärztlichen Praxis' (2010) 18 *Deutsches Ärzteblatt* 877.

78 See, for example, the Alabama Code § 22–8A-4(e) (2011): 'The advance directive for health care of a declarant who is known by the attending physician to be pregnant shall have no effect during the course of the declarant's pregnancy'.

79 S.25(2)(C) MCA 2005; § 1901a I BGB.

80 *HE v A Hospital NHS Trust, AE* [2003] EWHC 1017 (Fam) at para 43.

81 A. Spickhoff, 'Rechtssicherheit kraft Gesetzes durch sog. Patientenverfügungen?' (2009) *FamRZ* 1949, at 1951.

82 P. Balz, *Lebenserhaltung als Haftungsgrund*, Berlin: Springer, 2010, at 67.

will be unable to demonstrate the continuing validity of her refusal – great care must be taken not to subvert the utility of an advance directive. Doubts raised about the continuing applicability of the advance decision must be subjected to a stringent burden of proof, requiring that it be proved beyond reasonable doubt that the patient would no longer intend the decision to apply in her pregnant state. Andreas Spickhoff discusses the case of a pregnant woman, injured and in a serious condition with a poor prognosis following an accident. He argues that despite her advance directive refusing all forms of intensive care, she should be treated and that the directive cannot be said to be applicable due to the change in circumstance brought about by her pregnancy.[83] However, it is suggested that merely raising doubts about the validity of her directive will not suffice and that, instead, clear and convincing evidence must be adduced to show that she, rather than the 'reasonable woman', would not have intended her directive to apply in the case of pregnancy.

Pregnancy represents a unique life-changing event in that it is a transitory state, in which, for the duration of the pregnancy, the survival of another entity is entirely dependent upon the maintenance of that state. Therefore, pregnancy raises issues of a different nature to those occurring from other changes in circumstance, such as those mentioned by Munby J – getting married or having a child. In both these examples a new legal relationship has been formed since the writing of the directive, but the change of circumstance occasioned thereby would appear irrelevant in the circumstances that Spickhoff outlines. Thus, if the patient has an apposite advance directive stipulating that, in the case of loss of capacity, if she is in an apallic state, she refuses all life-sustaining treatment including ANH, ventilation and antibiotics, that directive is likely to be unaffected by the fact that she has married or given birth to a child in the intervening period since drafting the directive. By contrast, it could be suggested that the fact that she has become pregnant since drafting the directive would constitute a material change of circumstance, a suggestion made by both the Law Commission[84] and the British Medical Association.[85] In such a situation it would be possible to argue that the patient would have wanted to be kept alive for as long as was necessary to sustain the pregnancy until the child could be delivered.[86]

Thus, in both England and Wales and Germany, pregnancy is likely to lead to an assessment of whether the advance decision is still valid and applicable. Whilst this does not amount to the suspension of an advance directive for the duration of the pregnancy found in most American states, given that the principle of *in dubio*

83 A. Spickhoff (note 81), at 1951–2.

84 Law Commission, *Mental Incapacity* (Law Com No. 231, 1995), at paras 5.25–5.26, proposing that a presumption of non-applicability should apply in the absence of an indication to the contrary, Draft Bill, clause 9(3).

85 BMA, *Advance decisions and proxy decision-making in medical treatment and research: Guidance from the BMA's Medical Ethics Department*, 2007, at 6.

86 S. Halliday, 'Legislating to Give Effect to Precedent Autonomy: Comparative Reflections on Legislative Incompetence' (2011) 11 *Medical Law International* 127, at 157f.

pro vita underpins both of the legislative responses to anticipatory decision-making, this potential invalidity offers significant scope to undermine precedent autonomy. Nevertheless, there is no sound basis for the suggestion that pregnancy should automatically invalidate a woman's advance directive; such a suggestion overemphasises the woman's function as a foetal incubator, neglecting to consider her own rights and the negative impact upon her dignity that treating her as such would entail. The validity of a woman's advance directive cannot depend upon the contents of her uterus; thus it is submitted that there is a rebuttable presumption that an advance directive should survive pregnancy, requiring clear and convincing evidence that the woman would not have wanted her advance decision to operate during her pregnancy in order to justify setting the directive aside. If clear and convincing evidence does exist that the woman would have wished to receive treatment to enable the pregnancy to continue to term, implementation of the advance directive should be postponed until after the child has been delivered, and thereafter treatment can be discontinued in accordance with the directive.

b. Contemporaneous decision-making

In the case of contemporaneous decision-making there is much less clarity about the existence of such an exception in practical rather than merely theoretical terms. It will be remembered that in some of the US states the courts have held that medical intervention can be compelled on the basis of the state's interest in potential life, purporting to apply the third-trimester rule set out in *Roe v Wade*;[87] in others the woman's refusal of consent has been upheld subject to the requirement that she have the capacity to decide. Unlike the English courts, where the woman lacks capacity to decide the American courts apply the substituted judgement approach, seeking to establish what the individual would have wanted rather than what her best interests demand. There are no reported cases in this area, although, given that advance directives are almost always invalidated during pregnancy, it is likely that the judgment substituted would reflect what the court considers the 'good' expectant woman would have decided, accepting all treatment. Some guidance about how the woman's will might be ascertained can be derived from the District of Columbia Court of Appeals' decision in *re AC*.[88] The court stressed that, if competent, a woman's refusal of treatment will (usually) be determinative[89] and that, in the case of a woman lacking capacity to decide, the substituted judgment approach must be used to ascertain what the patient would want, finding that:

> To determine the subjective desires of the patient, the court must consider the totality of the evidence, focusing particularly on written or oral directions concerning treatment to family, friends, and health-care professionals. The court should also take into account the patient's past decisions regarding

87 *Roe v Wade* (note 71).
88 *Re AC* (note 41).
89 Ibid., at 1249ff.

> medical treatment, and attempt to ascertain from what is known about the patient's value system, goals, and desires what the patient would decide if competent.[90]

The patient's previously expressed wishes will be extremely important, but her previous treatment decisions may not demonstrate a clear preference for or against treatment. This was clearly the case in *re AC*; as the court recognised, she had sought antenatal care and had, in her earlier fight with cancer, accepted extremely invasive treatment (including amputation of her leg, radiation and chemotherapy). She became pregnant following three years in remission and was looking forward to the birth of her child, but a tumour was discovered on her lung during the 25th week of pregnancy and she was advised that it was inoperable. She chose to receive palliative care, knowing that it posed a risk to the foetus, on the basis that it would make her more comfortable and, she hoped, enable her to survive for three weeks, allowing the foetus to be delivered at 28 weeks, when it was felt it had the best chance of surviving. She was equivocal about whether she still wanted to have the baby. Thus her previous medical decisions did not provide reliable evidence of what she would have wanted, but there is a suggestion that take-up of antenatal care, without an express refusal of treatment, might support a finding that the woman would have wanted to have treatment for the foetus.

The court recognised that a subjective consideration of what the patient would want might not yield a clear answer and went on to say that:

> When the patient is pregnant, however, she may not be concerned exclusively with her own welfare. Thus it is proper for the court, in a case such as this, to weigh (along with all the other factors) the mother's prognosis, the viability of the fetus, the probable result of treatment or non-treatment for both mother and fetus, and the mother's likely interest in avoiding impairment for her child together with her own instincts for survival.[91]

It is suggested that this 'objective' consideration of what the woman would have wanted will dominate the assessment, and that although the substituted judgment standard is supposed to prioritise autonomy, normative considerations of what a 'good' mother would decide will prove irresistible to a court faced with a foetus that can be saved.

In England and Wales the courts have held that a pregnant woman's ability to consent, or refuse consent, is unaffected by her pregnancy, although in every case where a foetus was at risk due to the woman's refusal of consent, the woman has been held to lack capacity and the operation has been authorised as furthering her best interests. The scope for overruling a treatment refusal, or indeed for taking only minimal account of the woman's wishes under the best interests standard, is particularly apparent in the latest tranche of cases, where the women's autonomy

90 Ibid., at 1251.
91 Ibid.

was undermined by mental illness. These were not refusals based on ideological or religious grounds; in fact, in many of the cases there was no refusal of consent. The majority were pre-emptive applications based on the potential need for intervention rather than existing medical situations, with hospitals seeking permissive orders to allow doctors to intervene if they deemed it necessary, without the need for the woman's consent. The only basis upon which this can lawfully occur is to promote the woman's best interests. However, in a large number of the cases on both sides of the Atlantic the woman's health or life has not been endangered; rather, the risk to be averted has been to the foetus. It must be questioned whether the imposition of risk and pain through the performance of major abdominal surgery for the benefit of the foetus is consistent with furthering the woman's best interests, particularly where there is no risk to her physical health. In a number of the latest English cases the judges incorporated a consideration of what the woman would want into the best interests assessment. Clearly, the woman's own wishes and values are extremely relevant to that assessment, but rather than considering her subjective wishes, all too often the judges referred to what the woman would want by considering the question objectively, namely on the basis of what 'any pregnant woman' would want, concluding that the answer was the safe delivery of the foetus by whatever means necessary. Giving voice to this presumption, Butler-Sloss LJ stated in *Re MB*: 'It must be in the best interests of a woman carrying a full-term child whom she wants to be born alive and healthy that such a result should if possible be achieved'.[92] Similarly, the Royal College of Obstetricians and Gynaecologists recommends that in determining the patient's best interests

> The underlying moral presumptions are first in favour of life and second in favour of a mother's normal will to do what is best for the fetus. For example, in the absence of an advance directive and with neurological evidence of brain death in the mother, it would be appropriate to act on behalf of the fetus.[93]

Such altruistic desires are routinely ascribed to pregnant women and mothers,[94] and it is suggested that even though the English law has not recognised an exception to the general rule that consent is required, in practice such an exception would appear to exist, in the guise of the woman's best interests.

92 *Re MB (Medical Treatment)* (note 11), at 439.

93 Royal College of Obstetricians and Gynaecologists, *A Consideration of the Law and Ethics in Relation to Court-Authorised Obstetric Intervention*, 2nd edn, London, 2006, at 4.

94 A similar expectation that a woman lacking capacity should be prepared to put the needs of her children extant before her own can be seen in *Re X, Y and Z (minors)* [2014] EWHC 87 (COP). In this instance the fulfilment of financial responsibilities towards those children was found to be an important element of her best interests, despite the extremely negative impact it would have upon her own financial situation. I am grateful to Peter Bartlett for alerting me to this case and the interesting parallel that it affords.

In Germany there have been no reported cases concerning compelled obstetric intervention. In the literature, however, it is widely accepted that the duty owed by a pregnant woman to protect the foetus will encompass a *prima facie* duty for her to consent to medical treatment required to avert risk to the foetal life or risk of injury; a similar duty to provide such treatment is imposed upon her doctor.[95] Both the woman and her doctor may incur criminal liability for terminating a pregnancy by omission if they fail to fulfil their respective duties to protect the foetus and the foetus dies as a result (§§ 218, 13 StGB); indeed, if the dilating contractions have begun, they could potentially incur liability for homicide by omission (§§ 212, 13 StGB) or negligent homicide (§§ 222, 13 StGB). Thus, in theory, German law recognises an exception to the woman's right to refuse treatment. However, the ambit of the duty she owes towards her foetus is limited by what can reasonably be expected of her and, as argued above, this is likely to restrict a duty to tolerate obstetric intervention to exceptional cases where the intervention is minimal in terms of both invasiveness and risks to her own life and health, is not contrary to her firmly held beliefs and is immediately necessary to avert serious harm to the foetus. Even in such a situation it is clear that the woman will not be subjected to treatment against her will. Thus the manner in which *Zumutbarkeit* operates to obviate the duty to accept treatment where it cannot be reasonably expected of the woman, together with the fact that, even where a duty to tolerate obstetric intervention exists, there is no effective means of compelling compliance, renders the woman's refusal much more likely to be respected in Germany than in either the USA or England and Wales.

Where the woman lacks capacity and does not have a valid and applicable advance directive, or proxy decision-maker, German law requires that she be treated in accordance with her *mutmaßlicher Wille*. This approach (similar to the American substituted judgment approach) requires consideration of the woman's known wishes, beliefs and values to determine what she would have wanted were she able to make a valid decision.[96] The fact that a woman is willingly pregnant and looking forward to the birth of her child is likely to be taken to support the argument that she would have consented to any treatment necessary for the foetus. However, as Hans-Georg Koch argued in relation to this argument being applied to the case of a brain-dead woman maintained on life support for the benefit of her foetus (the Erlangen baby case), the woman was looking forward to developing a mother–child relationship with her baby; giving birth to an orphan was not something she could be said to have desired.[97] Similarly, if the woman is unlikely to regain capacity, this may militate against the presumption that she would have wanted to undergo the treatment for the benefit of the foetus. Nevertheless, if the subjective assessment is inconclusive, an objective assessment

95 See discussion above at B III 3 c and d.

96 § 1901a BGB.

97 H.-G. Koch, 'Hirntod und Schwangerschaft: Überlegungen aus rechtlicher Sicht,' in J. Bednarikova and F. C. Chapman (eds) *Festschrift für Jan Stepan zum 80. Geburtstag*, Zurich: Schulthess, 1994, 187, at 196.

of her wishes will be undertaken and the same presumption that has been applied in the English cases is likely to dominate this assessment – namely that women will accept all treatment necessary to protect foetal well-being. Thus the *Deutsche Gesellschaft für Gynäkologie und Geburtshilfe*'s working party on medical law advises that account should be taken of the fact that the majority of women are prepared to accept risks to their own health to protect the foetus from permanent and serious injury.[98]

3. A critical assessment of justifications advanced in support of a duty to consent to treatment for the benefit of the foetus

Whilst the practical contours of an exception to the general principle that consent is necessary are unclear, there does at least appear to be some support in each jurisdiction for imposing a duty to consent upon the pregnant woman. The justifications proposed for such an imposition will now be considered.

a. A duty to rescue

Any action to protect the foetus will necessarily also affect the pregnant woman. The question remains as to why a woman should be subject to interference for the sake of the foetus, to the extent that she may be required to undergo major surgery, when that same requirement will not be imposed upon her for the protection of her existing children. It is, of course, true that children can be treated without parental consent,[99] but any treatment afforded to a child will not impinge directly upon their parents' bodies, nor will parents be forced to undergo surgery for the sake of their child. Anglo-American law does not generally recognise any duty to rescue; thus in the famous case of *McFall* v *Shimp*[100] the court refused to order Shimp to donate some of his bone marrow to his cousin McFall, even though it would save his life. Certainly, it would have been nice of Shimp to donate his bone marrow to his cousin, and one might even say that because a close relative would die as a result of his refusal he should be ethically obliged to donate, but he was under no legal obligation to do so.

Similarly, the German textbook scenario, the blood donation,[101] demonstrates that individuals can lawfully refuse to donate blood required for the survival of

98 Deutsche Gesellschaft für Gynäkologie und Geburtshilfe, AG Medizinrecht, *Empfehlungen zu den ärztlichen Beratungs- und Aufklärungspflichten während der Schwangerenbetreuung und bei der Geburtshilfe*, 1996, confirmed 2010, at § 2.6.

99 See, for example, *Re E (A Minor)(Wardship: Medical Treatment)* [1993] 1 FLR 386; *Prince v Massachusetts* 321 U.S. 158 (1944), US Supreme Court; *OLG Hamm*, NJW 1968, 212.

100 10 PaD. & C. 3d 90 (1978) (Allegheny County Court).

101 See, for example, W. Gallas, 'Pflichtenkollision als Schuldausschliessungsgrund' in K. Engisch and R. Maurach (eds) *Festschrift für Edmund Mezger zum 70. Geburtstag am 15.10.1954*, München: C.H. Beck, 1954, 311ff.; W. Gropp, *Strafrecht Allgemeiner Teil*, 4th edn, Berlin: Springer, 2015, § 6, Rn. 143.

another person.[102] It is clear that a strong argument can be made that the life of the person requiring a blood transfusion weighs significantly more heavily than the potential donor's interest in bodily integrity. Nevertheless, the overwhelming majority of commentators believe that there is no legal duty to donate, nor would it be permissible to extract blood against the wishes of a potential blood donor, concluding that the interests of the potential donor in bodily integrity, self-determination and dignity outweigh the interest in the other's life.[103]

Just as Shimp was the only family member with potentially compatible bone marrow, and so the only person who could save McFall, the hypothetical patient was the only person with the same blood group as the incoming patient and thus the only person who could save her. In the same way, the pregnant woman is the only person who can save the foetus by allowing a caesarean to be performed. It may be argued that a pregnant woman is a member of a unique category of persons, in the sense that the foetus's life may be entirely dependent upon her consent to intervention.[104] However, whilst the unique quality of the relationship between a pregnant woman and the foetus must be recognised, as the Illinois Supreme Court stated, 'That this is so is not a pregnant woman's fault: it is a fact of life'.[105] In each of the three jurisdictions under consideration it is settled law that a parent cannot be legally required to undergo surgery for her child's sake. That being so, it is difficult to justify the adoption of a different approach in the context of a pregnant woman and her foetus. Nevertheless, precisely such a distinction can be seen in the German law. Whilst German law does not impose a duty upon a woman to rescue her existing children by, for example, donating a kidney, the comparable duty to accept medical treatment for the benefit of the foetus is, at least *prima facie*, widely held to exist.[106]

As guarantor, the pregnant woman has an enhanced duty to protect the foetus's life and welfare, but this does not require her to sacrifice her own rights and interests in order to protect the foetus. Where there is no other way of safeguarding the foetus, the key question will be whether it would be reasonable to expect the woman to endure obstetric intervention for the sake of the foetus. Thus, as discussed above,[107] the woman's duty to tolerate obstetric intervention for the benefit of the foetus is limited by the requirement of reasonableness – it must be reasonable to expect the woman to undergo the intervention; where that is not the case the duty will lapse.[108] As the *Bundesverfassungsgericht* made clear in

102 See above, B III 3 a cc.
103 See, for example, W. Gropp, *AT* (note 101), § 6, Rn. 144; W. Gallas (note 101), at 326; W. Perron, in *Schönke/Schröder*, § 34, Rn. 41e with further references.
104 See, for example, Belson J dissenting in *re AC* (note 41), at 1256, referring to the foetus being 'literally captive within the mother's body'.
105 *Stallman v Youngquist* (note 63), at 279.
106 See, for example, P. Kröger, in *LK*, § 218, Rn. 20, 21; R. Merkel, in *NK-StGB*, Rn. 97ff; L.-M. Bleiler, *Strafbarkeitsrisiken des Arztes bei religiös motiviertem Behandlungsveto*, Heidelberg: Springer, 2010, at 203ff.
107 B III 3 c.
108 R. Merkel, in *NK-StGB*, § 218, Rn. 113, cf. W. Gropp, in *MüKo-StGB*, § 218, Rn. 54, arguing that *Unzumutbarkeit* will justify the woman's non-performance (§ 34 StGB).

its abortion decisions, a finding of *Unzumutbarkeit* (unreasonableness) will require more than the usual burdens associated with pregnancy,[109] but it is suggested that obstetric intervention, whether it takes the form of a surgical or instrumental delivery, a blood transfusion or indeed an injection, is not a usual part of pregnancy and labour. Although these examples of obstetric intervention are not rare, they each constitute an additional burden upon the woman, going beyond those usual burdens associated with pregnancy. Moreover, none of the aforementioned examples are naturally occurring burdens of pregnancy.

An assessment of what can reasonably be expected of the pregnant woman will entail balancing her rights and interests (in bodily integrity, self-determination and dignity) against those of the foetus. Where her interests significantly outweigh those of the foetus, it will be unreasonable to expect her to accept the treatment. It has been argued above that there is almost no scope to find a reasonable expectation that the woman will accept obstetric intervention for the benefit of the foetus against her wishes. At most it is suggested that such an expectation can only arise in the case of a very minor intervention that has no lasting effects upon the woman's health or life, that does not contradict her firmly held values and that offers great potential benefit to the foetus. One such scenario might be the administration of corticosteroids by injection during premature labour to stimulate development of the foetal lungs and thereby reduce the risk of neonatal respiratory distress syndrome, a serious and potentially fatal condition. The injections have no negative effects for the woman or foetus/child and significantly reduce the risk of the child suffering respiratory distress syndrome.[110]

Even where it would be reasonable to expect the woman to accept the indicated treatment, there is no scope to compel performance of her duty to rescue the foetus; indeed, as the court in *re AC* noted, enforced performance can only be accomplished through physical force.[111] Whilst reasonable force has been authorised in England and Wales, and force has been used in the United States to compel treatment, there is no scope for a German court to authorise the use of force to compel the woman to accept treatment, even in the situation where the court has overridden her refusal of consent on behalf of the foetus, in accordance with § 1666 BGB. Whilst a fine may be imposed for non-compliance,[112] it would appear unlikely to convince the woman to accept the treatment. Moreover, even though the attending doctor also enjoys guarantor status with respect to the foetus and is therefore under a duty to safeguard its life and medical welfare, she will not be able to treat the foetus against the will of the pregnant woman.[113] Should a doctor decide to take matters into her own hands and override the woman's refusal of

109 *BVerfGE* 39, 1, at 48; 88, 203, at 257.

110 D. Roberts and S. R. Dalziel, 'Antenatal Corticosteroids for Accelerating Fetal Lung Maturation for Women at Risk of Preterm Birth' (2006) 3 *Cochrane Database of Systematic Reviews* Art. No.: CD004454.

111 *In re AC* (note 41), at 1244.

112 § 1666 BGB, together with § 35 FamFG.

113 The doctor's duty to act will lapse due to impossibility if the woman refuses to consent to the intervention.

consent, her action will constitute a battery, contrary to § 223 StGB. No defence will be available to her, even if the woman's refusal of consent can be termed an unlawful attack on the foetus, due to the fact that it would be reasonable to expect her to accept the treatment.[114] Such action would not only infringe upon the woman's rights to bodily integrity and self-determination; it would also undermine her dignity, treating her as a mere vehicle for delivering treatment to the foetus. Moreover, strong public policy reasons require that a woman's refusal of consent is respected, not least due to the fact that the protection of the foetus will be fatally undermined if a pregnant woman avoids antenatal care due to a fear that she will be subjected to compulsory treatment. In such a situation there is no scope to protect the foetus, or indeed to help the pregnant woman.

Should the woman persist in refusing treatment and the foetus die, she could face criminal liability for terminating a pregnancy by omission (§§ 218, 13 StGB); however, successful prosecution is extremely unlikely. First, in order to secure a conviction, it would have to be shown that the woman's refusal of consent led to the death of the foetus, but it is highly unlikely that it could be proved that the treatment refused could have saved the life of the foetus with the requisite degree of probability bordering upon certainty (the equivalent of beyond reasonable doubt).[115] Second, it is unlikely that public policy considerations would support the prosecution of women in such circumstances, the preference being for persuasion rather than compulsion in cases of foetal endangerment through drugs, alcohol and smoking.[116]

Although the duty to rescue is clearly extremely limited in application, the recognition of such a duty is significant. It expresses the public interest in the foetus and the mere existence of a legal duty makes it clear to the pregnant woman that she must consider the foetus in her decision-making and that she will be accountable for her decisions that impact upon the foetus. Thus the significance of the duty lies in its symbolic importance rather than its implementation. Some authors have suggested that it is also important in 'encouraging' women to make the right decision; thus, for example, Wolfgang Kapp refers to the potential use of judicial proceedings serving a warning function,[117] and Lisa-Marie Bleiler argues that the ability to cite a legal duty to accept treatment for the benefit of the foetus will be a powerful tool in the doctor's armoury for persuading the woman to comply.[118] Both suggestions carry negative connotations of coercion and it is

114 See above B III d cc and ff.

115 See also R. Merkel, in *NK-StGB*, § 218, Rn. 106.

116 In this respect cf. the final report of the working group considering § 1666 BGB: Bundesministerium der Justiz Arbeitsgruppe (Federal Ministry of Justice Working Party) *Familiengerichtliche Maßnahmen bei Gefährdung des Kindeswohls – § 1666 BGB, Abschlussbericht*, 14 July 2009, available at: www.bmj.de/SharedDocs/Downloads/DE/pdfs/Abschlussbericht_der_Arbeitsgruppe_Familiengerichtliche_Massnahmen_bei_Gefaehrdung_des_Kindeswohls_1666_BGB.pdf?__blob=publicationFile (accessed 13 August 2015). Discussed above at B III 3 d cc.

117 W. Kapp, 'Der Fötus als Patient' (1986) 5 *Medizinrecht* 276, at 280.

118 L.-M. Bleiler, *Strafbarkeitsrisiken des Arztes bei religiös motiviertem Behandlungsveto*, Heidelberg: Springer, 2010, at 212ff.

suggested that a more positive emphasis upon the support and assistance available to the pregnant woman is more likely to promote the protection of foetal life.

In the light of the above, it is clear that the justification for imposing treatment upon pregnant women cannot lie in a duty to rescue within Anglo-American law and, as has been shown, the enforcement of such a duty cannot be compelled in Germany. Indeed, in the majority of cases that have been determined by the courts in England and Wales and the US, it is submitted that the intervention involved (a caesarean or a blood transfusion) was so invasive that the woman could not reasonably have been expected to accept the treatment against her wishes and thus that she would not have had a duty to act in German law.

b. The protection of (the state's interest in) potential life

Whilst the German state is under a duty to protect foetal life, including from the pregnant woman herself,[119] it can fulfil that duty by providing education, counselling and support to the pregnant woman to encourage her to tolerate treatment for the benefit of the foetus. As the *Bundesverfassungsgericht* recognised in the abortion context, a more effective protection of foetal life may result from cooperation with the pregnant woman than from the imposition of criminal penalties.[120] Moreover, compelled medical treatment would not be consistent with the state's duty to respect the woman's right to self-determination or the guarantee of human dignity, and thus there is no prospect that the German state could seek to compel medical treatment on the basis of its own interest in foetal life. In England and Wales the right to life has not been applied to the foetus and, as the law currently stands, there is no basis for state intervention in pregnancy to protect the state's interest in potential life, or indeed the foetal interests. In *Re F. (in utero)* Balcombe LJ considered whether or not a court could order a woman to undergo a caesarean for the benefit of her foetus and stressed that this was not an area for judicial activism, stating:

> If Parliament were to think it appropriate that a pregnant woman should be subject to control for the benefit of her unborn child, then doubtless it will stipulate the circumstances in which such controls may be applied and the safeguards appropriate for the mother's protection. In such a sensitive field, affecting as it does the liberty of the individual, it is not for the judiciary to extend the law.[121]

Parliament has not chosen to legislate in this area and the courts have had to consider whether or not to authorise a caesarean against the woman's wishes on a number of occasions. However, on each occasion except the case of *Re S*, the courts have stressed that the foetus has no rights capable of protection and that

119 *BVerfGE* 39, 1, at 42; 88, 203, at 255.
120 *BVerfGE* 88, 203, at 266–7.
121 [1988] Fam. 122, at 144.

the woman has the right to refuse treatment, even that necessary to save the life of the foetus, provided that she has the requisite capacity. As the Court of Appeal stressed in *St George's*:

> When human life is at stake the pressure to provide an affirmative answer authorising unwanted medical intervention is very powerful. Nevertheless the autonomy of each individual requires continuing protection even, perhaps particularly, when the motive for interfering with it is readily understandable, and indeed to many would appear commendable ... An unborn child is not a separate person from its mother. Its need for medical assistance does not prevail over her rights. She is entitled not to be forced to submit to an invasion of her body against her will, whether her own life or that of her unborn child depends on it. Her right is not reduced or diminished merely because her decision to exercise it may appear morally repugnant.[122]

Whilst this appears to be a clear endorsement of the woman's autonomy, it hinges upon her retaining capacity. The assessment of capacity is extremely fluid and there is at least some suggestion that the courts have been willing to find women to lack capacity in order to safeguard the foetus. Once such case is *Rochdale Healthcare NHS Trust* v *C*[123] where it will be remembered that Johnson J discounted the doctor's opinion that C was competent and held that she lacked the necessary capacity to refuse consent to the caesarean. He held that being in the throes of labour, with all the pain and stress that involves, and seemingly being willing to accept the possibility of death rather than undergo another caesarean demonstrated that she was unable to weigh the information given to her in order to make a decision. This view that the pain associated with labour might suffice to render a woman (any woman disagreeing with medical advice) incapable of refusing consent to treatment was repeated in *Re MB*[124] and clearly has the potential to undermine the capacity of any woman in labour, but *is* contradicted by research findings that suggest that a woman's capacity is not diminished due to pain in labour.[125] Nevertheless, the presumption that pain might undermine a woman's capacity during labour clearly demonstrates the extremely flexible nature of the assessment of capacity and the scope for intervening to protect the foetus under the guise of promoting the woman's best interests. It underlines the need for the woman to consider what treatment she might be prepared to accept in advance of labour, at a time when her capacity cannot possibly be threatened by the pain and stress involved.

122 *St George's Healthcare NHS Trust* v*S; R* v *Collins and others, ex parte S* (note 8), *per* Judge LJ, at 46–50.
123 *Rochdale Healthcare NHS Trust* v*C* (note 16).
124 *Re MB* (note 11), *per* Butler-Sloss LJ, at 437.
125 See, for example, J. C. Gerancher et al., 'An Evaluation of Informed Consent Prior to Epidural Analgesia for Labour and Delivery' (2000) 9 *International Journal of Obstetric Anesthesia* 168; H. Brooks and W. J. Sullivan, 'The Importance of Patient Autonomy at Birth' (2002) 11 *International Journal of Obstetric Anesthesia* 196.

By contrast with the position in England and Wales and in Germany, some courts in the United States have been extremely willing to override a woman's refusal of consent on the basis of the state's interest in potential life. For example, in *Pemberton v Tallahassee Memorial Regional Medical Center* Hinkle J held: 'Whatever the scope of Ms. Pemberton's personal constitutional rights in this situation, they clearly did not outweigh the interests of the State of Florida in preserving the life of the unborn child'.[126] In *Roe v Wade*[127] the Supreme Court recognised that the state has an important and legitimate interest in protecting the potentiality of human life throughout pregnancy and that this interest becomes compelling from the third trimester onwards.[128] Therefore it has been argued that if a caesarean is medically indicated and vaginal delivery would have the same effect as an abortion, in that it would result in the death of the foetus, the court may order that a caesarean be performed, notwithstanding the woman's refusal of consent. Relying on the third-trimester rule in *Jefferson v Griffin Spalding County Hospital Authority*, the Georgia Supreme Court ordered Jessie Mae Jefferson to submit to an ultrasound examination and thereafter to submit to a caesarean if the scan showed that the placenta was obstructing her cervix.[129] Thus the court interpreted the state's ability to prohibit abortion to include the ability for states to proactively intervene in pregnancy to compel women to undergo medical procedures for the benefit of the foetus.

As Nancy Rhoden has explained, 'There is a quantum leap in logic between prohibiting destruction and requiring surgical preservation that courts and commentators relying on abortion law have ignored'.[130] This distinction between affirmative intervention and the mere prohibition of abortion was addressed directly by Hinkle J in *Pemberton*,[131] where he purported to apply the third-trimester rule in holding that Laura Pemberton's rights had to be weighed against the interests of the State of Florida in preserving the life of the unborn child. He dismissed the distinction between affirmative intervention and mere prohibition of abortion as superficial,[132] reasoning that:

> a third-trimester mother can be forced against her will to bear a child she does not want; this is in fact a substantially greater imposition on the mother's

126 *Pemberton v Tallahassee Memorial Regional Medical Center* (note 17), at 1251.
127 *Roe v Wade* (note 71).
128 *Roe v Wade* (note 71), at 162–4. In *Webster v Reproductive Health Services* 492 U.S. 490 (1989) and *Planned Parenthood v Casey* 505 US 833 (1992) the Supreme Court held that the state's interest in potential life becomes compelling at 24 weeks' gestation – that is, when the foetus achieves viability. This is not really inconsistent with the decision in *Roe v Wade*; it simply acknowledges that advances in medical science have led to a foetus being considered viable at an earlier stage of pregnancy than in 1973. Moreover, in *Casey* the Supreme Court stressed that the state has 'a substantial interest in potential life *throughout* pregnancy', at 876.
129 *Jefferson v Griffin Spalding County Hospital Authority* (note 4), at 460.
130 N. K. Rhoden, 'Caesareans and Samaritans' (1987) 15(3) *Law, Medicine and Healthcare* 118.
131 *Pemberton v Tallahassee Memorial Regional Medical Center* (note 17).
132 Ibid. (note 17), at 1251.

> constitutional interests than requiring a mother to give birth by one method rather than another.[133]

However, the Appellate Court of Illinois has taken a very different approach to the third-trimester rule.[134] In *In re Baby Boy Doe, a Fetus v Mother Doe*[135] DiVito J held that

> Roe … merely stated that, in the context of abortion, the state's interest in the potential life of the fetus becomes compelling at the point of viability, and therefore the state is permitted to prohibit post-viability abortions, except where necessary to preserve the life or health of the woman. The fact that the state may prohibit post-viability pregnancy terminations does not translate into the proposition that the state may intrude upon the woman's right to remain free from unwanted physical invasion of her person when she chooses to carry her pregnancy to term. *Roe* and its progeny, in particular *Planned Parenthood of Southeastern Pennsylvania v. Casey* (1992) … make it clear that, even in the context of abortion, the state's compelling interest in the potential life of the fetus is insufficient to override the woman's interest in preserving her health.[136]

It is suggested that DiVito J's understanding of *Roe* should be regarded as more satisfactory. Although the state's interest in potential life becomes compelling at viability, it never becomes absolute. In *Roe* and its progeny, the Supreme Court stressed that, whilst the state's compelling interest in potential life meant that it could restrict or even prohibit abortion after viability, the state's interest could never outweigh the woman's right to elect an abortion where the continuance of her pregnancy posed a threat to her life or health.[137] Moreover, in *Thornburgh* the Supreme Court held that the state's interest in potential life could not justify subjecting the pregnant woman to an increased risk, striking down a requirement that doctors utilise the abortion method most likely to ensure the live birth, unless that would 'present a significantly greater medical risk to the life or health of the pregnant woman'.[138] The fact that the state may restrict or even prohibit abortion in cases where there is no threat to the life or health of the woman is a very different proposition to that suggested above, whereby courts have suggested that the state's interest may suffice to mandate treatment for the benefit of the foetus, exposing the woman to an (increased) risk to her life and health.

133 Ibid. (note 17), at 1251.

134 In *In re Brown* (note 72), the Illinois Court of Appeals accepted that abortion is not the same as a refusal of treatment, at 405.

135 *In re Baby Boy Doe, a Fetus v Mother Doe* (note 9).

136 Ibid., at 334.

137 *Roe v Wade* (note 71), at 165, *per* Blackmum J; *Planned Parenthood v Casey* (note 128), at 846.

138 *Thornburgh v American College of Obstetricians and Gynecologists* (note 39), at 768–9.

In the English case *Re MB* the Court of Appeal suggested that it was illogical that a woman could not lawfully terminate a pregnancy after 24 weeks without satisfying the medical or embryopathic indications set out in the Abortion Act 1967, but that she could make an irrational decision to refuse treatment that could avert the threat to the life of a viable foetus. Nevertheless, it did not suggest that this factor could justify the overriding of the woman's refusal of consent.[139] It is argued that the distinction between the inability to have an abortion (a negative duty) and the positive duty to accept treatment for the benefit of the foetus is entirely logical[140] and reflects the fundamental distinction at the other end of life between acts and omissions. There is no duty to continue to live and therefore to accept all possible treatments, no matter what the quality of life, but an active intervention to cause death, no matter how compassionate the motive, will constitute homicide in each of the three jurisdictions. Equally, the case of a woman seeking an abortion is entirely distinct from that of a woman refusing treatment intended to benefit her foetus. By refusing treatment she does not actively harm the foetus or intentionally terminate the pregnancy; instead, she asserts her autonomy, making healthcare decisions in line with her beliefs and values. It is submitted that the *Bundesverfassungsgericht*'s approach in Abortion II[141] is correct: ultimately, the state's interest in the foetus is best served by it working to support and ameliorate pregnant women's welfare. There is no scope for influence or persuasion if a woman fears being compelled to have the very treatment she has rejected. Instead, the state and doctors need to work with women, rather than against them, and support them in their decisions, even if the cost is the death of the foetus.

c. The relevance of abortion waiver

It has been suggested that a pregnant woman will owe a duty towards the foetus not to harm it, in this instance by refusing medical treatment that would benefit it, because she has waived her right to abortion. One proponent of this view is John Robertson, who wrote:

> Conflicts over management of the pregnancy arise only after she has decided to become or remain pregnant. Once she decides to forgo abortion and the State chooses to protect the fetus, the woman loses the liberty to act in ways that would adversely affect the fetus.[142]

Similarly, in the Canadian case *Winnipeg Child and Family Services (Northwest Area)* v *G. (D.F.)*[143] Major J (dissenting) recognised that, whilst the grant of remedies in order to protect the foetus

139 *Re MB (Medical Treatment)* (note 11), at 441, *per* Butler-Sloss LJ.

140 Instead, it is illogical that a woman's decision to have a pre-viability abortion has to be ratified by two doctors under the Abortion Act 1967.

141 *BVerfGE* 88, 203, at 266–7.

142 J. A. Robertson, 'Procreative Liberty and the Control of Conception, Pregnancy and Childbirth' (1983) 69 *Virginia Law Review* 403, at 437.

143 *Winnipeg Child and Family Services (Northwest Area) v G. (D.F.)* (note 53).

> may interfere with the mother's liberty interests, in my view, those interests must bend when faced with a situation where devastating harm and a life of suffering can so easily be prevented. In any event, this interference is always subject to the mother's right to end it by deciding to have an abortion.[144]

There are various problems with asserting that by 'waiving her right to abortion' women have accepted an enhanced duty towards the foetus, to accept any medical treatment believed necessary to further its welfare. Unlike in the United States of America and Germany, in England and Wales a woman does not have a *right* to elect an abortion at any time during the pregnancy. In certain circumstances, prescribed by the Abortion Act 1967, as amended by the Human Fertilisation and Embryology Act 1990, she will be able to request an abortion. Certainly up to the 13th week of pregnancy, a woman desiring an abortion will satisfy the socio-medical indication set out in s.1(1)(a) Abortion Act 1967, namely that 'the continuance of the pregnancy would involve risk, greater than if the pregnancy were terminated, of injury to [her] physical or mental health'; however, her request for an abortion must be approved by two registered medical practitioners. Under English law women never have a right to elect an abortion; the only person with any right under the Abortion Act 1967 is the healthcare professional who may exercise her right to conscientious objection.

In Germany women are able to exercise their right to self-determination, electing to have an abortion within the first 12 weeks, subject only to complying with the counselling requirement and the termination being performed by a doctor (§ 218a I StGB). Nevertheless, even where a woman has a right to elect a termination of pregnancy, it is misleading to talk of abortion waiver – in the majority of the cases discussed above the woman was willingly pregnant and intended to parent the child.[145] Thus those women are unlikely to have even contemplated an abortion, much less waived the right to have one. More generally, even in the United States of America, it cannot be assumed that every pregnant woman has waived the right to abortion – some women will be opposed to abortion and some will be unable to access abortion. Although the American Supreme Court held that a woman's right to autonomy includes the right to elect a pre-viability abortion,[146] it is illusionary to talk of a right to abortion where restrictions are such that abortion cannot be accessed due to a lack of funding, a lack of parental consent, a lack of abortion facilities in the locality or any of the other restrictions upon a woman's ability to access abortion that exist in the United States of America. Indeed, given the background of the women involved in the US cases, it is unlikely that many of them would have been able to afford to exercise their 'right' to elect a pre-viability abortion. As the US courts have emphasised time and time again, the state is not

144 Ibid., at para 93.

145 In *St George's Healthcare NHS Trust v S; R v Collins and others, ex parte S* (note 8) the social worker reported that S's relationship with her partner had recently ended, that she didn't want the baby and that she intended to give the baby up to her ex-partner after it was born, at 37.

146 *Planned Parenthood v Casey* (note 128), at 846.

required to facilitate access to abortion, but the right to elect a pre-viability abortion is rendered rather empty if it is beyond the reach of those seeking to exercise it.[147]

Finally, in all the caesarean cases and most of the blood transfusion cases discussed in the preceding chapters, the foetus had achieved viability; restrictions upon abortion in each of the jurisdictions mean that there can be no talk of choosing abortion at that stage of pregnancy where abortion is limited to cases that are medically or embryopathically indicated. Therefore, it is suggested that talk of an abortion waiver is inherently misleading and it is ironic to think that women fought (and continue to fight) for the right to abortion, only to be faced now with court-authorised intervention on the basis that they did not terminate a pregnancy![148]

4. Interim conclusions on constructing the 'maternal'–foetal relationship

As the discussion above makes clear, the ability to treat the foetus as a patient leads to some very difficult questions. Morally, it might be argued that a woman has a duty to do everything possible to safeguard and indeed promote the welfare of the foetus. Most women will do just that, accepting risks to their health and even life in the hope of benefitting the foetus with whom they have already formed a strong emotional bond. However, the existence of a moral obligation is insufficient to ground a legal obligation. As the Court of Appeal (grudgingly) recognised in *Re MB* and *St George's*, there is a dichotomy between law and morality.[149] In both cases the court stressed that there was no legal obligation to consent to medical treatment for the benefit of the foetus, but suggested that failure to do so would be immoral.[150] The Court of Appeal clearly disapproved of S's behaviour, stating that 'no normal mother-to-be could think' like she did, that her refusal was 'morally repugnant' and that her bizarre thinking was 'contrary to the views of the overwhelming majority of the community at large'.[151] In fact, Judge LJ praised the courage of the social worker Ms Collins and accepted that

147 See, for example, *Harris v McRae* 448 US 297 (1980): 'The financial constraints that restrict an indigent woman's ability to enjoy the full range of constitutionally protected freedom of choice are the product not of governmental restrictions on access to abortion, but rather of her indigency', *per* Stewart J, at 316; *Webster v Reproductive Health Services* 492 U.S. 490 (1989): 'Missouri's refusal to allow public employees to perform abortions in public hospitals leaves a pregnant woman with the same choices as if the State had chosen not to operate any public hospitals at all', *per* Rehnquist CJ, at 509.

148 See also S. Rogers, '*Winnipeg Child and Family Services v D.F.G.*: Juridical Interference with Pregnant Women in the Alleged Interest of the Fetus' (1997) 36 *Alberta Law Review* 711, at 718.

149 Similarly, in *In re Brown* (note 72) the Appellate Court of Illinois stated 'we note the mother's apparent disparate ethical and legal obligations. Under the law of this State, however, we cannot impose a legal obligation upon a pregnant woman to consent to an invasive medical procedure for the benefit of her viable fetus', at 405.

150 *Re MB (Medical Treatment)* (note 11), *per* Butler-Sloss LJ, at 440; *St George's Healthcare NHS Trust* v*S; R* v*Collins and others, ex parte S* (note 8), *per* Judge LJ, at 50.

151 Ibid.

both she and the doctors had acted in accordance with a genuine desire to do what was best for S and the foetus, despite the fact that they had abused the Mental Health Act and unlawfully subjected S to major surgery.[152]

As a general principle of libertarian theory, the state may only require an individual to do or refrain from doing something in order to protect a third party from harm. As John Stuart Mill argued:

> The only purpose for which power can rightfully be exercised over any member of a civilised community against his will is to prevent harm to others. His own good, either physical or moral, is not a sufficient warrant. He cannot rightfully be compelled to do or forebear because it would be better for him to do so, because it would make him happy or because, in the opinion of others, to do so would be wise, or even right.[153]

Although it could be suggested that only persons can be 'others', Julian Savalescu has sought to apply Mill's harm principle to the court-authorised obstetric treatment debate and argued that 'others' may include future others – that is, the foetus.[154] He argues that that compulsion can be justified if

1 the harm to the pregnant woman of intervening is below some acceptable threshold;
2 the harm to the foetus of not-intervening is great;
3 the pregnant woman has a duty or obligation to the foetus;

and that 'Rather than devaluing or disregarding women's interests and rights, this approach gives equal consideration to the interests of both present and future individuals'.[155]

To an extent, this is reminiscent of the reasonableness requirement incorporated into the pregnant woman's duty to protect the foetus under German law, whereby it must be reasonable to expect the woman to accept the treatment. It may be possible to accept Julian Savalescu's argument if the threshold for harm to the pregnant woman is set extremely low, such as would be the case if a woman were required to accept the single administration of drugs without side effects or risk to her life or health. However, it is difficult to envisage circumstances in which an invasive intervention such as a caesarean or blood transfusion could ever be considered to fall below an acceptable level of harm. Moreover, even where there is a reasonable expectation that the woman should tolerate treatment for the benefit of the foetus, there is a fundamental difference between imposing an obligation to do so and forcibly compelling compliance with the duty. If we accept the argument that

152 Ibid., at 52.
153 J. S. Mill, *On Liberty*, London: John W. Parker, 1859, at 22.
154 J. Savulescu, 'Future People, Involuntary Medical Treatment in Pregnancy and the Duty of Easy Rescue' (2007) 19(1) *Utilitas* 1.
155 Ibid., at 17–18.

a woman must accept interventions for the benefit of the foetus, we necessarily subjugate her needs and values to the needs and welfare of the foetus. In her seminal article 'A defense of abortion',[156] Judith Jarvis Thomson wrote of bad Samaritans who refused to permit the use of their body for nine months, but the imposition of treatment upon a pregnant woman would cause much greater harm, creating captive (unwilling) Samaritans, instrumentalising the woman's body and enslaving her to the contents of her uterus. As Judge LJ recognised in *St George's*, even the smallest incursion into the woman's autonomy may lead over time to the total abandonment of the principle.[157]

Basic respect for the woman as a person requires that she should be able to decide what happens to her own body, for whatever reason, as Lord Donaldson recognised in *Re T*: 'The right of choice is not limited to decisions which others might regard as sensible. It exists notwithstanding that the reasons for making the choices are rational, irrational, unknown or even non-existent'.[158] This was recognised by the Appellate Court of Illinois in *In re Baby Boy Doe*,[159] where it was held that pregnancy does not curtail a woman's rights to bodily integrity and religious liberty, and the Court of Appeal came to a similar conclusion in both *Re MB* and *St George's*.[160] In fact, by treating the pregnant woman's body as a mere obstacle to be breached in order to access the foetal patient, Nelson and Miliken have suggested that we accord pregnant women less respect than a corpse, because before badly needed organs are removed consent is sought from the next of kin and refusals will be honoured, no matter how valuable those organs might be in saving a number of lives.[161] In the case of a pregnant woman the consent of her next of kin is, of course, irrelevant, but the fact remains that in many of the cases discussed above her refusal of consent and the views of her family were regarded as irrelevant. In none of the cases is there any suggestion that the woman was not supported in her refusal by her partner or family.

What is clear is that in many of the cases discussed above the foetus was regarded as a second patient in need of protection from its host, the woman. For example, both *S* and *Jefferson*, and their religious beliefs, were regarded as unimportant, their autonomy irrelevant, because they were a means to an end – that is, a live baby. As Rachel Roth argues:

> In the very era when people have been gaining power over their medical care, then, pregnant women wind up with greater responsibility and less authority than anyone else. With pregnant women ordered to do for fetuses what no

156 J. J. Thomson, 'A Defense of Abortion' (1971) 1(1) *Philosophy and Public Affairs* 47.
157 *St George's Healthcare NHS Trust* v*S; R* v*Collins and others, ex parte S* (note 8), at 46.
158 *Re T* (note 11), at 653; see also *BVerfGE* 89, 120, at 130.
159 *In re Baby Boy Doe, a Fetus v Mother Doe* (note 9).
160 *Re MB (Medical Treatment)* (note 11) and *St George's Healthcare NHS Trust* v*S; R* v*Collins and others, ex parte S* (note 8).
161 L. J. Nelson and N. Milliken, 'Compelled Medical Treatment of Pregnant Women' (1988) 259(7) *Journal of the Ameican Medical Association* 1060, 1065.

> one is ordered to do for children or adults, the fetus has been endowed with super-rights that exceed those of any living human being.[162]

The cases demonstrate how easily women may be 'de-personalised', at the same time as foetuses are increasingly endowed with quasi-personhood through their status as patient, how, as Donna Greschner suggests, women have become little more than machines, producing babies. As such the pregnant woman is separate from the end product, the baby, and should be manipulated so as to produce the best possible end product.[163]

Whilst it must be accepted that the foetus, particularly a viable foetus capable of life outside the uterus, has an inherent value, respect for women's equality and autonomy is also of great importance and must not be sacrificed. It is suggested that the Appellate Court of Illinois, the District of Columbia Court of Appeals and the English Court of Appeal are right to have concluded that a woman with capacity has the right to refuse all medical treatment, including that which would save the life of the foetus. However, care must be taken to ensure that the requirement of capacity is not manipulated in order to undermine this key holding – the presumption of capacity should not be displaced by the fact of pregnancy, and the mere refusal to follow medical advice should not become an automatic trigger for a capacity assessment. In attempting to navigate the conflict between the need to protect foetal life and the need to recognise the woman's rights and dignity, the German approach has much to commend it, recognising that a pregnant woman does have a duty to protect the foetus, but that the duty is limited by consideration of what can be reasonably expected of her. Even though this approach will ultimately prioritise the dignity, bodily integrity and autonomy of the pregnant woman, it does so whilst recognising the value of foetal life and seeks to persuade, rather than compel, acts that might be expected of a 'good Samaritan'.

Ultimately, it must be accepted that in this unique relationship, which is neither one nor two, there is only one person with rights and responsibilities. The state's role should be to support the woman in exercising those rights and meeting those responsibilities by respecting her autonomy and allowing her to make decisions reflecting her beliefs and values, even if she should later come to regret those decisions. Respect for human dignity requires that the focus of our attention remains upon the woman; she must be permitted to determine for herself what constitutes an acceptable level of risk, conducting her own cost–benefit analysis in determining whether or not to allow treatment to take place. As the recent decision of the UK's Supreme Court in *Montgomery v Lanarkshire Health Board* stressed, 'Patients are now widely regarded as persons holding rights, rather than as the passive recipients of the care of the medical profession'.[164] The case

162 R. Roth, *Making Women Pay: The Hidden Costs of Fetal Rights*, Ithaca, NY: Cornell University Press, 2000, at 134.

163 D. Greschner, 'Abortion and Democracy for Women; a Critique of *Tremblay v Daigle*' (1990) 35 *McGill LJ* 633, 647–8.

164 *Montgomery v Lanarkshire Health Board* [2015] UKSC 11, *per* Lord Kerr and Lord Reid, at [75].

involved a diabetic pregnant woman expecting a larger than usual baby, but she was not told of the risk of shoulder dystocia arising from vaginal delivery (estimated to be 9–10 per cent) because, as the treating doctor said:

> If you were to mention to any mother who faces labour that there is a very small risk of the baby dying in labour, then everyone would ask for a caesarean section, and it's not in the maternal interests for women to have caesarean sections.[165]

The risk of serious injury to the baby due to shoulder dystocia is less than 1 per cent, but the risks to the woman are significantly higher, including an 11 per cent risk of postpartum haemorrhage and a 3.8 per cent risk of fourth-degree perineal tears. Nevertheless, her obstetrician did not inform the woman of the risks; indeed, as the quotation above shows, her sole focus was upon any risk to the foetus. As Lady Hale stressed:

> In this day and age, we are not only concerned about risks to the baby. We are equally, if not more, concerned about risks to the mother. And those include the risks associated with giving birth, as well as any after-effects. One of the problems in this case was that for too long the focus was on the risks to the baby, without also taking into account what the mother might face in the process of giving birth.[166]

This case is significant because it finally recognised that informed consent is required in UK law, departing from *Sidaway v Bethlem Royal Hospital and the Maudsley Hospital Heath Authority.*[167] However, it is also important because it recognises that in the obstetric context doctors cannot only consider what is best for the foetus; risks to the woman must also be taken into account. More importantly, the right of the woman to weigh the risks involved and make her own decision was underlined:

> A patient is entitled to take into account her own values, her own assessment of the comparative merits of giving birth in the 'natural' and traditional way and of giving birth by caesarean section, whatever medical opinion may say, alongside the medical evaluation of the risks to herself and her baby. She may place great value on giving birth in the natural way and be prepared to take the risks to herself and her baby which this entails. The medical profession must respect her choice, unless she lacks the legal capacity to decide … There is no good reason why the same should not apply in reverse, if she is prepared to forgo the joys of natural childbirth in order to avoid some not insignificant risks to herself or her baby. She cannot force her doctor to offer treatment which he or she considers futile or inappropriate. But she is at least entitled to the information which will enable her to take a proper part in that decision.[168]

165 Ibid., at [13].
166 Ibid., *per* Lord Kerr and Lord Reid, at [111].
167 [1985] AC 871.
168 *Montgomery v Lanarkshire Health Board* (note 164), *per* Lady Hale, at [115].

This restatement of the position is to be welcomed. The very fact of pregnancy does not deprive a woman of her status as a person; she remains a person before, during and after the interval of pregnancy and must be treated as such. As Mary Ann Warren so memorably wrote. 'There is room for only one person with full and equal rights inside a single human skin'.[169]

IV. Framing the relationship between the woman and her doctor

A reading of the case law demonstrates the key role played by the woman's doctor both in the United States of America and in England and Wales. First, she assesses the needs of her two patients, the woman and the foetus; then she advises the woman on what treatment is necessary. If the woman refuses to comply with her recommendations, she will consider whether or not she has the capacity to refuse consent. If she believes the woman lacks capacity, the doctor may seek a court order;[170] if so, the judge will almost certainly agree that the woman lacks the capacity to refuse (if she had capacity, she would surely follow the medical advice), and agree that the proposed treatment will further the woman's best interests. Even if the doctor does not believe that the woman lacks capacity, in Germany and the United States the doctor can seek a court order overriding the woman's refusal of consent to treatment for the foetus. Throughout the proceedings the doctor is given a starring role, rivalled only by that given to the foetus. Her views and assessment of the risks are taken seriously and her motives are not treated as suspect. Unfortunately, she is the woman's adversary, rather than her confidante and trusted advisor. Therefore, it is suggested that the characterisation of compelled obstetric intervention as a response to conflict between the woman's right to autonomy and the life of the foetus is at best incomplete, overlooking the conflict between patient autonomy and medical paternalism that lies at its centre. In this section I will consider how the relationship between the pregnant woman and her doctor has been framed in terms of conflict and the way in which the courts have negotiated this conflict in determining whether to authorise obstetric interventions, highlighting the way in which the medical model of pregnancy has come to dominate the courts' thinking in this area.

1. The impact of technology upon pregnancy and childbirth and the doctor's predisposition to intervene

In each jurisdiction it is accepted that the woman's attending physician is also responsible for the care of the foetus. Technology has increasingly enabled doctors to identify, and sometimes treat, a large number of problems occurring during

169 M. A. Warren, 'The Moral Significance of Birth' (1989) 4(3) *Hypatia* 46, at 63.

170 In Germany, if the doctor believes that the woman lacks capacity, she should seek the appointment of a guardian (a *Betreuer*) unless a *Bevollmächtigte* (a surrogate decision-maker) has been appointed by the patient and has the power to make the necessary decision (§ 1896 II BGB).

pregnancy. However, the use of technology is argued to have transformed 'the naturalness of pregnancy and childbirth ... into an illness, an unnatural condition, with an assumption of risk to fetal and maternal health that only the medical profession can rectify and control'.[171] In this manner, pregnancy is subject to technological imperatives; it has come to be regarded as a condition to be managed – certainly a condition that is too difficult for a woman to navigate alone, without the guiding hand of a member of the medical profession. As Ann Oakley explained, the overwhelming view that emerged from her study of the medical care of pregnant women was that 'pregnant women were themselves deficient: they lacked the necessary intelligence, foresight, education, or responsibility to see that the only proper pathway to successful motherhood was the one repeatedly surveyed by medical expertise'.[172] Undoubtedly, the use of technology has served to ensure that healthcare professionals play a key role in the management of pregnancy in general, and more particularly in the delivery. Indeed, it is worth noting that the increasing use of obstetric interventions ensures that the central role is accorded to doctors, rather than midwives, in the delivery room. Thus, as Emily Martin argues, with 'the uterus as a machine that produces the baby and the woman as labourer who produces the baby ... What role is the doctor given? I think it is clear that he is predominantly seen as the supervisor or foreman of the labour process'.[173]

It is well recognised that the increasing use of technology is associated with increasing numbers of obstetric interventions in childbirth,[174] a factor reflected in the 60 per cent increase in the US caesarean rate from 1996 to 2009, with caesareans accounting for 32.8 per cent of all births in 2011.[175] Similar increases can be seen in the caesarean rates for both England and Wales and Germany; in fact, the rates in all three jurisdictions are significantly higher than that identified by the World Health Organization as the optimal rate of 10–15 per cent.[176] However, the increasing use of technology is not the only factor associated with increased caesarean delivery rate; rather, it is argued that in this high-risk branch of medicine the number of malpractice claims is driving the caesarean rate up.[177] Whilst a caesarean poses a greater risk to a woman than vaginal delivery, it does increase the doctor's control of the birthing process and so is regarded by some

171 L. R. Woliver, *The Political Geographies of Pregnancy*, Urbana: University of Illinois Press, 2002, at 30.

172 A. Oakley, *The Captured Womb: A History of the Medical Care of Pregnant Women*, Oxford: Basil Blackwell, 1984, at 72.

173 E. Martin, *The Woman in the Body*, Boston: Beacon Press, 1987, at 63.

174 F. G. Cunningham et al., *Williams Obstetrics*, 24th edn, New York: McGraw-Hill Education, 2014, at 587.

175 J. A. Martin et al., 'Births: Final Data for 2011' *National Vital Statistics Reports*, vol. 62, no. 1, 2013, Hyattsville, MD: National Center for Health Statistics, at 13.

176 WHO, 'Appropriate technology for birth' (1985) *Lancet* ii 436–7. The rate of births by caesarean section 2006–12 was 33 per cent in the USA, 32 per cent in Germany and 25 per cent in England, Table 4, WHO *World health statistics 2014*, available at http://apps.who.int/iris/bitstream/10665/112738/1/9789240692671_eng.pdf?ua=1 (accessed 13 August 2015).

177 F. G. Cunningham et al., *Williams Obstetrics* (note 174), at 588.

doctors as preferable *per se*; indeed, as Marsden Wagner wrote, 'If a [caesarean section] is done, the woman and the baby take the risks while if the CS is not done, the doctor takes the risk'.[178] Whilst a caesarean is a very common procedure, it is major abdominal surgery and not only involves a long recovery period but also poses significant risks to the woman, including 'infection, haemorrhage, thromboembolism, bladder and uterine lacerations and even death'.[179] Upon reading the cases, it is noticeable that there is a qualitative difference in the risk assessments provided in relation to the woman and the foetus. Those setting out the risk to the foetus of not intervening are typically much more detailed, quantifying and stressing the risk of foetal death or serious injury, whilst the risk to the woman of not intervening tends to be expressed in much more general terms. For example, in *Re L* it was said that if the caesarean were not performed, 'the carrying of a dead unborn child would be injurious to L's health and well-being'.[180] The risks involved in obstetric intervention are increasingly acknowledged by the judges, but are often underplayed and the focus is upon the current risks with no account being taken of the longer-term risks to the woman's health, life or even future reproductive capacity, all of which can be significantly affected by obstetric intervention. Moreover, in the recent English cases the acknowledged risks involved in a caesarean have been offset by other, unquantifiable risks of harm to the woman's mental health if the foetus were not to survive, without consideration of the similarly unquantifiable risks to the woman's mental health that could result from being compelled to accept obstetric intervention, particularly where she is not even aware that such an intervention is being proposed.

The potential for being sued is a matter of significant concern to many obstetricians and is liable to lead to the practice of defensive medicine. As Sheena Meredith argues:

> The threshold for intervention has plummeted, the obstetrician may be criticised for failing to act, and responsibility for adverse outcomes may appear to devolve accordingly; once intervention commences however, the obstetrician has done his or her best, the risks often become those of the birth or of the procedure itself and, short of negligence in performing the procedure, the obstetrician is thereby absolved.[181]

Moreover, doctors will not only be motivated by fears of malpractice litigation; risk aversion is also a powerful incentive to intervene in childbirth. As John Seymour points out:

> Doctors are trained to anticipate and minimize risk. They will frequently take the view that it is good medicine to seek to avoid a known risk, even a

178 M. Wagner, 'Choosing Caesarean Section' (2000) 356 *Lancet* 1677, at 1677.
179 F. G. Cunningham et al., *Williams Obstetrics* (note 174), at 587.
180 *Re L (Patient: non-consensual treatment)* [1997] 2 FLR 837, at 838.
181 S. Meredith, *Policing Pregnancy: The Law and Ethics of Obstetric Conflict*, Aldershot: Ashgate, 2005, at 194.

statistically remote one; their instinct will therefore be to err on the side of intervention.[182]

It may be that obstetricians are more risk-averse than doctors working in other specialties, simply because if the risk eventuates, the magnitude of that risk is greater than in other areas of medicine. However, caesareans were sought in a number of the cases discussed above not because the foetus was at risk but because there was a potential for a risk to the foetus to occur. For example, in *Madyun*[183] there was no evidence of infection. There was a potential cause for alarm, a risk that might or might not eventuate, but the court accepted the need for a caesarean, despite the woman's refusal of consent. Similarly, in the case of Amber Marlowe[184] the foetus was large, but it was not in distress. There was no need to perform a caesarean at the time the application was made; rather, the application was made in anticipation of the need to perform a caesarean. In fact, the Marlowes left the hospital and Amber Marlowe successfully delivered the baby vaginally in another hospital. Moreover, in the English case of *Tameside and Glossop Acute Services Trust v CH*[185] CH had not refused a caesarean or forceps delivery, but it was anticipated that she might refuse to cooperate with her doctors and a declaration was made for the eventuality that a caesarean was necessary. This approach was also adopted in a number of the more recent English cases that focused on the need for permissive orders to allow doctors to respond as necessary, rather than to existing threats. In each of these cases it is possible to view the applications for court authorisation as symptomatic of the doctors' aversion to risk, but it was the women who would be subjected to the risks of a caesarean section, regardless of whether the risk outlined eventuated. Thus the technological imperative can be seen to dominate the medical and legal consideration, elevating the medical professional's assessment of risk to almost statements of fact, whilst minimising the woman's own risk assessment and indeed her reasons for refusal.

John Robertson has argued that it is acceptable to force a woman to undergo a caesarean because she will have to undergo the physical burdens of parturition anyway,[186] an argument that appears to have been particularly persuasive in *Pemberton*.[187] However, the fact that she will have to give birth does not in itself justify the increased burden placed upon a pregnant woman by a caesarean. A woman's autonomy demands that *she* be permitted to choose how to give birth, not that she should be forced to accede to the doctor's recommendations. Nevertheless, the most recent case reported in the United States suggests that doctors may be willing to subject women to a caesarean even without a court

182 J. Seymour (note 31), at 220.
183 *Re Madyun* (note 50).
184 *WVHCS-Hosp., Inc. v. Doe* (note 25).
185 [1996] 1 FLR 762
186 J. A. Robertson (note 142), at 457.
187 *Pemberton v Tallahassee Memorial Regional Medical Center* (note 17), at 1251–2.

order,[188] and in England and Wales there is at least one reported case of a woman signing a consent form for a caesarean section under duress.[189] Writing in *Obstetrics and Gynecology*, the journal of the American College of Obstetricians and Gynecologists, Frank Chervenak has suggested that an obstetrician can 'justifiably coerce emergency caesarean delivery without a court order' subject to three criteria being met, namely that 'a cesarean is expected to prevent serious infant morbidity, 2) lack of physical resistance that could significantly increase the risks of maternal or fetal harm from coerced cesarean delivery, and 3) insufficient time to consider a court order'.[190] Any consideration of the woman's own interests, including risks to her life or health, or indeed the proportionality of the intervention is noticeably absent from these criteria, but the most remarkable element must be the second criterion, which clearly demonstrates the imbalance of power between the woman (arguably at one of the most vulnerable times of her life) and the doctor, the professional who will stop at nothing to save the foetus, but only if the woman is considered unlikely to fight back. As Sheena Meredith has pointed out, this criterion

> suggests, variously, a tendency to pick on women who cannot or will not defend themselves, a (welcome) reluctance to impose medical decisions by physical force, and a willingness to back off if the fight seems likely to be a bloody one. What it does not suggest is a universal, needs-based standard of intervention based on sound legal (or medical) principles and applied with proper regard to the due processes of the law.[191]

The suggestion that a doctor might justifiably force a woman to accept intervention for the benefit of her foetus is particularly surprising as it contrasts with the stance adopted by the medical professional bodies in each of the jurisdictions. For example, in the UK the Royal College of Obstetricians and Gynaecologists advise:

> It is inappropriate to invoke judicial intervention to overrule an informed and competent woman's refusal of a proposed medical treatment, even if it seems to others to be irrational. If an adult with capacity makes a voluntary and appropriately informed decision to refuse treatment this decision must be

188 A. Hartocollis, 'Mother Accuses Doctors of Forcing a C-Section', *New York Times*, 16.05.2014, A18.

189 Caroline Speer obtained £7000 in an out-of-court settlement after commencing legal action, claiming that her consent was vitiated by duress, S. Ebner, 'The unkindest cut' 02.06.1997 *Guardian* B5. Following the delivery, C was granted legal aid to challenge the decision authorising the performance of a caesarean, *Rochdale Healthcare NHS Trust v C* (note 16); C. Dyer, 'Mother vs Big Brother', *Guardian* 19.12.1996, T4.

190 F. A. Chervenak, L. B. McCullough and D. W. Skupski, 'An Ethical Justification for Emergency, Coerced Cesarean Delivery' (1993) 82(6) *Obstetrics & Gynecology* 1029, at 1029.

191 S. Meredith (note 181), at 196.

> respected, even where this may result in the death of the patient and/or the death of an unborn child, whatever the stage of the pregnancy.[192]

Similarly, the American College of Obstetricians and Gynecologists recommends:

> Pregnant women's autonomous decisions should be respected... . In the absence of extraordinary circumstances, circumstances that, in fact, the Committee on Ethics cannot currently imagine, judicial authority should not be used to implement treatment regimens aimed at protecting the fetus, for such actions violate the pregnant woman's autonomy.[193]

The *Deutsche Gesellschaft für Gynäkologie und Geburtshilfe* states:

> The doctor must respect the bodily integrity of the woman giving birth. Even in the case of an unambiguous indication he may not perform a surgical intervention against her express will, unless a gross error would be the consequence and sufficient reasons suggest that the woman no longer has the capacity to decide.[194]

Given the apparent clarity of the above statements, it is rather concerning that so many instances of doctors being willing to override a woman's express refusal, with or without court authorisation, have been reported. There can be no doubt that it is extremely difficult for a doctor to sit back and watch a woman and foetus die for want of a caesarean or a blood transfusion, both common and, at least from the medical point of view, largely straightforward procedures.[195] That difficulty is compounded by what Talcott Parsons referred to as medically ritualised optimism and bias in favour of active intervention.[196] However, the fact that treatment is possible does not translate to a right to treat; it does not justify a shift from patient choice to professional control. Obstetrics cannot be allowed to return to a 'golden age' of paternalism where women acquiesce and accept that doctors know best, particularly given the high level of medical errors and false indications for intervention caused by misinterpreting information, especially that derived from electronic foetal monitoring.[197]

192 Royal College of Obstetricians and Gynaecologists (note 93), at 7.
193 American College of Obstetricians and Gynecologists Committee on Ethics, *Committee Opinion No. 321: Maternal Decision Making, Ethics, and the Law* (2005), at 9.
194 Deutsche Gesellschaft für Gynäkologie und Geburtshilfe, AG Medizinrecht (note 98), at § 2.2.
195 In an interesting letter to the editors, A. Biscoe and G. Kidson-Gerber described how when a pregnant woman refused blood products, leading to the death of both herself and the foetus, 'staff were distressed, grappling with what was perceived as two "avoidable" deaths', 'Avoidable Death of a Pregnant Jehovah's Witness with Acute Promyelocytic Leukaemia: Ethical Considerations and the Internal Conflicts and Challenges Encountered by Practitioners' (2015) 45 *Internal Medicine Journal* 461.
196 T. Parson, *The Social System,* Glenco: Free Press, 195, chapter 10.
197 See S. A. Law, 'Childbirth: An Opportunity for Choice that Should be Supported' (2008) 32 *NYU Review of Law and Social Change* 345, at 360–2 for a useful discussion of the efficacy problems associated with EFM.

2. The overemphasis of medical advice by the courts and medical fallibility

A common theme in the cases discussed above is that medical opinion concerning appropriate treatment was considered to be conclusive, regardless of the woman's views. Medical evidence is seen as scientific, rational and objective. As Irving Zola has suggested, medicine 'is becoming the new repository of truth, the place where absolute and often final judgments are made by supposedly morally neutral and objective experts'.[198] By contrast, the women are portrayed as incapable of making a responsible decision. Just as doctors are portrayed as experts, as aids to responsible decision-making in the abortion context, they appear to be taking on the same role in assessing whether or not obstetric interventions should take place. Thus women who refuse to consent to treatment for the benefit of the foetus are constructed as selfish hedonists willing to sacrifice the life of the foetus rather than having an operation, as irresponsible individuals making decisions that are morally repugnant.

In refusing to consent, the women deviate from the social construct of motherhood, that self-effacing, altruistic condition that requires 'mothers', or in this case pregnant women,[199] to do whatever is necessary and accept all recommended treatment for the benefit of her foetus. By contrast, doctors are portrayed as merely wanting to do that which is best for the woman and to save the foetus, even in cases where they have misused the Mental Health Act and acted unlawfully.[200] The only inversion of this narrative in the case law is seen in *re AC*,[201] where subjecting Angela Carder to a caesarean against her wishes, in the knowledge that it was likely to hasten her death, the court's order that a caesarean be performed served only to deliver a baby that died within two hours of delivery and to hasten the death of AC who died two days later. As Jane Bryan notes in the D.C. Court of Appeals' judgment, 'The depiction of the pregnant woman as intelligent, compassionate and maternal, and the medical authorities as hasty and insensitive was an important counter-balance to the usual images in such cases, unsettling the narrative of the doctor as guardian of the foetus'.[202] However, in this, as in so many other respects, *Re AC* was atypical of the compelled obstetric cases. The descriptions of the women in the other cases are rather different; there they are described as selfish and immoral, or as immature and in need of guidance. Indeed, some of the judges have concluded their judgments by reference to the fact that the women concerned were sorry to have been a bother and grateful for

198 I. K. Zola, 'Medicine as an Institution of Social Control' (1972) 20 *Sociological Review* 487, at 487a.

199 Despite the fact the courts in each of the jurisdictions have referred to the woman concerned as a 'mother', unless she already has the status of mother in relation to a child extant, she is not a mother and, in any case, even if she is not a *prima gravida*, she is not a mother to the foetus until it is born.

200 See, for example, the praise for doctors seeking only to do the right thing in *St George's Healthcare NHS Trust* v *S; R* v *Collins and others, ex parte S* (note 8).

201 *Re AC* (note 41).

202 J. Bryan (note 23), at 132.

the court intervention, reinforcing the notion that the woman is the source of trouble and requires managing, rather than in trouble and in need of support.

The fact that some women are apparently grateful to the court does not excuse the subjection of women to major abdominal surgery for the sake of the foetus. It may well be that both she and her baby can be reported to be doing well after the intervention, but that does not negate the harm she suffered at the hands of the state. By treating her in a way that a non-pregnant person would not be treated, the woman is reduced to a uterine environment, a patient who must follow medical advice. Moreover, it is clear that not all women are grateful for the court's intervention: the woman who appealed against the declaration authorising doctors at St George's to perform a caesarean against her will was not grateful for the way she had been treated; nor would it appear was Fatima Chowdhary, the woman forced to undergo a caesarean despite protestations that she would rather die. In that case Johnson J concluded his judgment with the following statement:

> After I had said that I made the declaration Mr Leigh [the Trust's solicitor] left court and communicated my decision to the hospital by mobile telephone. In fact in the time it had taken Mr Leigh to come to the court the patient had changed her mind and given her consent to the procedure. Accordingly, the operation was in fact performed with her consent. The operation was successful and both patient and child are doing well. In the words of Mr Leigh, 'this story may show that justice is more accessible than psychiatry'.[203]

It will be remembered that during the emergency hearing there was no time for a psychiatrist to conduct a capacity assessment, but Fatima Chowdhary's obstetrician said that he believed her to be fully competent to refuse the caesarean. Nevertheless, Johnson J found that she lacked the ability to weigh up the information that she was given in order to make a choice, stating:

> The patient was in the throes of labour with all that is involved in terms of pain and emotional stress. I concluded that a patient who could, in those circumstances, speak in terms which seemed to accept the inevitability of her own death, was not a patient who was able properly to weigh-up the considerations that arose so as to make any valid decision, about anything of even the most trivial kind, surely still less one which involved her own life.[204]

However, it appears that having declared her incompetent and found that her best interests required that a caesarean be performed, he subsequently formed the opinion that she did have the capacity to make a decision, provided that it accorded with the medical advice given! Moreover, although he wrote that Mrs Chowdhary had changed her mind and consented to the operation, she later gave a very different account, saying that she had merely acquiesced, and she was granted legal

203 *Rochdale Healthcare NHS Trust* v *C* (note 16), at 275–6.
204 Ibid., at 275.

aid to challenge the ruling, suggesting that she did not believe that justice had been accessible, or indeed that justice had been done.[205]

All these cases illustrate the extreme deference shown by the courts to the views of the medical profession. Medical advice and the assessment of risks are accepted without question. For example, in *Re Madyun* Levie J dismissed the couple's considered view that they did not want a caesarean section to be performed at that time, feeling that such intervention was not yet necessary, saying, 'To ignore the undisputed opinion of a skilled and trained physician to indulge the desires of the parents where, as here, there is a substantial risk to the unborn infant, is something the Court cannot do'.[206] Levie J clearly displayed contempt for the 'self-indulgence' of the parents-*to-be* – that is, Ayesha Madyun's choice to attempt a vaginal delivery despite conflicting medical advice – instead accepting the validity of the medical assessment without question. On the other side of the Atlantic, writing extra-judicially, Thorpe LJ has suggested deference to medical opinions is inevitable, stating:

> Whatever emphasis legal principle may place upon adult autonomy with the consequent right to choose between treatments, at some level the judicial outcome will be influenced by the expert evidence as to which treatment affords the best chance of the happy announcement that both mother and baby are doing well.[207]

However, the role of the court in this context cannot be allowed to become merely an instrument to impose and enforce medical advice. A significant problem in this context is that orders are often sought in emergency situations where there is no or little opportunity to obtain second opinions or challenge medical evidence offered by the attending doctor. Alternatively, a number of the latest tranche of English cases have been pre-emptive in nature, but, like the emergency hearings, were conducted with little or no input from the woman herself and often without any clear statement of what the woman would have wanted, as opposed to what 'women' are presumed to want – that is, the safe delivery of the foetus at no matter what personal cost.

The evidence given to the court tends to emphasise the risks of not intervening; little is said of the risks involved in the intervention sought, and given that judges are generally not in a position to make a risk assessment for themselves, there is an inbuilt bias in favour of intervention.

In court proceedings the medical evidence is presented and handled as fact, but little account is taken of the now numerous occasions when the evidence presented has been shown to be wrong. As the Royal College of Obstetricians and Gynaecologists has stressed:

> There are limits to the accuracy and effectiveness of many diagnostic and therapeutic procedures during pregnancy and confinement and this should be

205 C. Dyer, 'Mother vs Big Brother', *Guardian*, 19.12.96, A4.
206 *Re Madyun* (note 50), at 1263.
207 M. A. Thorpe 'The Caesarean Section Debate' (1997) 27 *Family Law* 663, at 663–4.

> discussed with the mother. For example, the methods for detecting fetal compromise antenatally and during labour are not always reliable indicators of a poor outcome. The fine indices that determine whether the dynamic process of labour will culminate in a normal outcome are difficult to measure.[208]

It is well accepted that doctors are human, and thus are as fallible as any other person; for example, in *Jefferson* the medical evidence given to the court was that, due to the placenta previa,

> [t]here is a 99 to 100 percent certainty that the unborn child will die if she attempts to have the child by vaginal delivery. There is a 99 to 100 percent chance that the child will live if the baby is delivered by Caesarean section prior to the beginning of labor. There is a 50 percent chance that Mrs. Jefferson herself will die if vaginal delivery is attempted. There is an almost 100 percent chance that Mrs. Jefferson will survive if a delivery by Caeserean section is done prior to the beginning of labor.[209]

In fact, after Jessie Mae Jefferson was re-scanned it was discovered that her placenta was no longer lying over the cervix so that a caesarean delivery was no longer indicated. As Hill J noted, this is 'a most unusual occurrence';[210] indeed, it is respectfully submitted that the doctors had (correctly) testified that such movement is impossible. Thus it would appear that the application to the court was made on the basis of a mistaken reading of the ultrasound, highlighting the danger of courts merely accepting medical opinion without seeking independent confirmation of that evidence.

Similarly, in *In re Baby Boy Doe* medical opinion suggested that the chance of the foetus surviving natural childbirth was close to zero, but less than three weeks after the end of the initial court hearing Tabita Bricci delivered an apparently normal and healthy, if underweight, baby boy.[211] In the case of Laura Pemberton the medical evidence suggested that without a caesarean there was a risk of uterine rupture of 2–60 per cent. Nevertheless, since being subjected to a second caesarean she has had four successful vaginal deliveries.[212] The number of cases in which the doctor's risk assessment was wrong is a significant cause for concern and highlights the need for balanced medical evidence to be made available to the court. In some cases the risks as evaluated by doctors will eventuate and in other cases they will not, but the risk assessments presented to the courts should be treated as such – as expert opinions – and be subjected to rigorous scrutiny, rather than being treated as 'doctor's orders'.

208 Royal College of Obstetricians and Gynaecologists (note 93), at 5.3.
209 *Jefferson v Griffin Spalding County Hospital Authority* (note 4), at 459.
210 Ibid., at 461, footnote 1.
211 *In re Baby Boy Doe, a Fetus v Mother Doe* (note 9), at 329.
212 J. Flavin, *Our Bodies, Our Crimes: The Policing of Women's Reproduction in America*, New York: New York University Press, 2009, at 116.

Quite apart from the cases where mistakes were made, or risks overstated, it is a matter of considerable concern that the court in *St George's* could be misinformed that S was in labour and that the hearing was treated as an emergency hearing. The adage that 'doctor knows best' may well be true; however, this does not mean that treatment decisions should rest with doctors with no account taken of the patient's autonomy, or her beliefs and values. Just as in any other area, medical evidence must be subjected to scrutiny and not accepted at face value. In all but one of the cases considered above, the judges granted the order sought, despite well-publicised cases that demonstrated the medical assessment of risks had been wrong, suggesting that there is rather too much professional courtesy and a need to subject the medical advice to much more stringent review.

3. Interim conclusions on framing the relationship between the woman and her doctor

As the forgoing demonstrates, any consideration of whether or not obstetric intervention should take place is biased towards the views of the medical professional. Pregnant women are undoubtedly marginalised by technology. Doctors are no longer reliant upon information provided by the pregnant woman; instead, technology can supply the necessary information, in an objective, verifiable manner. Moreover, technology highlights the distance between the woman and the foetus: the fact that the foetus is not simply a part of the woman. This has led to the relationship between the two being cast as antagonistic rather than complementary, and the emphasis being placed upon the severability rather than the enduring nature of the connection between them. By contrast, technology reinforces the medical professional's position as an expert, an authoritative voice. In many ways this is inevitable. Doctors have the expertise to assess the risks involved and the best way of ensuring the desired outcome, a healthy mother and baby. However, in this as in any other area of medicine, patients will have views about the way in which they wish to be treated, or not treated, about what level of risk they are prepared to accept – views that should be determinative rather than mere factors for the doctor to consider before deciding how to proceed.

Despite the tendency of the technology to emphasise the separateness of the foetus, the woman must remain at the centre of the decision-making and indeed be the central decision-maker. Pregnancy does not reverse the presumption of capacity or obviate the right to refuse treatment; thus the central question is not what treatment is clinically indicated for the foetus, but what treatment will the pregnant woman accept. In this, as in any other area of medicine, women must be enabled and empowered to take decisions for themselves and should be able to rely on the support of their healthcare professional, support that properly given may sustain both 'maternal' and foetal welfare. There is little room for a constructive relationship with a doctor if she simply provides her advice and then threatens to seek a court order if the woman ignores it. Indeed, as the medical professional bodies advise, doctors should not seek court authorisation to compel women to accept their advice; rather, they should seek to establish a dialogue with the woman concerned, to try to persuade her to accept that advice.[213]

Technology has enabled us to view the contents of the uterus. The foetus is no longer invisible, but those early images of the foetus cannot be allowed to render the woman invisible. Whilst the contents of her uterus are clearly a matter of public interest, there is also a significant public interest in maintaining respect for the woman's bodily integrity, her autonomy and her dignity. It is suggested that the public interest is best satisfied by cooperation with the pregnant woman, by supporting and facilitating her ability to make decisions for herself (and her foetus), and respecting those choices. The alternative is to compel treatment, treating women as mere incubators and risking driving most affected women underground, unable or unwilling to seek prenatal care, and thus placing more foetuses and women unnecessarily at risk.

213 American College of Obstetricians and Gynecologists Committee on Ethics (note 194), at 9, Deutsche Gesellschaft für Gynäkologie und Geburtshilfe, *Absolute und relative Indikationen zur Sectio caesarea*, 2001, revised 2008, currently under revision, at § 4.2; Royal College of Obstetricians and Gynaecologists (note 93), at 5.2.

D. Conclusion: moving forward, putting the woman back centre-stage

Technology has changed the landscape of medical care during pregnancy, subverting the nature of the relationship between the woman and her doctor by shifting the emphasis from the provision of care to supervision, or even surveillance in some cases. Ultrasound imaging has provided a window into the womb, rendering that which was private, public; but all too often the public interest in the contents of the uterus has given voice to the need to protect the foetus from the woman, rather than to ways in which the interests and the welfare of both the woman and the foetus can be supported. As Gena Corea writes, 'Increasingly, it is the contents of the container that matter, not the container herself'.[1]

The narratives from the case law speak to the conceptualisation of pregnant women refusing treatment that could benefit the foetus as deviant. Her failure to comply with social expectations of (impending) motherhood and medical advice render not merely her choices suspect but her ability to make those choices moot. They tell the story of doctors trying to save their foetal patients rather than focusing upon supporting a woman who is willingly pregnant, looking forward to meeting her baby for the first time, but who for whatever reason cannot consent to treatment that is clinically indicated for the foetus. All too often the woman has been invisible in the ensuing debate. She has also been inaudible; her voice has either been sidelined or, worse, not heard at all. Therefore it is suggested that the way forward lies in putting the woman back at the centre of the decision-making. It is not a matter of regulating what others can legitimately do to the woman's body, but rather of protecting and enforcing her rights to bodily integrity and autonomy and respect for her human dignity. When obstetric intervention is clinically indicated for the benefit of the foetus, the question should not be framed in terms of who makes the decision about treatment. Instead, the issue is how the woman be supported and facilitated in making the decision through the provision of health and social support. The promotion of responsible and supported decision-making, even if that entails the death of a viable foetus, must be preferable to criminalisation and the complete disregard for the woman's dignity.

1 G. Corea, *The Mother Machine: Reproductive Technologies from Artificial Insemination to Artificial Wombs*, London: Women's Press, 1985, at 299.

Throughout this book it has been argued that respect for human dignity requires that the woman's bodily integrity and autonomy are respected and that, like any other patient, she should be allowed to make decisions that are 'wrong'. This, it is suggested, is the minimum content of the guarantee of human dignity, that no person can be instrumentalised and used as a means to an end. A key benefit of the German approach is the way that it combines respect for foetal life with respect for the woman's interests, without subordinating all other rights and interests to the protection of the foetal life. Thus the *Bundesverfassungsgericht* recognised that the foetus does not exist in a vacuum and the protection of its life will inevitably impinge upon the woman's rights and dignity, and although the court did not recognise that a pregnant woman has an absolute right to self-determination in terms of electing an abortion free of state control, it did find that her duty to protect the foetus is tempered by what can reasonably be expected of her.[2]

It is suggested that the approach adopted by the *Bundesverfassungsgericht* is correct, that the only effective way to safeguard foetal life lies in cooperation with the pregnant woman. Looking forward, this requires two important steps. First, the relationship between the woman and her doctor must be recalibrated, emphasising that whilst the doctor owes a duty of care towards the foetus, she cannot prioritise caring for the foetus above respect for the woman's autonomy and bodily integrity. A way must be found for doctors to cooperate with their pregnant patients, to seek a solution to problems that will protect the foetus to the greatest extent possible, whilst promoting and respecting the woman's autonomy. It is suggested that the best way to achieve this is by greater use of advance decision-making to enable treatment decisions to be made at a time where the woman's capacity is not in doubt. Second, the adjudication of disputes between the woman and the doctor must be refocused to centre upon the pregnant woman rather than the medical evidence. Too many of the cases discussed above exhibit grave procedural defects; almost all were dealt with in an emergency hearing, with no time for an adequate defence of the woman's rights, a detailed consideration of her wishes or even to scrutinise the medical evidence presented. Such procedural irregularities undermine the ability of the courts to respect the woman's dignity and call the validity of the decisions into question. No matter how unreasonable the woman's decision may appear, the judiciary must actively protect and promote the woman's rights to autonomy and bodily integrity, ensuring that procedural safeguards are upheld, rather than deferring to medical opinion and reducing judicial proceedings to little more than a rubber stamp exercise authorising the treatment proposed.

I. Re-centring the relationship between women and healthcare professionals through anticipatory decision-making

The number of cases brought before the courts is indicative not only of the doctors' fears of being sued, and thus their need for reassurance in the form of a court

2 *BVerfGE* 88, 203, at 255ff.

order, but also of a failure in communication between the doctor and her patient. In each jurisdiction the professional bodies have recognised that a doctor's role is to support the pregnant woman and respect her autonomy, and that it will almost never be appropriate to seek judicial authorisation to override the woman's refusal of consent.[3] Nevertheless, there are a surprising number of cases where orders have been sought, those reported representing a mere fraction of those that are heard by the courts. Moreover, whilst there are no reported cases from Germany, the results of Marina Cuttini's research suggests a significant disconnect between the professional guidance and professional attitudes and practice, with almost a third of German obstetricians reporting that they would be willing to seek an emergency court order to protect the life of the foetus, or to protect themselves from liability, and about 7 per cent of the German respondents answering that they would perform a caesarean where indicated by foetal distress, overriding a woman's refusal and without seeking a court order.[4]

In many of the reported cases it is clear that the conflict situation that arose was foreseeable and that it could have been resolved, or at least discussed, in a much calmer atmosphere in advance of the crisis situation that eventuated necessitating court intervention. For example, in the cases of *Re MB*[5] and *Bolton Hospitals NHS Trust v O*,[6] it was foreseeable that problems during the birth could occur due to the needle phobia that had prevented MB from having blood tests during her pregnancy (blood tests are a regular feature of antenatal care throughout pregnancy) and the fact that O was suffering from post-traumatic stress disorder following her previous caesarean delivery. In both cases early intervention such as cognitive behavioural therapy might have assisted the women to develop coping strategies, so that they would have been able to make a valid decision to accept, or indeed to refuse, a caesarean, instead of being deemed to lack capacity due to the panic they suffered. Similarly, in the case of a Jehovah's Witness, a discussion early in pregnancy about how she would like to be treated should a major haemorrhage occur during pregnancy or labour would enable an agreed treatment plan to be negotiated between the woman and her healthcare professionals. For example, a list of those blood products that she would be willing to accept should be drawn up and added

3 American College of Obstetricians and Gynecologists Committee on Ethics, *Committee Opinion No. 321: Maternal Decision Making, Ethics, and the Law* (2005), at 9; Deutsche Gesellschaft für Gynäkologie und Geburtshilfe, AG Medizinrecht, *Empfehlungen zu den ärztlichen Beratungs- und Aufklärungspflichten während der Schwangerenbetreuung und bei der Geburtshilfe*, 1996, confirmed 2010, at § 2.2; Royal College of Obstetricians and Gynaecologists, *A Consideration of the Law and Ethics in Relation to Court-Authorised Obstetric Intervention* 2nd edn, London, 2006, at 7.

4 M. Cuttini et al., 'Patient Refusal of Emergency Caesarean Delivery: A Study of Obstetricians' Attitudes in Europe' (2006) 108(5) *Obstetrics & Gynecology* 1121, at 1124. Responses from UK obstetricians demonstrated court orders would be sought to protect the doctor from liability (9 per cent) more often than to protect the foetus (4 per cent) and no respondents answered that they would proceed with a caesarean section against the wishes of the woman absent a court order.

5 [1997] 2 FLR 426.

6 [2002] EWHC 2871, [2003] 1 FLR 824.

to her medical notes; it should be considered whether it would be appropriate for the woman to take iron supplements throughout pregnancy in order to maximise stores of iron; and she should be advised to give birth in an obstetrician-led (rather than midwife-led) unit in order to ensure that the necessary specialist care will be immediately available if a haemorrhage were to occur.[7]

The case for the exercise of precedent autonomy is even clearer in the case of women with a history of mental illness where an advance decision will enable them to make autonomous choices about the care they will receive at a time when their capacity is not compromised. As discussed above,[8] difficult decisions will need to be made about whether to continue treating the woman's illness, and thereby risk causing harm to the foetus, or to discontinue/reduce the woman's medication in order to safeguard the foetus, but at the same time increasing the likelihood of the woman suffering a relapse and no longer being considered to have the capacity to make treatment decisions for herself. In many cases it will be appropriate to reduce or discontinue treatment for the mental disorder with the woman's agreement, but it is vital that a detailed care plan is developed through collaboration between the woman and both her obstetric and her psychiatric teams, detailing how she wishes to be treated during the pregnancy, the birth and the time thereafter should her capacity be compromised. The most obvious way to achieve this is through an advance medical treatment decision incorporated into the woman's birth plan.

Advance decisions/directives are commonly used at the end of life, and to a lesser degree in relation to psychiatric care, in each of the three jurisdictions. It is suggested that just as anticipatory decision-making has promoted dialogue between patients and their doctors at the end of life, it also has a significant role to play in the obstetric context. An advance directive is an important mechanism for conveying precedent autonomy, being designed to act as a communication bridge in the event of incapacity and providing a clear statement of how the patient wants to be treated, or more usually what treatment the patient does not wish to be afforded. It can provide a clear statement of the patient's wishes, enabling not only patient-centred care and respect for the patient's autonomy and bodily integrity, but more fundamentally respect for the patient as an individual, acknowledging and protecting her dignity.

It is common practice for women to write a birth plan whilst pregnant, to set out how they would like to be treated during labour, but what is being suggested here is a much more detailed and formal anticipatory decision about the treatment she wants to receive or refuse, a decision that is intended to be binding upon her doctors in the event that she lacks the capacity to make her own contemporaneous treatment decision. The manner in which a woman chooses to give birth is a deeply personal and intimate decision, encompassing much more than medical

7 Established guidance recommends such advance planning; see, for example, Royal College of Obstetricians and Gynaecologists, *Blood Transfusion in Obstetrics*, London, 2015, at § 11.

8 B II 4.

considerations. Thus birth plans operate at two levels. They can be described as aspirational, setting out the kind of birth experience that the woman would like to have, including, for example, which labour positions she would like to use, who she would like to be present and what form of pain relief she would like. Such considerations are entirely valid and extremely important, but inevitably they are broader in scope and less definite than a birth plan that takes the form of advance medical treatment decision. Whilst a general birth plan will evolve to respond to situations as they develop, an advance decision will not evolve in the same way as it will only come into effect if the woman lacks the requisite capacity to make a contemporaneous decision – that is, at a time when the woman is unable to assess the situation and make a valid treatment decision.

Similarly, a valid and applicable advance decision is intended to bind the attending doctor, whilst a birth plan is framed in much more tentative terms, outlining treatment preferences that will certainly give clear evidence of what the woman would want, but will not bind the doctor, or indeed the woman in the sense of a Ulysses contract, despite suggestions to the contrary in some of the obstetric literature.[9] A woman should always be presumed to have capacity until the reverse is clearly demonstrated, and whenever she has capacity her contemporaneous decisions will bind healthcare professionals, regardless of what is written in her birth plan. Thus, for example, if a woman desires a 'natural' birth, she may write in her birth plan, 'I do not wish to receive any pain relief during labour in any circumstance; any expressions to the contrary during labour should be ignored'. Such a statement will not bind her healthcare professionals should the woman find the lived experience of labour harder than she expected and request pain relief. In such a situation her contemporaneous decision will clearly overrule the statement in her birth plan and pain relief must be provided, even if her partner is helpfully reminding both the woman and the attending doctor that she said she did not want pain relief! In the case of an advance decision, a woman can revoke it at any time whilst she has the capacity to do so. Given that capacity is decision-specific and that the degree of capacity required depends upon the gravity of the decision, it is to be expected that a much lower level of capacity will suffice to revoke an anticipatory refusal of indicated treatment than would be required to make a valid refusal. Such an understanding of the capacity requirement would support the preference for life that dominates the legal response to precedent autonomy in each of the jurisdictions, but also supports the principle of self-determination by requiring at least a minimal level of capacity to revoke anticipatory decisions made with capacity.[10]

9 See, for example, the discussion in H. Brooks and W. J. Sullivan, 'The Importance of Patient Autonomy at Birth' (2002) 11 *International Journal of Obstetric Anesthesia* 196, at 200f.; P. Burcher, 'The Ulysses Contract in Obstetrics: A Woman's Choices Before and During Labour' (2013) 39 *Journal of Medical Ethics* 27.

10 S.24 (3) Mental Capacity Act 2005, § 1901a I BGB. NB the German civil code does not address the issue of capacity in relation to the revocation of an advance directive. However, it cannot be the case that capacity is required to execute a valid directive, but be irrelevant when the same directive is to be revoked; therefore it is submitted that at

An advance decision should detail the treatments that the woman refuses and the circumstances in which her refusal should operate, explicitly stating whether the refusal is to apply if there is a threat of serious injury or to the life of either her or the foetus.[11] One of the key asymmetries between an anticipatory and a contemporaneous decision is the temporal and psychological distance that separates the anticipatory choice from the time at which it should be implemented. For that reason advance decisions may be inapplicable to the situation that arises with regard to the treatment refused and/or the circumstances in which the refusal should operate. In the case of a religious-based refusal of treatment, or where the woman suffers from a known condition where its likely trajectory is predictable, as, for example, in the case of a mental disorder, specificity problems are unlikely to occur. The applicability of an advance decision to the treatment situation and the indicated treatment options is likely to be more problematic in cases where there is no specific risk of incapacity occurring, making it all the more important that the woman undertakes the process of drawing up an advance decision in partnership with the obstetrician. Such collaboration should ensure that the anticipatory decision is relevant and provides clear and applicable instructions for what treatment the woman wants to refuse, or receive, and in which circumstances. The dialogue involved in such advance planning should enhance the potential for cooperation between the healthcare professional and the woman, providing the obstetrician not only with an opportunity to gain a clear understanding of what the woman wants, but also with the possibility to discuss alternatives and even to persuade her to accept treatment indicated for foetal well-being in what should be a calm and constructive atmosphere far removed from the emergency settings described in the case law above. In the obstetric setting the range of treatments and treatment scenarios is more limited than in the case envisaged by a general advance directive and therefore the specificity problem that besets anticipatory decision-making should largely be addressed by the collaboration of the woman and her doctor in this way. Nevertheless, women should also be encouraged to appoint a surrogate decision-maker (LPA) to make decisions upon their behalf if the situation that arises is not covered by their advance decisions.

The Mental Capacity Act only provides for the recognition of advance refusals of treatment, rather than requests for specific treatment. By contrast, in the USA some states do enable treatment requests to be made, and in Germany § 1901a I BGB recognises that patients can give an anticipatory consent to specific medical treatments, clinical investigations or medical interventions, although problems may arise in terms of whether the consent is sufficiently informed.[12] In any event, the

least a limited degree of capacity will be required to revoke a directive in each jurisdiction. For a detailed consideration of the revocation of advance decisions and capacity, see S. Halliday, 'Legislating to Give Effect to Precedent Autonomy: Comparative Reflections on Legislative Incompetence' (2011) 11 *Medical Law International* 127, at 133f., 139f., 156.

11 S.25(5) (6) MCA 2005.

12 This is a significant omission in the German context because, under German law, a consent to medical treatment is only valid if it is sufficiently informed, or if medical

parameters of a valid anticipatory decision are established in each of the jurisdictions by reference to clinical indications,[13] excluding the possibility of a patient using an advance decision to mandate non-indicated treatment and emphasising that the doctor's role is not limited to that of 'body mechanic'.[14] Therefore, although an anticipatory consent to a specific treatment may not bind the obstetrician, it should be given substantial weight in the consideration of the woman's best interests, or what she would have wanted under the presumed will or substituted judgment standard. A further limitation to the effectiveness of an advance directive may result from the very fact that it is intended to apply during pregnancy. As discussed above in relation to the United States of America,[15] a statutory exclusion clause operates to invalidate advance directives for the duration of pregnancy in many states; similarly, in both the UK and Germany there have been suggestions that an advance directive should not apply during pregnancy, or that it will be necessary to consider specifically whether the woman would have wanted the directive to continue to apply during pregnancy.[16] However, it has been suggested here that there should be a presumption that the woman intended her directive to apply, unless clear and convincing evidence can be adduced to the contrary. Moreover, by creating a specific advance decision to apply to obstetric care, or by including a standard advance directive as an appendix to the woman's birth plan with an express statement that it should apply notwithstanding pregnancy, any suggestion that the woman did not intend it to apply during pregnancy should be dispelled.

It is suggested therefore that much greater use needs to be made of anticipatory decisions, enabling a woman to set out her wishes at a time where there can be no question of her lacking capacity, where there is no stress, pain or emergency situation detracting from a calm discussion of the available options. The very process of drawing up such a decision will stimulate dialogue between the woman and her healthcare professional. Whilst standard form birth plans are susceptible to the charge of institutionalisation and of providing only the illusion of choice,[17] an

advice has been rejected (*BGHZ* 154, 205, at 215; *BGHZ* 163, 195, at 197; *BGHZ* 29, 46, at 49ff; *BGH* NJW 1980, 1333; *BGH* NJW 1993, 2372, at 2373). Thus, the explanatory notes to the Bill (*Entwurf eines Dritten Gesetzes zur Änderung des Betreuungsrechts*) that resulted in the amendments to the BGB recommend that medical advice should be sought, or that explicit reference should be made in the directive that the individual waived such advice, BT-Drs 16/8442, at 14.

13 See, for example, *R (Burke) v General Medical Council* [2005] EWCA Civ 1003, [2006] QB 273, *per* Lord Phillips MR at [31]; *BGH* NJW 2003, 1588, at 1592.

14 M. Bayles, 'Physicians as Body Mechanics' in J. W. Davis et al. (eds) *Contemporary Issues in Biomedical Ethics*, Clifton: Humana Press, 1978, at 167.

15 B I 4.

16 See, for example, A. Spickhoff, 'Rechtssicherheit kraft Gesetzes durch sog. Patientenverfügungen?' (2009) *FamRZ* 1949, at 1951; P. Balz, *Lebenserhaltung als Haftungsgrund*, Berlin: Springer, 2010, at 67; Law Commission, *Mental Incapacity* (Law Com No. 231, 1995), at para. 5.25–5.26; BMA, *Advance Decisions and Proxy Decision-Making in Medical Treatment and Research: Guidance from the BMA's Medical Ethics Department*, 2007, at 6. See discussion above at C III 2 a.

17 S. Kitzinger, 'Birth Plans: How Are They Being Used?' (1999) 7(5) *British Journal of Midwifery* 300, at 301f.

advance directive for obstetric care should be regarded in exactly the same way as other advance decisions. However, the ability of an advance decision to act as a communication tool, to effectively bridge the gap between capacity and incapacity, will ultimately depend upon the healthcare professionals involved and their willingness to respect the woman's decision, without feeling that their expertise is being challenged or undermined, or indeed that they are being subjected to what Dan Brock refers to as 'consumer sovereignty',[18] whereby doctors are simply required to implement orders given to them by patients. However, in each of the jurisdictions it is clear that the central tenet of medical law is the principle of autonomy; the age of medical paternalism has waned. As the Supreme Court's decision in *Montgomery v Lanarkshire Health Board*[19] demonstrates, the courts expect doctors to collaborate with patients, to facilitate informed decision-making and to respect the patient's right to make her own choice. As Lady Hale stressed, in the obstetric context,

> A patient is entitled to take into account her own values, her own assessment of the comparative merits of giving birth in the 'natural' and traditional way and of giving birth by caesarean section, whatever medical opinion may say, alongside the medical evaluation of the risks to herself and her baby. She may place great value on giving birth in the natural way and be prepared to take the risks to herself and her baby which this entails. The medical profession must respect her choice, unless she lacks the legal capacity to decide.

In the same way, it is suggested that the medical profession must respect a woman's valid and applicable anticipatory choice where she lacks the capacity to make a contemporaneous decision, regardless of any risk that might pose to her own, or the foetus's welfare.

II. Putting the woman back centre-stage in the adjudication of disputes: the need for effective procedural safeguards and respect for human dignity

In 1987 George Annas wrote:

> Without time to analyze the issues, without representation for the pregnant woman, without briefing or thoughtful reflection on the situation, in almost total ignorance of the relevant law, and in an unfamiliar setting faced by a relatively calm physician and a woman who can easily be labelled 'hysterical', the judge will almost always order whatever the physician advises.[20]

18 D. W. Brock, *Life and Death*, Cambridge: Cambridge University Press, 1993, at 58.
19 [2015] UKSC 11.
20 G. J. Annas, 'Protecting the Liberty of Pregnant Patients' (1987) 316(19) *New England Journal of Medicine* 1213.

Despite the passage of almost 30 years, the most recent case law on both sides of the Atlantic demonstrates that this observation remains true. The cases clearly demonstrate a number of key failings – there is no effective external audit of medical decisions and cases continue to be heard on an *ex parte* basis, without effective representation of the woman's views and interests, and often without the possibility for her to be heard. The Anglo-American case law suggests that the role played by the courts has largely been to validate the doctor's decision to intervene against the woman's will. The court order coats what is often best described as obstetric violence with the veneer of legitimacy, whilst protecting the doctor against a potential negligence claim. With the notable exception of *In re Baby Boy Doe*,[21] whenever the question of intervention was live, with the life or well-being of the foetus at risk, there is little indication of a balanced attempt to adjudicate between the woman and the doctor and to ensure that the woman's rights and interests are protected.

Whilst technology has enabled the foetus to be constructed as a second patient, as Lauren Freeman recently wrote,

> The problem is not with technology per se, but rather with the way that it is deployed and the motivation behind its deployment… . The traditional ways in which the technology is used is a part of a panoptics of the womb, which aims to gain control over women's bodies: the problem then is not restricted to the agential level of individual physicians but is also and perhaps more insidiously a structural problem within the institution of medicine.[22]

Freeman's conclusion is undoubtedly correct; however, it is argued that the problem is more extensive than she suggests in that it is not merely restricted to the institution of medicine, but rather that it also infects the institution of law, underlying the legal responses to what is presented as a 'maternal'–foetal conflict.

All too often in the reported cases, courts have let women down and have colluded with the medical professionals involved to force women to submit to treatment against their will, allowing doctors to determine the level of sacrifice that women may be forced to endure for the sake of the foetus. When one considers the circumstances and manner in which the cases have been determined, it is hardly surprising that the woman's rights have been undermined in order to protect the foetus. The unquestioning acceptance of medical evidence (other than that C was in fact competent to refuse treatment in the view of her obstetrician)[23] brings to mind a sketch from Monty Python's *The Meaning of Life* (1983) where, with birth imminent, the patient asks her obstetrician, 'What do I do?' only to be told, 'Nothing, dear, you're not qualified!' The medical model of pregnancy emphasises

21 *In re Baby Boy Doe, a Fetus v Mother Doe* 632 N.E. 2d 326 (1994), at 333.

22 L. Freeman, 'Confronting Diminished Epistemic Privilege and Epistemic Injustice in Pregnancy by Challenging a "Panoptics of the Womb"' (2015) 40 *Journal of Medicine and Philosophy* 44, at 54.

23 *Rochdale Healthcare (NHS) Trust v C* [1997] 1 FCR 274.

risk, both to the woman and the foetus, and has constructed pregnancy and birth as a process to be managed, rather than a natural event. As experts, doctors have claimed the authority for making decisions about how birth should be managed, a claim that the courts have all too often accepted, without subjecting the medical testimony to rigorous scrutiny. As Nancy Rhoden argued:

> In some cases, there may be much to say against the doctor's recommendations and predictions. But it will not get said. Judges will never hear from the woman who has crept back home to deliver safely, or unsafely, there. Nor are they likely to hear lucid constitutional arguments from the one in the hospital, in the sweaty agonies of labor, or from her counsel, appointed one hour before the hearing. If informed consent in obstetrics is gradually replaced by enforced acquiescence, this transformation will most likely occur without there ever being a truly two-sided, fully litigated hearing. In any individual case, the immediacy of the potentially tragic consequences will be enormously compelling. It will be extremely hard for judges to refrain from overriding refusals in order to prevent these consequences. But on a broader societal scale, preventing these tragedies comes at the cost of embracing an unprecedented and problematic tyranny whose potential scope knows no bounds.[24]

Although this commentary pertains to the American case law, it is equally applicable to the cases in England and Wales. Whilst the medical model of pregnancy emphasises risk, just as in any other sphere of life the woman must be permitted to make her own risk assessments, to make decisions that may appear unwise or downright wrong. Despite repeated assurances that the woman's rights and best interests are the English courts' sole concern, the fact remains that a woman refusing a clinically indicated caesarean has yet to be found to have the capacity to refuse consent, and if the woman is found to lack capacity, there is unlikely to be anyone who will champion her right to refuse a caesarean. The Official Solicitor's role is to represent her best interests, not to act as her advocate demanding that her voice be heard. As the case law demonstrates, the Official Solicitor has consistently argued that the women lacked capacity to make the decision for themselves, and has argued in favour of a caesarean as best fitting her best interests even where less restrictive options appear to have been available. In almost all the cases the woman did not take part in the hearing. Too many of the applications have been made, and granted, on an *ex parte* basis, depriving the woman of the opportunity to be heard. Even those cases that were not emergencies, such as *Re AA (Mental Capacity: Enforced Caesarean)*,[25] have been dealt with on the basis of urgency, without full information being available to the courts and even absent an independent assessment of the woman's capacity to refuse the treatment proposed. As the custodians of liberty, it is imperative that judges ensure that the procedural

24 N. K. Rhoden, 'The Judge in the Delivery Room: The Emergence of Court-ordered Caesareans' (1986) 74 *California Law Review* 1951, at 2029f.

25 [2012] EWHC 4378 (COP), [2014] 2 FLR 237.

safeguards routinely applied to the question of whether an individual has capacity to make the decision to refuse treatment, and, if not, whether such treatment is required to further her best interests, are maintained in the context of obstetric intervention. The safeguards should serve to ensure that the woman's dignity is respected, that her rights and interests are protected; they should not be undermined by undue deference to medical opinion or by a willingness to grant orders without a full consideration of the evidence, including a detailed examination of the woman's capacity and known wishes, absent an emergency.

As Judge LJ recognised in *St George's Healthcare NHS Trust* v *S; R* v *Collins and others, ex parte S*:[26]

> How can a forced invasion of a competent adult's body against her will even for the most laudable of motives (the preservation of life) be ordered without irremediably damaging the principle of self-determination? When human life is at stake the pressure to provide an affirmative answer authorising unwanted medical intervention is very powerful. Nevertheless the autonomy of each individual requires continuing protection even, perhaps particularly, when the motive for interfering with it is readily understandable, and indeed to many would appear commendable: hence the importance of remembering Lord Reid's warning against making 'even minor concessions'. If it has not already done so medical science will no doubt one day advance to the stage when a very minor procedure undergone by an adult would save the life of his or her child, or perhaps the life of a child of a complete stranger. The refusal would rightly be described as unreasonable, the benefit to another human life would be beyond value, and the motives of the doctors admirable. If, however, the adult were compelled to agree, or rendered helpless to resist, the principle of autonomy would be extinguished.

This must be correct: the pregnant woman cannot be subjected to a higher duty to be a good Samaritan than that imposed upon other members of society. The judiciary must ensure that women's rights are protected, that women's dignity is respected, that they are treated as persons rather than uterine environments. Undoubtedly, this will be difficult in practice; as Thorpe LJ observed, writing extra-judicially, 'Some may perceive the judges as more confident in defining the principle of autonomy than in applying it to a mother and fetus for whom death is at the door'.[27] However, pregnant women cannot be singled out for special treatment; until such a time as men can be required to undergo surgery for the sake of an existing child, or indeed strangers can be required to undergo the much less invasive procedure of donating blood to save the life of a stranger, a woman's right to bodily integrity and autonomy must be maintained. The result may be

26 [1999] Fam. 26, at 46f.

27 M. A. Thorpe, 'Consent for Caesarean Section: Part 2 – Autonomy, Capacity, Best Interests, Reasonable Force and Procedural Guidelines' (1999) 5 *Clinical Risk* 209, at 211.

undesirable: a foetus may die, and this would undoubtedly be distressing for all concerned, but the alternative would be to diminish the personhood of the pregnant woman, to accept that for a period of 40 weeks she is obligated to protect the entity inside her body and do anything necessary to safeguard its welfare, sacrificing her own rights and indeed her identity in the process.

In Margaret Atwood's *The Handmaid's Tale* the handmaids are required to be 'a worthy vessel', to take daily vitamins, to avoid caffeine – in short, to provide the optimum foetal environment. It has been argued that whilst none of the jurisdictions under consideration have reached the extremes of Gilead, each requires a rather different standard of behaviour from those who are pregnant to those who are not. The fact of pregnancy and the implications of the woman's choices for the foetus will certainly complicate decision-making for a pregnant woman. Respect for human dignity requires that the foetus be protected, irrespective of whether that protection is afforded on the basis of protecting the foetus itself, or, as in the United States, in order to protect the state's interest in potential life. However, a balance needs to be struck whereby the protection afforded to the foetus remains consistent with respect for the woman's dignity and the protection of her rights. Thus the woman must take account of the foetus in making her decisions about what treatment to accept, but ultimately the decision to accept, or reject, obstetric intervention remains hers alone, regardless of the level of risk or invasion of her body involved.

The means that protecting the foetus and promoting its welfare lies in fostering a culture of cooperation between the woman and her health and social care professionals; undeniably, the basis for such a cooperation lies in trust, not compulsion. By establishing a dialogue with the woman, healthcare professionals will be able to seek to persuade her to accept treatment for the benefit of the foetus; if she fears being forced to accept treatment against her will, she is unlikely to seek medical attention, providing no opportunity to protect the foetus. Therefore the way forward is clear: the only way to safeguard the foetus, without reducing the woman to the status of an 'incubator on legs', is to provide the woman with health and social support, and to treat her as the senior partner in the endeavour of promoting foetal welfare. The imposition of a duty requiring the pregnant women to act in the best interests of the foetus at all times, whether that be by giving up smoking or by consenting to a caesarean, is to descend to the dystopia that is Gilead.

In the context of obstetric intervention for the benefit of the foetus, the public interest supports the need for a woman to retain autonomy over her own body and to be recognised as an equal member of society, with her own rights and interests that are undiminished by pregnancy. Moreover, it has been argued that the public interest in the maintenance of respect for human dignity and autonomy cannot be satisfied by merely allowing a pregnant woman to defend her bodily integrity against unwelcome medical intervention. Instead, she must be empowered to make effective choices about her pregnancy and labour that will be respected even if she lacks capacity and even where those choices will lead to the death of a viable foetus. The challenge for doctors and the judiciary will be to accept women's refusals when they are valid and applicable to the events that unfold, or, in the absence of such a decision, to resist the temptation to reduce the woman's best interests to the safe delivery of the foetus. Undoubtedly, it will be very difficult to watch a woman and/or a foetus die, to allow that to happen by upholding her refusal of consent, but that is the nature of autonomy and it is incumbent upon both judges and doctors to resist the temptation to play the hero, to save the foetus, or, indeed, the woman from herself. Women must be allowed to exercise their rights to autonomy, even if that means that they make decisions that appear morally repugnant, or that they have to later face the guilt of knowing that the foetus died due to their refusal of treatment. A failure to respect a woman's autonomy, driven by an emotional response to this complex situation, would diminish a women's dignity, making it dependent upon her reproductive capacity. Courts, legislatures and healthcare professionals would do well to consider Wilson J's statement in *R* v *Morgentaler*:[28]

> Liberty in a free and democratic society does not require the state to approve the personal decisions made by its citizens; it does, however, require the state to respect them.

28 [1988] 44 DLR (4th) 385, at 487.

Bibliography

American College of Obstetricians and Gynecologists, Committee on Ethics, Committee Opinion 321, 'Maternal Decision Making, Ethics and the Law' (2005) 106 *Obstetrics & Gynecology* 1127.

American Medical Association Board of Trustees Report, 'Legal Interventions during Pregnancy' (1990) 264 *Journal of the American Medical Association* 2663.

G. J. Annas, 'Protecting the Liberty of Pregnant Patients' (1987) 316(19) *New England Journal of Medicine* 1213.

G. J. Annas, 'She's Going to Die: The Case of Angela C' (1988) 18(1) *Hastings Center Report* 23.

M. Atwood, *The Handmaid's Tale*, Boston: Houghton Mifflin, 1986.

M. Baldus, 'Menschenwürdegarantie und Absolutheitsthese Zwischenbericht zu einer zukunftsweisenden Debatte' (2011) 134(4) *Archiv des öffentlichen Rechts* 529.

S. Balisy, 'Maternal Substance Abuse: The Need to Provide Legal Protection for the Fetus' (1987) 60 *Southern California Law Review* 1209.

P. Balz, *Lebenserhaltung als Haftungsgrund*, Berlin: Springer, 2010.

M. Bayles, 'Physicians as Body Mechanics' in J. W. Davis et al. (eds) *Contemporary Issues in Biomedical Ethics*, Clifton: Humana Press, 1978, 167–177.

R. Beckmann, 'Der Parlamentarische Rat und das "keimende Leben"' (2008) 47(4) *Der Staat* 551.

D. Beyleveld and R. Brownsword, *Human Dignity in Bioethics and Biolaw*, Oxford: Oxford University Press, 2001.

A. Biscoe and G. Kidson-Gerber, 'Avoidable Death of a Pregnant Jehovah's Witness with Acute Promyelocytic Leukaemia: Ethical Considerations and the Internal Conflicts and Challenges Encountered by Practitioners' (2015) 45 *Internal Medicine Journal* 461.

M. Blake, 'Policing of Pregnancy: Rights and Wrongs' in M. Freeman and A. Lewis (eds) *Law and Medicine: Current Legal Issues vol. 3*, 2000, Oxford: Oxford University Press, 283–301.

L.-M. Bleiler, *Strafbarkeitsrisiken des Arztes bei religiös motiviertem Behandlungsveto* Heidelberg: Springer, 2010.

P. Bockelmann, *Strafrecht des Arztes*, Stuttgart: Thieme, 1968.

P. Bockelmann, 'Der ärztliche Heileingriff in Beiträgen zur Zeitschrift für die gesamte Strafrechtswissenschaft im ersten Jahrhundert ihres Bestehens' (1981) 93 *Zeitschrift für die gesamte Strafrechtswissenschaft* 103.

M. Brazier, 'Hard Cases Make Bad Law?' (1997) 23 *Journal of Medical Ethics* 341.

British Medical Association, *Advance Decisions and Proxy Decision-making in Medical Treatment and Research: Guidance from the BMA's Medical Ethics Department*, 2007.

D. W. Brock, *Life and Death*, Cambridge: Cambridge University Press, 1993.

H. Brooks and W. J. Sullivan, 'The Importance of Patient Autonomy at Birth' (2002) 11 *International Journal of Obstetric Anesthesia* 196.

J. Bryan, 'Reading Beyond the Ratio: Searching for the Subtext in the "Enforced Caesarean" Cases' in D. Carpi (ed.) *Bioethics and Biolaw through Literature*, Berlin: Walter de Gruyter, 2011, 115–134.

Bundesärztekammer, 'Richtlinien zur pränatalen Diagnostik von Krankheiten und Krankheitsdispositionen' (1998) 95(50) *Deutsches Ärzteblatt* A-3236.

Bundesärztekammer, 'Empfehlungen der Bundesärztekammer und der Zentralen Ethikkommission bei der Bundesärztekammer zum Umgang mit Vorsorgevollmacht und Patientenverfügung in der ärztlichen Praxis' (2010) 18 *Deutsches Ärzteblatt* 877.

Bundesministerium der Justiz Arbeitsgruppe Familiengerichtliche Maßnahmen bei Gefährdung des Kindeswohls § 1666 BGB, *Abschlussbericht*, 14 July 2009.

T. Burch, 'Incubator or Individual: The Legal and Policy Deficiencies of Pregnancy Clauses in Living Will and Advance Health Care Directive Statutes' (1995) 54 *Maryland Law Review* 528.

P. Burcher, 'The Ulysses Contract in Obstetrics: A Woman's Choices Before and During Labour' (2013) 39 *Journal of Medical Ethics* 27.

B. A. Burkstrand-Reid, 'The Invisible Woman: Availability and Culpability in Reproductive Health Jurisprudence' (2010) 81 *University of Colorado Law Review* 97.

M. J. Casper, 'At the Margins of Humanity: Fetal Positions in Science and Medicine' (1994) 19(3) *Science, Technology, & Human Values* 307.

M. J. Casper, *The Making of the Unborn Patient*, New Brunswick: Rutgers University Press, 1998.

A. L. Cherry, 'Roe's Legacy: The Nonconsensual Medical Treatment of Pregnant Women and Implications for Female Citizenship' (2004) 6 *University of Pennsylvania Journal of Constitutional Law* 723.

F. A. Chervenak, L. B. McCullough and D. W. Skupski, 'An Ethical Justification for Emergency, Coerced Cesarean Delivery' (1993) 82(6) *Obstetrics & Gynecology* 1029.

M. Coester, 'Kinderschutz: Übersicht zu den typischen Gefährdungslagen und aktuellen Problemen' (2009) *Famile Partnerschaft Recht* 549.

G. Corea, *The Mother Machine: Reproductive Technologies from Artificial Insemination to Artificial Wombs*, London: Women's Press, 1985.

P. Cramer, 'Ein Sonderstraftatbestand für die eigenmächtige Heilbehandlung. Einige Bemerkungen zu §§ 229, 230 des Entwurfs eines 6. Gesetzes zur Reform des Strafrechts (6. StrRG)' in A. Eser, U. Schittenhelm and H. Schumann (eds) *Festschrift für Theodor Lenckner zum 70. Geburtstag*, München: C.H. Beck, 1998, 761–80.

F. G. Cunningham, K. J. Leveno, S. L. Bloom et al., *Williams Obstetrics*, 23rd edn, New York: McGraw-Hill Education, 2010.

F. G. Cunningham et al., *Williams Obstetrics*, 24th edn, New York: McGraw-Hill Education, 2014.

M. Cuttini et al. 'Patient Refusal of Emergency Caesarean Delivery: A Study of Obstetricians' Attitudes in Europe' (2006) 108(5) *Obstetrics & Gynecology* 1121.

W. van den Daele, 'Der Fötus als Subjekt und die Autonomie der Frau: Wissenschaftlich-technische Optionen und soziale Kontrollen in der Schwangerschaft' (1988) 21 *Kritische Justiz* 16.

C. R. Daniels, *At Women's Expense: State Power and the Politics of Foetal Rights*, Cambridge, MA: Harvard University Press, 1993.

Deutsche Gesellschaft für Gynäkologie und Geburtshilfe (DGGG), Arbeitsgemeinschaft Medizinrecht (AG MedR), *Empfehlungen zu den ärztlichen Beratungs- und Aufklärungspflichten während der Schwangerenbetreuung und bei der Geburtshilfe*, 1996, confirmed 2010.

Deutsche Gesellschaft für Gynäkologie und Geburtshilfe (DGGG), *Absolute und relative Indikationen zur Sectio caesarea*, 2001, revised 2008, currently under revision.

A. B. Dolderer, *Menschenwürde und Spätabbruch*, Berlin: Springer, 2012.

M. Donnelly, 'Best Interests, Patient Participation and the Mental Capacity Act 2005' (2009) 17 *Medical Law Review* 1.

H. Dreier, 'Menschenwürdegarantie und Schwangerschaftsabbruch' (1995) 24 *Die Öffentliche Verwaltung* 1036.

H. Dreier, 'Stufungen des vorgeburtlichen Lebensschutzes' (2002) 35(9) *Zeitschrift für Rechtspolitik* 377.

H. Dreier, *Grundgesetz Kommentar*, 2nd edn, Tübingen: Mohr Siebeck, 2004 (cited: Contributor, in *Dreier*).

H. Dreier, 'Grenzen des Tötungsverbotes – Teil 1' (2007) *Juristen Zeitung* 261.

H. Dreier, *Bioethik: Politik und Verfassung*, Tübingen: Mohr Siebeck, 2013.

M. A. Driessen, 'Avoiding the Melissa Rowland Dilemma: Why Disobeying a Doctor Should Not Be a Crime' (2006) 10 *MSU Journal of Medicine and Law* 1.

E. Drigotas, 'Forced Caesarean Sections: Do the Ends Justify the Means?' (1991) 70 *North Carolina Law Review* 297.

C. Dupré, *Importing the Law in Post-Communist Transitions: The Hungarian Constitutional Court and the Right to Human Dignity*, Oxford: Hart, 2003.

G. Dürig, 'Der Grundsatz von der Menschenwürde' (1956) 81 *Archiv des öffentlichen Rechts* 117.

R. Dworkin, *Life's Dominion: An Argument about Abortion, Euthanasia and Individual Freedom*, London: Harper Collins, 1993.

C. Dyer, 'Mother vs Big Brother', 19.12.96, *Guardian*, A4.

M. Dyke, 'A Matter of Life and Death: Pregnancy Clauses in Living Will Statutes' (1990) *Boston University Law Review* 867.

S. Ebner, 'The Unkindest Cut' 02.06.1997, *Guardian* B5.

J. Ehrlich, 'Breaking the Law by Giving Birth: The War on Drugs, the War on Reproductive Rights, and the War on Women' (2008) 32 *N.Y.U. Review of Law & Social Change* 381.

K. Engisch, 'Ärztlicher Eingriff zu Heilzwecken und Einwilligung' (1939) 58 *Zeitschrift für die gesamte Strafrechtswissenschaft* 1.

J. Epstein, 'The Pregnant Imagination, Fetal Rights, and Women's Bodies: A Historical Inquiry' (1995) 7 *Yale Journal of Law & the Humanities* 139.

L. C. Fentiman, 'The New Fetal Protection: The Wrong Answer to the Crisis of Inadequate Health Care for Women and Children' (2006) *Denver University Law Review* 537.

T. Fischer, *Strafgesetzbuch und Nebengesetze*, 62nd edn, München: C.H. Beck, 2014 (cited: *Fischer*).

J. Flavin, *Our Bodies, Our Crimes: The Policing of Women's Reproduction in America*, New York: New York University Press, 2009.

S. Fovargue and J. Miola, 'Policing Pregnancy: Implications of the Attorney General's Reference (No. 3 of 1994)' (1998) 6 *Medical Law Review* 265.

L. Freeman, 'Confronting Diminished Epistemic Privilege and Epistemic Injustice in Pregnancy by Challenging a "Panoptics of the Womb"' (2015) 40 *Journal of Medicine and Philosophy* 44.

J. Gallagher, 'Prenatal Invasions & Interventions: What's Wrong With Fetal Rights?' (1987) 10 *Harvard Women's Law Journal* 9.

J. Gallagher, 'Fetus as Patient' in S. Cohen and N. Taub (eds) *Reproductive Laws for the 1990s*, New Brunswick, NJ: Rutgers University Press, 1989, 185–235.

W. Gallas, 'Pflichtenkollision als Schuldausschließungsgrund' in K. Engisch and R. Maurach (eds) *Festschrift für Edmund Mezger zum 70. Geburtstag am 15.10.1954*, München: C.H. Beck, 1954, 311ff.

General Medical Council, *Treatment and Care towards the End of Life: Good Practice in Decision-making*, London: GMC, 2010.

J. C. Gerancher et al., 'An Evaluation of Informed Consent Prior to Epidural Analgesia for Labour and Delivery' (2000) 9 *International Journal of Obstetric Anesthesia* 168.

L. Gies, 'Contesting the Rule of Emotions? The Press and Enforced Caesareans' (2000) 9 *Social & Legal Studies* 515.

L. Greenhouse and R. B. Siegel (eds), *Before Roe v Wade: Voices that Shaped the Abortion Debate Before the Supreme Court's Ruling*, New York: Kaplan Publishing, 2010.

D. Greschner, 'Abortion and Democracy for Women: A Critique of *Tremblay v Daigle*' (1990) 35 *McGill Law Journal* 633.

W. Gropp, 'Der Embryo als Mensch: Überlegungen zum pränatalen Schutz des Lebens und der körperlichen Unversehrtheit' (2000) *Goltdammer's Archiv für Strafrecht* 1.

W. Gropp, 'Atypische rechtmäßige Schwangerschaftsabbrüche' in K. Amelung et al. (eds) *Strafrecht, Biorecht, Rechsphilosophie: Festschrift für Hans-Ludwig Schreiber zum 70. Geburtstag am 10. Mai 2003*, Heidelberg: C. F. Müller, 2005, 113–126.

W. Gropp, 'Strafrechtlicher Schutz des Lebens vor und nach der "Geburt"' in E. Schumann (ed.) *Verantwortungsbewusste Konfliktlösungen bei embryopathischem Befund*, Göttingen: Göttinger Schriften zum Medizinrecht Band 4, 2008, 19–40.

W. Gropp, *Strafrecht Allgemeiner Teil*, 4th edn, Berlin: Springer, 2015.

B. Hale, 'A Pretty Pass: When is There a Right to Die?' (2003) 32 *Common Law World Review* 1.

M. H. Hall and S. Bewley, 'Maternal Mortality and Mode of Delivery' (1999) 354 *Lancet* 776.

S. Halliday, 'Legislating to Give Effect to Precedent Autonomy: Comparative Reflections on Legislative Incompetence' (2011) 11 *Medical Law International* 127.

S. Halliday, 'Comparative Reflections upon the Assisted Dying Bill 2013: A Plea for a More European Approach' (2013) 13 *Medical Law International* 135.

S. Halliday and L. Witteck, 'Die Regelung von Nichtaufnahme und Abbruch einer medizinischen Behandlung am Lebensende in Deutschland und England' (2002) 15 *Juristen Zeitung* 752.

W. Hardwig, 'Betrachtungen zur Frage des Heileingriffes' (1965) *Goltdammer's Archiv für Strafrecht* 161.

A. Hartocollis, 'Mother Accuses Doctors of Forcing a C-Section', 16/05/2014, *New York Times*, A18.

Health Service Executive, *National Consent Policy*, 2013. Available at www.hse.ie/eng/about/Who/qualityandpatientsafety/National_Consent_Policy/National%20Consent%20PolicyMay14.pdf (accessed 11 November 2015).

N. Heinemann, *Frau und Fötus in der Prä- und Perinatalmedizin aus strafrechtlicher Sicht*, Baden-Baden: Nomos, 2000.

R. Herzberg and A. I. Herzberg, 'Der Beginn des Menschseins im Strafrecht: Die Vollendung der Geburt' (2001) 22 *Juristen Zeitung* 1106.

B. Hewson, 'How to Escape the Surgeon's Knife' (1997) 147 *New Law Journal* 752.

E. Hilgendorf, 'Zwischen Humanexperiment und Rettung ungeborenen Lebens – Der Erlanger Schwangerschaftsfall' (1993) *Juristische Schulung* 97.

E. Hilgendorf, 'Scheinargumente in der Abtreibungsdiskussion – am Beispiel des Erlanger Schwangerschaftsfalls' (1996) *Neue Juristische Wochenschrift* 758.

H. J. Hirsch, 'Die Grenze zwischen Schwangerschaftsabbruch und allgemeinen Tötungsdelikten nach der Streichung des Privilegierungstatbestands der Kindestötung (§ 217 StGB a.F.),' in J. Arnold, B. Burkhartd, W. Gropp et al (eds) *Menschengerechtes Strafrecht: Festschrift für Albin Eser zum 70. Geburtstag*, München: C.H. Beck, 2005, 309–322.

A. Hochreuter, 'Gebärzwang und tote Frau als Brüterin – patriarchale Ethik?' (1994) 27 *Kritische Justiz* 67.

N. Hoerster, 'Zur Bedeutung des Prinzips der Menschenwürde' (1983) *Juristische Schulung* 93.

N. Hoerster, *Ethik des Embryonenschutzes: Ein rechtsphilosophischer Essay*, Stuttgart: Reclam, 2002.

B. J. Horttor, 'A Survey of Living Will and Advanced Health Care Directives' (1998) 74 *North Dakota Law Review* 233.

J. Hruschka, *Strafrecht nach logisch-analytischer Methode: Systematisch entwickelte Fälle mit Lösungen zum Allgemeinen Teil*, 2nd edn, Berlin: Walter De Gruyter, 1988.

F. Hufen, 'In dubio pro dignitate' (2001) *Neue Juristische Wochenschrift*, 849.

L. C. Ikemoto, 'The Code of Perfect Pregnancy: At the Intersection of the Ideology of Motherhood, the Practice of Defaulting to Science and the Interventionist Mindset of Law' (1992) 53(5) *Ohio State Law Journal* 1206.

J. Ipsen, 'Der "verfassungsrechtliche Status" des Embryos in vitro: Anmerkungen zu einer aktuellen Debatte' (2001) *Juristen Zeitung* 989.

J. Isensee, 'Menschenwürde: die säkulare Gesellschaft auf der Suche nach dem Absoluten' (2006) 131(2) *Archiv des öffentlichen Rechts* 173.

B. Jähnke, H. W. Laufhütte and W. Odersky, *Leipziger Kommentar, Strafgesetzbuch Großkommentar: Fünfter Band §§ 146 bis 222*, 11th edn, Berlin: Walter de Gruyter (cited: Contributor, in *LK*).

J. M. Jordan, 'Incubating for the State: The Precarious Autonomy of Persistently Vegetative and Brain-dead Pregnant Women' (1988) 22 *Georgia Law Review* 1103.

D. Kaiser, K. Schnitzler, P. Friederci and R. Schilling (eds) *Nomos Kommentar zum Bürgerlichen Gesetzbuch: Familienrecht, vol. 4*, 3rd edn, Baden-Baden: Nomos, 2014 (cited: Contributor, in *NK-BGB*).

I. Kant, 'Grundlegung zur Metaphysik der Sitten' in J. Timmermann (ed.) *Sammlung Philosophie*, Göttingen: Vandenhoeck & Ruprecht, 2004, vol. 3.

M. Kaplan, '"A Special Class of Persons": Pregnant Women's Right to Refuse Medical Treatment After Gonzales v. Carhart' (2010) 13 *University of Pennsylvania Journal of Constitutional Law* 145.

W. Kapp, 'Der Fötus als Patient' (1986) 5 *Medizinrecht* 276.

A. Karnein, *The Theory of Unborn Life from Abortion to Genetic Manipulation*, Oxford: Oxford University Press, 2012.

I. Karpin, 'Legislating the Female Body: Reproductive Technology and the Reconstructed Woman' (1992) 3 *Columbia Journal of Gender and Law* 325.

H. Keane, 'Foetal Personhood and Representations of the Absent Child in Pregnancy Loss Memorialization' (2009) 10(2) *Feminist Theory* 153.

A. Kent, 'Psychiatric Disorders in Pregnancy' (2011) 21(11) *Obstetrics, Gynaecology and Reproductive Medicine* 317.

R. Kiesecker, *Die Schwangerschaft einer Toten: Strafrecht an der Grenze von Leben und Tod – der Erlanger und der Stuttgarter Baby-Fall*, Frankfurt am Main: Peter Lang, 1996.

M. D. Kilby, 'Prenatal Diagnosis: The Way Ahead?' (1998) 59(10) *Hospital Medicine* 752.

U. Kindhäuser, U. Neumann and H.-U. Paeffgen (eds) *Nomos Kommentar zum Strafgesetzbuch*, 4th edn, Baden-Baden: Nomos, 2013 (cited: Contributor, in *NK-StGB*).

S. Kitzinger, 'Birth Plans: How Are They Being Used?' (1999) 7(5) *British Journal of Midwifery* 300.

H.-G. Koch, 'Hirntod und Schwangerschaft: Überlegungen aus rechtlicher Sicht' in J. Bednarikova and F. C. Chapman (eds) *Festschrift für Jan Štěpán zum 80. Geburtstag*, Zürich: Schulthess, 1994, 187–201.

V. E. B. Kolder, J. Gallagher and M. T. Parsons, 'Court-ordered Obstetrical Interventions' (1987) 316 *New England Journal of Medicine* 1192.

V. Krey and M. Heinrich, *Strafrecht Besonderer Teil: Band 1, Besonderer Teil ohne Vermögensdelikte*, 15th edn, Stuttgart: Kohlhammer, 2012.

W. Küper, 'Mensch oder Embryo? Der Anfang des "Menschseins" nach neuem Strafrecht' (2001) *Goltdammer's Archiv für Strafrecht* 515.

W. Küper, 'Vollendung, Versuch und Rücktritt im "Interferenzbereich" zwischen Schwangerschaftsabbruch und allgemeinem Tötungsdelikt – Ein imaginäres Lehrgespräch' (2010) 3 *Zeitschrift für Internationale Strafrechtsdogmatik* 197.

G. Küpper, *Strafrecht Besonderer Teil I: Delikte gegen Rechtsgüter der Person und Gemeinschaft*, 3rd edn, Berlin: Springer, 2007.

L. Kutner, 'Due Process of Euthanasia: The Living Will, a Proposal' (1969) 44 *Indiana Law Journal* 539.

K. Lackner and K. Kühl, *Strafgesetzbuch, Kommentar*, 28th edn, München: C.H. Beck, 2014 (cited *Lackner/Kühl*).

A. Laufs and W. Uhlenbruck, *Handbuch des Arztrechts*, 3rd edn, München: C.H. Beck, 2002.

Law Commission, *Mental Incapacity* (Law Com No. 231, 1995).

S. A. Law, 'Childbirth: An Opportunity for Choice that Should be Supported' (2008) 32 *NYU Review of Law and Social Change* 345.

J. Levy, 'Jehovah's Witnesses, Pregnancy, and Blood Transfusions: A Paradigm for the Autonomy Rights of All Pregnant Women' (1999) 27 *Journal of Law, Medicine and Ethics* 171.

A. W. Liley, 'The Foetus as a Personality' (1972) 6 *Australian and New Zealand Journal of Psychiatry* 99.

H. Lim, 'Caesareans and Cyborgs' (1999) 7 *Feminist Legal Studies* 133.

A. D. Lyerly and M. B. Mahowald, 'Maternal-Fetal Surgery for Treatment of Myelomeningocele' (2003) 31(1) *Clinics in Perinatology* 155.

C. McCrudden, 'Human Dignity and Judicial Interpretation of Human Rights' (2008) 19 (4) *European Journal of International Law* 655.

E. McDonagh, *Breaking the Abortion Deadlock: From Choice to Consent*, Oxford: Oxford University Press, 1996.

V. MacDonnell, 'The Protective Function and Section 7 of the Canadian Charter of Rights and Freedoms' (2012) 17(1) *Review of Constitutional Studies* 53.

V. MacDonnell and J. Hughes, 'The German Abortion Decisions and the Protective Function in German and Canadian Constitutional Law' (2013) 50(4) *Osgoode Hall Law Journal* 999.

C. A. MacKinnon, 'Reflections on Sex Equality under Law' (1991) 5 *Yale Law Journal* 1281.

A. Maclean, 'Caesarean Sections, Competence and the Illusion of Autonomy' (1999) 1 *Web Journal of Current Legal Issues* 4.

S. A. M. McLean, *Autonomy, Consent and the Law*, London: Routledge-Cavendish, 2010.

S. A. M. McLean and K. Peterson, 'Patient Status: The Foetus and the Pregnant Woman' (1996) 2 *Australian Journal of Human Rights* 6.

J. Mair, 'Maternal Foetal Conflict: Defined or Defused?' in S. A. M. McLean (ed.) *Contemporary Issues in Law, Medicine and Ethics*, Aldershot: Dartmouth, 1996, 79–97.

E. Martin, *The Woman in the Body*, Boston: Beacon Press, 1987.

J. A. Martin et al., 'Births: Final Data for 2011' *National Vital Statistics Reports*, vol. 62, no. 1, Hyattsville, MD: National Center for Health Statistics, 2013.

S. S. Mattingly, 'The Maternal-Fetal Dyad: Exploring the Two-Patient Obstetric Model' (1992) 22(1) *Hastings Center Report* 13.

T. Maunz and G. Dürig, *Grundgesetz-Kommentar*, München: C.H. Beck, 70. Ergänzungslieferung, 2013 (cited: Contributor, in *Maunz/Dürig*).

S. Meredith, *Policing Pregnancy: The Law and Ethics of Obstetric Conflict*, Aldershot: Ashgate, 2005.

R. Merkel, 'Rechte für Embryonen?' *Die Zeit* 25.01.2001, 37.

R. Merkel, 'Grundrechte für frühe Embryonen?' in G. Britz et al., *Grundfragen staatlichen Strafens: Festschrift für Heinz Müller-Dietz zum 70. Geburtstag*, München: C.H. Beck, 2001, 493–521.

R. Merkel, *Früheuthanasie: rechtsethische und strafrechtliche Grundlagen ärztlicher Entscheidungen über Leben und Tod in der Neonatalmedizin*, Baden-Baden: Nomos, 2001.

J. S. Mill, *On Liberty*, London: John W. Parker, 1859.

M. Mills, 'Fetal Abuse Prosecutions: The Triumph of Reaction over Reason' (1998) 47 *DePaul Law Review* 989.

W. Mitsch, *Strafrechtlicher Schutz gegen medizinische Behandlung. Zur Problematik des ärztlichen Heileingriffs*, Baden-Baden: Nomos, 2000.

W. Mitsch, 'Notwehr gegen Schwangere' (2006) 11 *Juristische Rundschau* 450.

K. Moller, 'On Treating Persons as Ends: The German Aviation Security Act, Human Dignity, and the German Federal Constitutional Court' (2006) *Public Law* 457.

K. Moss, 'Substance Abuse during Pregnancy' (1990) 13 *Harvard Women's Law Journal* 278.

R. Müller-Terpitz, *Der Schutz des pränatalen Lebens: eine verfassungs-, völker- und gemeinschaftsrechtliche Statusbetrachtung an der Schwelle zum biomedizinischen Zeitalter*, Tübingen: Mohr Siebeck, 2007.

National Institute for Health and Clinical Excellence, *Clinical Guideline 45: Antenatal and Postnatal Mental Health: Clinical Management and Service Guidance*, London: NICE, 2007.

National Institute for Health and Clinical Excellence, *National Clinical Guideline 192: Antenatal and Postnatal Mental Health: Clinical Management and Service Guidance*, London: NICE, 2014.

C. Neff, 'Woman, Womb, and Bodily Integrity' (1991) 3 *Yale Journal of Law and Feminism* 327.

H. L. Nelson, 'The Architect and the Bee – Some Reflections on Post-mortem Pregnancy' (1994) 8(3) *Bioethics* 247.

L. J. Nelson, B. P. Buggy and C. J. Weil, 'Forced Medical Treatment of Pregnant Women: Compelling Each to Live as Seems Good to the Rest' (1986) *Hastings Law Journal* 703.

L. J. Nelson and N. Milliken, 'Compelled Medical Treatment of Pregnant Women – Life, Liberty and Law in Conflict' (1988) 259(7) *Journal of the American Medical Association* 1060.

A. Oakley, *The Captured Womb: A History of the Medical Care of Pregnant Women*, Oxford: Basil Blackwell, 1984.

C. Overall, 'Mother/Fetus/State Conflicts' (1988) *Health Law in Canada* 101.

J. Palmer, 'Seeing and Knowing: Ultrasound Images in the Contemporary Abortion Debate' (2009) 10(2) *Feminist Theory* 173.

L. Paltrow, 'Pregnant Drug Users, Fetal Persons, and the Threat to *Roe v Wade*' (1999) 62 *Albany Law Review* 999.

K. Parsi, 'Metaphorical Imagination: The Moral and Legal Status of Foetuses and Embryos' (1999) 2 *DePaul Journal of Health Care Law* 703.

T. Parson, *The Social System*, Glenco: Free Press, 1951.

N. S. Peart et al., 'Maintaining a Pregnancy Following Loss of Capacity' (2000) 8 *Medical Law Review* 275.

E. D. Pellegrino et al. (eds), *Human Dignity and Bioethics*, Notre Dame: University of Notre Dame Press, 2009.

R. P. Petchesky, 'Fetal Images: The Power of Visual Culture in the Politics of Reproduction' (1987) 13 *Feminist Studies* 263.

J. Phelan, 'The Maternal Abdominal Wall: A Fortress against Fetal Health Care?' (1986) 65 *Southern California Law Review* 461.

J. Raz, *The Authority of Law: Essays on Law and Morality*, 2nd edn, Oxford: Oxford University Press, 2009.

N. K. Rhoden, 'The Judge in the Delivery Room: The Emergence of Court-ordered Caesareans' (1986) 74 *California Law Review* 1951.

N. K. Rhoden, 'Caesareans and Samaritans' (1987) 15(3) *Law, Medicine and Healthcare* 118.

N. K. Rhoden, 'Informed Consent in Obstetrics: Some Special Problems' (1987) 9 *Western New England Law Review* 67

C. Robben, *Pränatale Schädigungen mit postnatalen Folgen: Überlegungen zu einem neuen Schutz- und Haftungskonzept unter Berücksichtigung der US-amerikanischen Rechtslage*, Frankfurt am Main: Peter Lang, 2014.

J. A. Roberston, 'Procreative Liberty and the Control of Conception, Pregnancy and Childbirth' (1993) 69(3) *Virginia Law Review* 405.

D. Roberts and S. R. Dalziel, 'Antenatal Corticosteroids for Accelerating Fetal Lung Maturation for Women at Risk of Preterm Birth' (2006) 3 *Cochrane Database of Systematic Reviews* Art. No.: CD004454.

J. A. Robertson, 'Posthumous Reproduction' (1994) 69 *Indiana Law Journal* 1027.

S. Rogers, '*Winnipeg Child and Family Services v D.F.G.*: Juridical Interference with Pregnant Women in the Alleged Interest of the Fetus' (1997) 36 *Alberta Law Review* 711.

R. Roth, *Making Women Pay: The Hidden Costs of Fetal Rights*, Ithaca, NY: Cornell University Press, 2000.

B. K. Rothman, *Recreating Motherhood*, New Brunswick, NJ: Rutgers University Press, 2000.

C. Roxin, *Strafrecht Allgemeiner Teil: Grundlagen. Der Aufbau der Verbrechenslehre, Band I*, 4th edn, München: C.H. Beck, 2005

Royal College of Obstetricians and Gynaecologists, *A Consideration of the Law and Ethics in Relation to Court-authorised Obstetric Intervention*, 2nd edn, London, 2006.

Royal College of Obstetricians and Gynaecologists, *Blood Transfusion in Obstetrics*, London, 2015.

M. Sachs (ed.), *Grundgesetz Kommentar*, 7th edn, München: C.H. Beck, 2014 (cited: Contributor, in *Sachs*).

F. J. Säcker (ed.), *Münchener Kommentar zum Bürgerlichen Gesetzbuch: Band 1, Allgemeiner Teil, §§ 1-240; ProstG, AGG*, 6th edn, München: C.H. Beck, 2012 (cited: Contributor, in *MüKo-BGB*).

G. M. Sander (ed.), *Münchener Kommentar zum Strafgesetzbuch Band 4: §§ 185-262 StGB*, 2nd edn, München: C.H. Beck, 2012 (cited: Contributor, in *MüKo-StGB*).

K. Savell, 'The Mother of the Legal Person' in S. James and S. Palmer (eds) *Visible Women: Essays on Feminist Legal Theory and Political Philosophy*, Oxford: Hart, 2002, 29–67.

J. Savulescu, 'Future People, Involuntary Medical Treatment in Pregnancy and the Duty of Easy Rescue' (2007) 19(1) *Utilitas* 1.

B. Schlink, *Aktuelle Fragen des pränatalen Lebensschutzes*, Berlin: Walter De Gruyter, 2002.

E. Schmidt, 'Das Reichsgericht und der "übergesetzliche Notstand"' (1929) 49 *Zeitschrift für die gesamte Strafrechtswissenschaft* 350.

E. Schmidt, *Der Arzt im Strafrecht*, Leipzig: T. Weicher, 1939.

A. Schönke and H. Schröder (eds), *Strafgesetzbuch, Kommentar*, 29th edn, München: C.H. Beck, 2014 (cited: Contributor, in *Schönke/Schröder*).

A. Schopenhauer, *Die beiden Grundprobleme der Ethik behandelt in zwei akademischen Preischriften*, 2nd edn, Leipzig: Brockhaus, 1860.

D. Schwab (ed.), *Münchener Kommentar zum Bürgerlichen Gesetzbuch: Band 8: Familienrecht II, §§ 1589-1921; SGB VIII*, 6th edn, München: C.H. Beck, 2012 (cited: Contributor, in *MüKo-BGB*).

R. Scott, 'The Pregnant Woman and the Good Samaritan: Can a Woman Have a Duty to Undergo a Caesarean Section?' (2000) 20 *Oxford Journal of Legal Studies* 407.

R. Scott, *Rights, Duties and the Body: Law and Ethics of the Maternal-fetal Conflict*, Oxford: Hart, 2002.

J. Seymour, *Childbirth and the Law*, Oxford: Oxford University Press, 2000.

S. Sheldon, 'Who is the Mother to Make the Judgement? The Construction of Woman in English Abortion Law' (1993) 1(1) *Feminist Legal Studies* 3.

S. Sheldon, *Beyond Control: Medical Power and Abortion Law*, London: Pluto Press, 1997.

D. Sperling, 'Maternal Brain Death' (2004) 30 *American Journal of Law & Medicine* 453.

D. Sperling, 'Do Pregnant Women Have (Living) Will?' (2005) 8(2) *Journal of Health Care Law & Policy* 331.

D. Sperling, *Management of Post-mortem Pregnancy: Legal and Philosophical Aspects*, Aldershot: Ashgate, 2006.

A. Spickhoff, 'Rechtssicherheit kraft Gesetzes durch sog. Patientenverfügungen?' (2009) *FamRZ* 1949.

Statistisches Bundesamt, *Gesundheit: Grunddaten der Krankenhäuser 2013*, Fachserie 12, Reihe 6.1.1, Wiesbaden, 2014, Table 2.15.

Statistisches Bundesamt, *Schwangerschaftsabbrüche 2014*, Fachserie 12, Reihe 3, Wiesbaden, 2015.

M. Stauch, 'Court-authorised Caesareans and the Principle of Patient Autonomy' (1997) 6 *Nottingham Law Journal* 74.

J. von Staudinger, *Kommentar zum Bürgerlichen Gesetzbuch mit Einführungsgesetz und Nebengesetzen, Einleitung zum Bürgerlichen Gesetzbuch*, München: Walter De Gruyter (cited: Contributor, in *Staudinger): Buch 1, Allgemeiner Teil, §§ 1–14*, München: Walter De Gruyter, 2004; *Buch 4, Familienrecht: §§ 1638–1683*, München: Walter De Gruyter, 2009.

B. Steinbock, 'Maternal-fetal Conflict and in Utero Fetal Therapy' (1994) 57 *Albany Law Review* 781.

U. Steiner, *Der Schutz des Lebens durch das Grundgesetz*, Berlin: Walter de Gruyter, 1991.

B. Tag, *Der Körperverletzungstatbestand im Spannungsfeld zwischen Patientenautonomie und Lex Artis: Eine arztstrafrechtliche Untersuchung*, Heidelberg: Springer, 2000.

J. S. Taylor, 'The Public Fetus and the Family Car: From Abortion Politics to a Volvo Advertisement' (1992) 4 *Public Culture* 67.

K. Taylor, 'Compelling Pregnancy at Death's Door' (1997) 7 *Columbia Journal of Gender and Law* 85.

J. J. Thomson, 'A Defense of Abortion' (1971) 1(1) *Philosophy and Public Affairs* 47.

M. A. Thorpe, 'The Caesarean Section Debate' (1997) 27 *Family Law* 663.

M. A. Thorpe, 'Consent for Caesarean Section: Part 1 – Development of the Law' (1999) 5 *Clinical Risk* 173.

M. A. Thorpe, 'Consent for Caesarean Section: Part 2 – Autonomy, Capacity, Best Interests, Reasonable Force and Procedural Guidelines' (1999) 5 *Clinical Risk* 209.

C. L. Townsend et al., 'Earlier Initiation of ART and Further Decline in Mother-to-child HIV Transmission Rates, 2000–2011' (2014) 28 *AIDS* 1049.

M. Wagner, 'Choosing Caesarean Section' (2000) 356 *Lancet* 1677.

M. Wagner, *Born in the USA: How a Broken Maternity System Must Be Fixed to Put Women and Children First*, Berkeley: University of California Press, 2008.

M. A. Warren, 'The Moral Significance of Birth' (1989) 4(3) *Hypatia* 46.

C. Wells, 'On the Outside Looking in: Perspectives on Enforced Caesareans' in S. Sheldon and M. Thomson (eds) *Feminist Perspectives in Health Care Law*, London: Cavendish Publishing, 1998, 237–257.

J. Wessels, W. Beulke and H. Satzger, *Strafrecht Allgemeiner Teil: Die Straftat und ihr Aufbau*, 44th edn, Heidelberg: C. F. Müller, 2014.

J. W. Williams, L. M. Hellman and J. A. Pritchard (eds) *Williams Obstetrics*, 14th edn, New York: Appleton-Century Crofts, 1971.

L. R. Woliver, *The Political Georgraphies of Pregnancy*, Urbana: University of Illinois Press, 2002.

World Health Organisation, 'Appropriate Technology for Birth' (1985) *Lancet* ii 436–7.

I. Zechmeister, 'Foetal Images: The Power of Visual Technology in Antenatal Care and the Implications for Women's Reproductive Freedom' (2001) 9 *Health Care Analysis* 387.

I. K. Zola, 'Medicine as an Institution of Social Control' (1972) 20 *Sociological Review* 487.

Index